A Feminist Companion
to Patristic Literature

Feminist Companion to the New Testament
and Early Christian Writings, 12

Other titles published in this series:

A Feminist Companion to Matthew
A Feminist Companion to Mark
A Feminist Companion to Luke
A Feminist Companion to John, volume 1
A Feminist Companion to John, volume 2
A Feminist Companion to Paul
A Feminist Companion to the Deutero-Pauline Epistles
A Feminist Companion to the Catholic Epistles and Hebrews
A Feminist Companion to the Acts of the Apostles
A Feminist Companion to Mariology
A Feminist Companion to the New Testament Apocrypha

Forthcoming:
A Feminist Companion to the Apocalypse of John
A Feminist Companion to the Historical Jesus

A Feminist Companion to

Patristic Literature

edited by

Amy-Jill Levine

with Maria Mayo Robbins

t & t clark

Published by T&T Clark International
A Continuum Imprint
The Tower Building, 11 York Road, London SE1 7NX
80 Maiden Lane, Suite 704, New York, NY 10038

www.continuumbooks.com

British Library Cataloguing-in-Publication Data
A catalogue record for this book is available from the British Library

Typeset by Fakenham Photosetting Ltd, Fakenham, Norfolk
Printed on acid-free paper in Great Britain by Athenaeum Press Ltd, Gateshead,
Tyne and Wear

ISBN 10: 0567045552 (Paperback)
ISBN 13: 9780567045553 (Paperback)
ISBN 10: 0567045544 (Hardback)
ISBN 13: 9780567045546 (Hardback)

CONTENTS

Preface   vii

Acknowledgements   ix

Abbreviations   x

List of Contributors   xii

AMY-JILL LEVINE
   Introduction   1

BARBARA E. BOWE
   'Many Women Have Been Empowered Through God's Grace. . .' (*1 Clem.*
   55.3): Feminist Contradictions and Curiosities in Clement of Rome   15

DENISE KIMBER BUELL
   Ambiguous Legacy: A Feminist Commentary on Clement of Alexandria's
   Works   26

VIRGINIA BURRUS
   Torture and Travail: Producing the Christian Martyr   56

ELIZABETH A. CASTELLI
   Virginity and its Meaning for Women's Sexuality in Early Christianity   72

ELIZABETH A. CLARK
   Ideology, History and the Construction of 'Woman' in Late Ancient
   Christianity   101

KATHY L. GACA
   The Pentateuch or Plato: Two Competing Paradigms of Christian Sexual
   Morality in the Second Century CE   125

ROBIN M. JENSEN
   Mater Ecclesia and *Fons Aeterna*: The Church and Her Womb
   in Ancient Christian Tradition   137

ROSS S. KRAEMER
   When is a Text About a Woman a Text About a Woman?: The Cases of
   Aseneth and Perpetua   156

CAROLYN OSIEK
   The Patronage of Women in Early Christianity   173

TERESA M. SHAW
   The Virgin Charioteer and the Bride of Christ: Gender and the
   Passions in Late Ancient Ethics and Early Christian Writings on Virginity   193

Bibliography   211

Index   237

PREFACE

A Feminist Companion to Patristic Literature, along with its sister volumes on the other documents of the New Testament and early Christian literature, signals the extent to which feminist critique has become a core element of biblical, historical and theological study.

Letters of invitation to contribute to this series went well beyond scholars known from their essays in explicitly feminist or women-identified collections, such as the two volumes of *Searching the Scriptures*[1] and the *Women's Bible Commentary*,[2] or from books and articles with 'feminist' in the title. Authors already established as having feminist interests were asked to suggest additional voices, and so interpreters at the beginning of their academic careers joined their senior colleagues in the pages of the volumes.

Invitations went beyond North America and Western Europe to East and South Asia, Africa, Eastern Europe, Central and South America, and Australia/ New Zealand. Along with an intentional focus on cultural diversity, we targeted as well authors who might speak explicitly from two perspectives sometimes overlooked even in feminist biblical collections, namely, sexual identity (e.g., lesbian critique) and religious tradition (e.g., Evangelicals, Jews). Some chose to write explicitly from their social location, and some did not. For either new or previously published work not in English, Vanderbilt Divinity School/the Carpenter Program in Religion, Gender and Sexuality provided funds for translation.

Not all those invited were able to contribute, but readers should be able to hear echoed in the footnotes – and by extension in the sources those notes utilize – numerous and diverse feminist voices speaking in other volumes and venues.

In addition to publishing select 'classics' in feminist analysis, the series invited numerous senior scholars to reconsider their earlier approaches and conclusions. Through their revisions, changes in feminist thought can be tracked. The series also sought contributions from biblical experts not known for feminist interests or even, in some cases, sympathies: 'Write a "feminist" piece', we exhorted; when a few demurred ('I don't "do" feminist critique'; 'I don't know what feminist critique is'), we responded: 'You should find out about it; you should engage it; if you don't like it, explain why, for all disciplines can profit from engaged critique; if you do find it helpful, use it.'

We wish to thank Marianne Blickenstaff for help with editing. We also wish to thank the Carpenter Program in Religion, Gender and Sexuality at the Vanderbilt Divinity School for financial and technical support.

---

1 Elisabeth Schüssler Fiorenza (ed.), *Searching the Scriptures: A Feminist Introduction and Commentary* (2 vols.; New York: Crossroad, 1993, 1994).
2 Carol A. Newsom and Sharon H. Ringe (eds), *The Women's Bible Commentary* (Louisville, KY: Westminster/John Knox Press, 1992; rev. edn, 1998).

It is our hope that this new series will quickly establish itself as a standard work of reference to scholars, students, and also to others who are interested in the New Testament and Christian Origins.

Amy-Jill Levine and Maria Mayo Robbins
Vanderbilt Divinity School and Graduate Department of Religion

ACKNOWLEDGEMENTS

The editors and publisher are grateful to the following for permission to reproduce copyright material: *Journal of Feminist Studies in Religion* for 'Virginity and its Meaning for Women's Sexuality in Early Christianity' by Elizabeth A. Castelli, from *JFSR*, 2.1 (1986), pp. 61–88; *Journal of Early Christian Studies* for 'Ideology, History and the Construction of "Woman" in Late Ancient Christianity' by Elizabeth A. Clark, from *JECS*, 2.2 (1994), pp. 155–84; Fortress Press for 'The Patronage of Women in Early Christianity' by Carolyn Osiek, an earlier version of which was published as 'Women Patrons in the Life of House Churches' in Carolyn Osiek, Margaret Y. MacDonald, with Janet Tullock, *A Woman's Place: House Churches in Earliest Christianity* (Minneapolis: Fortress Press, 2005), pp. 194–219.

ABBREVIATIONS

ABD	David Noel Freedman (ed.), *The Anchor Bible Dictionary* (6 vols.; New York: Doubleday, 1992)
ACW	Ancient Christian Writers
AE	*Année épigraphique*
ANCL	*Ante-Nicene Christian Library: translations of the writings of the Fathers down to A.D. 325*. Edited by Roberts and Donaldson. Edinburgh, 1867–1872
ANRW	Hildegard Temporini and Wolfgang Haase (eds), *Aufstieg und Niedergang der römischen Welt: Geschichte und Kultur Roms im Spiegel der neueren Forschung* (Berlin: W. de Gruyter, 1972–)
ATR	*Anglican Theological Review*
BDAG	Bauer, W., F. W. Danker, W. F. Arndt and F. W. Gingrich. *Greek English Lexicon of the New Testament and Other Early Christian Literature*. 3d ed. Chicago, 1999
BGU	*Aegyptische Urkunden aus den Königlichen Staatlichen Museen zu Berlin, Griechische Urkunden*. 15 vols. Berlin, 1895–1983
Bib	*Biblica*
BJS	Brown Judaic Studies
BR	*Bible Review*
BTB	*Biblical Theology Bulletin*
CCL	Corpus Christianorum, series latina
CH	*Church History*
CIJ	*Corpus inscriptionum judaicarum*
CIL	*Corpus inscriptionum latinarum*
CSEL	Corpus scriptorum ecclesiasticorum latinorum
DHGE	Dictionnaire d'Histoire et de Géographie Ecclésiastique
EJL	Early Judaism and its Literature
FRLANT	Forschungen zur Religion und Literatur des Alten und Neuen Testaments
GCS	Die griechische christliche Schriftsteller der ersten [drei] Jahrhunderte
HDR	Harvard Dissertations in Religion
HNT	Handbuch zum Neuen Testament
HR	*History of Religions*
HTR	*Harvard Theological Review*
HUT	Hermeneutische Untersuchungen zur Theologie
ILS	*Inscriptiones latinae selectae* (Berlin 1892–1916)
JAAR	*Journal of the American Academy of Religion*
JAC	*Jahrbuch für Antike und Christentum*
JBL	*Journal of Biblical Literature*
JECS	*Journal of Early Christian Studies*
JFSR	*Journal of Feminist Studies in Religion*
JMEMS	*Journal of Medieval and Early Modern Studies*
JSNT	*Journal for the Study of the New Testament*
JRS	*Journal of Roman Studies*
JRelS	*Journal of Religious Studies*
JSJ	*Journal for the Study of Judaism*
JSNTSup	*Journal for the Study of the New Testament,* Supplement Series
JSPSup	*Journal for the Study of the Pseudepigrapha,* Supplement Series
JTS	*Journal of Theological Studies*
LEC	Library of Early Christianity
LCL	Loeb Classical Library
MAMA	*Monumenta Asiae Minoris Antiqua*. Manchester and London, 1928–1993
NewDocs	*New Documents Illustrating Early Christianity*. Edited by G. H. R. Horsley and S. Llewelyn. North Ryde, N.S.W., 1981

NPNF[1]	*Nicene and Post-Nicene Fathers*, Series 1
NRSV	New Revised Standard Version
NTS	*New Testament Studies*
PG	Patrologia Graeca
PL	J.-P. Migne (ed.), Patrologia cursus completus Series prima [latina] (221 vols.; Paris: J.-P. Migne, 1844–65)
Rech. Aug.	*Recherches Augustiniennes*
RAC	*Reallexikon für Antike und Christentum*. Edited by T. Kluser et al. Stuttgart, 1950–
RivB	*Rivista biblica italiana*
RSR	*Recherches de science religieuse*
SAOC	Studies in Ancient Oriental Civilizations
SBLDS	SBL Dissertation Series
SBLMS	SBL Monograph Series
SBLTT	SBL Texts and Translations
SC	Source Chrétiennes
SE	*Studia Evangelica*
SMSR	*Studi e materiali di storia delle religioni*
TU	Texte und Untersuchungen
VC	*Vigilae Christianae*
ZKG	*Zeitschrift für Kirchengeschichte*
ZPE	*Zeitschrift für Papyrologie und Epigraphik*

LIST OF CONTRIBUTORS

Barbara E. Bowe, Catholic Theological Union, Chicago, IL, USA
Denise Kimber Buell, Williams College, Williamstown, MA, USA
Virginia Burrus, Drew University, Madison, NJ, USA
Elizabeth A. Castelli, Columbia University, New York, NY, USA
Elizabeth A. Clark, Duke University, Durham, NC, USA
Kathy L. Gaca, Vanderbilt University, Nashville, TN, USA
Robin M. Jensen, Vanderbilt University, Nashville, TN, USA
Ross S. Kraemer, Brown University, Providence, RI, USA
Carolyn Osiek, Brite Divinity School, Fort Worth, TX, USA
Teresa M. Shaw, Claremont Graduate University, Claremont, CA, USA

INTRODUCTION

AMY-JILL LEVINE

The time of the Early Church, sometimes designated by the seminal terms 'the Patristic Period' or the time of the 'Church Fathers', witnessed various constructions of sexuality, gender, the body, the family and 'woman'. The letters and sermons, martyrologies and hagiographies, architecture and exegesis, from the late first through to the early fifth centuries receive similarly diverse treatments by historians today. Some interpreters debate the possibility of saying anything meaningful about the experiences and thoughts of women in antiquity; some look to missed opportunities for women in early Christianity's development; some locate women's presence in the fissures and inconsistencies of ecclesiastical rhetoric; others interrogate the rationales and the techniques wherein women's actions were constrained. Investigating the intersections of Christianity and philosophy, gender and class, metaphor and realia, body and society, the following ten articles demonstrate the enormous contributions feminist criticism has made to this complex corpus; more, they proffer new avenues of inquiry and new theoretical approaches for future research.

Ross S. Kraemer's 'When is a Text About a Woman a Text About a Woman?' opens with a helpful overview of how feminist investigation of women's history and Christian origins has changed in both focus and conclusion. Whereas much second-wave feminist analysis sought to recover the voices and experiences of 'real women', the shift to interest in gender construction tended to erase 'real women' from the object of inquiry, and focus on masculinity further de-emphasized interest in women's lives, real or imagined. Breaking out of this either/or impasse, and breaking through the traditional disciplinary borders among the study of Jewish Pseudepigrapha, Christian hagiography and Hellenistic novellae, Kraemer asks about both women's history and the construction of gender by putting into dialogue the *Book of Aseneth*, the *Martyrdom of Saints Perpetua and Felicitas*, and the conventions with which ancient writers depicted women.

Aseneth, the daughter of an Egyptian priest, becomes the wife of Joseph (Gen. 41.45); *Aseneth*, which Kraemer dates to the third or early fourth century CE, recounts this beautiful young virgin's rejection of idolatry and affiliation with Judaism. Some historians regard *Aseneth* as yielding information about elite life at the time of composition (itself a highly debated question), and regard Aseneth's conversion experience – despite its facilitation by a gorgeous angel, hyperactive bees, and a mystical honeycomb, and despite Aseneth's own overwrought behaviour – as reflecting the experiences of actual proselytes. Others regard the text as an allegory, whether of the Soul that achieves union with the Divine or of the Jewish temple in Leontopolis. For Kraemer, the best lenses through which to read *Aseneth* are the late Hellenistic and early Christian romances – stories that stake out ideological positions about gender constructions, class status, ethnic identity, self and other.

Whereas Aseneth does not lose her female identity – to the contrary, she is wife to Joseph, mother to his children, and object of sexual desire for Pharaoh's son – her conversion nevertheless signals the attainment of male markers. She discards her female-identified foolishness for self-control, her idolatrous silliness for wisdom. When she covers her head with a veil, the angel makes her remove it, for 'today you are a holy virgin, and your head is a young man's'. The male-identified Aseneth thus resembles the Therapeutrides described by Philo (themselves, as Kraemer notes, not necessarily 'real women'), evokes the letter of Porphyry to Marcella, and recalls the prophesying women in the first-century Corinthian Church. But the liminality and attendant masculinity of the conversion experience must end. Aseneth's veil and so gender distinction reappear in subsequent scenes, and her marriage to Joseph marks her as the sort of woman Clement of Alexandria might praise: spiritually virtuous and domestically submissive. That the idolatrous Egyptian outsider who transforms into faithful Jewish insider is female may reflect, as Kraemer observes, 'an idea of woman as a more natural exemplar of the other and therefore a better candidate for transformation'. Her otherness is heightened by its liminality and masculinization achieved at conversion, and then Aseneth is safely tucked back into the woman's role. Yet if the woman is the better candidate for transformation, what then becomes of the male convert? Is he not only circumcised, but also feminized? And, given the fluid gender-markers that complement early Christian discourse, might his feminization be seen as a positive thing?

The couplet of masculinity and liminality reappears in the *Passio Sanctarum Perpetuae et Felicitatis*, where again masculine codes do not erase female eroticism. As Aseneth becomes male, so too Perpetua becomes transformed into a male. Yet the North African saints Perpetua and Felicity do not share Aseneth's fate of marriage and family; these women are accorded no explicit husbands; they give up their children; they suffer martyrdom.

Although the *Passio* claims to incorporate first-person testimony from Perpetua – and thus would be the earliest known writing by a Christian woman – both the claim to female authorship and the historicity of the martyrdom accounts may be questioned. Neither the attestation of the ancient editor, nor appeals to a discernible female rhetoric, nor arguments of verisimilitude confirm female authorship. Kraemer further observes that the *Passio* can be understood in part as a narrative dramatization of Joel 2.28–29 (cf. Acts 2.18). Yet she refuses to forego the search for women's history, or retreat to a focus on the discourses of gender and so the categories of men and masculinity. As she demonstrates, accompanied by careful readings of such resources as donative inscriptions and papyrus contracts, narratives such as the *Passio* and even *Aseneth* may prove 'not entirely unusable' resources for reconstructing the actualities of women's lives.

Text and material culture might well allow the recovery of the specifics of life, including ritual practice; how individuals understood their participation in such practice must remain speculative. What Church theologians asserted, what their followers experienced, and what feminist readers discover are not necessarily equivalent. These various questions of material culture, theological reflection and feminist observation combine in Robin M. Jensen's '*Mater Ecclesia* and *Fons Aeterna*: The Church and her Womb in Ancient Christian Tradition'. Despite Jesus' explanation to Nicodemus in John 4 that to be 'born again' (γεννηθῆναι) is a spiritual rather than physical act, early commentators regard the Church as a new mother and describe baptism as a new birth. Concretizing such associations, Christian architects built baptismal fonts to resemble wombs that would give birth to infants in Christ. The Church herself, as Jensen demonstrates, is conceived by the Church Fathers as both fecund and virginal. Like the Virgin Mary, she is faithful consort and chaste daughter, nurturing and immaculate; a new Eve, she is the 'Mother of All Christians'. Irenaeus details the development from Mother Eve's sexual intercourse, conception and childbirth, to Mary's conception and birth without intercourse, to the Church's parturition, which requires no intercourse and which gives birth spiritually rather than physically. For Ambrose, the Church is 'immaculate in intercourse' (*immaculate coitu*) and thus contradicts the order of nature, just as did Mary's pregnancy.

Jensen notes that while the imagery values women's potential fertility and generativity, and while it does challenge elitism by making all Christians children of the same mother, it may also have negative implications for women's personal and cultural roles. For example, the imagery transfers value from biological mothers to the *Ekklesia* (and her male managers) as well as potentially devalues *human* pregnancy, parturition and parenting. As the gap between biological procreation and ecclesial conception widens, Mother Church becomes the ideal for consecrated virgins; her conception of children requires not semen or sex, but the reception of divine seed conveyed by the power of the Holy Spirit. Moreover, Mother Church's generativity is infinite: continually fertilized, continually giving birth, continually feeding her children, she is a Church Father's ideal, even as she may seem to a twenty-first feminist speculum grotesque.

Such symbolism also complicates the construction of female modesty by bringing private parts and private actions into public view. Augustine exhorts his catechumens, 'Look to the womb of Mother Church (*uterus matris ecclesie*).' Thus the symbolism overturns the shame connected with the first 'mother of all living', Eve. A number of texts equate the consecration of the baptismal water with its insemination by the Holy Spirit or by God the Father. Zeno asserts that 'a new people is forged in the "milky liquid of the genital font" (*lacteum genitalis fontis ad laticem*)', and Paulinus of Nola explains: 'The Holy Spirit descends from heaven into this river/And marries the water in the sacred, heavenly font.' That such symbolism functions in an institution that values sexual renunciation enhances its power.

Baptisteries then, and now, take various forms and so obtain various meanings: the rectangular shape resembling a tomb or coffin signals death to one's old life; a cruciform shape recalls the sacrifice of the Christ. Perhaps today a womb-like font could convey a positive valuation of women's bodies; perhaps it could reinforce the positive values the Church Fathers inseminated into their baptismal observations: the baptized as children of the same mother; the Church as the protected space where nurturance is guaranteed; the beginning of a new life in which the initiate is truly a 'little child'. But the symbolism cannot be controlled. Perhaps some commentators would find such imagery essentializing, or co-opting of women's physicality, or seeking to naturalize the cultural value placed on childbearing. More likely, and much sadder, far too many today would find such imagery pornographic.

From Kraemer's warnings about using narrative to reconstruct women's lives and experiences, to Jensen's observations on maternal symbolism in both sermon and architecture, this *Companion* turns to its most optimistic recuperation of women's history. Carolyn Osiek's 'The Patronage of Women in Early Christianity' draws upon Roman social history, numerous inscriptions and early Church teachings to recover women's roles as patrons and clients, and thus to see women's influence in social, political and ecclesial settings. Then, by tracing the forms patronage language and function took over the first several Christian centuries, Osiek draws conclusions about Christology, social connections among slaves, masters and freedpersons, the relationship of bishop to congregations, the role of confessors and martyrs and the benefits and debits of a system that benefits the rich with honour even as it accords the less-well-off with reward, rank, support and influence.

Women's patronage extended beyond the hospitality of the house church to financial and material support, recommendations and even bequests. Osiek describes how the system cut across class, for 'any non-elite woman who had accumulated even a modest amount of wealth and connections could be active in patronage relationships'. Similarly, the system cut across gender roles, for the laws and customs of patronage applied to women and men equally: a man could be a woman's patron, and vice versa. In the Roman social world, as opposed to earlier Greek society, 'status took precedence over gender as a marker of prestige and power'. Even in cases where women were prohibited by law from participating in certain civic functions, such as voting, through patronage they were still able to advertise for their favourite candidates and thereby influence elections.

Turning to questions of theology, Osiek suggests that, for Romans, providing economic assistance (*euergetism*) to a community (e.g., distributing food, constructing a public facility, funding civic celebrations) was motivated less by compassion than by the patronage system's focus on honour. She contrasts this approach to the Jewish and then Christian systems of social aid, based on compassion rather than reward; for this she cites Mt. 6.1–4. The Christian was exhorted to donate to others without expecting recognition in return. Further, Osiek sees Paul as adding a new dimension to the patronage system by according all honour, and therefore the role of patron, to God. It is possible that Paul's proclamation of strength through weakness and of servant-leadership may have had some effect in Corinth on a patronage system premised on the desire for public honour and praise. Yet the Church itself recognized the honour that comes with patronage, and women may have found nascent Christian communities ideal settings for gaining public recognition.

Perhaps it was women's increasing public influence in the Churches, achieved substantially through networking, that prompted changes in the patronage system. The texts that became canonical associate submission (ὑποτάσσειν) with the roles of slaves and wives; as Osiek shows, the term then migrates to the deference owed to Church leaders. Ecclesial authorities sought to consolidate patronal power by encouraging centralized charitable donations, by discouraging gifts to the poor made apart from clerical supervision, and by rejecting the charismatic claims of martyrs to forgive sins (here we might speculate how Perpetua or the martyrs from Lyon could be located within an extended patronage system). Likely some women lost patronal honours in the process, just as they did when the Fathers thwarted women's mutual aid systems and made widows dependent on episcopal networks. Yet other women – particularly those of great wealth – managed to thrive in this reformed patronage system: Jerome can be seen as a client of Paula, Chrysostom of Olympias and Rufinas of Melania; their relationships are explored in a number of other essays in this volume.

Osiek ends by noting that in a successful patronage relationship, the powerful protect the powerless; when the relationship does not work well, the powerless become exploited. Whether a system such as Mt. 6.3–4 promotes ('but when you give alms, do not let your left hand know what your right hand is doing, so that your alms may be done in secret; and your Father who sees in secret will reward you'), wherein benefaction is made apart from interest in honour or loyalty, is to be desired over a well-working patronage model in which networks are created, the rich and poor are in relationship, and at least some women can achieve influence and recognition, remains a matter of some debate.

Perhaps, had the Corinthians attended to Paul's revision of patronage ideals, the factionalism that marked the early Christian community there would have abated. But the opportunity appears to have been missed. In her study of *1 Clement*, a pastoral letter written from Rome at the end of the first century to that (still) faction-ridden community, Barbara E. Bowe explores how in this text hermeneutics and hierarchy intersect to empower apostolic – that is, male – authority.

Proposing that the Corinthians' ecclesial structures borrowed from synagogue leadership patterns, Bowe begins by inquiring into women's roles in first-century Diaspora Judaism. Quickly dispelling stereotypes of silent, subordinate and sequestered women remanded to synagogue galleries, she turns to the evidence for women serving as 'heads of synagogues' and in the 'council of elders' as possible support for the presence of women elders (πρεσβύτεροι) in late first-century Corinth. Women may have been among the Corinthian presbyters whose deposition forms the occasion of *1 Clement*. However, given the letter's view of proper gender roles, one might demur from the likelihood of this suggestion.

First Clement itself, although sixty-five chapters long, has little to say specifically about women in the Corinthian Church, and both the implied audience of men (ἄνδρες, ἀδελφοί) and the masculine persona of its author erase female presence. Even the disproportional focus on wifely responsibilities in *1 Clement*'s two invocations of household codes (*Haustafel* material) lacks a sustained argument and so may be seen as conventional. As Bowe puts it, '*1 Clement* does not offer an exclusively gender-specific paraenesis', for the author exhorts everyone to practice submissiveness. Whether those Corinthian women of Paul's time who had been prophesying, speaking in tongues, and otherwise asserting charismatic authority had been cowed into submission, gone under the ecclesial radar, left the church, or died without spiritual heirs, remains unknown.

The women who do receive *1 Clement*'s critical treatment are conventional examples of intra-familial or intra-communal strife. Unlike the hospitable and pious Lot, his unnamed wife 'turned aside' and did not remain in harmony (ὁμονοία). Now a pillar of salt, she cautions any who might question divine power, and so that power's ecclesial representatives. Miriam together with Aaron epitomizes jealousy; they are comparable to Dathan and Abiram, who rebelled against Moses.

Israel's heroines, Rahab, Esther and Judith, as well as female martyrs, are revisioned as 'proper' ladies rather than patrons or independent agents. Rahab the Canaanite, the politically astute businesswoman who sheltered the spies sent by Joshua to Jericho, receives praise for her faith (πίστις), hospitality (φιλοξενία) and especially prophecy (προφητεία). Yet despite her popularity in the early Church, as seen by her references also in Hebrews (11.3) and James (2.25), one might wonder how, and how many of, the Christian faithful identified with her. Were all women (and men) to see themselves as repentant prostitutes? Did men ignore her example in favour of identifying with heroic males, such as Abraham? Although *1 Clement* states that Judith and Esther were 'empowered by divine grace' to 'perform "deeds of manly valor" (ανδρεîος), courage, and fidelity', the descriptions of them are more of meekness than manliness. The forceful, fiercely independent Judith who scolds the town elders for faithlessness becomes, for *1 Clement*, a proper matron who asks the elders' permission for acting on Israel's behalf. Clement praises Esther's faith, fasting, humility and willingness to seek the good of her people over her own interests. As Bowe explains, Clement 'narrates their courageous acts, but values more their humble spirit as an example to be imitated'. Turning to more recent history, Clement adduces the women martyrs 'who were persecuted as Danaids and Dircae, and suffered terrible and unholy outrages', a reference that may allude to the practice of having the condemned enact death scenes from mythology and, perhaps, to women who rejected marriage. Bowe notes that these 'women are no weak, passive, or simpering examples of female submission. They are courageous actors, who intervene to save their people.' But *1 Clement* values them primarily because they conform to normative gender roles. Thus Clement rewrites history, and controls the bodies of the martyrs, to instruct the Church. Bowe concludes: 'Gone completely is any memory of Prisca's teaching, or Chloe's people, or Phoebe's patronage and ministry. ... As for the women in *1 Clement*, we find, instead, "the gentleness of their tongue manifest by their silence".'

Elizabeth A. Clark's 'Ideology, History and the Construction of "Woman" in Late Ancient Christianity' confirms and expands Bowe's observations on how *1 Clement* appropriates and reinterprets earlier texts. In discussing the mechanics of ideology, Clark explains how cultural narratives conceal and contradict, offer continuity as well as dissonance, project containment and attempt to control leakage. Therefore, to construct a stable subject and a fixed self, texts and cultures – or, given a focus on uneven economic and social roles, those who have the power and authority to write texts and manipulate cultures – stereotype, naturalize and universalize. What is a cultural judgement, such as the idea that women are submissive or men rational, becomes seen through narrative, myth and history-writing as true, natural and timeless; non-elite groups impacted by this master-narrative, such as women, submit to their inferior status, and the elites do not question the rightness of their superior social roles. Further, narratives direct attention to the idealized past, where the true, natural and timeless symbols and values escape the chaos of the present; intertextual readings then prevent the detritus of contradictory narratives from impacting the idealized construct. No wonder *1 Clement* and other patristic works based their exhortations to women substantially on biblical accounts, historical narratives, and thus nostalgia for a(n invented) past. The task of the critic then becomes one of interrogating the gaps, making visible what is not said, denaturalizing and rehistori-cizing.

Clark engages the critical task by examining patristic stereotyping, universal-izing and naturalizing of 'woman' and so the construction and containment of female subjectivity. For example, through an appeal to Eve (see 1 Tim. 2.11–1), Tertullian can say of, and to, all women: 'you are the Devil's gateway ... you so lightly crushed the image of God, the man Adam; because of your punishment, that is, death, even the Son of God had to die' (*cult. fem.* 1.1.2). Jerome uses the *topos* of woman's 'weakness' both to ground exhortations against second marriage and for living in community; he further uses the trope to shame men who do not follow the exemplary renunciation that *even women*, such as Paula and Eustochium, model. John Chrysostom, exhorting men to avoid marriage, describes women as 'wicked, false, insulting, garrulous, irrational, and given to drink'; their innate being then threatens men, for women will make male ascetics 'softer, more hot-headed, shameful, mindless, irascible, insolent...', in effect, 'women'. Only select women, like Jerome's patrons Paula and Eustochium, and Chrysostom's friend Olympias, escape the stereotypes since, as the Fathers understand the term, they cease to be 'women'. Perhaps echoes of the masculinized *Aseneth* and Perpetua, or even Phoebe and Junia, can be heard in the background of their discussions.

To secure their teachings, the Fathers required exemplary figures, whether biblical (e.g., Sarah, Rebecca, Mary and Martha) or classical (e.g., Lucretia, Dido), who either could be imitated or, as with Eve or Lot's wife, could serve as negative models. Consequently, biblical figures took on a mythic – that is, timeless – quality. The Fathers evoked 'the good old days' when men ruled, women stayed home, and both men and women knew their place; they lamented (or ignored) the present, in which women owned property, served as their children's guardians and could initiate divorce. They could do no more, since their efforts to inscribe their morality into Roman law were unsuccessful. This same approach appears in *1 Clement*, as Bowe indicates: the letter speaks of the 'good old days' of the Corinthian congregations; a glance at Paul's epistles to the Corinthians reveals the artificiality of the appeal. Clark shows how John Chrysostom reads Genesis 1 in light of 1 Corinthians 11 to conclude that only man was created in the divine image, and then to explain that the image equals authority, which only men have. Similarly, 1 Corinthians allows Chrysostom to understand Genesis as promoting a 'natural' hierarchy in which man is the 'head' of creation and woman the 'body' that both entraps and needs to be controlled. Jerome reads 1 Corinthians 7 with the intertext of Proverbs 6, 7 and 9 to warn men about the dangers of women who 'touch' and so cause loss of understanding. As Clark explains, the male restraint Paul advocates is transformed into a message of female danger. Texts such as the exhortation for young widows to remarry (1 Timothy 5) are not discarded; rather, they receive their 'proper' interpretation through intertextual readings with occasional help from allegory.

Yet this naturalizing and universalizing break down. Chrysostom locates women's weakness not just in their nature, but also in their upbringing; what had been seen as 'natural' becomes recognized as culturally created. Other fissures show in the appeal to the past, which itself has to be controlled and so moulded to serve present needs. While Methodius can speak of a progressive morality developing from Genesis, a morality that saw sequential prohibitions of incest, polygamy, adultery, and finally the teaching of virginity and continence, the 'progress' needed to be stopped at some point, lest contemporary women – say, Montanists – would think they excelled their predecessors. One solution was a proposed downward trajectory from biblical times for women, or what Clark calls the 'greater dissoluteness'. Whereas Rebecca could appear in public, interact with men, and not endanger her purity, and whereas New Testament women could be called 'apostles', women of the Fathers' time could not. Another view, popular in the fourth and fifth centuries, was that it was all downhill once sexual intercourse and marriage entered the world. Only in the Fathers' own time was humanity able to reclaim paradise through asceticism. The greater dissoluteness, however, contradicted the idea of the liberating effects of the cross; the downward trajectory from Eden threatened the denigration of the Old Testament. Gaps had to be filled; contradictions needed to be glossed.

Attending to the gaps, the strategies of containment, the silences in the writings of the Fathers, Clark then proposes a counter-narrative in which aristocratic women, converted to ascetic forms of Christianity, found in the Church a prime outlet for patronage. Thus, what Clark finds in the fourth and fifth-century Christians recapitulates in part what Osiek discovered for the first and early second-century house churches. In the post-Constantinian Church, elite women such as Paula and Melania the Younger served as patrons to the Fathers and to the Christian community, and the Fathers, such as Jerome and Chrysostom, were their clients. To what extent Paula and Olympias internalized the gender-coded teachings proffered by the Fathers, and how these upper-class women understood the stereotypes promulgated by their ecclesiastical teachers albeit social inferiors (in terms of birth and income), cannot be known. But we do know that Olympias used her wealth to support the church in Constantinople, and that Paula supported not only Jerome, but also communities of women. Moreover, despite their stereotyping, naturalizing and universalizing of women's subordinate nature, Jerome, Chrysostom and others nevertheless encouraged women toward extra-domestic activity and study. Therefore, Clark states, 'the little we know about the actual women who were represented in patristic writings make us question whether the ideological stance of the Fathers entirely won the day … [the Fathers] left us portraits of them that suggest that the patristic ideology of "womanhood" had been to some degree subverted from within, by the women themselves.'

Clark's warnings about the power of ideology, about the means by which stories are presented to reinforce and so naturalize cultural constructions, apply directly to the stories of female martyrs. On the one hand, in the early centuries of the Church, non-elite women, including slaves, as well as their upper-class sisters, could obtain power and influence through martyrdom: such women not only gained earthly honour among their fellow Christians and, perhaps, admiration from the pagan crowds, they were also taught that they had – and some likely experienced – special access to the divine. On the other, the stories of their deaths became the means by which female identity was shaped and contained. Looking at the *Passio Sanctarum Perpetuae et Felicitatis* as well as the narratives of two other female martyrs – Biblis and Blandina of Lyon – Virginia Burrus explores how gender, power, status and identity are tested and transformed through (the description of) torture. As the female martyr conceives a new masculinity, she simultaneously reinscribes her female identity; as the Church Fathers appropriate her tortured body, she is both freed and domesticated.

Such paradoxical appropriations are consistent with the public nature of torture. While spectacles of violence strip victims of honour, modesty and life, they also empower by providing victims a public face and the chance of acquiring public glory. Epitomizing this dichotomous role is the gladiator, who held a slave-like status even as he, like the martyr, became the object of both male and female desire. But as the boundaries between slave and free became more fluid – with slaves gaining freedom and power and Roman citizens playing at being gladiators, women and slaves – so too gender roles in the second century became destabilized. Simultaneously, the foregrounding of *patientia*, or 'endurance', as a virtue by Stoics, Jews and Christians, and the attendant recognition of a weakness that required discipline, created fluidity in understandings of gender, the body and power. Burrus argues that this emphasis on endurance denaturalized female submissiveness and so granted women agency. Her point is proved by the textual performances of women such as Biblis, Blandina and Perpetua.

Burrus explains how the elaborate descriptions of physical mutilation and the preoccupation with social status and gender in *The Letter of the Churches of Lyons and Vienne* relate to the construction of Christian witness. As the torturer obtains from Biblis the truth of her Christianity, he cedes to her the power of witness and is himself thus placed on trial. As the reader identifies with the tortured slave Blandina, whose body speaks the truth and so exemplifies freedom, social norms and gender roles are reversed if not dissolved. The female slave outlasts her torturers, for 'even those who were taking turns to torture her in every way from dawn to dusk were weary and exhausted'. Hung 'in the form of a cross' on a post, her fellow Christians 'saw in the person of their sister him who was crucified for them…'. Blandina even becomes a new Eve who 'would make irreversible the condemnation of the crooked serpent … for she had overcome the Adversary'. Victorious athlete, crucified Christ and redemptory Eve, Blandina surpasses her earthly role, even as she remains ever the female slave. Her heroism is admirable and striking, precisely because she is female, for the 'pagans themselves admitted that no woman had ever suffered so much in their experience'.

In *The Passion of Perpetua and Felicitas*, gender is more explicitly contested, in numerous senses of the term. Perpetua, like Blandina, is humiliated, tortured and dies; she is also a new Eve who treads on the head of a dragon. Like Blandina, her body articulates a new form of Christian subjectivity by assuming the masculine characteristics of endurance and steadfastness. But despite Perpetua's masculine self-image – facilitated by the miraculous weaning of her son, her dream of being a male athlete stripped for combat but unashamed, and her victory in battle – she remains the matron of a good family, the companion of the Felicitas, whose pregnancy and parturition reinforce female identification, and an eroticized naked woman. Despite her explicit female coding, Felicitas too confounds gender roles, as she speaks of how her sufferings in childbirth and in torture are displaced by the suffering of Jesus; he who 'will be inside me [and] who will suffer for me, just as I have suffered for him'. Like Blandina, her body becomes a screen that reveals the (male? female? androgynous?) body of her Lord.

That subjectivity comes via the twin expressions of torture and martyrdom is not particularly good news. That the bodies of Biblis, Blandina, Perpetua and Felicity become the ideal for Christian women is not particularly good news either. That they hold potentially eroticized roles and are to be taken as objects of desire grants a potentially pornographic aspect to their stories. Blandina, Biblis, Perpetua and Felicity defeat their enemies by embodying the truth; they gain freedom but at the cost of their lives. When Church Fathers secure orthodoxy by appropriating the (rhetorical) bodies of tortured women and slaves, the cost bears interest. Women's subjectivity, actual or constructed or both, comes at a heavy price.

Before, during and after the age of martyrdom, bodies remained the site of constructions of gender, mimesis and restraint. Christian rhetoricians explained that by disciplining the body, virgins and celibates could conquer the passions, subdue the devil, and move toward perfection; women adepts might even escape female identity and its attendant markers of pathos, physical corruption, weakness, or evil. In 'Virginity and its Meaning for Women's Sexuality in Early Christianity', Elizabeth A. Castelli explores how Christian discourse promoted asceticism and then seeks to discover how this discourse impacted women's lives.

Castelli begins with historiographical caveats; although her sources are different from those adduced by Kraemer, her warnings complement Kraemer's, for both reveal that what remains of women's lives in antiquity is accidental, filtered, haphazard and incomplete. Sources for women's asceticism are almost entirely literary: the *Apocryphal Acts of the Apostles*, letters to women by the Church Fathers, treatises and homilies on virginity from the third century and following, biographies of exceptional women such as Macrina and Melania the Younger, and anecdotal accounts about as well as sayings attributed to the desert mothers. The picture these works present may be no truer of Christian women in antiquity than the pronouncements of any religious leader, or the images in any book or movie, reflect the lives and experiences of women in Nashville or Auckland, Rome or Kinshasa.

The Fathers offered several arguments to persuade women to restrain their passions and adopt the celibate life: they stressed the marital woes of jealousy and strife, concern for familial illnesses, accidents and death, worries about fertility, miscarriage, pain and death in childbirth, and the suffering of the widowed. They analogized marriage to tragedy, disease and social evils. As Chrysostom insists, the virgin 'is not obliged to involve herself tiresomely in the affairs of her spouse and she does not fear being abused'. She not only escapes the 'curse' of suffering in childbirth, she also need not submit to an earthly husband. Her master is the Christ, her marriage is celestial, her fecundity is spiritual, and erotic language surrounds the description of her life with her heavenly bridegroom. Athanasius advises that virgins who abandon feminine mentality and so please God 'will be elevated to male ranks'. The import of virginity is sealed in the trope of the virgin threatened with rape for whom suicide is the preferred response. The drastic response is not based on the violence of the attack but on the fact that it would render the virgin unfit for her heavenly bridegroom.

The rhetoric to a great extent worked. By the fifth century, Christian virgins were living in communities or with continent men; Christian wives were living celibately with their husbands; Christian daughters practised asceticism in their homes. Renunciation of marriage provided elite women new intellectual opportunities and greater control over their wealth; those who led women's communities practised administrative skills that otherwise would have been invested in household management. However, as Castelli observes, the ideology of virginity, like the ideology of marriage, also domesticated and circumscribed women's sexuality. Because sexuality was perceived to be an intrinsic component of female identity, renunciation of sexuality threatened to promote self-alienation with the goal of self-dissolution. Conversely, for the Fathers, women's elevation to the (preferred) masculine role was spiritual only: women were to appear as female rather than cut their hair or wear men's clothes. As to whether the benefits of virginity outweighed the problems of psychological alienation and ecclesiastically based commodification, the virgins of antiquity, and their nonvirginal sisters, mothers and friends, would likely offer a variety of answers.

Teresa M. Shaw's 'The Virgin Charioteer and the Bride of Christ: Gender and the Passions in Late Ancient Ethics and Early Christian Writings on Virginity' similarly concludes that virginity 'both subverts and reinforces traditional notions of female virtue'. Looking at virginity through the discourse of late ancient moral theory, including the pathologized relationship between behaviour and the health of the soul, Shaw details how Christian writers refashioned the marital advice given by Galen, Musonius Rufus, Epictetus and Plutarch.

The earlier moralists recommended the exercise of self-control (σωφροσύνη) and abstinence (ἐγκράτεια), sexual moderation and detachment from desire; achieving these goals required a 'combination of mental exercise, self-examination, moral guidance and physical renunciation'. Just as the charioteer controls his horses, so the rational mind controls the impulsive parts of the irrational soul, and both Christian moralists and their non-Christian counterparts saw men and women as equally capable of attaining such self-control.

Gender, however, complicates both the achievement of σωφροσύνη and its results. For example, women display σωφροσύνη through decorum, refraining from gossip and chastity. Applied to men, σωφροσύνη connotes self-mastery and self-knowledge, moderation and resistance to uncontrolled passion. And yet, the malleability of the ethical system allows women to become masculinized by the exercise of ἀνδρεία just as a man becomes feminized by cultivating σωφροσύνη. Further complicating the discourse of asceticism in both Christian and Pagan contexts is the categorization of the soul as effeminate and so both as stimulated by external sensations and as subject to pollution by the passions (the irrational) just as semen pollutes the womb.

Shaw details the gendered imagery that describes the passions and the training (ἄσκησις, whence 'asceticism') required to resist them in three Greek Christian texts: the short instructions by Evagrius of Pontus (c. 345–399) entitled *Sententide ad virginem* and two anonymous works influenced by Evagrius's ascetic theory, the *Life of Syncletica*, and the *Discourse on Salvation to a Virgin*. According to these works, women can achieve the goals of self-control (σωφροσύνη), manliness (ἀνδρεία) and even ἀπάθεια (freedom from passions), purity of prayer and illumination. However, to do so they must project an image of physical integrity and protect their virtue through traditional female behaviour: staying out of the public sphere, avoiding gossip (thereby keeping a closed mouth along with the rest of the closed body), having downcast eyes, practising modesty, humility and the like. For the female virgin, the reward of training (ἄσκησις) is union with the heavenly bridegroom; for her male counterparts, it is knowledge of God. Thus, as Shaw demonstrates, gender continues to shape 'even the most radical ascetic eschatology'.

It shaped Christian philosophy as well. Repeating Paul's insistence that in Christ there is 'neither slave nor free, and not male or female' (Gal. 3.28), Clement of Alexandria, the second-century Christian Platonist, concludes that women as well as children and slaves should 'philosophize equally with [free] men'; he develops his pneumatology by using imagery of birth and lactation, and he goes as far as to proclaim that God 'became female' for the sake of human salvation. Yet Clement also follows the *Haustafel* model that relegates women and slaves to positions of subordination. While he avers that women can become 'Gnostics' and so hold the highest rank in his Christian system, he also sets as requisite for attaining this state not only eradication of passions but also 'becoming male'. To sort through these apparently mixed messages and thus reveal how Clement constructs his own authority, Denise Buell extends the feminist focus on gender to address how Clement treats ethnicity and class, sexual practice and history.

Interrogating four of Clement's works – the *Protreptikos*, the *Paidagogos*, the *Stromateis* (or *Miscellanies*) and *Who is the Rich Person Who is Being Saved?* – Buell's 'Ambiguous Legacy: A Feminist Commentary on Clement of Alexandria's Works' confirms Clark's observations on stereotype, naturalizing, universalizing and intertextuality. For example, the *Protreptikos* uses conventional images in depicting the Christian Word (*Logos*) as making fertile the desert and the womb whereas non-Christians, and their beliefs and practices, are barren and sterile. Clement's non-Christian readers, described as atheists, are eunuchs, whereas those who follow the Christ produce a fertile lineage. The images of the true convert, taken from farming, sea-faring, the military and the household, are, like those of *1 Clement*, premised on the conventional experiences of free adult men. Despite his concern to reorient readers from custom to Christ, Clement reinforces the privilege of the Christian 'citizen' rather than undermines normative hierarchies; how slaves, women or children might become appropriate imitators of these models is not Clement's concern; that the mimetic ideal necessarily reinforces inequality is not antithetical to Clement's views.

Clement does see the act of conversion to Christianity as crossing an ethnic boundary (the same could be said of *Aseneth*), but he seeks to erase the fluidity that might keep the path open between Christian identity determined by the Church and the identities of Jew, Greek and Barbarian. If one can cross over, then one might cross back; as the unstable nature of gender remained a social threat, so too the unstable identities of ethnic classification and social status continued to threaten the pure identity of the Christians. To secure the Christian identity of his new converts and protect their boundaries, Clement describes them having been granted citizenship in the heavenly city, as being heirs of the heavenly Father, and as free from the 'slavery' of other religious practices and beliefs. To return to their original identity would then mean loss of citizenship, disinheritance and enslavement.

The problem of gender fluidity, seen in several articles in this collection, arises also in Clement's writings. His theology advocates a deity who manifests both male- and female-coded actions, and his soteriology allows the morphing of the female into the male in terms of human perfection. Again, the potential benefits to 'women' are in the spiritual realm only. Seeking to close the gender markers, Clement solidifies social boundaries between men and women in the Church.

Nevertheless, the *Protreptikos* does offer, according to Buell, at least two avenues of potential feminist recuperation. The first is Clement's 'apologetic for Christian novelty', which Buell connects with feminist reimaginings of the past and visions for the future. The second is his homogenizing vision, echoing both Paul's Epistle to the Galatians and Homer's *Iliad*, that 'the whole Christ, so to speak, is not divided; there is … neither male nor female, but a new human transformed by the Holy Spirit of God' (11.112.3). Although Buell notes the supersessionist and triumphalistic aspects of Clement's rhetoric, feminist potential remains even in his willingness to draw from non-Christian sources.

Feminist readings of the *Paidagogos* encounter similar appeals to status and gender along with familial imagery for the divine and an emphasis on obedience and imitation. Following Paul's nursing imagery (see 1 Cor. 3.2) as well as Classical images of education, Clement develops the metaphoric potential of pregnancy, parturition and lactation. Then, physiologically connecting milk and blood, and drawing again on both Paul and Homer, he develops the image of the Christ who nourishes his children *in utero*, gives birth to them, and continues to feed them. The imagery suggests more than sustenance; it also, like the baptisteries and teachings described by Jensen, promotes the unity of all Christians: as children of the same 'maternal Logos' they share not only food, but also substance.

This is not to say that Clement elides sexual difference. Men and women are separated by embodiedness manifest particularly in sexual desire, and it is in this arena that Clement draws on stock figures, such as the 'silly woman' and the 'effeminate man', and the convention of the active male and the passive female. For Clement, appropriate sexual behaviour is explicitly heterosexual, connubial, procreative and characterized by self-restraint, and it projects the proper Christian life as requiring constant self-monitoring.

Turning to the *Stromateis*, Buell explores how Clement emphasizes the elimination of human desires within his discussion of sexual practices, marriage and procreation. Steering a middle ground between what he perceives as Carpocration licentiousness and the too stringent asceticism of Marcion and John Cassian, Clement promotes marriage and procreation and so the male householder as the ideal Christian. Yet Buell also notes how 'Clement's own logic introduces a tension between this hierarchical social ideal and the requirements for becoming the ideal Gnostic Christian.' Despite epitomizing the male householder, Clement also insists that gender, status, age and ethnicity 'are not disqualifying impediments'. Whereas bodily differentiation destines a woman for childbearing, housekeeping and subordination to a husband, a woman's (dis-embodied) soul is neither male nor female, and women who do attain perfection are transformed (spiritually) into males. The discussion of martyrdom in particular facilitates Clement's comments on equality (or, less generously put, erasure of difference) between men and women; when discussion focuses on domestic arrangements, hierarchies are reinforced. As we have seen, the erasure of difference through martyrdom comes at a very high price.

In Kathy L. Gaca's study of paradigms of sexual morality, Clement emerges once again as offering teachings of both freedom and constraint. Attempting to counter the teachings of Epiphanes, a 'Gnostic' philosopher who followed Plato in advocating communal sexual norms, Clement draws upon the patriarchal norms of marriage found in the Decalogue and Paul's Epistles. The disagreement is one of hermeneutics (and so the discussion again supports Clark's observations on ideology).

Although in substantial theological agreement on the one, true (masculine) God, the two Christian philosophers offer a different theological construct. Although substantially agreeing on the order of creation and recognizing that sexual rules are pivotal for social and moral order, ranging from kinship structures to the distribution of wealth to the shaping of society to the formulations of justice (cf. today's culture wars concerning same-sex marriage, polygamy and birth control), they offer different sets of sexual desiderata. Epiphanes, arguing for Plato's god and so Plato's moral system, argued for an equitable structure of justice encompassing women as well as men. Sounding much like both Luke (Acts 2:42–45) and Plato (*Rep.* 424a1–2, 449c4–5), he asserted the principles of 'communal sharing on an equitable basis (κοινωνία μετ᾽ ἰσότητος)'. Therefore, laws are unjust if they lead to private property, and an equitable society requires humans to abandon the desire to acquire persons and goods. In terms of familial construction, Epiphanes, following Plato, stated that men must cease taking wives as property, and so cease to promote patriarchal marriage and the family; instead, they should practise communal sexual mores. Plato himself insisted that communalizing women and reproductive labour removes kinship-based factionalism and severs sexual desire from consumerism; women freed from consumer-driven goals and kinship loyalties, and aided by communal childcare, could contribute to the city's greater good.

Such a position inevitably prompts Epiphanes to pronounce the tenth commandment, which supports male ownership of property, including wives, quite ludicrous (γελοιοτερόν). In his view, the deity is revealed through Plato, not Moses. Epiphanes evokes Pauline phrasing on the relationship of sin and law – but not Paul's teachings on either celibacy or conjugal sex – to argue that sin entered the world through the law (νόμος) of men taking wives.

In fact, Epiphanes had a chance of holding the orthodox position. In the second century, Christianity remained partially shaped by the communal social ideas idealized in Acts 2.42–45, and the monastic orders show their ongoing persuasiveness. The developing interest in asceticism continued to challenge the familial norms, and Plato's teaching that virtue comes from their restraining of their sensuous and acquisitive desires will later echo in the teachings of *askesis*. Epiphanes' reading of Genesis anticipates one of the views Clark describes as surfacing in the fourth and early fifth centuries. Much later, his communitarian views would find resonance in American utopian communities.

But just as Plato's communal sexual proposals were ridiculed, so too Epiphanes was caricatured as, in Gaca's terms, a 'libidinous heretic'. Yet this name-calling betrays gaps in Clement's own hermeneutic. Whereas Clement accuses Epiphanes of misreading Plato's *Republic*, it is his own hermeneutic, guided by his canonical texts, that forces him to do the misreading. For Clement, Plato was Moses' disciple and therefore, logically, Plato could not argue for the communalization of wives.

Patriarchal marriage became the Christian norm, and Plato's vision of a society that eschewed private property, had communal childcare, freed women from domestic labour and the replication of domestic tasks, became labelled as heretical. Then again, perhaps matters would be worse with the Platonic utopian model, in which women become an aggregate set of wombs to be utilized by the men in the community.

From history to ideology, patrons to martyrs and back to patrons, rhetoric to ritual, asceticism to architecture, the essays in this volume can only hint at the enormous work that has been done in the study of the early Church. Read together with the Companions to the New Testament Apocrypha and Mariology, these essays complement, and complicate, the approaches to the materials of the early Church, and conclusions drawn from them.

'Many Women Have Been Empowered Through God's Grace…' (*1 Clem.* 55.3): Feminist Contradictions and Curiosities in Clement of Rome

Barbara E. Bowe

The Setting

In the history of early Christianity, the letter known as *1 Clement* stands as a Janus-like figure presiding over the turn of the first century.[1] On the one hand, pointing back to apostolic times, it shares with Paul a concern for the unity of the fledgling Christian community. It describes, with glowing hyperbole (albeit questionable accuracy), a recounting of Christian beginnings in Corinth (*1 Clem.* 1.2–3.1) when harmony and concord characterized the Church's gatherings. Clement draws repeatedly from the Septuagint and especially from the Pauline tradition and derives from them principles and strategies to respond to the challenges of a new generation. On the other hand, the letter looks forward to and contains harbingers of the future as it points to the second-century Christian community. This future would be marked by more institutionalized and hierarchical patterns of organization and leadership – not only to guarantee and safeguard communal cohesion but also to preserve unity in doctrine and praxis – from which women increasingly would be excluded. *First Clement* stood on the edge of that development and, somewhat unwittingly, enhanced its arrival.

First Clement is among the earliest Christian documents outside the New Testament canon, although it appears in the fourth-century biblical Codex Alexandrinus. A genuine *letter* from the Roman church to the church in Corinth written about the turn of the first century, it employs all the formal characteristics of deliberative rhetoric: (1) a focus on future time as the subject of deliberation; (2) employment of a determined set of appeals or ends, the most distinctive of which is the advantageous (τὸ συμφέρον); (3) proof by example (παράδειγμα); and (4) appropriate subjects for deliberation, of which factionalism and concord are especially common.[2] In an earlier study, I showed that the authors, intentionally imitating Paul, employed deliberative rhetoric's traditional vocabulary and strategies to urge the Corinthian readers to abandon their factionalism and embrace concord.[3]

---

1 The dating of this text remains inexact, but the limits of ca. 80–140 CE have been convincingly argued by L. L. Welborn, 'On the Date of First Clement', *BR* 29 (1984), pp. 35–54. Surprisingly, the recent commentary by Andreas Lindemann (*Die Clemensbriefe* [HNT, 17; Die Apostolischen Väter, 1; Tübingen: Mohr/Siebeck, 1992], pp. 12–13) accepts the standard dating of ca. 96 CE which is based on the assumption that the reference in *1 Clem.* 1.1 to 'sudden and repeated misfortunes and calamities' refers to sporadic persecutions under Domitian. He is apparently unaware of Welborn's arguments.

2 Margaret M. Mitchell, *Paul and the Rhetoric of Reconciliation* (HUT, 28; Tübingen: Mohr/Siebeck, 1991), p. 23.

3 Barbara E. Bowe, *A Church in Crisis. Ecclesiology and Paraenesis in Clement of Rome* (HDR, 23; Minneapolis, MN: Fortress Press, 1988), esp. pp. 58–74.

The occasion that prompted Roman Christians to write this letter was the report that had reached them (*1 Clem.* 47.7) of the outbreak in Corinth of factions similar to the situation Paul addressed (1 Cor. 1–4). The factions in Clement's day had apparently been triggered by the deposition of some (not all) Corinthian presbyters (44.6). Despite recent arguments to the contrary,[4] the letter does not at all make clear who was responsible for their deposition, what the motive was for their ouster, or how widespread the support for this deposition was in the larger community. In keeping with acceptable rhetorical strategy, the letter provides only vague allusions to the exact cause and nature of the dispute. However, it considers the effects serious enough to warrant an appeal for the restoration of peace and concord (63.2). The letter was carried to Corinth by couriers from Rome, Claudius Ephebus, Valerius Vito and Fortunatus (*1 Clem.* 65.1 and see 63.3), who no doubt were delegated to act as mediators.

The identity of the author(s) remains obscure – the letter contains no specific reference either to an author or to specific recipients – but Eusebius in the early fourth century (*Hist. eccl.* 3.16.1; 3.38.1) quotes a letter from Bishop Dionysius of Corinth in 170 CE (*Hist. eccl.* 4.23.9), which attributes the text to one 'Clement'. Who this Clement might have been is still uncertain, although many claim that he was an imperial freedman of the household of Titus Flavius Clemens and a (the?) leader among Roman presbyters.[5] He might have been the same Clement mentioned by the *Shepherd of Hermas* (*Vis.* 2.4.3) whose duty it was to send communication from Rome 'to the cities abroad'. It is certain that he did not function in the role of monarchical bishop, as Irenaeus later claimed (*Adv. Haer,* 3.3.3), since other early sources (notably Ignatius's *Letter to Rome*) confirm that the monarchical episcopate was not introduced in Rome until at least the middle of the second century. Moreover, this judgement is supported by the fact that *1 Clement* uses the terms 'bishops' (ἐπίσκοποι) and 'presbyters' (πρεσβύτεροι) interchangeably and always in the plural.

Whoever the actual author(s) were, their worldview is unambiguous. The letter offers a positive assessment of Roman society and government (*1 Clem.* 61.1–3), and it demonstrates a concern for the maintenance of order (often hierarchically conceived) consistent with the prevailing perspective of Rome's well-educated 'social elite'.[6] Eusebius reports (*Hist. eccl.* 4.22.1; 4.23.11) that *1 Clement* successfully ended the Corinthian crisis, so persuasive was its plea for harmony. Furthermore, by its apparent success the letter contributed significantly to the development of an ecclesial structure that became increasingly hierarchical and that gradually and systematically excluded women from all forms of communal leadership. Appeal to *1 Clement* to bolster arguments for orthodoxy, institutional order and apostolic (i.e., male) authority (e.g., Irenaeus, *Haer.* 3.3.3; Eusebius, *Hist. eccl.* 4.22.1; 5.7.3) attests to its influence and participation in that development.

4 See most recently, for example, David G. Horrell, *The Social Ethos of the Corinthian Correspondence. Interests and Ideology from 1 Corinthians to 1 Clement* (Edinburgh: T & T Clark, 1996), pp. 244–50.

5 See J. B. Lightfoot, *Apostolic Fathers* (5 vols; 2nd edn; London: Macmillan, 1889–1890), 1.1, pp. 14–103.

6 For this view, see especially James S. Jeffers, *Conflict at Rome. Social Order and Hierarchy in Early Christianity* (Minneapolis, MN: Fortress Press, 1991), esp. pp. 90–105.

Women in Jewish and Christian Communities

To place *1 Clement* in context it is important to review briefly the data concerning women's leadership in Jewish and Christian circles prior to the letter's composition. If the ecclesial structures emerging in Corinth borrowed from the synagogue, as some maintain, then women's roles in first-century Judaism offer a possible parallel for the Christian women in Corinth. Bernadette Brooten's ground-breaking study of women as leaders in ancient synagogues has dispelled well-worn assumptions about the so-called 'women's galleries' in synagogues and the subordinate role of women in Jewish life in the first century CE.[7] Her discussion of the role of women elders is particularly germane to the situation presupposed in *1 Clement*. Inscriptional evidence attests to women serving as 'heads of synagogues' (ἀρχισυναγώγοι),[8] as members of the council of elders (γερουσία),[9] and as patrons and benefactors of the synagogues. Brooten concludes that Jewish women 'could fulfill certain official functions' and were 'most likely members of a council of elders' [that] may have had some oversight of synagogue finances...'.[10] If it is correct to assume that Christian groups at first adopted the structures of leadership known in the synagogue communities, then *1 Clement* must be read admitting the *possibility* that women as well as men served as elders (πρεσβύτεροι) in Corinth.[11]

Concerning Christian practice, the Pauline corpus provides ample evidence of women's leadership. Women were teachers and missionaries like Priscilla (Acts 18.18, 26; 1 Cor. 16.19; Rom. 16.3), 'workers in the Lord' like Tryphaena, Tryphosa and Persis (Rom. 16.12), deacons like Phoebe (Rom. 16.1–2), hosts of house churches like Nympha of Laodicea (Col. 4.3), Lydia of Thyatira who lived in Philippi (Acts 16.11–16), and possibly both Phoebe in Cenchreae and Chloe in Corinth (1 Cor. 1.11). They were part of 'missionary teams', whether married or working partners, like Andronicus and Junia, who are praised as 'outstanding among the apostles' (Rom. 16.7), or like Julia and Philogus (Rom. 16.15), Nereus and his 'sister' (Rom. 16.15), and Apphia and Philemon in Colossae (Phlm. 2). Influential women like Euodia and Syntyche could disrupt the well being of the whole Christian community (Phil. 4.2–3). And despite Paul's wrestling in Corinth with gender distinctions (1 Cor. 11.2–16; 14.33–35), this evidence of women's leadership in early Christian communities remains compelling. In fact, in Corinth, as Ann Wire argues, this leadership may well have stemmed from women's claims of prophetic inspiration that conflicted with Pauline efforts to encourage 'decency and order' (1

---

7 Bernadette Brooten, *Women Leaders in the Ancient Synagogue. Inscriptional Evidence and Background Issues* (BJS, 36; Chico, CA: Scholars Press, 1982).

8 Brooten, *Women Leaders*, pp. 5–33; Ross S. Kraemer (ed.), *Maenads, Martyrs, Matrons, Monastics. A Sourcebook on Women's Religions in the Greco-Roman World* (Philadelphia, PA: Fortress Press, 1988), p. 218.

9 Kraemer, *Maenads*, pp. 219–21.

10 Brooten, *Women Leaders*, p. 55. See also the additional piece of evidence for women elders in Ross S. Kraemer, 'A New Inscription from Malta and the Question of Women Elders in the Diaspora Jewish Communities', *HTR* 78 (1985), pp. 431–38.

11 Kraemer (*Maenads*, pp. 219–21) gives six epitaphs of Jewish women elders dated to the first six centuries CE as well as two examples of Christian women given that same title.

Cor. 14.40).[12] Roman and Corinthian Christians of *1 Clement*'s day were no doubt familiar with this history, even as Christian ministries and paraenesis were already exhorting women to submission within the household (Col. 3.18–4.1; Eph. 5.22–6.9; 1 Pet. 2.18–3.7), urging older women to teach the younger 'feminine' virtues (Tit. 2.3–5), and commending to them their 'appropriate' roles as mothers and wives (1 Tim. 2.11–15; 5.11–15).

Women in First Clement

Just how scant the evidence is in *1 Clement* for any specific data concerning the activities, roles and social portraits of Christian women is striking. Compared to the more sustained effort of the Pastorals – documents roughly contemporary with *1 Clement* – to establish societal controls for women's activities, the letter gives only meagre, direct attention to women in its sixty-five chapters.

The letter, however, betrays an implied audience in which men are more literally and grammatically 'visible' than women.[13] While women can be subsumed under the masculine plural grammatical form, the author specifies his audience as 'brothers' (ἄνδρες ἀδελφοί) in his summary remarks in 62.1. This male perspective is even more evident in the two references to household duties in *1 Clem.* 1.3 and 21.6–8 (discussed below).

Several passages do, however, introduce women as examples (both positive and negative): Miriam (4.11), the 'Danaids and Dircae' (6.2), Lot's wife (11.2), Rahab (12.1–8), Judith and Esther (55.3–6).[14] A brief survey reveals their persuasive logic. The first example, that of Miriam, occurs within a long list of biblical figures illustrating the effects of 'jealousy and envy' (ζῆλος καὶ φθόνος). Beginning with Cain and Abel, *1 Clement* mentions Jacob and Esau, Joseph and his brothers, Moses and his fellow Hebrews. At last the series comes to Aaron and Miriam – 'Through jealousy Aaron and Miriam were lodged outside the camp' (διὰ ζῆλος Ἀαρὼν καὶ Μαριὰμ ἔξω τῆς παρεμβολῆς ηὐλίσθησαν [4.11]) – before concluding with Dathan and Abiram, and finally the jealousy between David and Saul.

Each example underscores the scandal of intra-familial or intra-communal strife and serves to warn the Corinthians of the impending consequences of their own discord. Whereas in Numbers 12, Miriam *alone* suffers the punishment of removal from the camp (in addition to her leprous condition), *1 Clement* links her with Aaron as *both* deserving punishment for their challenge to Moses' prophetic authority. The passive form of the verb 'to lodge' (ηὐλίσθησαν) suggests that it functions as a divine passive and therefore is meant to imply punishment. The letter gives no special emphasis to Miriam; rather, by linking her with Aaron it distributes equally the punishment that Numbers 12 reserves for her alone. On the other hand, because *1 Clement* does not quote the text of Numbers but only alludes to it, we lose the clue

12 See Antoinette Clark Wire, *Corinthian Women Prophets. A Reconstruction through Paul's Rhetoric* (Minneapolis, MN: Fortress Press, 1990).

13 See the pointed and perhaps intentionally restrictive use of ἀνήρ (39.4; 44.2, 3; 45.3; 62.1, 3) or the vocatives ἄνδρες ἀγαπητοί (16.17) and ἄνδρες ἀδελφοί (14.1; 37.1; 43.4; 62.1).

14 Compare the discussion of the importance of rhetorical example in Hebrews 11 outlined in Pamela Michelle Eisenbaum, *The Jewish Heroes of Christian History. Hebrews 11 in Literary Context* (SBLDS, 156; Atlanta, GA: Scholars Press, 1997), pp. 60–73.

in the third person feminine singular verb 'spoke' (Num. 12.1) pointing to Miriam's special and individual role in the complaint.

After considering the effects of jealousy on the 'good apostles' and holy martyrs Peter and Paul (*1 Clem.* 5), the text turns to the examples of the Christian martyrs: 'the great multitude of the chosen who because of jealousy suffered many outrages and tortures' (6.1). Reference to the Christian community as the 'elect' (ἐκλεκτός) with the specific naming of women in the next verses establishes an implicit gender-inclusive consciousness. Verse 2 singles out exemplary women martyrs 'who were persecuted as Danaids and Dircae, and suffered terrible and unholy outrages, and having run with steadfast faith (ἐπὶ τὸν πίστεω βέβαιον δρόμον) they finished [the race] and received a noble reward, despite being weak in body (αἱ ἀσθενεῖς τῷ σώματι)' (6.2).[15]

The reference to the 'Danaids and Dircae' probably refers to the practice of using the condemned to enact the deaths of mythological figures in the amphitheatre. These spectacles involved atrocities against both women and men who, we are told, endured them with dignity (Suetonius, *Nero* 6.11–12; Tertullian, *Apol.* 15, 50; *de Spec.* 19, 22).[16] The letter applauds such acts of bravery by Christian women even as it condemns the jealousy that caused them, a jealousy that 'has estranged wives from husbands, overthrown great cities and uprooted great nations' (*1 Clem.* 6.3–4). David Balch[17] speculates that the 'Danaids and Dirce' supply *1 Clement* with an example of women rejecting marriage, presumably out of jealousy, behaviour that is elsewhere attested in the NT (1 Cor. 7.10–16; Luke 18.29; Acts 9.39; 1 Tim. 4.3). While this is possible, I am less certain that we can ever know the exact reason for this reference.

The list of exemplary figures continues with Noah and Jonah (ch. 7), the unnamed prophets (ch. 8), Enoch, Noah again (ch. 9), Abraham (ch. 10) and finally Lot (ch.

---

15 The example of heroism and courage in women was thought to be especially convincing and probative as Quintilian (*Inst. Ort.* 5.11.10) noted: 'Courage is more remarkable in a woman than in a man. Thus, if we wish to kindle someone's ambition to the performance of heroic deeds, we shall find that parallels drawn from the cases of Horatius and Torquatus will carry less weight than that of the woman by whose hand Pyrrhus was slain...'. This logic of course assumes the moral inferiority of women whose demonstrations of courage would thereby be even more remarkable. See Eisenbaum, *Jewish Heroes*, pp. 60–61 and Kathleen O'Brien Wicker, '*Mulierum Virtutes* (*Moralia* 242E–263C)', in Hans Dieter Betz (ed.), *Plutarch's Ethical Writings and Early Christian Literature* (Leiden: Brill, 1978), pp. 106–34.

16 Compare Clement of Alexandria, *Strom.* 4.19, which cites the same example of the daughters of Danaus who suffered torture nobly and became models for Christians of endurance and faith. On this difficult verse, see J. B. Lightfoot, *Apostolic Fathers* pp. 32–34; Robert M. Grant and Holt H. Graham, *The Apostolic Fathers. A New Translation and Commentary. Volume 2: First and Second Clement* (New York: Thomas Nelson & Sons, 1965), p. 27; Lindemann, *Die Clemensbriefe*, pp. 41–42; H.C. Brennecke, 'Danaiden und Dirken. Zu 1 Clem 6.2', *ZKG* 88 (1977), pp. 302–8.

17 David L. Balch, 'Zeus, Vengeful Protector of the Political and Domestic Order. Frescoes in Dining Rooms N and P of the House of the Vettii in Pompeii, Mark 13.12–13, and *I Clement* 6:2', in Annette Weissenrieder, Friederike Wendt and Petra von Gemünden (eds), *Picturing the New Testament. Studies in Ancient Visual Images* (Tübingen: Mohr-Siebeck, 2005), pp. 67–95. See the numerous references to renunciation of marriage in Aeschylus, *Suppl.* (4–10, 27–39, 77–85, 104–11, 141–61, 332, 335, 341, 392–96, 476–77, 531–34, 580–81, 643–45, 762–63, 792–807, 817–35, 872–908, 924–25, 932–33, 940–49, 1013–17, 1030–33, 1050–53, 1062–73), cited by Balch, p. 93.

11). The author commends Lot as an example of hospitality and piety (φιλοξενία καὶ εὐσέβεια) but quickly contrasts his actions with those of his wife:

> For of this [i.e, turning aside] a sign was given when his wife went with him but changed her mind (ἑτερογνώμονος), and did not remain in harmony (ὁμονοία), so that she became a pillar of salt to this day, to make known to all, that those who are double-minded (δίψυχοι), and question (διστάζοντες) concerning the power of God, incur judgment and become a warning to all generations. (11.2)

The terms noted in Greek are central to the argument of the letter and show how the tradition of Lot's wife (Gen. 19.16, 26) is reinterpreted to serve *1 Clement's* rhetorical purpose.[18] The simple description that she 'looked behind her' (καὶ ἐπέβλεψεν ἡ γυνὴ αὐτοῦ εἰς τὰ ὀπίσω καὶ ἐγένετο στήλη ἁλός, Gen. 19.26 LXX) receives a more pointed meaning in *1 Clem.* 11.2. Lot's wife exemplifies those who 'turn aside', 'change their mind', 'threaten harmony', are 'double-minded', and 'raise doubts' about God's power. It would be wrong, however, to assume that criticism of Lot's wife signals a wholesale reproach of women's conduct.

Having used the negative example of Lot's wife, the letter turns immediately (12.1) to Rahab the prostitute – who according to Joshua 2 hid the Israelite spies and confessed her belief that the Lord had given the land to them – as an example of faith, hospitality and prophecy.[19] Jewish legend had already transformed Rahab from 'harlot' [ἡ πόρνη] to 'innkeeper' (ἐν τῷ τῆς Ῥαάβης καταγωγίῳ [Josephus, *Ant.* 5.8])[20] and hailed her exemplary courage. In later tradition, Rahab was regarded as a proselyte, wife to Joshua, and ancestor of eight male prophets as well as of the female prophet Huldah (*b. Meg.* 14b; *Ruth R.* 2.1; *Num. R.* 8.9).[21]

Christian tradition employed the figure of Rahab to illustrate her central role in God's plan of salvation (Mt. 1.5), the exemplary character of her faith (Heb. 11.31), and her extraordinary works that demonstrated her faith and righteousness (Jas 2.25). In the same tradition, *1 Clement* praises Rahab for her three virtues: faith (πίστις), hospitality (φιλοξενία) and prophecy (προφητεία). Of all the women *1 Clement* mentions, Rahab receives the most extended description. The example of her prophecy, which appears as the final term describing her virtues (12.8), receives thereby the greatest emphasis. What she 'prophesies' is the belief that 'through the blood of the Lord, all who believe and hope in God will have redemption' (12.7). In 7.4, the author had already exhorted: 'Let us look intently on the blood of Christ, and let us know that it is precious to his Father, for it was poured out for our salvation, and bore the grace of repentance to all the world.' Rahab's example, therefore, is central to the argument that Christian identity marks one as redeemed by Christ's blood and as called into the grace of repentance. To draw the link between salvation

---

18 See Wis. 10.7; Josephus, *Ant.* 1. 203.

19 See similar treatment of Rahab in *b. Zeb.* 116a–b; *b. Meg.* 14b–15a; *Ruth R.* 2.1; *Num. R.* 8.9; *Eccl. R* 5.6; Josephus, *Ant.* 5.8–15, 26, 30; 7.11, 12; Mt. 1.5; Heb. 11.31; Jas 2.25.

20 Josephus follows the tradition of the Targum on Jos. 2.1 naming Rahab as innkeeper [πανδοκεύτρια].

21 See Edwin D. Freed, 'The Women in Matthew's Genealogy', *JSNT* 29 (1987), pp. 3–19; A.T. Hanson, 'Rahab the Harlot in Early Christian Tradition', *JSNT* 1 (1978), pp. 53–60; John Paul Heil, 'The Narrative Roles of the Women in Matthew's Genealogy', *Bib* 72 (1991), pp. 538–45.

and repentance, moreover, is essential for the letter's rhetorical strategy. Those in Corinth who conspired to depose some of the presbyters are invited to regard the example of Rahab, 'the harlot', who herself repented and then pointed the way to redemption.

Toward the end, the letter urges those responsible for the strife and divisions to embrace voluntary exile for the sake of the restoration of peace (54.1–4). It again draws on examples of self-sacrifice to bolster the exhortation that the Corinthians think first of the whole body (τὸ πλῆθος) and not their own interests (cf. 48.6). It cites 'many kings and rulers' who died or sought exile (55.1). Next it mentions many (πολλοί [the masculine plural perhaps conceals women]) unnamed Christians who 'handed themselves over into bondage' and thereby provided food for others for the price they received for themselves (55.2).

Finally, by way of climax and rhetorical emphasis, are examples of many heroic 'women [who] have been empowered through the grace of God and have performed many deeds of manly valor' (ἀνδρεῖος, 55.3). *First Clement* mentions only two by name: Judith and Esther. As the letter recounts the story, Judith 'the blessed' (ἡ μακαρία) asked the elders (πρεσβύτεροι) if they would allow her to go into the strangers' camp. She risked danger to herself for the sake of her love for her country and her people, and 'the Lord delivered over Holofernes by the hand of a female' (55.5 = LXX Jdt. 13.15). As with the case of Lot's wife, *1 Clement* again takes liberties in retelling the story. Gone is Judith's dramatic speech to the elders who come to her when she summons them: 'Listen to me, rulers of the people of Bethulia!' (Jdt. 8.11); 'Listen to me. I am about to do a thing that will go down through all generations of our descendants' (8.32). It serves the author's purposes better to describe Judith as one who asks the elders' permission. Nevertheless, *1 Clement* faithfully represents Judith's courage, her love of her people and country, and the Lord's fidelity to her in delivering Holofernes.

Esther, too, is described as 'perfect in faith' [ἡ τελεία κατὰ πίστιν Ἐσθήρ] and as one who put herself in danger for the sake of the nation of Israel (*1 Clem.* 55.6). The letter singles out her willingness to use 'fasting and humility' (νηστεία καὶ ταπείνωσις, cf. Est. 4.8) in begging God to save her people. And it reports twice that she risked danger to herself (55.6 [2x]) for the sake of her people. Without altering the substance of the scripture, *1 Clement* finds in Esther the attitude and virtue it especially seeks to recommend to the Corinthians: a willingness to put the good of the people before one's own interests together with a humble spirit (ταπείνωσις). The latter term, in various forms, occurs nearly thirty times in the letter in quotations or allusions to scripture and in the author's own exhortations.[22] Esther's example, therefore, undergirds *1 Clement*'s central argument.

Like Judith, Esther endangers herself for the sake of the community. These women are no weak, passive, or simpering examples of female submission. They are courageous actors who intervene to save their people. It is true that *1 Clement* casts them in the light of its central themes, namely, self-sacrifice, concern for the community

---

22 Ταπεινος 30.2, 55.6; 59.3, 4 (var.); ταπεινοφρονέω 2.1; 13.1, 3; 16.1, 2, 17; 17.2; 19.1 (var.); 30.3; 38.2; 48.6; 62.2; ταπεινοφροσύνη 21.8; 30.8; 31.4; 44.3; 56.1; 58.2; ταπεινόφρων 19.1; ταπεινόω 18.8, 17; 59.3; ταπείνωσις 16.7; 53.2; 55.6. On the use of this word group in *1 Clement* see Bowe, *Church in Crisis*, pp. 112–21 and the literature cited there.

above the individual, and firmness of faith. However, when it resumes its hortatory style (56.1), drawing a lesson from the examples of Judith and Esther, the letter underscores not their daring but their humility (ταπεινοφροσύνη) before God. As in the case of Miriam, *1 Clement* gives a mixed message. It narrates their courageous acts but values more their humble spirit as an example to be imitated.

The women mentioned – Miriam, 'Danaids and Dircae', Lot's wife, Rahab, Judith and Esther – all exhibit *1 Clement*'s prized virtue of self-sacrificing love, or its opposite. Women like these can stand side by side with male examples of heroic virtue or vice, and in the case of Miriam, can be presented in a more favourable light than even the scripture portrays them.

Gender Roles and the Household

Two passages in *1 Clement* deserve special scrutiny: 1.3 and 21.6–8. Both incorporate the language and, in modified form, the style of the *Haustafeln*, the codes of 'household duties' found in Col. 3.18–4.1; Eph. 5.21–6.9; 1 Pet. 2.11–3.12; 1 Tim. 2.8–15; 5.1–2; 6.1–2; and Tit. 2.1–10; 3.1. These codes, reflecting the concerns of numerous Hellenistic ethical, political and philosophical texts, discuss the 'appropriate' roles and obligations that must be maintained within the city, the state and the household, including gender relationships and the conduct of children and slaves.[23] In all cases, whether Christian, Jewish, Stoic, or Aristotelian, these traditions presume a social and political order where some 'naturally' ruled and others were to be ruled, some 'naturally' were superordinate and others subordinate. And, as Fitzgerald notes, 'The appearance of the *Haustafeln* in first-century Christianity reflects the theological conviction that the new life in Christ is to be lived within the framework of [these] existing natural and social orders.'[24] *First Clement* shares with many other early Christian texts a concern that Christian communities and households maintain this 'natural' and 'appropriate' social order as a safeguard against division and as a guarantee for continued harmony (cf. *1 Clem.* 63.2).

The letter's inclusion of two passages alluding to household duties is intricately bound to its larger rhetorical strategy. A brief discussion of these passages will illustrate both the similarities and differences between *1 Clement*'s use of the *Haustafeln* and the parallel texts in other NT (Col. 3.18; Eph. 5.21–22; Tit. 2.5, 9; 1 Pet. 2.18; 3.1, 5; 5.5) and early Christian writings like Ignatius of Antioch (*Eph.* 2.2; 5.3; *Mag.* 2.1; 13.2; *Tral.* 2.1–2; 13.2; *Letter to Polycarp* 2.1; 6.1), *Didache* 4.11, and *Barnabas* 19.7.

---

23 The literature on this topic is vast and ever expanding. For important summaries of the state of research see especially, James E. Crouch, *The Origin and Intention of the Colossian Haustafel* (FRLANT, 109; Göttingen: Vandenhoeck & Ruprecht, 1972); Dieter Lührmann, 'Wo man nicht mehr Sklave order Freier ist: Überlegungen zur Strucktur frühchristlicher Gemeinden', *Wort und Dienst* 13 (1975), pp. 53–83; David L. Balch, *'Let Wives Be Submissive'. The Domestic Code in 1 Peter* (SBLMS, 26; Chico, CA: Scholars Press, 1981); *idem*, 'Neopythagorean Moralists and the New Testament Household Codes', *ANRW* II.26.1 (1992), pp. 380–411; *idem*, 'Household Codes', ABD vol. III, pp. 318–20; John T. Fitzgerald, 'Haustafeln', ABD vol. III, pp. 80–81; P. Fiedler, 'Haustafel', *RAC* 13 (1986), pp. 1063–73; Carolyn Osiek and David L. Balch, *Families in the New Testament World. Households and House Churches* (Louisville, KY: Westminster/John Knox, 1997).

24 Fitzgerald, 'Haustafeln', p. 80.

In 1.3 and 21.6–8, *1 Clement* names four groups within the community or household, and in each case lists them in the same order: church leaders (ἡγούμενοι, 1.3; προηγούμενοι, 21.6), the aged (πρεσβύτεροι, 1.3; 21.6), the young (νέοι, 1.3; 21.6) and women, wives (γυνή, 1.3; 21.6). In addition, 21.8 adds a second reference to children (τὰ τέκνα). Although they share similar contents, the two texts differ in their grammatical forms. The first is a simple third-person narrative description of what the author believes [constructs or imagines?] to have been the case in the earliest years of the Corinthian community's life.

> For you did everything impartially, and walked in the laws of God, being submissive (ὑποτασσόμενοι) to your rulers, and paying appropriate honor to the older among you; you instructed the young to think measured and sober thoughts; women you have charged to conduct themselves with a blameless, reverent and pure conscience, showing affection (στεργούσας) for their husbands, as is fitting, and abiding by the rule of obedience (ὑποταγῆς) you have taught them to manage their households with dignity and discretion. (1.3)

This ideal picture is in no way an objective report; it is a pointed description designed to set up a contrast with the current state of affairs. Rhetorically, it serves as part of an opening *captatio benevolentiae* praising the Corinthians to gain their favourable reception for the letter's contents as a whole.[25] It is important to notice that the implied audience is an *exclusively male* audience: 'and to the women *you* gave instruction...' (1.3). Therefore, the exhortation to submission and obedience (which in the NT *Haustafeln* applies only to women) is here and elsewhere in the letter (cf. ὑποτάσσω, 34.5; 37.5; 38.1; 57.1, 2) directed to a predominantly *male* audience. If the letter is addressed to the whole church (1.1) then women are part of the implied addressees, but they remain largely invisible in the implied audience. The appropriate conduct and character here assigned to women includes terms that elsewhere are applied equally to men (the male addressees are also exhorted to humility and submission throughout the letter); therefore, *1 Clement* does not offer an exclusively gender-specific paraenesis.

At the same time, in both invocations of *Haustafel* material, *1 Clement* elaborates more carefully the statements concerning women than it does the references to rulers, the old and the young, and children (1.3; 21.6–8). Such elaboration might suggest the presence of social tensions generated by women who sought independence from their traditional roles, as Wire maintains was true in Corinth at Paul's time.[26] But the same situation is by no means certain for *1 Clement*. James Jeffers sees in this 'disproportionate amount of space [given] to the duties of wives' an indication of *1 Clement*'s concern to regulate the behaviour of women, and he speculates that this emphasis manifests a possible 'decline in the power of the *paterfamilias*, accompanied by a rise in the power and independence of women'.[27] That the letter does not marshal a

---

25 This section of *1 Clement* parallels closely, in form and function, the Pauline thanksgivings and may have been modelled on them. See Bowe, *Church in Crisis*, pp. 43–46, 97–104.

26 Wire, *Corinthian Women Prophets*, *passim*.

27 James S. Jeffers, 'Jewish and Christian Families in First Century Rome', in Karl P. Donfried and Peter Richardson (eds), *Judaism and Christianity in First-Century Rome* (Grand Rapids, MI: Eerdmans, 1998), pp. 128–50 (142).

sustained argument urging women to adopt their 'proper' roles (only the two texts noted 1.3; 21.6–8) suggests to me that while it reflects traditional attitudes toward women's subordinate position within the household, gender is not, for this text, the main issue debated in Corinth.

The second passage echoing the household code tradition, 21.6–8, confirms this judgement. Chapter 19 urges: 'Let us hasten on to the goal of peace...' (19.2). Chapter 20 follows with a long reflection on the peace and harmony in the universe, using Stoic vocabulary thoroughly stamped with the letter's own theocentric emphasis. Responding to this testimony of God's all-seeing presence, *1 Clement* admonishes its audience not to be 'deserters from [God's] will' (21.4) and encourages them to resist hubris and to adopt an attitude of reverence and respect (21.6). Here it employs the hortatory subjunctive so characteristic of the entire letter (used over fifty times), and exhorts an exclusively male-implied audience to adopt certain behaviours. Among these is the exhortation: 'let us lead our wives to that which is good' (21.6). The following verse adopts a third-person plural imperative concerning these women:

> Let them show the lovely habit of purity (ἁγνεία),
> let them exhibit a sincere desire for meekness (πραΰτῆ),
> let them make the gentleness (ἐπιεικής) of their tongue manifest by silence,
> let them give their affection not by factious preference,
> but, equally and in holiness, to all who fear God. (21.7)

The first three injunctions to ἁγνεία, πραΰτης and ἐπιείκεια are more general in character, whereas the final phrase speaks directly to the Corinthian situation – not by factious preference (μὴ κατὰ προσκλίσεις).[28] But, as in the case of *1 Clem.* 1.3, the letter applies all of these terms equally to men and therefore the injunctions do not constitute a gender-specific argument. Ἁγνεία describes the whole community in 64.1. Πραΰτης exemplifies those (masc.) blessed by God in 30.8 and becomes one of the virtues prayed for in rulers in 61.2. Ἐπιείκεια was taught by Jesus (*1 Clem.* 13.1), and should mark all those (masc.) blessed by God (30.8). Those (masc. αὐτούς who have transgressed (παραπτώμα need ἐπιείκεια (56.1). The one (masc. ὁ ποιήσας who has kept the ordinances of God with ἐπιείκεια will be enrolled in the number of the elect (58.2).

According to Osiek and Balch, among the late first and early second-century Christian writers, neither Ignatius, Polycarp, nor Hermas emphasizes that one Christian social group (wives or slaves) be subordinate to another: 'The author of *1 Clement* is the only one who repeats this emphasis on one social group subordinate to another.'[29] While their statement is true for the submission language in *1 Clem.* 1.3, the same emphasis on submission is *absent* from the similar household exhortation in 21.6–8. Indeed, Osiek and Balch rightly observe, in a note on this text: 'The superscript of this section (*1 Clem.* 19.1 and 20.1) focuses the ethic on subordination, but strikingly, neither wives nor children are exhorted to be submissive; slaves are not

---

28 See *1 Clem.* 50.2 which makes the same plea to the entire community: 'Let us then beg and pray of his mercy that we may be found in love, without human partisanship (προσκλίσεως), free from blame.'

29 Osiek and Balch, *Families*, p. 2.

mentioned. *All* [emphasis mine] are to be submissive, not one social class to another, so that *1 Clement* 20–21 is unlike the deutero-Pauline codes.'[30]

Conclusion

Such conflicting data and contradictory perspectives in the same letter yield a composite picture that does not fit easily with the deutero-Pauline and Pastoral Epistles or with a contemporary Roman document like 1 Peter. These texts, despite their attempt to Christianize the household code tradition by introducing specifically Christian motivation (see esp. Eph. 5.21–6.9 for behaviour) reinforced social patterns that curtailed women's roles within the Christian community. *First Clement* is more ambivalent toward gender-specific issues, giving on the one hand and taking away on the other – praising women's courageous acts and leadership, but employing their example to inculcate gentleness and submissiveness, and excluding them implicitly from ministerial roles (44.2, 3).

The letter undergirds powerfully a general ethic of hierarchical order within the cosmos (*1 Clem.* 20), the Christian household (1.3; 21.6–8) and the Church (42.1–5). But the gender-specific *maleness* of the implied audience forces us to read *1 Clement*'s language of submission and obedience over against the (implicitly) male struggle for power in Corinth and not in the context of gender disputes between men and women. When the discussion turns to the deposed presbyter-bishops in Corinth (44.1–6) and structures of leadership and ministry, the language is again exclusively male, as the repeated (and pointed) repetition of ἀνδρές makes clear.

Perhaps the most lamentable feature of this letter is not that women are singled out for special opprobrium or social control, but that they are for the most part invisible to the author. Women remain hidden behind the masculine-gendered implied audience, spoken about but not spoken to, and where mentioned they are confirmed in their protected household roles. Although *1 Clement* can praise the heroic deeds of Judith and Esther, their willingness for self-sacrifice is prized most of all, not their leadership and courage. Gone completely is any memory of Prisca's teaching, or Chloe's people, or Phoebe's patronage and ministry, all active women in the Corinthian church of Paul's day. As for the women in *1 Clement*, we find, instead, 'the gentleness of their tongue manifest by their silence' (21.7).

---

30 Osiek and Balch, *Families*, p. 278, n. 47. See also p. 260, n. 69 which mentions several texts in *1 Clement* for their 'striking' *absence* of language demanding submission: 34.5; 37.2; 38.1; 57.1–2.

Ambiguous Legacy: A Feminist Commentary on Clement of Alexandria's Works

Denise Kimber Buell

Women are therefore to philosophize equally with men, but males are preferable at everything, unless they have become effeminate. (*Strom.* 4.8.62.4)

[M]ilk is the fountain of nourishment by which a woman makes clear that she has really given birth and is a mother … Because of this, the Holy Spirit says mystically, 'I have given you milk to drink' (1 Cor. 3.2) through the Apostle, using the voice of the Lord. If we have been reborn to Christ, then the one who gives us this new birth nurses us with his own milk – the Logos. (*Paid.* 1.6.49.2–3)

Clement of Alexandria (ca. 150–215 CE) has attracted sporadic attention from feminist scholars, particularly with respect to his views about the significance of gender as a marker of human difference, social and sexual norms, and his imagery for the divine. The portions of his surviving corpus that have received the most attention from scholars interested either in feminist analysis or his views about women include: (1) a long section of the first book of the *Paidagogos*, in which Clement develops analogies between pregnancy, birth, lactation and the relationship between the divine and Christians; (2) his detailed instructions for proper Christian behaviour (books two and three of the *Paidagogos*); (3) an extended discussion of the merits of both marriage and virginity for women and men (the end of the second and virtually the entire third book of the *Stromateis*); and (4) his assertions about female equality with and difference from males in the context of a discussion of martyrdom (fourth book of the *Stromateis*).

Because feminist analysis is concerned with more than gender, that is, with disclosing the operations of power – including gender – in a particular context, this commentary addresses the functions and possible implications of Clement's treatment of status, age and ethnicity as well as gender. These categories are central to how he constructs his own authority; attention to how he employs them has important consequences not only for how we assess his writings but also for how we can reimagine the history of Christian development.

Clement repeatedly proclaims the Pauline slogan of equality in Christ (Gal. 3.26–28 and par.) to argue that women as well as children and slaves should 'philosophize' (Clement's term for the practice leading to the summit of Christian existence), yet he insists on the deutero-Pauline household codes and the teachings of the Pastoral Epistles as authoritative guides for how to model human relationships. Clement's writings complicate the dichotomous model proposed by Ross Kraemer for early Christian communities:

By the early second century, two distinctive interpretations of Christian life emerged that are reflected in the texts at hand [the Pastorals and the *Acts of Thecla*]. Those who wrote, read, and promulgated the Pastorals favored marriage, social conformity, hierarchy, and structure, and bitterly opposed any leadership roles on the part of women. Those who told stories like that of Thecla and ultimately committed them to writing and circulated them favored asceticism, rejected social conventions, denied the value of contemporary hierarchy, and believed that women could baptize and teach just as men.[1]

At first glance, Clement would appear to fit the former group quite nicely, since he cites 1 Timothy approvingly but gives no indication that he even knows the *Acts of Thecla*. Nonetheless, Clement never cites 1 Timothy's admonishments against female teaching, let alone 1 Cor. 14.34b–35 on women keeping silent in church; indeed, Clement explicitly states that women are capable of becoming 'Gnostics', the highest rank of Christian in his system. I do not mean to imply, however, that Clement's arguments are free of dissonance. His model for Christian perfection presupposes an androcentric ideal: to attain the state of a Gnostic, both males and females must transform themselves through eradication of the passions, but Clement describes this process as 'becoming male' specifically with reference to female perfection (*Strom.* 6.12.100.3).[2] Clement does not rail against female leadership, but neither does his espousal of gendered hierarchy as natural and appropriate for social relations make clear what sort of leadership position a woman achieving Gnostic perfection might occupy. Such pervasive ambiguities show how even useful categories such as Kraemer's cannot account for all second-century Christian views about female social roles and religious leadership.

Clement's corpus also contains an unparalleled quantity of feminine, particularly maternal, imagery for the divine that makes Clement a primary representative of 'an atypical tradition, where God's activity is described with female metaphors'.[3] For example, Clement asserts that God 'became female' for the sake of human salvation, in order to produce the Logos: 'For God Godself is love, and became visible to us because of love. The ineffable part of God is father, while the part that has sympathy toward us is mother. Since he loved, the father became feminine (θηλύνειν; pass.), a great sign of this being that he bore from himself' (*Quis* 37.2).[4] This type of imagery for the divine would seem to offer a valuable resource for feminist theologians who seek precedents for imagining the divine apart from mere 'father' or 'master' language.[5] But Clement's language plays upon and reinforces certain stereotypes about gender:

---

1 Ross S. Kraemer, *Her Share of the Blessings: Women's Religions Among Pagans, Jews, and Christians in the Greco-Roman World* (New York: Oxford University Press, 1992), p. 154.

2 See also Kari Vogt, '"Becoming Male": One Aspect of an Early Christian Anthropology', in Elisabeth Schüssler Fiorenza and Mary Collins (eds), *Women – Invisible in Theology and Church* (Concilium, 182; Edinburgh: T & T Clark, 1985), pp. 72–83 (74–75).

3 Kari Elisabeth Børresen, 'God's Image, Man's Image? Female Metaphors Describing God in the Christian Tradition', *Temenos* 19 (1983), pp. 17–32 (19). As she goes on to note (p. 20), this imagery is generally based in a few biblical references (Isa. 49.14–15 and 66.13; Hos. 13.18; Mt. 13.33 and par.; Lk. 15. 8–10; Mt. 23.27 and par.; Gal. 4.19; 1 Cor. 3.1–2; 1 Thess. 2.7–9; Heb. 5.12–13; and 1 Pet. 2.2).

4 *Quis* is the standard abbreviation for Clement's work entitled *Who is the Rich Person Who Is Being Saved?*

5 In this vein, scholars such as Walter Wagner and Kathleen McVey praise Clement; see Wagner, 'Divine Femaleness: Two Second Century Contributions', *JRelS* 17 (1991), pp. 19–43, especially 19–20, and 29–40; McVey, 'Christianity and Culture, Dead White European Males, and the Study of Patristics', *The Princeton Seminary Bulletin*, n.s. 15 (1994), pp. 103–30, esp. 123–8 and 130.

notably, that femaleness is particular, while maleness is 'ineffable', irreducible to bounded language.[6] The following analysis, informed by a brief discussion of Clement's historical and cultural context, elaborates these complexities.

Clement's Context: Late Second-Century Alexandria

Titus Flavius Clemens was not from Alexandria, but he made his name there.[7] Clement lived in this 'most important commercial city of the Mediterranean world'[8] during the reigns of the emperors Commodus (176–192) and Septimius Severus (197–211). Where he lived prior to his arrival in Alexandria is uncertain; he left near the end of his life, apparently in reaction to a wave of persecutions against Christians.

In Clement's day, there was no established Christian 'orthodoxy', and no persuasive evidence exists for an indisputable, central Christian authority in Alexandria. Christianity was a work-in-progress. To establish oneself as a teacher in Alexandria ca. 180 CE would have meant jumping into the bustling intellectual marketplace of a city with a reputation for erudition. The second century appears to have been a time of intellectual and philosophical regrouping in Alexandria, a regrouping in which Christian teachers like Clement participated. His adaptation of Platonic thought, together with Stoicism and Aristotelianism, anticipates Alexandria's third and fourth-century reputation as a centre of neo-Platonic philosophy.

Clement's writings indicate that some Christians in the city used the philosophical model of schools, consisting of a teacher and students, to locate themselves and to construe a pattern for Christian living. Not only does Clement speak of Christianity as the true philosophy in contrast to other, only partially accurate, philosophical schools (including Stoics and Platonists), he also applies this to his own self-positioning in two distinct ways. First, he refers to most rival Christians using the language of allegiance to a school. He explicitly compares those Christians whom he condemns as heretics to members of non-Christian philosophical schools, saying that he would prefer the latter over the former (*Strom.* 1.19.95.4) and that 'heretics' value their allegiances to their (Christian) 'schools' (διατριβαί) over that due the church (*Strom.* 7.15.92.7).[9]

---

6 See Børresen, 'God's Image', pp. 26–28; see also Denise Kimber Buell, *Making Christians: Clement of Alexandria and the Rhetoric of Legitimacy* (Princeton, NJ: Princeton University Press, 1999), pp. 177–79.

7 See Annewies van den Hoek, 'How Alexandrian Was Clement of Alexandria? Reflections on Clement and His Alexandrian Background', *Heythrop Journal* 31 (1990), pp. 179–94.

8 Alan K. Bowman, *Egypt After the Pharaohs: 332 BC–AD 642* (Berkeley: University of California Press, 1986), p. 218; Alexandria gained this commercial advantage due in large part to its protected double harbour and interior waterway connections to the Red Sea and Nile River.

9 At a number of points in his writings (especially in the *Stromateis*), Clement mentions the views of other Christians either in passing or in detail. The followers of Basilides and Valentinus are most frequently singled out for comparison, but other Christians are named as well, including Encratites, Nicolatians, Phrygians (i.e., New Prophecy movement or Montanists), and the followers of Prodicus and Marcion. Although viewed through the lens of Clement's own rhetorical aims, these moments suggest some of the issues debated by Christians in Alexandria in the late second century: the character and role of faith, fear and the passions; the relationship between God and humans; the status of Mosaic Law; marriage and procreation; asceticism; and martyrdom. As we shall see, Clement elaborates many of these topics using gendered metaphors or examples.

Despite his appeal to Christian 'schools' as a technique of intra-Christian polemic, Clement also positively defends the notion of Christian 'schools' both by arguing that Jews and Greeks also have their own philosophical schools (αἱρέσεις) (*Strom.* 7.15.89.3) and by scripting the ideal path for Christians in terms taken from philosophical education (imitation of and training by one's teacher, with the ultimate goal of becoming a teacher oneself).

Clement has traditionally been known as the head of the 'catechetical' school of the 'official' church in Alexandria, but this view is largely rejected today as a useful fabrication preserved by the Christian bishop Eusebius (ca. 260–339 CE).[10] Given how little evidence there is for any dominant form of Christianity in Alexandria in the late second century, let alone for such a school in Clement's day, it is better to understand Clement's position as that of a 'Gnostic' teacher seeking to attract and keep students much like other rival Christian teachers (who traced their authority via Basilides, Valentinus, or others, back to the apostles).[11] His appropriation of concepts drawn from philosophical education thus offers a glimpse of how he shaped his own vision for Christian perfection as well as how he sought to negotiate and instantiate boundaries within Christianity (between 'simple believers' and 'Gnostics'; between legitimate and illegitimate Christian philosophizing).

Philosophical training and divisions among Christians are not the only aspects of Alexandrian culture we should consider; ethnic or racial categories also play a significant role. Throughout most of his corpus, Clement writes as if he is addressing 'Greeks' or gentile Christians. For example, the full title of his work commonly known as the *Protreptikos* is Προτρεπτικὸς πρὸς Ἕλληνας or 'Exhortation to the Greeks'. In his two other major surviving works, the *Paidagogos* and the *Stromateis*, Clement's examples and quotations suggest that he expects his audience to be familiar with classical Greek texts (Homer, Euripides, Plato), and to identify with being 'Greek' (at least prior to conversion to Christianity) in contrast to 'Egyptian' or 'barbarian' (as evidenced by his use of 'barbarian' to mean the behaviour of 'others' including, in a number of places, Jews).[12]

---

10 See Eusebius, *Ecclesiastical History* 6.6.1. For further discussion, see Gustave Bardy, 'Aux origines de l'école d'Alexandrie', *RSR* 27 (1937), pp. 65–90; Alain le Boulluec, 'L'École d'Alexandrie. De quelques aventures d'un concept historiographique', in *Alexandrina. Hellénisme, judaïsme et christianisme à Alexandrie: Mélanges offerts au P. Claude Mondésert* (Paris: Les Éditions du Cerf, 1987), pp. 403–17; van den Hoek, 'How Alexandrian', pp. 179–82; and *idem*, 'The "Catechetical" School of Early Christian Alexandria and Its Philonic Heritage', *HTR* 90 (1997), pp. 59–87.

11 See Buell, *Making Christians*, pp. 10–12; 79–94; and David Dawson, *Allegorical Readers and Cultural Revision in Ancient Alexandria* (Berkeley: University of California Press, 1992), pp. 219–34. For a longer historical view on this topic, see David Brakke, 'Canon Formation and Social Conflict in Fourth-Century Egypt: Athanasius of Alexandria's Thirty-Ninth *Festal Letter*', *HTR* 87 (1994), pp. 398–410.

12 Clement asserts quite programmatically, 'Of humans, all are either Greek or barbarian', a point that he uses to claim the universality of the Christian God (*Strom.* 5.14. 133.8). Occasionally, Clement uses the adjective 'barbarian' to refer to Christian teachings, but more frequently he insists that Christianity makes barbarians and Greeks into one 'peculiar people' (e.g., *Strom.* 6.17.159.8–9; *Prot.* 12.120.2). Once, he uses the phrase 'barbarian gentiles' to refer to those who are neither Jew nor Greek (*Strom.* 6.2.4.2).

Alexandria's strange relationship with the rest of Egypt, as signalled by its epithet 'Alexandria by (*ad*) Egypt', offers some historical perspective on this aspect of his writings. The only one of the many namesake settlements of Alexander the Great to achieve long-standing fame, Alexandria (founded 331 BCE) was the centre for both Ptolemaic control (305 BCE–30 BCE) and Roman rule (30 BCE–642 CE) over Egypt. Many inhabitants of Egypt settled in Alexandria, including Greeks, Persians, Syrians, Jews and others who already had a well-established history in the country, but the new capital city also became a boom town for large numbers of Macedonians and other fortune-seekers from the Mediterranean basin in the third and second centuries BCE. Although residents of Alexandria interacted with the rest of Egypt through family connections, trade, control of agricultural lands, etc., surviving texts treat Alexandria as a distinct unit. This may account for Clement's relative lack of interest in Egypt as a whole.

There is another aspect to Alexandria's diverse population that is significant for understanding Clement's work. As is the case for the identity markers 'male' and 'female', whose potential fluidity greatly troubled some ancient authors (particularly because of the spectre of effeminization), ethnic or racial markers were understood as both boundary setting and permeable. Although Clement employs positively the notion of crossing gender boundaries, in both directions,[13] he generally seeks to keep these boundaries firmly in place when it comes to social practices (such as maintaining one's body hair). Clement also regularly depicts the process of becoming a Christian as one of crossing an 'ethnic' boundary from Jew, barbarian or Greek to Christian.[14] In contrast to his view of the continued relevance of sexual difference among Christians, however, Clement emphasizes that the primary salience of ethnicity or race for a Christian lies not among Christians but in defining the boundary between Christians and non-Christians.

During Ptolemaic rule in Egypt, one way to mark social distinction was by ethnic or racial categories; the content and attribution of ethnicity was far from simple, however, as the phenomenon of double names (people using both a Greek and an Egyptian name) shows.[15] There was some flexibility in how individuals styled themselves and were perceived by others. Tax status, profession, or the person with whom one corresponded (or litigated) each might affect one's declaration of identity. Although debate continues about precisely how Jews in Alexandria perceived

---

13 Male to female, speaking of actions of God (*Quis* 37.2); female to male, speaking of human spiritual perfection (*Strom.* 6.12.100.3).

14 For further discussion of Clement and other early Christian authors on this point, see Denise Kimber Buell, *Why This New Race: Ethnic Reasoning in Early Christianity* (New York: Columbia University Press, 2005).

15 See Naphtali Lewis, *Greeks in Ptolemaic Egypt* (Oxford: Clarendon Press, 1986); Dorothy J. Thompson, 'Language and Literacy in Early Hellenistic Egypt', in Per Bilde et al. (eds), *Ethnicity in Hellenistic Egypt* (Studies in Hellenistic Civilization, III; Aarhus: Aarhus University Press, 1992), pp. 39–52; Willy Clarysse, 'Some Greeks in Egypt', in Janet H. Johnson (ed.), *Life in a Multi-Cultural Society: Egypt from Cambyses to Constantine and Beyond* (SAOC, 51; Chicago: Oriental Institute of the University of Chicago, 1992), pp. 51–56; Jan Quaegebeur, 'Greco-Egyptian Double Names as a Feature of a Bi-Cultural Society: The Case Ψοσνευς ὁ καὶ Τρίαδελφος', in Johnson (ed.), *Life in a Multi-Cultural Society*, pp. 265–72.

themselves and were perceived, this ethnic permeability seems to have extended also to Jews.[16]

With Roman rule, these choices became more circumscribed. Rome declared that only those persons who were citizens of Alexandria and the three other 'Greek' cities in Egypt (Ptolemais, Naukratis and later Antinoopolis) would count as 'Greek'; all others were classified as Romans (few at first), Jews, or Egyptians. Thus, many categorized as 'Egyptian' would not necessarily or always have understood themselves this way. Naphtali Lewis has suggested that 'Hellenism' became the marker used by those classed in this category as a means to provide 'their own social gradations with the total group'.[17] Consequently, Clement's appeal to 'Greeks' and his many references to Greek literature and philosophy are not clues that his actual audience consisted of recent emigrés from Asia Minor or Athens or even of those who could trace their heritage to such places; rather, he writes to people who have surrounded themselves with things Greek, who speak Greek, who are at least passingly familiar with Homer, Euripides and the veneration of Greek deities, and who are quite keenly aware of Alexandria's fashionable culture. The categories of Egyptian and barbarian are multivalent in Clement's writing – they can function positively and negatively, as can 'Greek' – but 'Greek' social customs, religious practices and educational system are presumed to be the standard against which Clement's audience will measure his teachings.

Finally, within the web of power in Roman Egypt, free, freed, slave, soldier and citizen are the most significant status distinctions. Status clearly intersects with ethnic/racial and gender boundaries under Roman rule insofar as enlisting in the Roman army would immediately change one's ethnicity (from 'Greek' to 'Roman' in the case of a citizen of a πόλις). And, as noted, being a citizen corresponded to being counted as 'Greek'. Clement indicates his awareness of another kind of link by condemning the idea that people be enslaved based on their ethnicity or race (*Strom.* 2.18.94.4). From the perspective of Roman legal discourse, these boundaries had significant consequences: 'If a Roman man or woman is joined in marriage with an urban Greek or an Egyptian, their children follow the inferior status', or 'Egyptians who, when married to discharged soldiers, style themselves Romans are subject to the provision of violation of status' (*BGU* 1210).[18] Clement, while never challenging the propriety of societal status differentiation, offers converts a 'new status' that plays upon all of these categories – citizenship in the heavenly πόλις, the prospect

16 See especially Joseph Mélèze-Modrzejewski, 'How to Be a Greek and Yet a Jew in Hellenistic Alexandria', in Shaye J.D. Cohen and Ernest S. Frerichs (eds), *Diasporas in Antiquity* (BJS, 288; Atlanta: Scholars Press, 1993), pp. 65–92; *idem, The Jews of Egypt: From Rameses II to Emperor Hadrian* (trans. Robert Cornman; French original 1992; Princeton, NJ: Princeton University Press, 1997); Sylvie Honigman, 'The Birth of a Diaspora: The Emergence of a Jewish Self-Definition in Ptolemaic Egypt in the Light of Onomastics', in Cohen and Frerichs (eds), *Diasporas in Antiquity*, pp. 93–127; Aryeh Kasher, 'The Civic Status of the Jews in Ptolemaic Egypt', in Bilde et al. (eds), *Ethnicity in Hellenistic Egypt*, pp. 100–21; Peder Borgen, 'Philo and the Jews in Alexandria', in Bilde et al. (eds), *Ethnicity in Hellenistic Egypt*, pp. 122–38; and Erich S. Gruen, *Heritage and Hellenism: The Reinvention of Jewish Tradition* (Hellenistic Culture and Society, 30; Berkeley: University of California Press, 1998).

17 Naphtali Lewis, *Life in Egypt Under Roman Rule* (Oxford: Clarendon Press, 1983), pp. 31–32.

18 Lewis, *Life in Egypt*, pp. 32–34.

of inheriting from the ultimate Father, freedom from the 'slavery' of atheism or traditional religious custom, as well as translation into a new people and common humanity.

Clement's Works: Commentaries

Eusebius lists ten works by Clement, five of which survive:[19] (1) the *Protreptikos pros Hellēnas* (or *Exhortation to the Greeks*); (2) the three-part *Paidagōgos* (or *Tutor*); (3) the eight-part *Strōmateis* (or *Miscellanies*); (4) a sermon-like text focused on Mk 10.17–31 entitled *Tis ho Sōzomenos Plousios* (or *Who is the Rich Person Who Is Being Saved?*); and (5) a very brief discourse with a double name, *Protreptikos eis Hupmonēn ē Pros tous Neōsti Bebaptismenous* (or *Exhortation to Endurance or To the Recently Baptized*). Three additional items attributed to Clement have survived, which Eusebius does not mention. The first two are notebooks: *Ek tōn Theodotous ... Epitomai* (*Excerpts of Theodotos*) consists of quotations from and comments about the teachings of the Valentinian Christian Theodotos; and *Ek tōn Prophētikōn Eklogai* (*Eclogues of the Prophets*) contains comments on the prophetic writings from the Septuagint. The final item is a letter, possibly containing a variant of the Gospel of Mark.[20] This commentary will analyse the first four texts.[21]

Protreptikos[22]

This interesting work, addressed 'to the Greeks', is written to persuade a non-Christian audience to convert. Clement relies upon two techniques to make his argument most effective. First, he regularly invokes familiar categories and practices to subvert their usual meanings (e.g., cult images are meaningless sticks and stones, but humans are the real cult images, as the image and likeness of God; the mysteries are mere custom and opinion, but Jesus is the high priest of the true mystery religion). Second, dialectical contrasts create a related dramatic effect (works of the serpent or devil vs. those of the divine; human custom vs. divine law; slavery vs. sonship; barrenness vs.

---

19 See Eusebius, *Ecclesiastical History* 6.13.1–3. The standard critical edition for Clement's works is Otto Stählin (ed.), Clement of Alexandria, *Opera* (4 vols.; Die griechischen christlichen Schriftsteller der ersten drei Jahrhunderte, 12, 15, 17, 39; Leipzig: Hinrichs, 1905–1909). See also the excellent critical editions of the Greek text with French translations in the Sources chrétiennes series, numbers 2, 23, 30, 38, 70, 108, 158, 278, 279, 428, 446, 463 (Paris: Les Éditions du Cerf), which includes most of Clement's corpus (except book 8 of the *Stromateis*, the *Eclogues of the Prophets*, and his miscellaneous shorter writings). Easily available English translations of Clement's works are noted as they are discussed below.

20 On this controversial last item, see Morton Smith, *Clement of Alexandria and the Secret Gospel of Mark* (Cambridge, MA: Harvard University Press, 1973).

21 The *Excerpts of Theodotos* contains a number of passages of interest to feminist readers, but its format makes it very difficult to perform a sustained analysis of Clement's views, both because he has not shaped the work as an argument and because it is sometimes unclear where his ideas begin and Theodotos's end. For an English translation of the work, see Robert Pierce Casey (ed. and trans.), *The Excerpta ex Theodoto* (London: Christophers, 1934).

22 The most readily available translation of this work can be found in the LCL series (Clement of Alexandria, *An Exhortation to the Greeks, The Rich Man's Salvation, and the Fragment of An Address Entitled 'To the Newly Baptized'* [trans. G.W. Butterworth; LCL; London: Heinemann/New York: G.P. Putnam's Sons, 1919], pp. 2–263).

fruitfulness; Egyptian or barbarian vs. Greek). These two strategies converge in his argument for the universality and antiquity of the Christian message (e.g., the 'song of salvation' described by Clement is newer than that of Orpheus, but it is actually most original).

In arguing for the fraudulence of non-Christian religious practices and for the benefits (indeed necessity) of conversion to Christianity, Clement appeals to notions about gender, ethnicity, sexual practices and history. For example, he flatters his readers that they are 'in every way' better than Egyptians (2.39.4), thereby capitalizing on ethnic stereotypes; then, not leaving this division in place, he accuses Greeks of being no less wrong in their religious practices. Clement also plays upon the widespread suspicion of novelty both to explain the 'newness' of Christianity and to argue that it is the oldest and truest form of worship.

Similarly, Clement utilizes notions of gender and sexual norms in order to draw the lines between Christianity and the religious practices of his audience. Let me give two examples. In the first instance,[23] he juxtaposes fertility and infertility with the respective results of Christian and non-Christian allegiances (1.9.2–5). Clement asserts that two voices preceded the manifestation of the Logos in the world: John the Baptist's 'crying in the desert' and the angel's (Gabriel) annunciation to 'a barren woman' (i.e., Elizabeth). Clement interprets these two references together with a citation from Isaiah (54.1): 'We are they to whom the angel brought the good tidings; we are they whom John exhorted to recognize the farmer and to seek the husband. For he is one and the same, the husband of the barren woman and the farmer of the desert' (1.9.4–5). This interpretation is then extended: 'So then by reason of the Word *both become mothers*, the desert of fruits and the woman of believing children; even now the words "barren" and "desert" remain for unbelievers' (1.9.5, my emphasis).

Clement uses this gendered language metaphorically, the Logos as impregnating male and cultivating farmer, humans as either fruitful or barren women or land. We should read Clement's selection of this imagery not as an oblique reference to rival cultic practices but rather as designed to resonate primarily on a figurative level. Nevertheless, its ability to resonate at all derives from cultural concerns about fertility of both women and fields. In his day, a very popular cult to Isis at Menouthis drew many Alexandrian residents twenty kilometres outside of the city, especially to seek assistance with fertility.[24]

In the second example, it becomes apparent that, at least on the rhetorical level, Clement seeks the kind of fertility that produces legitimate lineages of believers, and that he has male listeners in mind (2.25.1–2). In this passage, Clement calls his non-Christian readers eunuchs, sexually mutilated men, or offspring of a whore (i.e., bastards). To understand his use of this reference to Deut. 23.1–2, we need to know that Clement has just labelled non-Christian religious practices as either the worship of δαιμόνες or atheism, which he defines in two ways: ignorance of the true God or

---

23 For a discussion of how this passage illustrates Clement's 'revisionary hermeneutic' see Dawson, *Allegorical Readers*, pp. 205–10.

24 David Frankfurter states: 'The temple of Isis at Menouthis was such a major source of maternity and health in the western Delta during the fifth century that it could only be replaced by a Christian healing cult, of Saints John and Cyrus' (*Religion in Roman Egypt: Assimilation and Resistance* [Princeton, NJ: Princeton University Press, 1998], p. 47; see also pp. 40–41, 162–65, 177–79 and 271).

belief in things that have no real existence (2.23.1). We might expect this definition to apply to the image of the bastard, who does not know the identity of its father and might attribute paternity to any number of possible figures. Clement does indeed interpret the bastard as one who 'lays claim to many gods, falsely so called, in place of the only real God' (2.25.2). He charges eunuchs and mutilated males with atheism. In a manner that explicitly recalls our first example: 'By the first two expressions [i.e., eunuch and mutilated male] he [Moses] refers in a figure to the atheistic manner of life, which has been deprived of divine power and fruitfulness' (2.25.2). Thus the atheist eunuch or 'mutilant' represents one who cannot produce a lineage while the bastard stands for one who worships δαίμωνχ, spirits who are not gods. Although these two types are distinguished here to suit his biblical interpretation, Clement later uses the terms 'atheist' and 'δαίμον-worshipper' interchangeably.

Clement's vision for Christian existence appears to offer a fertile salvation for its converts, but it also requires conformity within one lineage, in obedience to the one true Father. While the text offers no extended reflection about power relations among Christians and insists that Christian salvation is open to all, its appeals imply that the listener is a mature, free man. Three examples make this clear. After asserting that it is the particular feature of humans to 'be in close fellowship with God' (10.100.2; see also 2.25.3) and to 'come to knowledge of God' (10.100.3), Clement illustrates how this emblem of humanity relates to professional life:

> Till the ground, we say, if you are a farmer, but recognize God in your farming. Sail the sea, you who love sea-faring, but always call upon the heavenly pilot. Were you a soldier on campaign when the knowledge of God laid hold of you? Then listen to the commander who commands righteousness. (10.100.4)

This choice of professions, almost always held by men in antiquity,[25] may have no correspondence with the livelihoods of his audience, but it does emphasize divine power over land, sea and military operations; moreover, these occupations would be very familiar to residents of Alexandria, regardless of their respective stations in life.

Slightly later, Clement describes how knowledge of God benefits Christians by using household imagery that positions his hearers as adult, free, slave-owning husbands:

> For it is because of wisdom that they whose course has led them to the Father are good fathers of their children, that they who have come to know the Son are good sons to their parents, that they who have been mindful of the Bridegroom are good husbands to their wives, that they who have been ransomed from deepest slavery are good masters of their servants. (10.107.3)

Once again, the interplay between human action and divine model says more about how Clement wishes to direct his listeners' perceptions than it does about the actual audience composition. Nonetheless, in a model for Christian living that is framed

---

25 The primary exception to this list would be cultivation, as women participated in tending the fields; metaphorically, however, farming has a masculine connotation, especially when used in a sexual context (i.e., procreation as the act of a farmer sowing seeds into a field).

as much around imitation as obedience, this choice of imagery not only reinforces a familiar household kyriarchy but offers little in the way of imitation for enslaved men and women or free females (children or adults). Despite Clement's fierce opposition to custom as a hallmark of error leading away from God, the result of salvation according to these two examples would seem to offer little manifest change in either occupation or household arrangement. The re-orienting of one's allegiances metaphorically reinscribes existing social hierarchies while promising comparable salvation for all. Clement offers a way for aspiring or actual Alexandrian citizens to identify with a power other than Rome without requiring sacrifice of privilege, apart from the not-insignificant alignment with a marginal group.

After a few sentences that positively contrast wild animals, fish and birds with his ignorant addressees (in which the animals are deemed better off), Clement resumes this argument from a slightly different angle:

> When you think of this [the superiority of the wildlife], are you not ashamed to have made yourselves less reasonable than even the creatures without reason, you who have wasted so many stages of life in atheism? You have been children (παῖδες), then boys (μειρακία), then young men (ἐφέβοι), then men (ἄνδρες), but you have never been good. Have respect for your old age (γέρας); become sober now that you have reached the sunset of life; even at the end of life acknowledge God, so that at the end of your life you may regain a beginning of salvation. Grow old to the worship of δαιμόνες. Return as young men (νέοι) to the fear of God; God will enroll you as innocent children (παῖδες). (10.108.2–3)

Clement implies that Christian existence can be thought of in terms of the familiar stages of life for a free male, which begin again at conversion. The *Paidagogos* develops this analogy.

Enrolment as a citizen was one of the consequences of birth for a free citizen male, which conferred privileges and obligations. Clement stresses both as he continues, 'Let the Athenian, then, follow the laws of Solon, the Argive those of Phoroneus, and the Spartan those of Lycurgus, but if you record yourself among God's people, then heaven is your fatherland (πατρίς) and God your lawgiver' (10.108.4). The *Protreptikos* repeatedly contrasts the varieties of peoples, customs, laws and teachings with the one universal version offered by the Christian God. But this universal vision is figuratively expressed in terms that exclude women and most males (i.e., non-citizens).

Two other aspects of the *Protreptikos* are of interest to feminist readers: its comparison of the actions of the divine with female animals and its defence of Christianity's newness. The first may seem of obvious interest, but the second is of possibly greater importance.

In the first case, we turn to Clement's response to the hypothetical charge that he requires listeners to foresake ancestral customs. He opens with another argument based on an analogy between human life span and religious affiliation. But instead of claiming that his old listeners should become young again by conversion, Clement argues that his audience should grow up (10.89.1). Urging them to acknowledge the Christian God as their 'real Father', he contends that their present religious practices are not merely childish but a wicked and false 'deadly drug' (10.89.2).

To demonstrate this, he challenges their view that the 'holy word of God [is] accursed' (10.89.3) by stating that punishment awaits them if they maintain this position, but that God – like a 'mother bird' – wants to help all the human nestlings back into heaven even when they have fallen away and mourns those who are consumed by predators (10.91.3). Clement leaves no doubt about how to understand this comparison: 'For God, out of his great love, still keeps hold of humans, just as, when a nestling falls from the nest, the mother bird flutters above, and if perchance a serpent gapes for it, "flitting around with cries, the mother mourns for her offspring" [Homer, *Iliad* 2.315]. Now God is a father and seeks his creature. He remedies the falling away, drives off the reptile, restores the nestling to strength again, and urges it to fly back to the nest' (*Prot.* 10.91.3). While the divine may encompass stereotypically maternal characteristics such as fierce protectiveness of her young, Clement's God remains paternal – the father who adopts converts to make them eligible for the inheritance of salvation (see 12.122.4–123.1). Similar reasoning appears in the *Paidagogos*.

The argument in this passage also relates to Christian novelty in that Clement depicts his audience as baby birds who have fallen away from the original, true nest of Christianity; Clement's role is to help God recover the chicks. While I would not suggest that feminists find an ally in the *content* of Clement's arguments, we do share with him an interest in analysing what is wrong with the world as it is and the impulse to transform it.

Clement has to negotiate a thought world in which things labelled 'new' were far more likely to be condemned than embraced. Feminists today also have to contend with the question of how to view and use history in order to articulate our assessments of the present and to craft our visions for the future. The welcome adumbration of feminist foremothers or glimpses of alternative ways of structuring our worlds (both by positive and negative example) continue to fuel much feminist writing.[26] Many feminists seek also to revolutionize the ways we imagine a narrative of the emergence of Christianity.[27] Attention to how early Christians such as Clement render the relationship between Christianity and other religious and cultural formations can help feminists articulate our own reconstructions more responsibly and self-consciously.

In the *Protreptikos*, Clement depicts Christianity as the new song of Moses sung

---

26 Recent works on this topic include Kraemer, *Her Share of the Blessings*; Karen Jo Torjesen, *When Women Were Priests: Women's Leadership in the Early Church and the Scandal of Their Subordination in the Rise of Christianity* (San Francisco, CA: HarperSanFrancisco, 1993); and the recent collection of essays edited by Ross Shepard Kraemer and Mary Rose D'Angelo, *Women and Christian Origins* (Oxford: Oxford University Press, 1999). Amy Richlin's article pertaining to feminist study of classics is also relevant here as she calls attention to the epistemological and methodological differences among feminists that lead some of us to look hopefully to the past for precedents while others of us see only a legacy of oppression to be overcome ('The Ethnographer's Dilemma and the Dream of a Golden Age', in Nancy Sorkin Rabinowitz and Amy Richlin [eds], *Feminist Theory and the Classics* [New York: Routledge, 1993], pp. 272–303).

27 The classic text for this task is Elisabeth Schüssler Fiorenza's *In Memory of Her: A Feminist Theological Reconstruction of Christian Origins* (New York: Crossroad, 1983); but see also the inspiring methodological desiderata articulated by Elizabeth A. Castelli and Hal Taussig, 'Drawing Large and Startling Figures: Reimagining Christian Origins by Painting Like Picasso', in *idem* (eds), *Reimagining Christian Origins: A Colloquium Honoring Burton L. Mack* (Valley Forge, PA: Trinity Press International, 1996), pp. 3–20.

not by Moses but rather by the Logos: 'This is the new song, namely, the manifestation that has just now shone among us, of the Logos who was in the beginning, pre-existent' (1.7.3). To present Christianity as the 'new song' is to draw upon Hebrew Scripture (see especially 8.77.1–88.4) and a vast range of 'pagan' literature to argue that the divine has spoken through all of this prior material but has more recently revealed itself in the most complete manner through the incarnated Logos:[28] 'The Logos himself now speaks to you plainly ... yes, I say, the Logos of God speaks, having become human so that you may learn from a human how it is even possible for a human to become a god' (1.8.4). The positive aspect of this method is a porous inclusivity that makes Christianity compatible with existing practices and norms; the negative aspect is its totalizing and homogenizing tendency and supersessionist agenda relative to both Jewish and 'Greek' religious practices. Ultimately, Clement's message is that the one God, communicated by the teachings of the Logos, trumps all others by either absorption (as with some types of philosophy) or elimination. Members of all nations and peoples are welcome, but at the expense of particularity.

Moreover, Clement asserts that none of the peoples who claim to be the oldest race or who are attributed with this honour is as old as Christians:

> Not one of these [peoples] existed before our world (κόσμος). But we were before the foundation of the world, we who, because we were destined to be in him, were begotten beforehand by God. We are the rational images formed by God's Logos, or Reason (λογική), and we date from the beginning because of our connection with him, because 'the Word was in the beginning'. Since the Logos was from the first, he is the divine beginning of all things, but because he lately took a name – ... the Christ – I have called him a new song. (1.6.4–5)

Lest his readers misunderstand this notion of preselection, Clement repeatedly emphasizes that distinctions in religious practices, like ethnic divisions, result from a mistaking of the part for the whole (a theme that recurs in the *Stromateis*); all are properly members of this one people:

> The Word was not hidden from any; he is a universal light; he shines on all people ... Let us hasten to salvation, to the new birth. Let us, who are many, hasten to be gathered together into one love corresponding to the union of the One Being. Similarly, let us follow after unity by the practice of good works, seeking the good Monad. And the union of many into one, bringing a divine harmony out of many scattered sounds, becomes one symphony, following one leader and teacher, the Logos, and never ceasing until it reaches the truth itself, with the cry 'Abba Father'. (9.88.2–3)

Clement affirms this sentiment by playing first on a Pauline slogan ('the whole Christ, so to speak, is not divided: there is neither barbarian nor Jew nor Greek, neither male nor female, but a new human transformed by the Holy Spirit of God' [11.112.3]) and then on a citation from Homer: 'Give ear, you myriad peoples' [*Iliad* 17.220], or rather, all reason-endowed humans, both barbarian and Greeks; the entire

---

28 David Dawson discusses the Middle Platonic context for this type of reasoning and explores more fully how Clement (and Justin Martyr before him) develops it (*Allegorical Readers*, pp. 186–218; see especially 210).

human race I call, I who was their creator by the father's will. Come to me that you may be marshalled under one God and the one Word of God' (12.120.2–3).

The *Protreptikos* has received virtually no attention from feminist scholars. Yet Clement's homogenizing vision and apologetic for Christian novelty offer rich bases for analysis and critique beyond the few moments in the text in which he employs feminine imagery for divine or human behaviour.

Paidagogos[29]

While the *Protreptikos* attempts to persuade listeners to pursue Christian life, the three-volume *Paidagogos* offers some specifics about this life. For Clement, these works correspond to the first two of three major steps on the Christian path: conversion, training and higher study (see the opening of the *Paidagogos*). In each step, the Logos plays a different role.

When seeking to introduce people to Christianity, the Logos exhorts, calling listeners to piety; the *Protreptikos* embodies this type of instruction. But piety merely lays the foundation for one's life as a Christian. For the next step, the Logos takes on a different aspect, as a kind of personal tutor; the training it provides is designed to transform one's way of living: 'For the life of Christians, in which we are now trained, is a system of reasonable actions ... the system is the commandments of the Lord, which, as divine statutes and spiritual counsels, have been written for us, being adapted for us and our neighbors' (*Paid*. 1.13.102.4–103.1). This training focuses on the actions of the body, but its ultimate goal is preparation for removal of passions from the soul (1.1.1.2, 4). The *Paidagogos* outlines the second step, this practical conditioning (see 1.1.1.4; 1.1.2.1) for μετριοπάθεια, the moderation and control of the passions. In Clement's system, the move from control to cure of passions (ἀπάθεια) occurs during the third step – intellectual training in the spiritual mysteries of Christianity. In this final step, the Logos becomes a teacher who explains and reveals matters of doctrine.[30]

The *Paidagogos* offers two very different kinds of materials – a metaphorically rich discourse on the process of becoming a Christian (book one) and a series of very detailed prescriptions for daily life (books two and three). An overarching analogy between Christian life and a human life span helps to bridge the apparent gap. The first, more abstract volume takes the reader through the conception, gestation, infancy and childhood of a Christian while the latter two volumes *seem* to contain the instructions necessary for 'adulthood'.

But this perception is misleading. Since the entire *Paidagogos* is devoted to the second step of Christian development (the 'training'), its detailed precepts should

---

29 The most readily available English translation is contained in the *ANCL* (volume 2), but it is lacking because the translators render into Latin rather than English those portions of the text that they deemed too racy. I recommend the Fathers of the Church Series: Clement of Alexandria, *Christ the Educator* (trans. Simon P. Wood; New York: Fathers of the Church, 1954).

30 One would expect this work to be entitled the *Didaskalos* (Teacher) (see *Paid*. 1.1.2.1; 1.1.3.3; 3.12.97.3). Because no such work is extant, many scholars have suggested that we view the *Stromateis* as the completion to the trilogy, but this hypothesis has more detractors than supporters at present. Although the *Stromateis* (discussed below) does offer an example of this type of theoretical approach to scripture, it does not seem to constitute the final book in the trilogy begun by the *Protreptikos* and the *Paidagogos*. A work like the now lost *Hypotyposes*, which was Clement's biblical commentary, would be a more likely candidate for this role.

be interpreted as the content of this training; the first book offers its theoretical/ theological foundation. Thus, the work as a whole corresponds to Christian 'youth' rather than adulthood. Those who reach 'adulthood' in Christianity become eligible for higher instruction by the Logos.

The second and third books proceed by topic (eating, drinking, etc.), with a few thematic asides (e.g., the benefit of negative and positive examples for training). Most remarks concern behaviour that would take place under the eyes of others; Clement frequently appeals to this implied gaze in order to persuade his readers of his points. The first several chapters of book two all involve social activities (eating, drinking, laughing and speaking) or choices displayed in social contexts (use of costly vessels for dining, ointments, perfumes, hair dye, flower crowns), as do the final chapters of the book, which address clothing, shoes and jewellery. Even when he turns to sleep and sex in the central portion of this book, Clement still appeals to an implied gaze but relies more on the cultivation of self-scrutiny.[31] For example, Clement charges his listeners to sleep lightly and briefly, cultivating constant wakefulness through various practices:

'Those who have the sleepless Logos dwelling in them, ought not to sleep the entire night' [Homer, *Iliad* 2.24]; rather, they should rise by night, especially in old age, and one devote himself to literature and another begin his art, while the women should handle the distaff; all of us should, so to speak, fight against sleep, accustoming ourselves to this gently and gradually, so that through wakefulness we may partake of life for a longer period. (*Paid.* 2.9.81.4–5)

This passage creates a vivid image not only of the struggle to fend off sleep but also of how to negotiate this struggle through gender-appropriate activities.

The third book also includes new prescriptions for behaviour (particularly about care for one's hair, bathing and exercising), as well as a summary section that reiterates and amplifies topics already addressed. Clement makes the moralizing frame for these topics more visible than in many parts of the previous book; for example, he discusses self-ornamentation in the first few chapters by theorizing about beauty, authentic religion and gender roles.

For a feminist reading of the *Paidagogos*, three aspects emerge as central: (1) Clement's use of familial imagery for the divine and the divine/human relation, in the first book and final hymn of the third book; (2) 'incidental' and explicit appeals to gender and status, with their implications for appropriate power relations among Christians; and (3) the primary characteristics of Christian orientation to the divine: obedience and imitation.

In the first book, Clement develops his argument for how Christians should understand themselves as infants or children in relation to God. Although Clement generally favours an analogy between the divine and human fathers, in the lengthy

---

31 In adopting this ideal of self-scrutiny, Clement Christianizes a concept already well established in rhetorical competition and philosophical discourse. See Maud Gleason, *Making Men: Sophists and Self-Presentation in Ancient Rome* (Princeton, NJ: Princeton University Press, 1995); Harry O. Meier, 'Clement of Alexandria and the Care of the Self', *JAAR* 62 (1994), pp. 719–45; Peter Brown, *The Body and Society: Men, Women and Sexual Renunciation in Early Christianity* (Lectures on the History of Religions, 13; New York: Columbia University Press, 1988), pp. 122–39; Michel Foucault, *The Care of the Self. The History of Sexuality, Vol. 3* (trans. Robert Hurley; New York: Pantheon, 1986).

sixth chapter he develops a complicated analogy among God, the Logos and human mothers.[32] Maternal metaphors become salient for at least two reasons. Most obviously, the bulk of this chapter offers an elaborate interpretation of Paul's giving his 'infant' readers 'milk to drink' (1 Cor. 3.2). In contrast to Clement's uses of this verse elsewhere in his corpus, here it serves to demonstrate that baptism confers equal perfection upon all Christians. For his readers, giving infants milk not only conjures up an image of mother or wet nurse suckling a newborn, it is also an image familiar as a metaphor for the early phases of classical education, or παιδεία, as well as for the transmission of divine instruction.[33] Clement capitalizes upon both of these associations, crafting them so as to contrast 'real' mothers with the actions of the Logos and the divine father: 'While women who have conceived and become mothers produce milk, the Lord Christ – the fruit of the virgin – did not bless women's breasts or judge them to be nourishers; rather, since the loving and kind father rained down the Logos, he himself has become the spiritual nourishment of the self-controlled' (1.6.41.3). As I have argued elsewhere,

> Women's pregnant, birthing, and lactating bodies are necessary for the success of Clement's theological argument as the basis for his comparison, but they are devalued by contrast with their spiritual analogues. Indeed, these spiritual analogues exclude women while appropriating these maternal characteristics: the Christian seeks after the father's breasts, which provide breast milk in the form of the Logos (1.6.43.3–4; 1.46.1); the Lord has conceived and given birth to 'the new people' through the pangs of his flesh (1.42.2; see also 1.35.2–3); the one who gives rebirth nourishes us with his own milk, the Logos (1.49.3).[34]

The relevance of maternal metaphors extends beyond this link between nursing and spiritual education. In order to emphasize the commonality among Christians and the strength of their bond with their 'new' parent(s),[35] Clement appeals to the notion that a foetus is formed from the material substance of its mother's blood. Drawing upon a range of eclectic sources to argue that milk is blood, Clement concludes:

> [M]ilk is the fountain of nourishment by which a woman makes clear that she has really given birth and is a mother ... Because of this, the Holy Spirit says mystically, 'I have given you milk to drink' (1 Cor. 3.2) through the Apostle, using the voice of the Lord. If we have been reborn to Christ, then the one who gives us this new birth nurses us with his own milk – the Logos ... Thus, blood and milk are the same thing, a symbol of the Lord's passion and teachings. For this very reason, we infants may each boast in the Lord, by quoting, 'I profess to be of a good father and [his] blood.' (Homer, *Iliad* 14.113) (1.49.2–3, 4–50.1)

This move repeats the assimilation of human maternal features into a depiction of a divine figure who is ultimately perceived as a father figure.

---

32 For a close reading of this portion of the text, see Buell, *Making Christians*, pp. 119–79. See also Annewies van den Hoek (van de Bunt), 'Milk and Honey in the Theology of Clement of Alexandria', in Hans Jörg Auf der Maur et al. (eds), *Fides Sacramenti Sacramentum Fidei: Studies in honour of Pieter Smulders* (Assen: Van Gorcum, 1981), pp. 27–39.

33 See discussion in Buell, *Making Christians*, pp. 119–30.

34 Buell, *Making Christians*, p. 161.

35 'Parent(s)', because Clement alternates between subsuming the role of the Logos within the single parent God and differentiating between God as father and the Logos as mother.

Clement employs this abundance of maternal imagery, with particular emphasis on nourishment *in utero* and in infancy, in order to emphasize the unity of all Christians. All Christians metaphorically share *substance* in common: a noble 'bloodline' (via the blood of Christ's passion and adoption by God) and divine nourishment (Christian teachings); more so than paternity in antiquity, maternity implied the transmission of materiality from parent to child. Thus, when Clement wants to stress that Christians are more alike than different, he has a powerful referent in widespread ideas about children born of the same mother (or at least suckled at the same breast). We see this emphasis in the evocative hymn that concludes the work: 'Christ Jesus, Heavenly Milk, pressed from the bride's sweet breasts, the gifts of your wisdom, under the weight of sorrows. For us infants, with tender mouths, always suckling at the breast of the maternal Logos...' (*Paid.* 3, hymn 42–51). By contrast, when he wishes to call attention to differences among Christians (particularly of authority) or the authority of divine over human, he creates metaphors from father/son or master/ slave relations.

Early in the *Paidagogos* Clement raises the issue of sexual difference. Immediately after explaining that the Logos, by becoming flesh, offers an embodied example of the 'likeness and image' that humans should seek to emulate (through obedience and imitation), Clement asserts that men and women have the same virtue, same God, same life, same salvation, and hence require the same training (1.4.10.1–2). Sexual desire, according to Clement, is what separates humans into two sexes in this life: 'There [in "that world"] the rewards of this social and holy life, which is based on conjugal union, are laid up, not for male and female, but for humans, the sexual desire that divides humanity being removed. Common therefore, also, to men and women, is the name "human"' (1.4.10.3). As becomes clearer in the *Stromateis*, Clement theorizes sexual difference in relation to embodiedness – to have a body is to have a sex.[36] By positing a common category of humanity, which he most closely links to the nature of souls, Clement produces an awkward situation for those whose embodiedness is perceived to disadvantage them: on the one hand, 'sex' is a finite condition but, on the other hand, it has concrete social consequences while embodied.

The second and third books of the work reveal some of these implications of sexual desire for the specifics of Christian living. Addressing how 'each of us ought to ... regulate the body' (2.1.1.2), Clement finds many instances in which sexual desires are at issue and hence in which the regulations for conduct differ for males and females. For example, in a passage unusual for its calling attention to sex explicitly, Clement argues for a common standard in clothing: 'For it is common to both [men and women] to be covered, as it is to eat and drink. The necessity, then, being common, we judge that the provision ought to be similar' (2.10.106.4–107.1). When he elaborates this similarity, however, we see that 'similar' does not mean 'same'. Both male and female Christians should wear simple white garments (2.10.108.1; 3.11.53.4), but women are permitted softer garments (2.10.107.3) and should fully cover their heads and veil their faces when out of the home (2.10.107.1; 2.10.114.2–3; 3.11.79.4). Softer cloth is explained by appeal to the 'natural' softness

---

36 See Daniel Boyarin's provocative case for two different religious models for theorizing sex and gender in antiquity, 'Gender', in Mark C. Taylor (ed.), *Critical Terms for Religious Studies* (Chicago: University of Chicago Press, 1998), pp. 117–35.

and passivity of female relative to male, whereas veiling/head covering is explicitly linked to male and female sexual desire (2.10.107.1–2; 3.11.56.1–2; 3.11.79.4; see also 3.11.82.5–83.4).[37]

This gap between 'similar' and 'same' reinscribes gender stereotypes for both men and women.[38] 'Silly women' or 'silly rich women' as well as effeminate men are stock characters used to present a foil for proper Christian behaviour; so too are slaves, barbarians and animals in other contexts.

In discussing sexual behaviour, the desire for which Clement locates at the very root of sexual differentiation (1.4.10.3), it is not surprising to find him arguing that females and males should occupy different roles. For Clement, as for virtually all of his contemporaries, the crucial axis for difference in sexual behaviour is that of active and passive. Just as women are 'given in marriage' (pass.) and men 'marry' (act.), so too should women play the passive role in sexual relations and men the active role – a prescription vividly illustrated by agricultural metaphors, such as Clement's admonition that men should '"Abstain from working in every female field" except your own, the great Plato advised (Plato, *Laws* 8.839A), having culled from holy scriptures, selecting the law, "do not have sex with your neighbor's wife and be polluted because of her"' (Lev. 18:20; *Paid.* 2.10.91.1) and 'do not sow where "you do not want what is sown to grow"' (*Laws* 8.841D; *Paid.* 2.10.91.2).

The force of these metaphors entails a further dimension of Clement's teachings about appropriate sexual behaviour: it should be with procreation in mind. Indeed, the chapter in which he treats sexual activity is entitled 'Concerning Procreation'. He does not merely prescribe heteroerotic norms but also constrains these within the social structure of marriage, the cultural value of producing a lineage, and the moral value of self-restraint.[39] This portion of Clement's text also offers the first post-Pauline Christian mention of female homoeroticism, which Clement condemns along with male homoeroticism.[40]

The active/passive division extends as well to clothing and coiffure. I have mentioned clothing above, but Clement's comments about hair are quite striking as well. At the opening of book three, he turns first to women and then to men to argue against a number of ways in which people adorn and sculpt their bodies. He has particularly harsh words for men who shave or depilate the hair from their faces or bodies (although he advocates shaving one's head). He links this pronouncement to an active/passive distinction between male and female bodies:

37 To persuade his listeners of the importance of veiling, Clement refers obliquely to 1 Cor. 11.5–6 (3.11.79.4), but his more elaborate examples are non-Christian. For example, Clement cites (without naming her as he does elsewhere) an anecdote about a Pythagorean philosopher, Theano, who responded to a compliment about her arm by saying that it was not for public enjoyment (2.10.114.2); later, Clement invokes an otherwise unattested anecdote: 'They say that the wife of Aeneas did not ... even in her terror at the capture of Troy, uncover herself, but kept on her veil as she fled through the fire' (3.11.79.5).

38 M. Eleanor Irwin also notes this effect, but defends Clement's conserving approach to gender as reasonable; see her 'Clement of Alexandria: Instructions on How Women Should Live', in Wendy E. Helleman (ed.), *Hellenization Revisited: Shaping a Christian Response within the Greco-Roman World* (Lanham, MD: University Press of America, 1994), pp. 395–407.

39 For an extended analysis of this chapter, see Buell, *Making Christians*, pp. 32–49.

40 Bernadette J. Brooten, *Love Between Women: Early Christian Responses to Female Homoeroticism* (Chicago: University of Chicago Press, 1996), pp. 320–38.

This, then, is the mark of the man, the beard, by which he is seen to be a man, older than Eve, and is the token of the superior nature. In this God deemed it right that he should excel, and dispersed hair over man's whole body. Whatever smoothness and softness was in him God abstracted from his side when he formed the woman Eve, *physically receptive,* his partner in offspring, his help in household management, while he (for he had parted with all smoothness) remained a man, and shows himself man. *And to him has been assigned action, as to her receiving.* (my emphasis, 3.3.19.1–2)

Speculating about the consequences of male hair removal, Clement visualizes a range of practices he deems contrary to nature, wicked, horrible and licentious; such practices include men or boys taking a passive role in intercourse with other men, female prostitution, women marrying other women (taking active as well as passive roles), and fathers having sex unknowingly with their sons or daughters (whom the fathers had abandoned at birth) (3.3.21.3–5). Clement concludes this tirade with an interesting complaint: 'These things your wise laws allow' (3.3.22.1), thereby producing a dramatic distance between the laws *he* is advocating and those of his audience. That his listeners are interested Christians is beside the point. Clement is here engaging in a shaming discourse to underscore Christianity's moral high ground, despite the fact that many other ancient philosophers shared Clement's views about gender and sexual norms.[41]

Clement writes as if his audience consists primarily of free men and women with financial and human resources – that is, money and domestic slaves. Indeed, two closely related running themes of the book are the avoidance of luxury and the proper management of wealth. That Clement has well-off Christians in mind is made clear by his persistent concern that his readers might be tempted to indulge in, or even care about, such delicacies as Median peafowl (2.1.3.2) and sweet Syracusan wine (2.2.30.3); moreover, they might wish to consume such luxury goods from equally extravagant gold or silver containers (2.3.35.1–3), let alone 'get gold receptacles made for excrement' (2.3.39.2). Not only does Clement offer medical and/or ethical arguments for restraint in food, drink, clothing, bathing, home furnishings, slave-holding, personal adornment and shoes, but he also addresses each of these topics with an eye to the use of wealth. As in his *Who is the Rich Person Who is Being Saved?* (see discussion below), Clement does not vilify material wealth *per se* but seeks to redirect the attitudes and practices of his audience with regard to wealth.

In general, Clement condemns owning many slaves because it makes both male and female owners lazy (3.4.26.1–30.4), although he nowhere condemns slave-holding itself. Most frequently, he discusses slaves to criticize the behaviour of free women. For example, he asserts that drunken women behave like slaves (2.2.33.2) and that women who deck themselves out in gold necklaces and other jewellery unwittingly resemble chained prisoners and slaves (2.12.122.2–123.2). The social

---

41 Clement's indebtedness to Stoic and Middle Platonic ideas is well-known (see, e.g., Michel Spanneut, *Le Stoïcisme des Pères de l'Église: De Clément de Rome à Clément d'Alexandrie* [Patristica Sorbonensia, 1; Paris: Seuil, 1957]; Robert M. Berchman, *From Philo to Origen: Middle Platonism in Transition* [BJS, 69; Chico, CA: Scholars Press, 1984]; in addition, Clement frequently praises Pythagoreans (especially Theano, see n. 37 above). Many of Clement's precepts for female dress and behaviour in this work closely resemble those of the Neopythagorean Treatise on 'Chastity', translated in Mary R. Lefkowitz and Maureen Fant (eds), *Women's Life in Greece and Rome* (1982; Baltimore: Johns Hopkins University Press, 1992; 2nd edn), pp. 163–64.

contrast between free women and slaves serves to shame his wealthy listeners into compliance.

In a related tactic, Clement juxtaposes the categories of free women and slaves by playing upon the concept of slavery in the context of Christian identity: 'Women who wear gold seem to me to be afraid that, if they remove their gold, they will be mistaken for slaves without their jewellery' (3.11.58.3). Regardless of the possible accuracy of this tendentious charge, Clement's point is that 'we should prefer to be free rather than only to appear to be free' (3.11.58.3); that is, he redefines freedom as the quality of those who are tutored and adopted by God, rather than one that can be designated by jewellery. This example highlights the degree to which Clement has in mind privileged, free readers. While Christians who are slaves might benefit from a standard for Christian dress and food that flattens some of the markers of social difference, Clement nowhere questions the morality of slaveholding *per se*; a Christian slave must apparently be content with this-worldly enslavement and freedom under God.[42]

In addition, Clement links free women and slaves to imply that the combination leads to sexual impropriety (in the baths, 3.5.32.3; eunuchs who arrange love affairs, 3.4.26.3) or decadence (women buy slaves to make them up, cart them around the city for all to see, tell them erotic tales, 3.4.26.3–30.4). In this type of example, Clement blames both the free women for their superficiality and immorality and the slaves for being a bad influence. The passage implies, however, that the free women are responsible for their actions whereas the slaves remain simply foils for his criticisms. All three of these types of juxtapositions are in part enabled by a perceived comparability of the subordinate groups of stereotypical dichotomies in antiquity (animals, children, barbarians, gentiles, females and slaves vs. humans, adults, Greeks, Jews, males and free persons); furthermore, this particular juxtaposition may have been of particular poignancy in Alexandria, a city in which the vast majority of slaves were domestic slaves, likely to have been overseen by free females.[43]

Finally, obedience and imitation are central to Clement's notion of how a Christian should be oriented to the Logos. He elaborates the first concept most frequently by using familial or political metaphors (God as father, ruler, Christians as children, subjects) and the second by appealing to educational metaphors or Gen. 1.26–27. These two intertwine: Christians should '[turn] away from some examples, and [imitate] others as much as we can, thus to perform the works of the παιδαγωγός according to his similitude and so fulfil what scripture says "in his image and likeness"' (1.3.9.1). The rhetoric of the entire work operates on this principle of self-monitoring using both negative examples (emphasizing degenerate luxury and licentiousness) and positive examples, drawn from both philosophical and scriptural references. The *Stromateis* employs these ideals for the relationship between Christian teacher and student, whereas in the *Paidagogos* they apply explicitly to divine/human relations.

---

42 Because enslavement was not generally a lifelong status, its consequences are somewhat different from those of sex. Unlike slavery, Clement views sex as an intrinsic feature of embodiedness. For further discussion of slavery including attention to gender, see Jennifer A. Glancy, *Slavery in Early Christianity* (Oxford: Oxford University Press, 2002).

43 Thus, feminists reconstructing early Christian women's experiences must be careful to attend to differences and possible tensions among women of different statuses.

The overall effect of the *Paidagogos* is to depict the proper Christian life in terms of a small household, composed of a married man and woman, possibly with children, and a few household slaves. A simple diet, simple white clothing, restricted sleep, constraint in sex, use of wealth for charity rather than display, beard and shaved head for men, long bound hair for women, regular baths, no make-up or hair dye, no earrings (but a sealing ring is permitted) all feature. As these mundane topics indicate, Christianity pervades all corners of one's life[44] – being a Christian, for Clement, entails constant vigilance and action.

But it is also crucial to remember that the overarching analogy for this work is that between Christian and human development. The *Paidagogos* addresses those who are still children relative to other, 'adult' Christians, even while Clement speaks of all Christians as children in relation to the divine. This analogy naturalizes power relations among Christians as well as between divine and humans, drawing most consistently upon father/son imagery.[45] We now turn to examine a text that purports to preserve its message for those 'who have been enrolled as men' (*Strom.* 6.1.1.3).

Stromateis[46]

'The Miscellanies' is one of the most common English designations for this multi-volume work,[47] whose full title is *Miscellanies of Gnostic Notes in Accordance with the True Philosophy.*[48] Clement explains its miscellaneous character by asserting that it is based upon the oral teachings he received from his teachers.[49] He claims that the work is selective rather than comprehensive, partly due to what he has forgotten but primarily to protect the 'pearls' of truth from unprepared readers. If one is able to comprehend Christian 'mysteries', the text functions both as a useful basis for remembering these mysteries and for their further elucidation (1.1.14.1–15.3; 1.12.55.1–56.3; 4.2.4.1–7.4; 7.18.110.4–111.3).

Two topics interest Clement most in this work: (1) a description of the Christian philosophy and its ideal practitioner, the 'Gnostic';[50] and (2) a demonstration of the

---

44 Despite its apparently exhaustive character, the *Paidagogos* does not address topics like child-rearing and professional labour; these omissions, among others, may correlate with the privileged status of his intended audience or figurative ideal of a Christian.

45 See also Mieke Bal, 'Metaphors He Lives By', *Semeia* 61 (1993), pp. 185–207.

46 An English translation of all but book three can be found in Alexander Roberts and James Donaldson (eds), *Fathers of the Second Century: Hermas, Tatian, Athenagoras, Theophilus, and Clement of Alexandria (entire)* (The Ante-Nicene Christian Fathers, 1885; Peabody, MA: Hendrickson, 1995), pp. 299–568. For an English translation of the first three books, see Clement of Alexandria, *Stromateis: Books One to Three* (trans. John Ferguson; Fathers of the Church; Washington DC: The Catholic University of America Press, 1991).

47 There are eight volumes, although the final volume does not fit neatly with the rest.

48 The most comprehensive analysis of this work remains André Méhat, *Études sur les 'Stromates' de Clément d'Alexandrie* (Patristica Sorbonensia, 7; Paris: Seuil, 1966).

49 See Annewies van den Hoek, 'Techniques of Quotation in Clement of Alexandria: A View of Ancient Literary Working Methods', *VC* 50 (1996), pp. 223–43.

50 Clement uses this term far more than other Christians who have been categorized as 'Gnostic' in early Christianity, where Gnostic also serves as a shorthand for 'heretic'. For a discussion of the categories 'Gnostic' and 'Gnosticism' see Karen L. King, *What is Gnosticism?* (Cambridge, MA: Harvard University Press, 2003).

truths contained within Greek and other non-Christian philosophical schools. These foci allow Clement not only to frame Christianity as a philosophy but also to adapt ideas about the pursuit of philosophical studies to his model for the ideal Christian life. By claiming the phrase 'true philosophy' for the highest form of Christian practice, Clement makes it rhetorically possible to appropriate from various philosophical writings while asserting the superiority of Christianity. He portrays Greek philosophy as comparable to the Law in Judaism – classifying both as preparation for the Gospel (e.g., 1.5.28.1–3). These two overarching goals mark Clement's discussion of a range of topics, most notably including arguments against rival Christian claims to authoritative explications of Christianity (see e.g., 4.1.2.2–3 and much of book seven).

In the third book of the *Stromateis*, Clement uses the topics of sexual practices, marriage and procreation to form a lens through which to examine the underlying goals of Christian living: to eliminate the passions and thereby to attain the 'likeness and image' of God. Sexual desires represent passions most vividly.[51] While a call to eliminate all human desires could easily be read as extreme, Clement locates himself as the moderate between two unreasonable extremes (i.e., between inappropriate sexual asceticism and licentious promiscuity). Clement insists that his form, the true form of Christianity, praises both virginity and marriage, so long as they are for the right reasons (3.9.66.3; 3.12.88.3).[52] The spectrum that Clement constructs cleverly conceals the fact that he objects to both 'extremes' for similar reasons – both reject the value of marriage and/or procreation.

The views of a range of different Christian teachers (including Valentinus, Basilides, the Carpocratians, Marcion, Tatian, Prodicus and Julius Cassian) indicate how complex the possible connections were between cosmological, theological and philosophical concepts and social/sexual practices; they also reveal how Clement authorizes his views. One of his most vitriolic critiques of rival Christians is reserved for the followers of Carpocrates and his son Epiphanes. Even reading Clement's descriptions with some scepticism, it appears that what Clement finds most offensive about the so-called Carpocratians is that they apply the principle of equality in Christ (Gal. 3.28 and par.) to social relations, with the result that sexual relations between men and women are not bounded by monogamous marriage (3.2.5.1–10.2); he seems most concerned by what he views as their licentious promotion of indiscriminate heteroerotic liaisons for the sake of procreation. By detaching procreation from marriage, the Carpocratians threaten the social system that Clement insists is a reflection of heavenly order. We get a hint of the destabilizing potential of the Carpocratian position for Clement's Christian vision in his cry, 'How can this fellow [Epiphanes, Carpocrates's son] still be listed in our church members' register when he openly does away with the Law and Gospels alike by these words [that detach procreation from marriage]?' (3.2.8.4). Even if

---

51 See Kathy L. Gaca, *The Making of Fornication: Eros, Ethics, and Political Reform in Greek Philosophy and Early Christianity* (Hellenistic Culture and Society, 40; Berkeley and Los Angeles: University of California Press, 2003), pp. 247–72; and David G. Hunter, 'The Language of Desire: Clement of Alexandria's Transformation of Ascetic Discourse', *Semeia* 57 (1992), pp. 95–111.

52 See also Jean-Paul Broudéhoux, *Mariage et famille chez Clément d'Alexandrie* (Théologie Historique, 11; Paris: Beauchesne et Ses Fils, 1972).

not literally, Clement implies that he and Epiphanes are deemed members of the same religious community.[53]

On the other end of the spectrum, Clement condemns other Christians as too extreme in their asceticism, including the followers of Marcion and Julius Cassian. He quotes Cassian's work *On Self-Control*: 'No one should say that because we have the parts of the body that we do, with the female shaped one way and the male another, one for receiving, the other for inseminating, sexual intercourse has God's approval' (3.13.91.1). Cassian apparently uses a distinction between bodies and souls in order to argue against sexual activity that would result in the production of more bodies. While Clement also holds the body and soul in tension, he does view them as a necessary team. What Clement does not discuss, but Cassian's quotation suggests, is how some second-century Christians could interpret the distinction between bodies and souls such that existing cultural assumptions about sex (here outlined clearly along an active/passive split) could be acknowledged but also denied; activity and passivity might characterize maleness and femaleness, but Cassian rejects the significance or presumed implications of sex for social and sexual relations.[54]

Despite Clement's approval of voluntary celibacy, he values marriage and procreation more highly. Whether arguing that Paul was married (3.6.53.1) or citing the pastoral prescription of marriage as a precondition of religious leadership for men (e.g., 3.18.108.2), 'Clement tended to view the world from the perspective of these householders'.[55] For Peter Brown, this is an asset:

> Clement's writings take us, for a welcome moment, out of the narrow confines of the radical groups [e.g., Marcion, Tatian, Encratites, Valentinians]. ... Clement's most daring act, in a time of increasingly vocal radicalism, was to have spoken up, in this ingenious and elegant manner, for the married Christian laity. ... Clement wrote, in part, to block the rise of a dangerous mystique of continence. He reassured married householders that they did not need to feel ashamed to have married leaders, nor, as married persons, need they feel unable to aspire to Christian perfection. They could also aspire to leadership within the Christian communities. Even Paul had been a married man, so Clement surmised, rather ingeniously. Certainly, Peter had been married.[56]

Brown does not explore the implications of this 'welcome' stance for anyone other than married persons, which by the end of the passage seems to mean married men. While Clement makes clear that women are capable of attaining Christian

---

53 For an evocative reconstruction of the Carpocratian position, see Gaca, *The Making of Fornication*, pp. 273–91.

54 Clement rebuts Cassian's interpretation of bodily differences by insisting on a metaphorical interpretation of sex, whereby male represents 'temper' and female 'desire' – two types of passions that the soul must master in order to attain Gnostic perfection (3.13.93.3; see also 3.10.69.2–4). Clement develops his position in part from a counter-interpretation of a dialogue between Salome and Jesus, attributed to a lost *Gospel of the Egyptians* (see 3.6.45.3); this passage apparently serves as a proof-text for Cassian and other pro-ascetic Christians. Clement challenges those who interpret Jesus' remark that he has 'come to destroy the works of the female' as a condemnation of procreation by interpreting 'female' as 'lack of self-control' (3.9.63.3). Kathy Gaca develops the views of Tatian, another of Clement's rivals on this allegedly too-ascetic end of the spectrum (see Gaca, *The Making of Fornication*, pp. 221–46).

55 Brown, *Body and Society*, p. 135.

56 Brown, *Body and Society*, pp. 137–38.

perfection and does not explicitly exclude them from leadership, his vision for the ideal Christian community is modelled upon a notion of the household that depends upon asymmetry in power relations; the division of roles lends itself toward structural emphasis on male leadership (imitating Paul or Peter). Yet Clement's own logic introduces a tension between this hierarchical social ideal and the requirements for becoming a Gnostic Christian.

For Clement, a Gnostic is one who, through imitation of and assimilation to God, can be said to have already become God or God-like in this life (2.19.97.1; 4.23.149.8; 4.23.151.3–152.3; 6.14.114.5–6; 7.3.13.3); indeed, the Gnostic is a 'third divine image' after that of the only-begotten image of the Logos (7.3.16.6). More specifically, the Gnostic is one who has built upon the foundation of faith and action (through obedience to the Logos's precepts), become not just continent but passionless (e.g., 3.5.43.1; 4.23.152.1; 6.9.71.1–79.2), and so has cultivated a life of true wisdom. Finally and crucially, the Gnostic is a teacher, one who helps to form and instruct others (1.10.49.1; 2.10.46.1; 2.19.97.2; 7.9.52.1–54.1).

One way in which a Christian can cultivate perfection is by imitating those who have already attained it, that is, who have become Gnostics. Clement grants significant authority to the Gnostic as one who 'makes up for the absence of the apostles by an upright life, accurate knowledge...' (7.12.77.4). This comparison indicates that Clement visualizes the process of perfection as the production and transmission of a lineage. He makes this more explicit in another passage: 'γνῶσις itself is that which has descended by transmission to a few, having been imparted unwritten by the apostles' (6.7.61.3). While Clement refrains from identifying this 'few' (although he does seem to include himself; see 1.1.11.3), he does not exclude anyone *per se*. After insisting that the original apostles were not chosen 'for some distinguished peculiarity of nature', he continues: 'then, also now, those who have exercised themselves in the Lord's commandments, and lived perfectly and gnostically according to the Gospel, may be enrolled in the chosen body of the apostles' (6.13.105.1; 106.1). Whether Clement intends to include women among those who can be counted as apostles remains unclear, but the theoretical framework of his argument would permit this reading.[57]

While Clement generally writes as if his ideal Gnostic is a married man, at other points he insists that gender, status, age and 'race' or ethnicity, are not disqualifying impediments for pursuing a Gnostic life.[58] In book four, Clement explicitly raises the question of gender, age and status. His response is worth a close look. 'We know that children, women and slaves have often, against their fathers', masters' and husbands' will, reached the highest degree of excellence' (4.8.68.2). Clement offers this statement as one of his proofs for why certain categories of people should 'philosophize equally'.

---

57 Some Valentinian Christians, with whom Clement agrees on many points despite the rhetorical distance he places between himself and them, did consider women eligible for the transmission of unwritten apostolic tradition (see 'Ptolemy's Letter to Flora', in Bentley Layton (ed. and trans.), *Gnostic Scriptures* [Garden City, NY: Doubleday, 1987], pp. 314–15).

58 See also Laura Rizzerio, 'La notion de γνωστικὴ φυσιολογία chez Clément d'Alexandrie', in Elizabeth A. Livingstone (ed.), *Studia Patristica vol. XXVI: Papers presented at the Eleventh International Conference on Patristic Studies held in Oxford 1991. Liturgica, Second Century, Alexandria before Nicaea, Athanasius and the Arian Controversy* (Leuven: Peeters, 1993), pp. 318–23.

It highlights the operations of social power by articulating the particular relationships of subordination pertaining to each of the former category of persons (with an evident presumption that the 'women' in question are free women). Never directly questioning the validity of these social hierarchies, Clement does play upon them to make two points: precedent, that children, women and slaves have already shown themselves capable of attaining Christian perfection (implying that this could happen again); and counter-intuition, that the 'least' can prevail despite opposition.

In addition to this brief proof, Clement offers three other kinds of proofs directed primarily to defend women's pursuit of the Gnostic ideal. First, Clement insists that all humans share a common nature and virtue, across 'race' and gender at the level of the soul: 'Accordingly, woman is to practise self-restraint and righteousness and every other virtue, just as man, both bond and free' (4.8.59.3). But, unlike ethnic or racial groupings, for which Clement offers no mitigating circumstances allowing for any difference (4.8.58.4), in the case of gender Clement demures:

> We do not say that woman's nature is the same as man's, since she is woman. For undoubtedly it stands to reason that some difference should exist between each of them. Pregnancy and child-bearing are in a woman's nature, as she is a woman, not as she is a human being. For if there were no difference between man and woman both would do and receive the same things [i.e., be active and passive in the same ways]. (4.8.59.4–5)

The differences that Clement selects as significant are 'pregnancy and child-bearing', which Clement attributes to the 'peculiar construction of the body'. This reasoning corresponds quite closely to that of the *Paidagogos*, in which both females and males are to be trained by the Logos and will have their differences dissolved in the next life, but they are presently differentiated by sexual desire and their roles in marriage.[59] In the *Stromateis*, Clement explains the consequences of this bodily difference in terms of women being 'destined for child-bearing and housekeeping (οἰκουρία)', subordination to their husbands, and general inferiority (4.8.60.1–2; 4.8.62.4–65.1).[60]

This first proof needs to be interpreted in light of an earlier point in Clement's discussion of martyrdom – his overarching topic in this portion of book four. He defines the body as the irrational portion of the human, the soul as the rational component, with the consequence that true life entails separating the soul from 'sinful' connection to the body through mastery of the soul over the body. Despite the hierarchical relationship between body and soul, however, Clement deems the body not as something to be rejected but as a necessary vehicle for salvation: 'the harmonious mechanism of the body contributes to the understanding which leads to goodness of nature' (4.4.17.4).[61]

---

59 See also *Strom* 6.12.100.3: 'souls, on their own, are equal. Souls are neither male nor female, when they no longer marry nor are given in marriage. And isn't a woman transformed into a man, when she has truly become equally manly and perfect?'

60 The link between bodily particularity and child bearing may seem more obvious to modern readers than that between bodily particularity and housekeeping; nonetheless, housekeeping remains, even today, largely 'women's work', frequently performed by economically and ethno-racially marginalized women.

61 Its context makes this passage particularly interesting. Clement appears aware that his line of argument could be read as disparaging the body. Instead, he claims that this is the position of other Christians, specifically that of 'falsely-named' Gnostics, and he offers this statement as well as a passage from Plato's *Republic* to clarify his view of the importance of the body.

Because of the central role of the body as the material with which a Christian must work to achieve perfection, any bodily differences that Clement deems peculiar to the nature of a particular group will alter the ways in which members of that group pursue the cultivation of their otherwise common human virtues. Thus, this proof about the underlying similarity in female and male souls permits Clement to argue on behalf of women's pursuit of virtue and philosophy while his insistence on the significance of bodily difference permits him to maintain gendered social distinctions.

Clement's second proof on women's behalf consists of appeals to 'barbarian' cultures and dogs whose females supposedly participate in activities that Clement views as gender-inappropriate: engaging in battle, 'manly toil', hunting and herding (4.8.62.1–3). Followed immediately by the assertion: 'Women are therefore to philosophize in a manner similar to men' (4.8.62.4), this proof seems to function as an anticipatory rebuttal to the hypothetical objection that the pursuit of philosophy is one of those activities unsuited to women's peculiar physical construction. The potential force of this statement is undercut, however, both by Clement's follow-up quip that 'males are preferable at everything, unless they have become effeminate' and by his citation of passages from Euripides, Paul and the deutero-Pauline household codes about female inferiority and the propriety of female subordination in the household and church (4.8.63.1–66.1).

A final kind of proof appears later in the discussion, which also has this double-edged character. In this case, Clement invokes a series of precedents from classical and biblical history in order to demonstrate that women as well as men can attain perfection. As is the case in the previous proof, the force of this catalogue of famous women (4.19.118.1–123.1) – which includes Sappho, Theano, Hipparchia (the Cynic philosopher), as well as the biblical heroines Judith and Esther – is diminished by the section that immediately follows in which Clement describes the virtues of a 'good wife' (4.19.123.2–4.20.129.1). Even though Clement frames these somewhat paradoxical portions of text with twinned assertions that male and female can both attain perfection (4.19.118.1) and have the same goal in attaining perfection (4.20.67.4), the virtues of female modesty and attentiveness to one's people or husband reveal a double standard.[62]

It is not coincidental that these proofs occur within the larger treatment of martyrdom. Accounts of early Christian martyrs are one of the few places in Christian literature where we find many women, slave and free, as well as enslaved men, depicted as heroic agents. As Annewies van den Hoek helpfully notes, 'in book four, the issue of martyrdom evokes women as heroines and brings out their equality with men; book three, on the other hand, deals with sexuality and marriage, and equality hardly comes up'.[63] Although Clement tempers his assertions of equality among Christians across social differences in book four (by appealing especially to Euripides, the household codes, and *1 Clement*), the context for discussion makes

---

62 In a thematically related, but contextually different portion of the *Stromateis*, he reasserts the possibility of Gnostic perfection for females but notes that females attain this perfection once they have been transformed into males first (6.12.100.3); see Vogt, '"Becoming Male"', pp. 73–75.

63 Annewies van den Hoek, 'Clement of Alexandria on Martyrdom', in Elizabeth A. Livingstone (ed.), *Studia Patristica*, vol. 26, pp. 338–39.

this portion of the *Stromateis* his most explicit and positive with respect to the possibilities of advanced spiritual achievement by the socially subordinate.

For a feminist reading of the *Stromateis*, two final issues are noteworthy: *mimesis* as the technique for assimilation into the 'likeness and image' of God, represented in the flesh by one's teacher (7.9.52.3); and filiation as the central model for Christian education.

Throughout the *Stromateis*, Clement insists that Christians must actively work to perfect themselves, to make themselves conform to the 'likeness and image' of the divine. Frequently, the necessity of this effort is presented in contrast to the rejected notion that humans (or only certain humans) have an inborn or natural perfection (e.g., 2.16.75.1–2; 6.9.78.4; 6.12.96.1–3).[64] This position makes Clement's version of the Gnostic path potentially open to all manner of people.

The process of becoming a Gnostic Christian depends upon the production and citation of authoritative lineages. In book six, Clement says, 'If there is instruction, you must seek for the teacher' (6.7.57.2). Not surprisingly, Clement insists that God, via the Logos, is the ultimate teacher to whom we must trace the 'teaching of all good things'. As he has done for much of the *Stromateis*, Clement claims that truth has been transmitted via both Jewish and gentile peoples but that, in the case of the latter, their alleged lineages are incomplete and their 'truths' partial.[65] This rhetorical move is particularly interesting because Clement also adapts it to secure his own claims to authority relative to other Christians, by tracing his own lineage back via some apostles (1.1.11.3) and by condemning other Christians who allegedly trace their lineage to a human teacher (i.e., followers of Marcion, Valentinus and Basilides; 7.17.108.1), even though he concedes that they too claim to preserve apostolic traditions.[66]

Clement employs both paternal and maternal metaphors to depict the educational process. He cites Paul's use of each (1 Cor. 4.15 and Gal. 4.19) to demonstrate that the apostles continued to produce 'children' after Jesus' death (3.15.99.2–3); his Gnostic interpretation of the decalogue reads divine knowledge as the 'mother' (God as the father) of the commandment to honour one's parents (6.16.146.1–2). As in the *Paidagogos*, these paternal and maternal metaphors also serve to describe the earliest stages of Christian perfection. When speaking of more advanced instruction and perfection, however, Clement more commonly elides teaching with fatherhood, depicting the Gnostic as one who 'begets' Christians through instruction, alluding to 1 Cor. 4.15 (7.9.53.5).[67] This emphasis on patrilineages reflects Clement's concern to authorize his form of 'Gnostic' teaching in relation to other options; moreover, by

---

64 See also Karen Jo Torjesen's brief remarks, 'Pedagogical Soteriology from Clement to Origen', in Lothar Lies (ed.), *Origeniana Quarta. Die Referate des 4. Internationalen Origeneskongresses (Innsbruck, 2–6 September 1985)* (Innsbruck: Tyrolia, 1987), pp. 370–73.

65 For example, in the immediate context of book six, Clement pursues his 'search for the teacher' by stating that 'Cleanthes claims Zeno, and Metrodorus Epicurus … But if I come to Pythagoras … and the first wise people I come to an impasse in my search for their teacher. Should you say the Egyptians, the Indians, the Babylonians, and the Magi themselves, I will not cease asking for their teacher. And I will lead you up to the first generation of humans; from that point I begin to investigate who their teacher is' (*Strom.* 6.7.57.3) finally concluding that it is the one called 'Sophia' by all the prophets who is the 'teacher of all created beings' (6.7.58.1).

66 For a longer analysis on these intra-Christian polemics, see Buell, *Making Christians*, pp. 79–98.

67 I discuss this practice at length in Buell, *Making Christians*, pp. 50–68.

depicting the appropriate relations between more junior and more senior Christians (would-be Gnostics and Gnostics) as that of son to father, where the ideal is for the son to be(come) exactly like the father, Clement naturalizes a hierarchical and androcentric model for power relations.

Nonetheless, feminists may find Clement's emphasis on the necessity of human growth and transformation worthy of further analysis. Although he unquestionably accepts stereotypes about social divisions (slave/free) and gender (female passivity/ male activity), his framework for Christian perfection presumes that even those who are privileged in this-worldly standards must actively change themselves to acquire spiritual knowledge and perfection. I suspect, however, that his message is precisely calibrated to the ears of such a privileged reader so that its intended force is less one of the liberating possibilities of self-transformation than of persuading the well-born and/or well-off of the need for his variety of self-transformation. Finally, it is important to note that the price of Gnostic perfection is conformity to one standard; whether depicted as 'becoming male' or becoming transformed into the likeness of one's teacher, Clement's vision does not view diversity among Christians as an asset.

Who is the Rich Person Who is Being Saved?

This text, an allegorical or 'spiritual' interpretation of Mk 10.17–31, offers both a fascinating example of Clement in his teacherly mode and a troubling sense of his vision for Christian living. In its message about wealth and its concern for curing the soul of its passions, it strongly resembles the *Paidagogos*. Clement here, in good Platonic fashion, distinguishes between literal/material and spiritual levels of both biblical interpretation and riches. Because 'the Saviour teaches his people nothing in a merely human way, but everything by a divine and mystical wisdom, we must not understand his words literally (σαρκικῶς), but with due inquiry and intelligence we must search out and master their hidden meaning' (5.2).

What is this 'hidden meaning'? Clement's answer does not suit any form of liberation theology, but it must have been quite agreeable to well-off Christians familiar with urban euergetism. Clement adapts this practice of spending personal wealth on public works to Stoic-like notions of self-mastery and control of one's passions to formulate a teaching 'new and peculiar to God' (12.1). Specifically, he renders Jesus' command 'if you will be perfect, sell all you have and distribute to the poor' (10.21) as a call to 'strip the soul itself and the will of their lurking passions and utterly to root out and cast away all alien thoughts from the mind' (12.1). Appealing to the status quo to justify the acquisition or inheritance of wealth ('Why need wealth ever have arisen at all out of earth, if it is the provider and agent of death?' [26.5]), Clement advocates that wealthy Christians spend their excess funds on other Christians while constantly training themselves to cut away passions under the guidance of a 'godly person' who can serve as their trainer (ἀλείπτης) and pilot (κυβερνήτης) (41.1).

Clement does entertain the idea of renouncing earthly wealth but dismisses it for three reasons. First, if it were necessary to renounce wealth to gain eternal life, then people who just happen to be destitute, 'though "ignorant" of God and "God's righteousness" (Rom. 10.3), [would] be most blessed and beloved of God and the only possessors of eternal life' (11.3). This argument is consistent with his insistence throughout his writings that people are not naturally saved or perfected but must act on their natural *potential*. Second, Clement notes that there are precedents for renouncing wealth (i.e., Anaxagoras, Democritus and Crates [11.4]) for a range of reasons, so renunciation is not automatically linked with the search for eternal life. Finally, Clement argues that renunciation of material possessions does not ensure that one will be free from material concerns: 'For when one lacks the necessities of life, that one cannot fail to be broken in spirit and to neglect the higher things, as they strive to procure these necessities by any means and from any source' (12.5). Such a claim makes it difficult to see how any poor person could achieve salvation!

Clement does presuppose, however, the presence of both needy and wealthy Christians in his community; his prescription for the wealthy ones is to 'open your heart to all who are enrolled as God's disciples, not gazing scornfully on their bodies, not being led to indifference by their age. And if one appear needy or ill-clad or ungainly or weak, do not take offense in your soul at this and turn away' (33.5). He then turns this lesson in charitable distribution of funds simultaneously into a lesson about human nature: 'This is a form thrown around us from without for the purpose of our entrance into the world, that we may be able to take our place in the universal school, but hidden within dwells the Father and his Son who died for us and rose with us' (33.6). Thus Clement both argues for a kind of spiritual equality of all Christians yet still upholds the usefulness of distinctions on the material level.

While the above summary addresses the main points of the homily, there are two other passages of particular interest for a feminist reader:[68] the interpretation of Mk 10.29 and Lk. 14.26 on the importance and rewards of leaving or hating one's family (22.1–23.5) and a very brief but striking image of God becoming female (37.2). In the first instance, Clement defuses the apparent literal meaning of these passages by saying that, unless it interferes with one's salvation, one should continue to honour one's father – as long as it is less than one honours Christ (22.5–7). Using a hypothetical law trial to clarify the matter, he notes that if one's father (and he later adds 'brother, child, wife, or anyone else') should appeal to family ties to encourage disobedience to 'the law of Christ', one should let Christ's appeal win – an appeal arguing that God, via Christ, is one's true father and nurse (23.1–5).[69] Recalling the argument in the *Protreptikos* (89.1–2) that his Greek readers should risk angering their fathers by seeking for their true father, this passage reinforces an image of appropriate Christian orientation to the divine as one of obedient child to parents, but with particular emphasis on paternal authority.

In the second, tantalizingly brief passage, Clement distinguishes between aspects of the Godhead, according to their type of relation to humanity. Just as paternity in the above example is linked with claims to authority and allegiance, maternity is invoked in the context of a discussion of God's love and care for humanity: 'the part [of God] that has sympathy with us is mother. By God's love, the father became female; a great sign of this is that he (αὐτός) begat from himself. And the fruit born of love is love' (*Quis*

---

68 For a feminist analysis of the entire work, see Denise Kimber Buell, '"Sell What You Have and Give to the Poor": A Feminist Interpretation of Clement of Alexandria's *Who is the Rich Person Who is Saved?*', in Shelly Matthews, Cynthia Briggs Kittredge and Melanie Johnson-DeBaufre (eds), *Walk in the Ways of Wisdom: Essays in Honor of Elisabeth Schüssler Fiorenza* (Harrisburg, PA: Trinity Press International, 2003), pp. 194–213.

69 See Buell, *Making Christians*, pp. 100–4.

37.2). As I noted in the introduction, while this assertion of divine femaleness is exceptional, it is also inextricably linked to gender stereotypes that need to be considered before such images are taken as signs of Clement's open-mindedness or appropriated for feminist work. Although this text has received almost no sustained feminist reading, its interest in maintaining and managing economic as well as spiritual differences among Christians makes it worth further feminist attention.

Conclusion: Analysing Clement across the Corpus

Clement is one of the few early Christian authors who employ maternal imagery to reflect on the nature of the divine and the relation between divine and human. While maternal imagery for divine beings was widely available in antiquity,[70] it is far less common to find this imagery explicitly invoked in early Christian texts.[71] As we have seen, Clement uses this maternal imagery in three portions of his corpus: a very brief reference in his homily on wealth; an extended argument in the first book of the *Paidagogos*; and in the closing hymn of the *Paidagogos*. Additionally, the *Proptreptikos* and *Paidagogos* compare the actions and attitudes of God to humans with that of female animals to their children, metaphorically appropriating maternal characteristics to the divine.

While some scholars emphasize the importance of a precedent in Christian writings for imaging the divine in gynocentric terms,[72] I agree with Gail Paterson Corrington Streete's more sceptical position that Clement appropriates nursing metaphors (and this would extend to pregnancy metaphors as well) to depict the actions of a *male* saviour and his divine *father*.[73] Such metaphors might indeed provide useful resources for feminist theological reimaginings, but only if these reimaginings are unfaithful to Clement's own rhetoric.[74]

For Kari Børresen, Clement ranks as a 'feminist' Church Father (along with Augustine), because he 'managed to include women in human Godlikeness already from creation by means of an asexual definition of *imago Dei*, that is despite non-Godlike femaleness'.[75]

---

70 See Gail Paterson Corrington Streete, *Her Image of Salvation: Female Saviors and Formative Christianity* (Louisville, KY: Westminster/John Knox, 1992). The popularity of Isis during the Roman period, not merely in Egypt, but around the Mediterranean basin, may also help to account for Clement's choice of feminine imagery for the divine although we find nothing in Clement's writings comparable to the spousal imagery so common for Isis.

71 Børresen sketches the main features of this 'atypical' Christian tradition in 'God's Image', pp. 17–31.

72 E.g., Wagner, 'Divine Femaleness', pp. 29–40; and McVey, 'Christianity and Culture', pp. 123–26.

73 Gail Paterson Corrington, 'The Milk of Salvation: Redemption by the Mother in Late Antiquity and Early Christianity', *HTR* 82 (1989), pp. 393–420 (412–13).

74 With Donna Haraway, I view the concept of being unfaithful to one's origins as an asset, not a liability; see Haraway's 'Cyborg Manifesto: Science, Technology, and Socialist-Feminism in the Late Twentieth Century', in *eadem, Simians, Cyborgs, and Women: The Reinvention of Nature* (New York: Routledge, 1990), pp. 149–82.

75 Kari Elisabeth Børresen, 'Recent and Current Research on Women in the Christian Tradition', in Elizabeth A. Livingstone (ed.), *Studia Patristica XXIX: Papers presented at the Twelfth International Conference on Patristic Studies held in Oxford 1995: Historica, Theologica et Philosophica, Critica et Philologica* (Leuven: Peeters, 1997), pp. 224–31 (226).

I would offer three cautions to this praise. First, and well-discussed, is that Clement links female attainment of *imago Dei* with the trope of 'becoming male' (*Strom.* 6.100.3),[76] which exposes the definition of *imago Dei* as not entirely 'asexual'. Second, Clement employs the principle of *imago Dei* to advocate the necessity of hierarchical relations among humans and between divine and human: the most advanced Christians – the Gnostics – become the likeness of God and hence models for other Christians; less advanced Christians must always seek to obey and imitate human and divine models.[77] Feminists should hardly embrace this model for power relations.[78]

Third, Clement does not employ feminine metaphors for the divine in contexts where he stresses that humans are created in the 'image and likeness' (Gen. 1.26–27) of the divine (I suspect that this is largely due to connotations of material connections between mothers and children that infuse his maternal and nursing imagery). Gen. 1.26–27 appears as a proof text for how Christian practice ideally affects human *souls*. The gap between 'human Godlikeness' and 'non-Godlike femaleness', enabled in large part by a reading of Gen. 1.26–27 in contradistinction from Gen. 2.7, 20–22, allows Clement to argue that the part of the self that is in the image and likeness of God (the soul) is common to both males and females but that the embodied self is characterized by sexual difference. This reading is bad news for theorists who seek to question the naturalness of sex – not just gender.[79]

Clement's wide-ranging corpus offers many entry points for feminist analysis. Certainly, multiple feminist readings are possible – feminists most interested in reconstructing the historical situation of women's lives in Clement's community will pose different questions from those more interested in the implications of his Christology. While their respective evaluations of Clement's views may vary, the most persuasive feminist interpretations will locate their analyses in relation to Clement's rhetorical aims.

---

76 Vogt, '"Becoming Male"', pp. 72–83; see also Elizabeth A. Castelli, '"I Will Make Mary Male": Pieties of the Body and Gender Transformation of Christian Women in Late Antiquity', in Julia Epstein and Kristina Straub (eds), *Body Guards: The Cultural Politics of Gender Ambiguity* (New York: Routledge, 1991), pp. 29–49.

77 See Elizabeth A. Castelli's analysis of power in Paul's writings in light of the principle of imitation, *Imitating Paul: A Discourse of Power* (Louisville, KY: Westminster/John Knox, 1991).

78 See Judith Plaskow's pithy essay, 'What's Wrong with Hierarchy?' in *eadem*, *The Coming of Lilith: Essays on Feminism, Judaism, and Sexual Ethics, 1972–2003* (Boston: Beacon, 2005), pp. 138–42.

79 Boyarin, 'Gender', pp. 117–28; Judith Butler, *Bodies That Matter: The Discursive Limits of 'Sex'* (New York: Routledge, 1993), esp. pp. 1–31, 187–222.

Torture and Travail: Producing the Christian Martyr

Virginia Burrus

There was a woman named Biblis among those who had denied Christ, and the Devil thought that he had already devoured her; hoping further to convict her as a slanderer, he brought her to the rack and tried to force her to say impious things about us, thinking she was unmanly and easily broken. But once on the rack she came to her senses and awoke as it were from a deep sleep. . . . And from then on she insisted she was a Christian, and so was counted among the number of the martyrs. (*MCL* 1.25–26)[1]

How are we to read this woman, Biblis? She both is and is not an open book. The diabolical prosecutor calls her to the witness stand, imagining that her unmanly spirit will be easily broken. Torture does not, however, produce the anticipated perjury. Refusing to testify against the Christians, Biblis boldly exposes the Accuser's lies by confessing her own Christian identity, thus proving herself whole and manly after all – indeed, one might almost say wholly a man. The task of this essay is to explore the implications of such an odd and striking scene, in which torture transforms falsehood into truth and renders a woman more masculine than the men who torture her. Labouring under the fruitful conditions of political persecution, ancient Christian writers like the one who recorded Biblis's story give birth to a new masculinity even as they make truth-telling martyrs of women. Is a new femininity thereby also born? Yes, though it – *she* – may emerge, as so often, as something of a by-product of the conception of man. En route to its ultimate textual destinations – the *Letter of the Churches of Lyons and Vienne* (177 CE) and the *Passion of Perpetua and Felicitas* (203 CE) – this present reading of the complex gendering of the Christian martyr will begin by retracing the arguments of scholarly works that may facilitate a fresh framing of the place of the martyr in the history of subjectivity, one aspect of which – the ambiguously masculine appropriation of the torturable female body – has already insinuated itself here at the outset.[2]

Slaves, Women, Gladiators, and Other Tortured Subjects

Let us begin, with Biblis, on the rack, where we encounter the intimate relation of torture and confession not only to the female but also to the slave body. As Page duBois

---

1 For both the *Letter of the Churches of Lyons and Vienne* (*MCL*) and the *Passion of Perpetua and Felicitas* (*PPF*) I am following the texts and translations of Herbert Musurillo, *Acts of the Christian Martyrs* (Oxford: Clarendon Press, 1972).

2 This essay has taken a long time to reach publication. It was first drafted as a conference paper in 1994, redrafted for another conference in 1996, and revised in more or less its present form in 1998. In the meantime, much has been written on the topics of martyrdom, slavery and gender in ancient Christianity – so much that I have not attempted to bring the annotations up to date (exceptions include but are not altogether limited to cases where I initially referenced an unpublished or early version of a work that has since appeared in print or expanded form). It has seemed best to let the essay remain for the most part embedded in its 'original' 1998 intertextuality.

has demonstrated, the juridical practices of the classical Greeks explicitly marked the body of the slave as a privileged site for the production of truth through torture:

> The slave on the rack waits like the metal, pure or alloyed, to be tested. The test, the touchstone [βάσανος], is the process of torture.... The βάσανος assumes first that the slave always lies, then that torture makes him or her always tell the truth, then that the truth produced through torture will always expose the truth or falsehood of the free man's evidence.[3]

According to this juridical logic, the free man meets torture with a noble silence and indeed is not finally a torturable subject, whereas the tortured slave has no choice but to 'break' into a truth that he or she contains but does not possess. Defined by torture, the slave *cannot* witness freely yet *must* give witness when coerced. As duBois points out, the slave body, typically scarred, branded, or tattooed, resonated with ancient Greek images of the 'text' or writing tablet as a site of truth's inscription.[4] It resonated too with ancient Greek images of the female: the tortured body containing a hidden or buried truth was indelibly marked with 'sexual difference', notes duBois.[5] Excavating various sites of meaning in ancient Greek culture – 'epic, oracles, sacred buildings, the medicalized body' – she finds that all 'lay out a pattern of obscure, hidden truth that must be interpreted', contributing to the construction of 'images of interiority' that are associated 'with female space, with the containment and potentiality of the female body'. Indeed, on duBois's reading of the ancient Greeks, 'the female is analogous to the slave'.[6] Like (and sometimes *as*) a pregnant woman, the slave was understood to be the container of a concealed truth that the master must extract through violence – the violence of torture, truth's conception and also its birthpangs. Practices and representations of torture in the Roman Imperial era drew from but also disrupted the cultural traditions of classical Greece, as public spectacles of violence partly displaced the dramas of civic assemblies and lawcourts as primal enactments of political power. In the Empire, the tortured body was everywhere on display, above all in the performances of the arena, which ranged from gladiatorial combat to fights between humans and wild animals to mock military battles to other forms of dramatized execution. There, rites of sacrifice to the gods, displays of military triumph over non-Romans, assertions of social order through the punishment of criminals, and manifestations of aristocratic munificence all converged in symbolically saturated performances that embraced (in principle at least) the breadth of a highly differentiated and intensely hierarchical society. To be publicly marked by the rites of torture was to be exposed in a most extreme way to the shame of one's own subjugation. However, it was also, paradoxically, to be endowed with a highly constrained but nonetheless potent agency, to be made an actor, a performer – to acquire a public 'face', even (possibly) to attain glory.

This culture of spectacle loosened but did not entirely break the link between torture and slavery, as the example of the gladiator reveals. By the first century of the Common Era, it was no longer the case that all gladiators were slaves; never-

---

3 Page duBois, *Torture and Truth* (New York: Routledge, 1991), pp. 35–36.
4 duBois, *Torture*, pp. 69–74. On tattooing, slavery, gender and the inscription of Christian identity, see now my 'Macrina's Tattoo', *JMEMS* 33 (2003), pp. 403–17.
5 DuBois, *Torture*, p. 77.
6 DuBois, *Torture*, p. 91.

theless, the stigma of slavery still clung to these conscripted swordsmen and indeed continued to be crucial to their social and cultural role, as Carlin Barton suggests. The gladiator's slave-like status was expressed most vividly in the *sacramentum* or oath in which the gladiator 'swore to endure being burned, bound, beaten and slain by the sword', thereby renouncing freedom while recreating the possibility for a circumscribed and paradoxical nobility, in an almost parodic enactment of the position in which every subject of empire found him- (or her-)self.[7] 'Men give [the gladiators] their souls, women their bodies too. ... On one and the same account, they glorify them and degrade and diminish them', Tertullian observes, commenting with the characteristic acerbity and insight of the social critic on the ambivalence aroused by the gladiator (*de spect.* 22).[8] The play of desire and repulsion, identification and alienation, evoked by this figure appears to have been fundamentally shaped by the experience of political autocracy (with its threat to make all subjects slavish), on the one hand,[9] and the dramatic upward social mobility of some slaves and former slaves (particularly those connected with the Imperial household), on the other.[10] A heightened preoccupation with the fluidity of the boundary between free and slave[11] injected the traditional discourse on slavery and torture with both fresh anxiety and increased imaginative flexibility.[12] The harsh reality of the coercive violence at the heart of Roman Imperial rule thus created ripples of attraction and repulsion

---

7 Carlin A. Barton, *The Sorrows of the Ancient Romans: The Gladiator and the Monster* (Princeton, NJ: Princeton University Press, 1993), p. 14. See also Thomas Wiedemann, *Emperors and Gladiators* (New York: Routledge, 1992), pp. 28–30, 102–24, on the legal and social status of gladiators.

8 Cited by Barton, *Sorrows*, p. 12.

9 See Barton, *Sorrows*, pp. 11–46.

10 See P.R.C. Weaver, *Familia Caesaris* (Cambridge, UK: Cambridge University Press, 1972), on Imperial slaves. Note, however, that K.R. Bradley, *Slaves and Masters in the Roman Empire* (New York: Oxford University Press, 1987), in dealing with the extensive Roman practice of manumission emphasizes not only its commonly noted role in creating possibilities of social mobility but also its usefulness as a mechanism for the social control of slaves. It is the congruence of experiences of relative social fluidity, on the one hand, and the varied and flexible practices of social control, on the other, that shape the context of Imperial Roman slavery.

11 The free/slave boundary was not the only social distinction subjected to scrutiny or redefinition in this period, but it did retain a particular cultural resonance. Peter Garnsey, in *Social Status and Legal Privilege in the Roman Empire* (Oxford: Oxford University Press, 1970), highlights the multiple and shifting social distinctions negotiated juridically, encompassing not only slave versus free, but also non-citizen versus citizen, and finally *honestior* versus *humilior*. Garnsey cites the *Letter of the Churches of Lyons and Vienne* as evidence of the continuing juridical significance of the citizen/non-citizen distinction in the Antonine period (pp. 269–70); his discussion of torture suggests a growing tendency to subject the freeborn to torture, although 'the torture of *honestiores* was not permitted in the Antonine and Severan periods' (p. 141). However, as Bradley points out, although slaves were not uniquely subject to torture in the Roman Empire, the juridical use of torture did have a unique function in relation to slaves: given that the slave could not be threatened with any reduction of legal status, 'extreme physical punishment of the slave was thus the only avenue open to the law, which exhibited no moral qualms about the infliction of brutality on slaves' (*Slaves*, p. 134). Bradley also insists that neither juridical ambiguity nor the social mobility of many slaves obscured for the Romans the distinctiveness and significance of slave status: 'the broad categorization could not be altered and was something more than merely juridical' (*Slaves*, p. 18).

12 As exemplified by the Pauline elaboration of the metaphor of slavery; see the fine analysis of Dale B. Martin, *Slavery as Salvation* (New Haven, CT: Yale University Press, 1990).

across a broad spectrum of cultural texts: reassuring in its traditional promise to reinforce social boundaries, political autocracy also threatened to disrupt those same boundaries, in a situation in which even the elite might find themselves capriciously subjected to physical torture and exuberantly 'mad' emperors might play at being gladiators.[13]

As the distinction between slave and free became less steady and clear, the gendering of the performed subject likewise took a new turn. Barton locates a fundamental destabilization of the ideal of the 'hard' (*durus*) or 'weighty' (*gravis*) man in the period of the Roman civil wars and early Empire, of which the rising popularity of gladiators was but one symptom. 'Now everyone was relieved of the necessity – or freedom – of *gravitas*. In the beseiged city one could sport. Now the "heavy" and "light" were equally weightless. The Roman male, liberated from rigid masculine sex roles, delights in the freedom of playing a slave and a woman.'[14] Focusing on the strategies of self-presentation deployed by rhetoricians of the so-called Second Sophistic (the cultural movement that perhaps most distinctly reflects the social and political conditions of the early Empire), Maud Gleason likewise finds evidence that masculine gender had been dislodged from stable foundations; in particular, she recounts the success of the 'natural' eunuch Favorinus in captivating audiences with riveting enactments of gender ambiguity that both unmasked and exploited the fragility and malleability of a maleness acknowledged to be in some sense fictive, constructed or performed.[15] Reading Christian texts against other texts witnessing to a widespread cultural preoccupation with the motif of the suffering body, Judith Perkins suggests that Christian discourse constituted only the most extreme instance of a broader shift in subjectivity: by the second century, the ancient 'self' was slipping from its moorings in a mind-over-matter subjectivity grounded in conventional patriarchal familial roles, precisely by becoming more fluid, able to encompass and turn to strategic advantage stances marked as 'feminine', such as embodiment, possibility and even penetrability.[16] Brent Shaw finds particular evidence for significant shifts

---

13 As Barton notes, 'Caligula, Titus, Hadrian, Lucius Verus, Commodus, Didius Julianus, Caracalla, and Geta were ... known to have "played" gladiator in and out of the arena' (*Sorrows*, p. 66). Also relevant to the theme of the class disruptions of play-acting emperors is the work of Shadi Bartsch, *Actors in the Audience: Theatricality and Doublespeak from Nero to Hadrian* (Cambridge, MA: Harvard University Press, 1994), which offers an insightful and multifaceted exploration of the theatrics of power in the early Roman Empire, raising the broader question of the distorting impact of autocratic rule on language and representation more generally.

14 Carlin Barton, 'All Things Beseem the Victor: Paradoxes of Masculinity in Early Imperial Rome', in Richard C. Trexler (ed.), *Gender Rhetorics: Postures of Dominance and Submission in History* (Binghamton, NY: Center for Medieval and Early Renaissance Studies, 1994), pp. 83–92 (citation at p. 92).

15 Maud Gleason, *Making Men: Sophists and Self-Presentation in Ancient Rome* (Princeton, NJ: Princeton University Press, 1995). While chapters 1 and 6 focus particularly on Favorinus, the 'constructedness' and malleability of manliness is the theme of this entire book on second-century rhetorical practice and theory.

16 Judith Perkins, *The Suffering Self: Pain and Narrative Representation in the Early Christian Era* (New York: Routledge, 1995). Perkins's work is actually more suggestive than explicit in its thematizing of gender, despite the considerable attention that she gives to the roles of 'heroines' in the Hellenistic novels, *Apocryphal Acts* and martyrdom texts; however, I think that the inferences I have drawn here are fair to the thesis she argues.

in understandings of gender, body and power in the innovative foregrounding of the
virtue of ὑπομονή or *patientia*, most commonly translated 'endurance', by a wide
range of Stoics, Jews and Christians in the early Roman Imperial era:

> The simultaneous rise to a position of predominance of the more conscious recognition of
> feminine or 'weak' virtues and the problematization of women in terms analogous to those
> usually set for men is found in a wide range of ideological writings between the Roman Musonius
> and the Greek Plutarch. … Certain elements of it were not absolutely new. … But the isolation
> and elevation of passive power and resistance to a position of centrality in written texts, and the
> forging of one of the central pillars of moral guidance for men, required wholly new emphases
> and degrees of consciousness. The act of passivity became a deliberative action for men, a choice
> they could make; for women it remained, as it had always been, a constant role.[17]

In a similar vein, Daniel Boyarin highlights the distinctive strategies by which a
colonized Jewish subculture represented its rabbis as 'feminized' in resistance to the
traditional 'phallic' masculinity of the dominant Roman culture.[18] Such slippages
in the gendering of strategically 'vulnerable' masculine subjects did not constitute,
however, a complete severance with, or even simple inversion of, classical configura-
tions of masculinity. If the 'suffering' and 'feminized' self was necessarily produced
as a stance of resistance, it thereby competed with traditional representations of the
'impassible' male by partially appropriating excluded or marginal positionalities
produced within the same discursive field, such as those of the conventionally
degraded figures of the erotically passive male or the aggressively desiring female. I
would argue (*pace* Shaw) that the translation of endurance or submission into a manly
virtue also denaturalized this virtue in the case of women, thereby making females as
well as males agents of the choice to submit, without however by any means simply
erasing sexual difference or eradicating gender hierarchies. In the mirroring oscil-
lations of complexly gendered subjectivities, conventional negotiations of relative
status and honour among men, as well as women, remained in play yet were thereby
also opened to ongoing, fertile operations of cultural deconstruction.[19]

A heightened scholarly awareness of the power of performance for the production

---

17 Brent Shaw, 'Body/Power/Identity: Passions of the Martyrs', *JECS* 4 (1996), pp. 269–312
(citation at p. 295). See now also Elizabeth A. Castelli, *Martyrdom and Memory: Early Christian
Culture Making* (New York: Columbia University Press, 2004), pp. 60–67, whose interpretation of
the gendering of martyrdom partly follows Shaw's lead. She concludes, somewhat cautiously, that
'the available evidence cautions us against making any sweeping assumptions about the transgressive
character of Christianity with respect to gender ideology. That women, too, could offer themselves in
the most extreme and unalterable form of self-sacrifice – that they, too, could be tortured and killed
– is a faint and, indeed, Pyrrhic victory in the struggle for gender equality' (p. 67).

18 Daniel Boyarin, *Carnal Israel: Reading Sex in Talmudic Culture* (Berkeley: University of
California Press, 1993), pp. 16–18 ('Rabbinic Culture as Colonized Culture') and pp. 197–225
('[Re]producing Men: Constructing the Rabbinic Male Body'). See also his *Unheroic Conduct: The
Rise of Heterosexuality and the Invention of the Jewish Man* (Berkeley: University of California
Press, 1997) and *Dying for God: Martyrdom and the Making of Christianity and Judaism* (Stanford,
CA: Stanford University Press, 1999).

19 In emphasizing the deconstruction of conventional gender categories (evidenced particularly
but not exclusively in martyrological texts), I partly diverge from the more 'pessimistic' reading of
Stephen D. Moore and Janice Capel Anderson, 'Taking it Like a Man: Masculinity in 4 Maccabees',
JBL 117 (1998), pp. 249–73.

of the 'self' in this period makes it possible for cultural historians – normally inclined to take for granted the 'textual' status of the literary works on which historical reconstructions necessarily depend – to raise the question of the role and status of textuality in the society of Imperial Rome. Such a question seems all the more relevant, given that the Second Sophistic is associated not only with stagings of rhetorical virtuosity (in which we may detect echoes of the performances of the arena) but also with the energetic production of novelistic literature, to which Jewish novellae and Christian works like the Apocryphal Acts and the martyrdom texts stand in close, if somewhat ambiguous, relation.[20] John Winkler's 'narratological' analysis of Apuleius's *Golden Ass* suggests that the novel's author stages a 'literary performance' suspensefully re-enacted with each reading of the text, in which the reader becomes the audience and indeed finally displaces the author himself, while the relation between author and narrating protagonist or 'actor' awaits the reader's resolution.[21] Kate Cooper's reading of Hellenistic novels and their Christian counterparts likewise understands these literary works as constituting persuasive performances, suggesting that the Greek romances create a powerful complicity among readerly audience, hero or heroine, and author.[22] If such narratives may be understood as 'performances' with staying power, restaged with every new reading, they additionally constitute 'performances' in which the very complexity of authorial mediation, by invoking the reader's or listener's complicity, also provides the opportunity for an exceptionally direct identification of audience with both actor and author. Thus, narrative texts (at least some of which may have most typically been encountered via oral readings) may constitute some of the most powerful sites in Roman culture for the dramaturgical production of a 'self'.[23] And insofar as a significant number of such texts place

20 G.W. Bowersock, long known for his work on the rhetoricians of the Second Sophistic, has recently turned his attention to novelistic literature (*Fiction as History: Nero to Julian* [Berkeley: University of California Press, 1994]), which he positions in close relation to martyrdom texts; his readings of martyrdom literature particularly emphasize the resonances of the martyr with the sophist and the extent to which Christian texts represent martyrdom as a spectacle offered and staged by God (*Martyrdom and Rome* [Cambridge, UK: Cambridge University Press, 1995], pp. 41–57). See also David Potter, 'Martyrdom as Spectacle', in Ruth Scodel (ed.), *Theater and Society in the Classical World* (Ann Arbor: University of Michigan Press, 1993), pp. 53–88, a fine study of the theatrics of trial and execution that constituted martyrdom as spectacle in the ancient city. Potter's concern is, however, with the 'acts' rather than the *Acta* and he does not directly address the question of the role of literature in 'producing' martyrdom.

21 John J. Winkler, *Auctor and Actor: A Narratological Reading of Apuleius* The Golden Ass (Berkeley: University of California Press, 1985); see, e.g., p. 15 (on text as performance), pp. 135–79 (on the relation of 'author' and 'actor').

22 Kate Cooper notes the 'peculiar power of romance to create complicity' among reader, hero/ine and author and also suggests that where ascetic behaviours may be understood as 'performances' so too do 'accounts of ascetic behavior themselves become performances, designed to elicit a new sense of allegiance from an audience' (*The Virgin and the Bride: Idealized Womanhood in Late Antiquity* [Cambridge, MA: Harvard University Press, 1996], pp. 31, 58).

23 Compare the similar suggestions made by Harry O. Maier in relation to apocalyptic narrative, with special reference to the biblical Book of Revelation ('Staging the Gaze: Early Christian Apocalypses and Narrative Self-Representation', *HTR* 90 [1997], pp. 131–54; and *Apocalypse Recalled: The Book of Revelation After Christendom* [Minneapolis, MN: Fortress Press, 2002], especially pp. 75–86. See now also Christopher A. Frilingos, *Spectacles of Empire: Monsters, Martyrs, and the Book of Revelation* (Philadelphia: University of Pennsylvania Press, 2004).

not heroes but persecuted heroines at the centre of their narratives, the seeming availability of female figures as objects of identification as well as desire for male authors and audiences would appear to open up a new perspective on the complex and fluid gendering of the masculine subject in this period.[24]

My reading of two Christian martyrdom accounts seeks, then, to position these works as performative texts taking part in a broad-based set of Roman cultural practices that in various ways contested the terms of more ancient discourses of torture, slavery and gender with which they remained nevertheless also continuous, not least to the extent that they implicitly positioned themselves as revisionary interpretations of those discourses.[25] In a period when even emperors might play with roles of submission, what new positionings of the subject became available through

---

24 Scholarly interpretations of the significance of such heroine figures have proliferated in recent years. Exemplary among those who explore the availability of the heroine for male identification are: Helen Elsom, whose psychoanalytic reading of the polytheistic romance heroine suggests that she functions as the site for the articulation of a displaced phallic subjectivity ('Callirhoe: Displaying the Phallic Woman', in Amy Richlin [ed.], *Pornography and Representation in Greece and Rome* [New York: Oxford University Press, 1992], pp. 212–30); Judith Perkins, who sees in the polytheistic romance a 'domestication' of the male hero via his appropriation of the female social role and virtue of chastity, in the period of the Hellenistic city's relative depoliticization (*Suffering Self*, p. 67); Amy-Jill Levine, whose analysis suggests that the heroines of the Jewish novel may function for Jewish males of the diaspora as the symbol of a displaced and resistant colonized communal identity ('Diaspora as Metaphor: Bodies and Boundaries in the Book of Tobit', in J. Andrew Overman and Robert S. MacLennan [eds], *Diaspora Jews and Judaism* [Atlanta: Scholars Press, 1992], pp. 105–17); and Kate Cooper, who positions the heroines of the Christian *Apocryphal Acts of the Apostles* as figures of attentive listening and discernment, with whom the male reader or listener is encouraged to identify, in the process of transferring his allegiance from the married householder to the ascetic apostle (*Virgin and Bride*, chapter 3). On virginal heroines in the ancient romance (pagan, Jewish, Christian), see now also my 'Mimicking Virgins: Colonial Ambivalence and the Ancient Romance', *Arethusa* 38 (2005), pp. 49–88.

25 One of the strengths of Perkins's *Suffering Self* is to make clear the extent to which Christian texts were participating in broader cultural currents. Interestingly, Bowersock, *Martyrdom and Rome*, likewise stresses both the 'newness' of the second-century Christian narratives of martyrdom and their strong continuity with contemporaneous Greco-Roman texts and genres, although Bowersock's intention seems to be (as Perkins's is not) to attribute an 'originating' force to the Christian texts, a point argued still more sharply in his *Fiction as History*. Carlin Barton offers one of the clearest articulations of the continuity between Christian and Roman representations of sacrifice and honour exemplified in the figures of martyr and gladiator, suggesting that such continuities have been obscured by long-standing habits of contrasting Caesar and Christ: 'we fail to see the degree to which the proud Roman *animus* was already turned against itself, nor how deeply in love with victory and glory was the humble Christian' ('Savage Miracles: The Redemption of Lost Honor in Roman Society and the Sacrament of the Gladiator and the Martyr', *Representations* 45 [1994], pp. 41–71 [citation at p. 60]).

Note that duBois's genealogy of torture and truth exploits the continuities between classical Athenian and modern Western philosophy (above all Heidegger). By here briefly continuing the account of the history of the ancient discourse of torture and truth to include the impact of 'Romanization' and 'Christianization', I am implicitly glossing duBois's *Torture and Truth* by locating my own work in a gap in her text. The point is neither to 'criticize' duBois's analysis nor to 'apply' it uncritically to the Christian martyrdom texts, but rather to place the classical Greek discourse so evocatively illumined by duBois in dialogue with the discursive practices of Christians and others in the early Roman period in such a way as to highlight both continuities and disruptions.

ambivalent strategies of identification with women and slaves, with the gladiators who made a spectacle of slavish nobility, or with those Christian doubles of the gladiators, the martyrs? More specifically, how was the torturable and therefore revelatory body of the slave-woman-martyr rewritten, reclaimed from the body's perspective,[26] as it were, and what disruptions of both social hierarchies and mind-body dualisms were thereby accomplished? What disturbing alignments of torture and truth were at the same time further solidified, as heroic Christian witnesses were represented as ambiguously complicit in their own bodily mutilation? Finally, to introduce a further note of political ambivalence (though this is only an ominous foreshadowing, retrospectively visible on the horizon of our Christian texts' future): does fresh danger not arise from within the introduced confusion of victor with victim, of torturer with slave, of male with female, insofar as such a confusion ultimately enabled the appropriation of the truth-telling claim of victimized female and slave bodies by the triumphalist male authors of an imperial orthodoxy that paradoxically invoked the privileges of both political power and persecuted witness?[27]

The Letter of the Churches of Lyons and Vienne

Two aspects of this late second-century martyrdom text are often noted: first, the unusually elaborate descriptions of physical mutilation that recreate torture's spectacle, re-establishing but also relocating the onlooker's gaze; second, the preoccupation with social status and gender that runs throughout the account. DuBois's illumination of the ancient association of slave torture, sexual difference, and truth prepares us to see these two particularities as neither incidental nor unrelated to the text's central concern with the true witness of Christianity, formulated in the context of political persecution and profiting from other currents of cultural revision and subversion in the Roman world, that (as we have seen) made possible a radical shift toward identification with the tortured slave. Although preserved by Eusbeius in a somewhat fragmentary and perhaps slightly edited form,[28] the surviving *Letter of the Churches of Lyons and Vienne* nevertheless offers a strikingly coherent and sophisticated reinterpretation of the classically delineated relation between torture and

---

26 One might go so far as to suggest that Christian martyrdom texts may be interpreted from the perspective of an implied 'slave' subject, thus constituting a kind of 'slave literature', the absence of which is frequently bemoaned by historians of Roman slavery (e.g., Bradley, *Slaves*, p. 18; note, however, that Bradley does make use of the *Letter of the Churches of Lyons and Vienne* to reflect on the effects of the threat of torture on slaves [pp. 132, 136]). However, more to the point is the extent to which the subject positioning of the slave was made available to all readers of these texts; compare Dale Martin's analysis of the Pauline texts (*Slavery as Salvation*).

27 On Christian constructions of masculinity post-Constantine, see now my *'Begotten, Not Made': Conceiving Manhood in Late Antiquity* (Stanford, CA: Stanford University Press, 2000).

28 A number of the papers published in *Les martyrs de Lyons (177)* (Colloque à Lyon 20–23 Septembre 1977; Paris: Centre National de la Recherche Scientifique, 1978) raise the question of the status of the text transmitted by Eusebius, although none finally seriously disputes its authenticity. See, e.g., T.D. Barnes, 'Eusebius and the date of Martyrdoms', pp. 137–41; G. Bowersock, 'Les êglises de Lyon et de Vienne: relations avec l'Asie', pp. 249–55; R.M. Grant, 'Eusebius and the Martyrs of Gaul', pp. 129–35; note that Bowersock has now retracted his earlier suspicions of the authenticity of the prescript (*Martyrdom and Rome*, pp. 85–98).

truth, slavery and speech, femaleness and redemption, within which a new Christian subjectivity defined itself.

The first individual represented in the letter is not among the anonymous Christians initially described as having been 'dragged into the forum and interrogated', 'locked up in prison to await the arrival of the governor', and then subsequently 'brought before the prefect' and shown 'all the cruelty he reserves for us'. Instead, Vettius Epagathus, 'a distinguished person', intrudes on the narrative in the role of the free citizen: 'one of our number came forward full of love of God and of his neighbor'. A just man, Vettius Epagathus 'could not endure the unreasonable judgment that was passed against us and he became highly indignant'; standing near the tribunal, 'he requested a hearing in order to speak in defense of the Christians'; and when the prefect asked if he too were a Christian, 'he admitted he was in the clearest tones' (*McL* 1.9–10). The value of the traditional philosophic representation of free male speech presented in this opening tableau is not directly questioned. However, in subsequent pages, the voluntary speech of this initial witness (who might be expected to tempt readerly identification) is overlaid with the coerced 'speech' of the body of the tortured slave woman, who (the text ultimately suggests) proves to be paradoxically the freest and truest speaker of all.

There are three major moments in the text's competing presentation of torture's truth, each constituting a scene of public humiliation and physical torture of Christians in the arena. The first scene establishes the relation among slavery, torture and truth in such a way as to relocate the slave's subjectivity within this ancient configuration. Crucial is the scene's framing with an account of an arrest of pagan slaves as part of a process of investigating their Christian masters. Fearing (and seemingly evading) torture, the domestic servants readily agree to implicate their owners in the crimes of cannibalism and incest (*MCL* 1.14). Later, however, the woman named Biblis is tortured and, as we have already seen, under the condition of torture she 'comes to her senses' and denies the charge of cannibalism, confessing herself 'from then on' a Christian (*MCL* 1.25–26). Although Biblis is not explicitly identified as a slave or as one of those domestic servants initially arrested, the text seems to invite, if not require, this interpretation, according to which Biblis's performance becomes a critique of the false witness of her fellow slaves.[29] The slaves who speak from fear but without the coercion of physical torture speak falsely, the letter suggests, whereas the one who is tortured sees clearly, not only denying the false charges but also giving witness to the divine truth of the Christians. The classical Greek reading of the coerced speech of the slave is thereby invoked, but with a crucial interpretive shift: the truth revealed in Biblis's confession is a truth not about her owner but about herself and her faith, and the power of judgement claimed by the torturer is wrested from him, as the narrative places the persecutor himself on trial.[30] It is Biblis's audacious claiming of her speech for her own vindication and her persecutor's condemnation that is celebrated in the summary comment: 'so she was counted among the number of the witnesses (μάρτυρῶν)'. (*MCL* 1.26)

Within this frame occurs the first scene of public torture of four Christians

29 Garth Thomas, 'La Condition social de l'êglise de Lyon en 177', in *Les martyrs de Lyon (177)* p. 95 n. 5, assumes it likely that Biblis was the Christian slave of pagan masters.
30 I am grateful for Kate Cooper's help in reframing this thought.

scripted into the slave's role: Sanctus, Maturus, Attalus and Blandina. Highlighted are the performances of Blandina and Sanctus, and again the text both exploits the connections among slavery, torture and truth and at the same time contests the social hierarchy that traditionally awards the slave's truth to the slave owner. In a well-known passage, Blandina is initially presented as an explicit symbol of social reversal, 'through whom Christ proved that the things that men think cheap, ugly, and contemptuous are deemed worthy of glory before God, by reason of her love for him which was not merely vaunted in appearance but demonstrated in achievement' (*MCL* 1.17). This reversal is made concrete in the context of torture, as we are informed that Blandina's mistress, also among the accused Christians, feared that she would not be able to confess her faith due to the weakness of her body; 'yet Blandina was filled with such power that even those who were taking turns to torture her in every way from dawn to dusk were weary and exhausted' (*MCL* 1.18). If the examples of Blandina and her mistress seem to privilege slavery over free status in the context of torture,[31] Sanctus's subsequent performance teases, raising the question of whether reversal does not constitute a dissolution of the categories: 'he would not even tell them his own name, his race, or the city he was from, whether he was a slave or a freedman; to all of their questions he answered in Latin, "I am a Christian"' (*MCL* 1.20). Here extorted speech is simultaneously the true speech of the coerced slave and a kind of 'no-speech', the silence that traditionally distinguishes nobility from slavery in the context of torture. The response of the persecutors to this asserted ambiguity is more torture, an excruciating reinscription – indeed branding – of slave status: 'they finally tried pressing red-hot bronze plates against the tenderest parts of his body' (*MCL* 1.21). Sanctus's broken body – 'being all one bruise and one wound, stretched and distorted out of any recognizably human shape' – proves nonetheless eloquent, no hollow container of spoken truth but rather itself a revelation of 'Christ suffering in him' (*MCL* 1.23). And indeed, that carnal truth continues to amaze its spectators: 'his body unbent and became straight under the subsequent tortures' (*MCL* 1.24). Sanctus's witness, straight and whole, is not at the torturer's disposal but brings salvation to the body of the slave itself, thereby questioning the truth of his slave's status.

A second scene explicitly invokes the comparison of the martyr to the professional fighter of wild beasts while at the same time turning the tables and suggesting that it is not the Christians but their persecutors who are made a 'spectacle' when the martyrs are matched with animals in the arena: 'Maturus, then Sanctus, Blandina, and Attalus were led into the amphitheatre to be exposed to the beasts and to give a public spectacle of the pagans' inhumanity, for a day of gladiatorial games (θηριομά-χιων) was expressly arranged for our sake' (*MCL* 1.37).[32] Again, the performances of Sanctus and Blandina are highlighted. Sanctus is once more subjected to multiple tortures, including but not limited to maulings by beasts and culminating finally in

---

31 This interpretation is perhaps strengthened if one reads Blandina's mistress's concern as being for her own 'bodily weakness', in which case the text seems to set up an explicit contrast between the free and slave women's capacities to give witness; the more likely reading that the text reflects concern for Blandina's weakness, however, does not shift the effect of a narrative that focuses attention on the slave woman's revelatory suffering.

32 On the close relation among exhibitions of fighting beasts, criminal executions and gladiatorial shows, see Wiedemann, *Emperors and Gladiators*, pp. 55–101.

a second fiery branding of flesh via the 'iron seat'. Again, the slave witness refuses to 'break' into the truth sought by his torturers but instead continues to repeat his monotonous confession of faith, and the text reiterates the blurring of 'no-speech', the noble refusal to be coerced into uttering the torturer's truth, with the true confession of the coerced slave witness: 'from Sanctus all they would hear was what he had repeated from the beginning, his confession of faith' (*MCL* 1.38–39). The figure of Blandina is also reintroduced, again in an interpretive context that gives Christological significance to social reversal: 'Blandina was hung on a post and exposed as bait for the wild animals that were let loose on her. She seemed to hang there in the form of a cross, and by her fervent prayer she aroused intense enthusiasm in those who were undergoing their ordeal, for in their torment with the physical eyes they saw in the person of their sister him who was crucified for them...' (*MCL* 1.41). Blandina's gender once more becomes fraught with significance, as she is scripted not only as the crucified Christ but also as a second Eve: 'for her victory in further contests she would make irreversible the condemnation of the crooked serpent, ... for she had overcome the Adversary in many contests' (*MCL* 1.42). Finally, in this second scene slave status and torturability are at once destabilized and reinscribed as Attalus is paraded through the arena like a slave, only to be removed when it is discovered he is a Roman citizen (*MCL* 1.43–44).

The third scene of public torture circles back to the opening portrait of Vettius Epagathus as a potential (but crucially contested) object of readerly identification, as one Alexander is introduced as a second figure of free male speech: 'He had been standing in front of the tribunal and by his attitude he had been urging the Christians to make their confession.' Alexander's maleness is, however, almost immediately disrupted, as he is depicted making his own confession 'as one who was giving birth'; his free status is likewise compromised when the letter records that the governor (himself demonstrating a distinct loss of masculine self-control) 'flew into a rage and condemned him to the beasts' (*MCL* 1.49–50). Ambiguity about social status persists as Alexander, though subject in a torturous spectacle, remains silent, the response of the noble man. In parallel, Attalus, reintroduced into the arena despite his earlier identification as a citizen, seems to claim his freedom not through the noble silence exhibited by Alexander but through speech: like Sanctus, he speaks the language of his persecutors (Latin), boldly turning their accusation of cannibalism back on them, as he sniffs his own roasting flesh (*MCL* 1.50–52). Finally, Blandina re-enters, proving herself the ultimate virtuoso of torture. Her witness dissolves into a purely non-verbal physical utterance, which may be read not only as the noble refusal to speak the torturer's truth, but also as the tortured slave's insistence on speaking the Christian truth with the body itself. 'Duplicating in her own body all her children's sufferings', Blandina finally dies, a distinctly maternal figure of Christological recapitulation. As the text notes, 'The pagans themselves admitted that no woman had ever suffered so much in their experience' (*MCL* 1.55–57).

It is Blandina, then, not Vettius Epagathus, who claims the centre stage of this text, suffering most and dying last, in a final displacement mediated by intervention of the free man Alexander, who explicitly appropriates the personae of both the birthing woman and the publicly tortured slave. In Blandina, truth proves best expressed not through the speech of the free man but through the silent confession of the coerced female slave body; there we may read slavery as nobility, torture as the pangs of labour through which truth is born. Yet at the same time the categories of freedom and slavery, maleness and femaleness, are by no means completely dissolved in the subtle play of this text. Blandina's power still resides in her 'otherness', and the truth which she bears remains at least partly veiled, the mute speech of a body that has become a strangely enigmatic text, awaiting a cycle of reappropriations by subsequent readers invited to identify with the Christ figure made accessible through the textualized body of the female slave.

The Passion of Perpetua and Felicitas

Shifting attention to the slightly later martyrdom account known as the *Passion of Perpetua and Felicitas*, we find gender more explicitly thematized and also more actively contested in the articulation of a 'new' Christian subjectivity, while the discourse of slavery plays a more muted but still (as we shall see) significant role in the text's rearticulation of the relationship between torture and truth. The *Passion* narrates four dreams of the martyr Perpetua. These dreams are embedded in a diary text, and the dialogic play between dream and diary emphasizes the maternal features of figures in both realms. The imprisoned Perpetua initially represents herself as 'tormented' (*macerabar*) on account of concern for her infant (*PPF* 3.6); when subsequently allowed to keep her son with her in prison, she is 'relieved ... of [her] worry and anxiety over the child' (*PPF* 3.9). In a dream vision received shortly thereafter, Perpetua – like Blandina – is scripted as a 'New Eve' who treads on the head of a monstrous dragon (*PPF* 4.7); this vision culminates in her arrival in a heavenly garden where a tall, grey-haired shepherd milking sheep feeds her a morsel of cheese (*PPF* 4.8–9), both echoing Perpetua's nurturant role and marking her as 'daughter' to a heavenly father figure who has appropriated her maternal attributes. When her 'worldly' father subsequently obtains custody of her son, divine intervention brings about her son's weaning and her own relief from the 'torment' of anxiety for her infant and the pain of engorged breasts (*PPF* 6.8). Once more, there are echoes of breastfeeding themes in two subsequent dreams that represent Perpetua's deceased brother Dinocrates first as ill and thirsting but unable to reach a nearby pool of water, full to the brim (*PPF* 7.3–8), and subsequently as healthy and miraculously quenched of his thirst (*PPF* 8.1–4).

The fourth and best-known dream vision narrates Perpetua's combat with an Egyptian 'of vicious appearance'. As the dream begins, Perpetua is taken by the hand and led to the amphitheatre by Pomponius, the deacon who had cared for her in prison; this Christ-like figure leaves Perpetua in the centre of the arena, assuring her, 'I am here, struggling with you' (*PPF* 10.1–4). Facing the Egyptian, and assisted by some 'handsome young men', Perpetua is stripped, at which point she becomes 'masculine' (*PPF* 10.6–7). The reader is thus presented with an image that confounds the imagination – Perpetua is at once a naked woman and a male athlete stripped for combat. In the meantime, a tall man enters the arena to announce the terms of the fight; he is clad (like Pomponius) in a beltless tunic and wonderfully wrought sandals and carries both a trainer's wand and a leafy branch. As Perpetua engages the Egyptian, she is once again figured as a New Eve, treading on the head of an adversarial masculine figure; her victory is acknowledged by the benignly paternal trainer who returns to Perpetua the power of her female eroticism and fertility in the form of 'a green branch on which were golden apples', kissing her and proclaiming, 'Peace be with you, daughter' (*PPF* 10.8–13). Rather than articulating either a repudiation or a simple male appropriation of femaleness, this dream, as suggestively interpreted by Patricia Cox Miller, seems to comprise the culmination of a sequential revising of a masculinity initially representative of a 'discourse of mastery and domination' marked as both sinister and pathological, and progressively refigured in the direction of 'an image of maleness whose highly valued stance is a recognition of female identity' and which is itself 'intensely feminized or radically eroticized in the direction of female desire', as Cox Miller puts it.[33] If Perpetua has become nakedly male for her victory in the arena, she is still also a 'daughter', and the carefully draped supportive male figures similarly take on aspects of femininity while remaining men.

Rich as the diary is, the complexity of gendered figurations in the *Passion* is far from exhausted by the play of dream texts with the framing autobiographical narrative. Indeed, a central site of intratextual dialogue emerges as the already multi-vocal diary text is itself embedded in a larger framework in which Perpetua is identified explicitly in terms of her privileged class status – a matron 'of good family and upbringing' – while a twin figure, the female slave Felicitas, is introduced and positioned in such a way as to reinscribe the very gendered figurations that are contested and blurred by the diary and dream texts (*PPF* 2.1).[34] Gender itself becomes both a more dominant and a less fluidly constituted trope, while femaleness and slavery are realigned, as in the *Letter of the Churches of Lyons and Vienne*, but now function partly to undermine the nuanced gender subversions of the diary and dream texts.[35]

The slave woman Felicitas is pregnant and through divine intervention is enabled to deliver her child prematurely so that she will be allowed to join her companions in martyrdom. Her unusual suffering in labour, drawing taunts from the guards, creates an opportunity to disrupt resonances between Felicitas's own birthing and the pains by which the Christians would give birth to themselves as martyrs in the arena. Seeming to promote not so much her identification with as her ultimate displacement by the suffering Christ, the young mother is said to answer her guards, 'What I am suffering now, I suffer by myself. But then another

---

33 Patricia Cox Miller, *Dreams in Late Antiquity: Studies in the Imagination of a Culture* (Princeton, NJ: Princeton University Press, 1994), p. 182.

34 I am assuming here that the designation *conserva* indicates Felicitas's slave status. Other readings are possible, given the metaphoric use of the language of co-servitude in Christian discourse and the added 'problem' that Felicitas appears free to hand over her daughter to be raised by a Christian 'sister' (*PPF* 15.7); Georg Schoellgen concludes: 'Felicitas und Revocatus wird man deshalb besser aus der Liste der Sklaven in der karthagischen Gemeinde streichen' [It is therefore better to strike Felicitas and Revocatus off the list of slaves in the Carthaginian community] (*Ecclesia sordida? Zur Frage der sozialen Schichtung frühchristlicher Gemeinden am Beispiel Karthagos zur Zeit Tertullians* [Münster Westfalen: Aschendorffsche Verlagsbuchhandlung, 1984], p. 249). The distinction may not, however, be absolutely crucial, if my argument is partly that the spectacle of torture scripts all martyrs as 'slaves', in which context the metaphoric use of the term *conserva* merely underlines the point. As David Potter remarks, 'A person sentenced to die in the arena lost human identity, lost control of his or her body, became a slave' ('Martyrdom as Spectacle', p. 65).

35 See also Brent Shaw, 'The Passion of Perpetua', *Past and Present* 139 (1993), pp. 30–45 (30–33), on the 'framing' of Perpetua.

will be inside me who will suffer for me, just as I shall have suffered for him' (*PPF* 15.5–7). A subtle shift in language seems to signify a downplaying of the martyr's agency: whereas the dreamed Pomponius had assured Perpetua that he would 'labour with' her, Felicitas's Christ will be 'in' her and 'suffer for' her, seemingly in (uneven) exchange for her own suffering in giving birth. Still more forcibly than in the *Letter of the Churches of Lyons and Vienne*, the readerly eye is directed to see through the figure of the tortured, 'birthing' slave woman to the image of the suffering Christ 'within'.

Unlike Perpetua, the slave woman bears a daughter, and indeed this final section of the *Passion* becomes almost parodic in its exaggerated strategies of feminization. The self-dreamed Perpetua is made male in order to meet an intensely masculinized adversary, but in the realm of the insistently 'literal', the doubled female figures of Perpetua and Felicitas face a 'mad heifer', an adversary that the narrator assures 'was an unusual animal', 'chosen that their sex might be matched with that of the beast' (*PPF* 20.1).[36] Stripped and enmeshed in nets, the bodies of the martyrs remain resolutely female, the one fragile and the other dripping with milk, their vulnerability arousing a horrified excitement in the onlooking crowd (*PPF* 20.2). In a teasing performance, the women are re-clothed, only to have Perpetua's body again exposed in her first tussle with the cow. Represented as more preoccupied with her modesty than with her suffering, Perpetua re-covers her thighs and re-pins her dishevelled hair (*PPF* 20.3–5). Undefeated and therefore by the logic of martyrdom not yet victorious in relation to a female adversary, Perpetua and Felicitas subsequently die by the sword of a man. When the executioner strikes Perpetua on the bone, she herself guides the weapon to her throat (*PPF* 21.7–10). Perkins reads this gesture as a sign that 'the "unruly woman" is in control until the end'.[37] Barton sees in it 'the gladiator's gesture of baring the throat'.[38] One might also note that the throat is the site, as Nicole Loraux has argued, where the demands of the classical genre of tragedy dictate a woman must meet her peculiarly 'female' death.[39] The door is left open for both flexible rearticulations of a feminized virility and virilized femininity and a chastising resubjugation of the Christian woman.

Concluding Comments

Among the surviving pre-Constantinian accounts of Christian martyrdom, the *Letter of the Churches of Lyons and Vienne* and the *Passion of Perpetua and Felicitas* offer a rare combination of narrative sophistication and seeming 'historical authenticity'

---

36 Emphasizing the element of shaming in the spectacle of martyrdom, Shaw suggests that the 'usual wild beast ... in this type of punishment' would have been a bull, signalling sexual dishonour; on this reading, the substitution of the heifer adds a further parodic twist, adding to the sexual shaming of the women the insinuation that they were not even 'real women' ('The Passion of Perpetua', pp. 7–8).

37 Perkins, *Suffering Self*, p. 112.

38 Barton, *Sorrows*, p. 67.

39 Nicole Loraux, *Tragic Ways of Killing a Woman* (Cambridge, MA: Harvard University Press, 1987).

that continues to lure readers, scholarly and otherwise.[40] The centrality of female figures in both accounts has scarcely gone unnoticed, whether read as a mark of the influence of the novelistic preoccupation with persecuted heroines, as a sign of the benign 'transcendence' of gender distinctions within certain marginalized communities or, more pointedly, as the assertion of a radical 'Christian' inversion of 'Roman' social hierarchies that invokes for the purposes of political subversion the carnivalesque image of a 'world upside down'.[41] I am here arguing for the historical and narratological plausibility of a somewhat more complicated (and perhaps less romanticizing) interpretation of the rescriptings of gender produced by these texts. At a particular moment in the cultural history of Mediterranean antiquity, the *Letter of the Churches of Lyons and Vienne* and the diary of Perpetua each invokes and revises the interpenetrating classical discourses of torture, gender and slavery, not least by exploiting the evocative image of the productive suffering of the maternal body, overlaid on the figure of the athlete or gladiator. The spectacularly displayed tortured body now claims the power to give birth to its own life-giving truth, in a radical disruption of a prior tradition that assigned truth to the torturer. It thereby also deconstructs the binaries of male and female, free and enslaved, by exposing the subject as actively submissive in the face of a coercive power that it does not so much *oppose* (via a logic of inversion) as *resist* (via a logic of subversion). Such a deconstruction necessarily reinvokes, even as it also resists, a culturally dominant inscription of gender: to put it simply, these texts' reconfigurations of gender do not 'work' unless the female (thus also the 'Christian') retains her status as 'other'.

Ancient accounts of female martyrs unquestionably open up spaces for the production of novel female subjectivities that may provide sites of ambivalent identification for female readers, now as then. For male authors and readers, they

---

40 The 'authenticity' or 'reliability' of the historical data provided by these texts is not significant for the argument of this essay; however, the texts' *claim* to represent 'real' events is crucial to their power and performative function. I find it somewhat curious that most scholars remain strongly committed to a relatively 'positive' interpretation of these texts. Even Bowersock, who argues for the close link between the genres of martyrdom and romance as 'fictional' literature, still positions the martyrdom accounts as 'precious repositories of authentic historical material' (*Martyrdom and Rome*, p. 38). Similarly, J.W. Halporn, 'Literary History and Generic Expectations in the *Passio* and *Acta Perpetuae*', *VC*, 45 (1991), pp. 223–41, constructs a subtle argument both for the futility of seeking a single authoritative *Urtext* among the various shifting accounts and translations of Perpetua's martyrdom and for these texts' similarities to novelistic literature, yet he still is able to state that 'their significance derives from the actual events to which they testify' (p. 234).

41 Perkins entertains all of these possibilities, particularly stressing the last (*Suffering Self*, pp. 104–23). See also Francine Cardman, 'Acts of the Women Martyrs', *ATR*, 70.2 (1988), pp. 144–50; Elizabeth A. Castelli, '"I Will Make Mary Male": Pieties of the Body and Gender Transformation of Christian Women in Late Antiquity', in J. Epstein and K. Straub (eds), *Body Guards: The Cultural Politics of Gender Ambiguity* (New York: Routledge, 1991), pp. 29–49, and *eadem*, 'Visions and Voyeurism: Holy Women and the Politics of Sight in Early Christianity', *Protocol of the Colloquy of the Center for Hermeneutical Studies* n.s. 2 (Berkeley, CA: Center for Hermeneutical Studies, 1995); W.H.C. Frend, 'Blandina and Perpetua: Two Early Christian Heroines', in *Les martyrs de Lyon (177)*, pp. 167–75; Mary R. Lefkowitz, 'The Motivations for St. Perpetua's Martyrdom', *JAAR*, 44 (1976), pp. 417–21; Mary Ann Rossi, 'The Passion of Perpetua, Everywoman of Late Antiquity', in R.C. Smith and J. Lounibos (eds), *Pagan and Christian Anxiety: A Response to E.R. Dodds* (Lanham, MD: University Press of America, 1984), pp. 53–86; and Shaw, 'The Passion of Perpetua'.

also, I suggest, offer an ambiguously 'feminized' male subjectivity that – in part via the mediation of secondary figures like Alexander or Pomponius – strategically appropriates the revelatory body of the suffering woman, who is thereby very nearly (but not quite completely) 'swallowed up' into a victoriously vulnerable manhood. Finally, the diary of Perpetua cannot be read outside of its framing in the *Passion of Perpetua and Felicitas*, which enacts a further battle of significations within the resistant discourse of martyrdom. This internal contestation leaves the question of the gendering of the Christian subject curiously unresolved, via a strategy of contradiction as well as ambiguity: the reader (whether male or female) seems ultimately invited to identify not only with the intensely feminized martyr but also with the (implicitly male) voyeur, in a doubling back and splitting of the penetrating gaze that produces the self as sufferer in this performative text. The disciplining framework of the *Passion of Perpetua and Felicitas* foreshadows the emergence in fourth-century Christian discourse of a figure of the female martyr that serves the purposes of articulating both a radically re-subjugated femininity and a partly 'feminized' male subjectivity that appropriates the female martyr's stance of victimized triumphalism.[42] But there remain strategic gaps in the controlling frame, productive failures in the impulse to reinscribe conventional gender categories, as evidenced not least in queerly sexed lives of the saints (both male and female) of later antiquity.[43]

---

42 See my 'Reading Agnes: The Rhetoric of Gender in Ambrose and Prudentius', *JECS*, 3 (1995), pp. 25–46.
43 See now my *The Sex Lives of Saints: An Erotics of Ancient Hagiography* (Philadelphia: University of Pennsylvania Press, 2004).

Virginity and its Meaning for Women's Sexuality in Early Christianity[*]

Elizabeth A. Castelli

The fervour with which large numbers of early Christian women pursued lives of asceticism and renunciation is a curious fact in the history of women in late antiquity. In recent years, several feminist scholars have attempted to explain the attraction of the ascetic life for early Christian women by demonstrating that renunciation of the world paradoxically offered women the possibility of moving outside the constraints of socially and sexually conventional roles, of exercising power, and of experiencing a sense of worth which was often unavailable to them within the traditional setting of marriage.[1] The purpose of this essay is to engage the question of the attraction of asceticism for women from a slightly different perspective, to try to determine the effect of worldly renunciation and celibacy on the lives and sexuality of early Christian women and on the culture that constructed women's limited options in the first place. The first section of the paper deals with the question of method and the problem of sources; the second section treats the idea of virginity as the Fathers of the Church and other male writers of the period portrayed it. The third section attempts to portray the diversity of women's practice of virginity and to set this experience in the context of the other options available to women at the moment in history; the fourth section seeks to draw conclusions about the meaning of virginity and renunciation for women's sexuality in late antiquity.

Problems of Method and Sources

To ask the question about women's history in any period is to embark on a treacherous and often disappointing search for buried treasure. When the period of history is remote and evidence has had centuries to be lost, misfiled, unindexed, rewritten and suppressed, the task grows yet more frustrating. And when, finally, one turns to the history of women in Christianity in a remote period, the situation takes on Heraclean contours. In attempting to understand a distant moment in the lives of Christian women, an historian faces not only the silence of misplaced information and absent texts, but the work of orthodoxy over the centuries. Orthodoxy's power

---

[*] An earlier version of this essay appeared in *JFSR*, 2.1 (1986), pp. 61–88; reprinted by permission.

1 Elizabeth A. Clark, 'Ascetic Renunciation and Feminine Advancement: A Paradox of Late Ancient Christianity', *ATR*, 63 (1981), pp. 240–57; Stevan L. Davies, *The Revolt of the Widows: The Social World of the Apocryphal Acts* (Carbondale, IL: Southern Illinois University Press, 1980); Ross S. Kraemer, 'The Conversion of Women to Ascetic Forms of Christianity', *Signs* 6 (1980/81), pp. 298–307; Aline Rousselle, *Porneia: De la maîtrise du corps à la privation sensorielle, IIe-IVe siècles de l'ère chrétienne* (Paris: Presses Universitaires de France, 1983); Rosemary Ruether, 'Mothers of the Church: Ascetic Women in the Late Patristic Age', in Rosemary Ruether and Eleanor McLaughlin (eds), *Women of Spirit: Female Leadership in the Jewish and Christian Traditions* (New York: Simon and Schuster, 1979), pp. 71–98; Anne Yarbrough, 'Christianization in the Fourth Century: The Examples of Roman Women', *CH*, 45 (1976), pp. 149–65.

derives from its own dogmatism and its claim to absolute truth; the vacillations of orthodox truth over time have produced the approved bibliography and the filters through which information has passed. It is true that certain heterodox texts have survived through historical accident; it is also true that details concerning women's historical experience may sometimes be deduced from the texts that do remain, as, for example, when the actions of a Church council or synod against a particular action by women provide evidence that women were acting outside of the prescribed conventions of the Church. But this sort of evidence is almost always fragmentary, and women's side of the story is never preserved.

Even evidence concerning the most orthodox women is often absent through neglect or oversight. Jerome's letters to Paula, Marcella, Eustochium and other learned and literate women were collected and preserved while not a single letter of any of these women remains.[2] The situation is the same with respect to John Chrysostom's correspondence with Olympias[3] as well as with other Church Fathers and the women to whom they wrote.[4] A poignant example of the accidental nature of historical knowledge of even the most exceptional and orthodox women of the early Church is the case of Macrina, the sister of Basil of Caesarea and Gregory of Nyssa. Thanks to Gregory's biography of Macrina,[5] the story of her life is part of the Church's history. According to Gregory's narrative, Macrina, at the age of twelve and through her own rhetorical finesse and theological understanding, evaded her parents' attempts to marry her off, and later single-handedly converted her worldly brother Basil to asceticism.[6] Of course, hagiographical fervour may account for some of Gregory's claims about his sister's life;[7] nevertheless, there is no reason to believe that the entire account of Macrina's influence over Basil's spiritual life is invention. Therefore, it is somewhat shocking to discover that, in all of Basil's writings, which comprise four volumes of Migne's *Patrologiae* and include 366 letters, Macrina

---

2 Jerome, *Epistolae/Lettres* (text established and French trans. Jerome Labourt; 8 vols.; Paris: Société d'Édition 'Belles Lettres', 1949–1963). To Eustochium, *Epp*. 22, 31; to Marcella, *Epp*. 23–29, 32, 34, 37–38, 40–44; to Paula, *Epp*. 30, 33, 39; to others, *Epp*. 45, 52, 54, 64, 65, 75, 78, 79, 97, 106, 107, 117, 120, 121, 123, 127, 128, 130. *Ep*. 46 in the collection of Jerome's letters bears the title, 'Paula and Eustochium to Marcella', though Labourt (2:100 n. 2) suggests that the letter may well be an exercise in feminine style on the part of Jerome.

3 John Chrysostom, *Epistolae ad Olympia/Lettres à Olympias*, 2nd edn, aug. with *Vita Olympiadis/ La Vie Anonyme d'Olympias* (text established and French trans. Anne-Marie Malingrey; SC no. 13; Paris: Cerf, 1968). Hereafter cited as *Ep*. and *Vita Olympiadis*. There is a certain irony, given the fact that none of Olympias's letters remains, that Malingrey says of John's letters, 'Il nous reste encore un grand nombre de lettres qui ont le merite d'être de veritables échanges de pensée et d'amitié', Malingrey, 'Introduction', p. 11. ('A large number of letters remain for us which have the value of being genuine exchanges of thought and friendship.')

4 Rouselle, *Porneia*, p. 231, n. 8 for a summary of the evidence on this point. One exception appears to be the letters of Melania the Elder to Evagrius Ponticus, some of which have been preserved, along with his sixty-two letters to her, in Armenian. This preservation seems to have occurred thanks to the special place Melania held in the Syrian tradition. Cf. Nicole Moine, 'Melaniana', *Rech. Aug.* 15 (1980), pp. 3–79 (64, n. 327).

5 Gregory of Nyssa, *Vita Macrinae/Vie de Sainte Macrine* (text established and French trans. Pierre Maraval; Sources Chrétiennes no. 178; Paris: Cerf, 1971). Hereafter cited as *Vita Macrinae*.

6 Gregory of Nyssa, *Vita Macrinae*, 5, 6ff.

7 Gregory of Nyssa, *Vita Macrinae*, cf. Maraval's Introduction, pp. 23–29, 92 on the text as a philosophical, *theios anêr*-type work.

is never mentioned once.[8] How many women lost their places in the written record of the Church because no one chose to write their biographies and because the men whose lives they influenced omitted any mention of them? How many exceptional women may have been only mentioned and been otherwise lost without a trace?[9] How many 'ordinary' virgins are absent from the record altogether?

The regrettable state of the historical record duly noted, there nevertheless remain sources that help in the construction of a partial portrait of women's experience of virginity and asceticism in the early centuries of Christianity, which suggests certain interpretations of that portrait. With a few notable exceptions,[10] the sources for the history of the idea and practice of virginity and asceticism among women are literary sources. One of the earliest sources is probably the _Apocryphal Acts of the Apostles_, a collection of narratives which provides evidence for the attraction of Christian asceticism for women in the second and third centuries.[11] Treatises and homilies on virginity and renunciation had their origins in the third century in Africa and seem to have become a favourite of writers in the fourth century and afterwards.[12] The lives of certain exceptional women remain, notably Macrina, Syncletica, Olympias

8 J.-P. Migne, _Patrologiae Cursus Completus, series graeco-latina_ (5 = PG), pp. 29–32; cf. Maraval's introduction, p. 43.

9 Cf. Cuthbert Butler, _The Lausiac History of Palladius_ (2 vols.; Texts and Studies: Contributions to Biblical and Patristic Literature no. 6.1–2; Cambridge, UK: Cambridge University, 1904), vol. 2, p. 219, n. 78: 'The other holy women mentioned [in _Historia Lausiaca_ 41, on _gynaikes andreiai_: Veneria, Theodora, Hosia, Idolia, Basianna, Photina and Sabiniana (deaconness and aunt of John Chrysostom)] are not otherwise known to history'. Butler is mistaken with regard to Sabiniana, who is mentioned in John Chrysostom, _Ep._6, 1d (Malingrey, 130, 1.1), though his point remains well-taken.

10 These exceptions are papyrus documents which lend credence to the fact that literary sources do not tell the whole story of women's experience of the ascetic life. The documents are _BGU_ 13897, _P. Oxy._ 1774 and 3203; cf. A. M. Emmett, 'Female Ascetics in the Greek Papyri', _Jahrbuch der österreichischen Byzantinistik_ 32 (1982), pp. 507–15.

11 Wilhelm Schneemelcher and Edgar Hennecke (eds), _New Testament Apocrypha_ (2 vols; trans. and ed. R. McL. Wilson; Philadelphia, PA: Westminster, 1966); Kraemer, 'The Conversion of Women'; Davies, _Revolt of the Widows, passim_. There are references to female virginity in the Apostolic Fathers: Clement of Rome, _Epistola 1 ad Corinthios_ 38, 2; Ignatius, _Epistola ad Smyrnaeos_ 13, 1; Ignatius, _Epistola ad Polycarpum_ 5, 2; Polycarp, _Epistola ad Philippenses_ 5, 3. See now Amy-Jill Levine (ed.), _A Feminist Companion to the New Testament Apocrypha_ (London: Continuum, 2006).

12 Tertullian, _De Virginibus Velandis_ (PL 2, 887–914), dated between 200 and 206; Cyprian, _De Habitu Virginum_ (PL 4, 439–64), dated to the middle of the third century, ca. 249. The most important treatises on virginity are the following: Ambrose, _De Virginibus_ (PL 16, 187–232); Athanasius, _De Virginitate Sive Ascesi_ (PG 28, 251–82); Augustine, _De Sancta Virginitate_ (PL 40, 395–428); Basil of Ancyra, _De Vera Virginitate_ (PL 30, 669–810); Pseudo-Clement, _Epistolae 1–2 ad Virgines_ (PG 1, 379–452); Eusebius of Emesa, _Homiliae VI et VII_, in E. M. Buytaert (ed.), _Eusèbe d'Emèse: Discours conservés en Latin_ (Spicilegium sacrum Lovaniense no. 26; Louvain: Université catholique et collèges théologiques O.P. et S.J. de Louvain, 1953); Gregory of Nyssa, _De Virginitate/ Traité de la Virginité_ (text established and French trans. Michel Aubineau; SC no. 119; Paris: Cerf, 1966) [hereafter cited as _De Virginitate_]; Jerome, _Adversus Jovinianum_ (PL 23, 211–388); Jerome, _Ep._ 22; John Chrysostom, _De Virginitate/La Virginit_ (text established by Herbert Musurillo; French trans. Bernard Grillet; SC no. 125; Paris: Cerf, 1966) [hereafter cited as _De Virginitate_]; Methodius, _Symposium Decem Virginem/Le Banquet_ (text established and French trans. Victor-Henry Debidour; SC no. 95; Paris: Cerf, 1963). For a summary of the development of the arguments of fourth-century treatises, cf. Thomas Camelot, 'Les traités _De Virginitate_ au IVe siècle', _Etudes Carmelitaines_ 13 (1952), pp. 273–92. Also, on general content of treatises, cf. François Bourassa, 'Excellence de la virginité: Arguments patristiques', _Sciences ecclésiastiques_ 5 (1953), pp. 29–41.

and Melania the Younger.[13] As noted above, there is a one-sided epistolary tradition involving virgins and ascetic women, women who received the carefully preserved letters of such important Church Fathers as Jerome, Paulinus of Nola, John Chrysostom and Basil.[14] The monastic movement in the east, a particular manifestation of the ascetic ideal, produced two anecdotal works that include information on women's experience of asceticism: Palladius's *Historia Lausiaca* and the anonymous *Historia Monachorum in Aegypto*.[15] Finally, the monastic desert also preserved a handful of sayings attributed to the holy women Theodora, Sara and Syncletica in the collection *Apophthegmata Patrum*.[16]

The question then is how to use these texts to understand and interpret the experience and meaning of asceticism and virginity for women, and for the culture as a whole. Of course, as Butler, Rousseau and Moine have ably shown, to act under the assumption that these texts portray history as today's scholars understand the concept would be naive.[17] Narratives and discourses full of miraculous healings, demons (real or imagined), hagiographical fervour, and a desire to recreate – through example and dogmatic definition both – an ideal of Christian perfection and the angelic life are not historically accurate in the modern sense, nor do they mean to be. Rather, they are orthodox attempts to frame and order experience and doctrine into a single, monolithic image of Christian existence. In a Christocentric, ecclesio-centric world order, each act and its motivation must be adapted to the dominant set of categories or be lost or called heretical. Thus, true virgins remained chaste for the love of Christ, in a desire to perfect themselves for an angelic future, for an ideal of humility and self-effacement. They did not do so to escape disagreeable home lives, to avoid painful sex, or to have access to a different set of possibilities than the limited ones offered them by a constricting social order. The texts offer a glimpse of women's experience of virginity, and a clear and well-developed picture of the frame that envelops the image, the frame comprised of the categories that constructed and attempted to appropriate and subsume the experience. The questions become these: Where did women's experience of virginity and asceticism coincide with the orthodox line and where did it rupture that line? Did women use the Christian categories to try to break the severely limiting conventions of the social order? Was

---

13 Gregory of Nyssa, *Vita Macrinae*; Pseudo-Athanasius, *Vita et Gesta Sanctae Beataeque Magistrae Syncleticae* (PG 28, 1487–1558), hereafter cited as *Vita Syncleticae: Vita Olympiadis*; *Vita Melaniae/Vie de Sainte Melanie* (text established and French trans. Denys Gorce; Sources Chrétiennes no. 90; Paris: Cerf, 1962), hereafter cited as *Vita Melaniae*.

14 For Jerome and Chrysostom, see notes 2 and 3 above. Basil of Caesarea, *Epistolae/Lettres* (3 vols.; text established and French trans. Yves Courtonne; Paris: Societé d'édition 'Belles Lettres', 1957–1966). Paulinus of Nola, *Epistolae/Lettres* (2 vols; trans. P. G. Walsh; Ancient Christian Writers nos. 35, 36; Westminster, MD: Newman, 1967).

15 Palladius, *Historia Lausiaca* (PG 34, 995–1262); critical ed., Butler, vol. 2; *Historia Monachorum in Aegypto* (text established and French trans. A.-J. Festugière; Subsidia Hagiographica no. 53; Brussels: Société de Bollandistes, 1971).

16 *Apophthegmata Patrum* (PG 65, 71–440); sayings of Theodora (PG 65, 201A–204B); sayings of Sara (PG 65, 419B–422A). English translation in Owen Chadwick (ed.), *Western Asceticism* (Philadelphia, PA: Westminster, 1958), pp. 33–189.

17 Butler, *Historia* I: 178–96; Philip Rousseau, *Ascetics, Authority and the Church in the Ages of Jerome and Cassian* (Oxford: Oxford University Press, 1978), pp. 11–18; Moine, 'Melaniana', *passim*.

such a rupture possible, given the shared notion of patriarchal dualism that created the material and ideological realities of both late antiquity in general and early Christianity in particular? And the final, specific question that motivates this inquiry entirely: What did the movement toward virginity and ascetic renunciation mean for women's sexuality?

The Roots of Asceticism and the Idea of Virginity

The roots of asceticism lie at the very heart of the Christian tradition, in Jesus' more radical exhortations on the requirements of discipleship and in Paul's advice to early Christian communities to follow his example of the celibate life so as not to detract from preparation for the coming kingdom of God.[18] How did these early roots bring forth such a flourishing of radical renunciation? How did the eschatologically motivated words of Paul and the historical exigencies of the early centuries of the Common Era combine to produce an ascetic ideology and practice virtually unheard of in antiquity and certainly never before practised by such large numbers of people representing such a spectrum of society?[19]

One convincing hypothesis suggests that the ascetic ideal flourished as a response to the end of the persecutions of Christians in the early fourth century. Brock, for example, argues this way:

> Movements can often best be understood in terms of reactions against some aspects of contemporary society, and, just as the idealism of modern aspirants to an 'alternative society' has largely been motivated by disgust at the materialistic affluence of the post-war society they live in, so that of their fourth-century counterparts was, to some extent at least, the product of a reaction against the degradation of the quality of Christian life after the last persecutions had ceased. As we shall see, the ascetic is in many ways the successor of the martyr. To the early church the martyr represented an ideal, and after the end of the persecutions, when this ideal was no longer attainable, it was replaced by that of the ascetic, whose whole life was in fact often regarded in terms of a martyrdom, and it is very significant that much of the terminology used in

18 Mk 8.34–9.1 (par.); Lk. 9.1–6 (par.); etc.; 1 Cor. 7.

19 Judaism offers two examples of communities self-consciously pursuing lives of ascetic renunciation and withdrawal, the Essenes and the Therapeutae and Therapeutrides. The ancient references to the Essenes may be found in Josephus, *Jewish Antiquities* XIII, 5, 9; XV, 10, 4–5; XVIII, 1, 2–6; *Jewish Wars* II, 8, 1–14; Pliny, *Historia Naturalis* 5, 17; Philo, *Quod omnis probus liber sit* 12–13. The sole witness for the community of the Therapeutae/Therapeutrides is Philo's *De Vita Contemplativa*. The Greek tradition is without a parallel notion of asceticism; cf. Anatole Moulard, *Saint Jean Chrysostom: Le defenseur du mariage et l'apôtre de la virginité* (Paris: Lecoffre, 1923), pp. 171ff., which cites certain exceptions: temporary asceticism among athletes, but without moral connotations, and some ritual virginity which was also always only temporary. The Roman tradition offers the example of the vestal virgins, whose virginity was tied to the well-being of the state. That the virtues and dangers of virginity as a permanent condition were being discussed in the first century of the Common Era is attested by Soranus, *Gynaeciorum Libri IV*, ed. Ioannes Ilberg, Corpus Medicorum Graecorum vol. 4 (Leipzig: Tuebner, 1927), paragraphs 30–32 (pp. 20–22). Finally, the philosophical tradition, particularly Stoicism, was exploring the question of the relationship between marriage and sexuality on the one hand and the pursuit of the good on the other; see below for the discussion of the Stoic influence on certain Christian notions related to virginity and asceticism.

connection with ascetics, such as 'contest', 'athlete', and so on, was previously applied to martyrs. In the case of the ascetic the human persecutor had simply been replaced by a spiritual, that is to say, demonic, counterpart. Moreover, if one sees the ascetics of the fourth century onwards as heirs to the martyrs, it helps one realise why they regarded their life as simply carrying on the norm of Christian life in pre-Constantinian times, when to be a Christian was usually a matter of real seriousness.[20]

Marcel Viller has traced the connection between martyrdom and asceticism from its origins in Christianity, showing how the ideology of asceticism made it possible for the faithful to follow Christ and achieve perfection even during persecutions without becoming martyrs. He also demonstrates how asceticism was elevated during the years following the persecutions to a position more honoured even than martyrdom itself, and how *new* notions such as that of the non-bloody martyrdom of renunciation arose after the fourth century to accommodate the new historical situation.[21]

Of course, one can probably not account completely for the rise of the ascetic ideal by invoking the historical move from cultural marginality to hegemony which the Christianizing of the empire represented. Nevertheless, it seems quite likely that the shift played an important role in the evolution and growth of asceticism in the fourth century. Certainly, the developing ideology of virginity and asceticism would sustain such an argument, since the special status of virgins, already asserted in the first centuries of Christianity,[22] becomes a commonplace in the fourth-century literature.[23]

---

20 S. P. Brock, 'Early Syrian Asceticism', *Numen* 20 (1973), pp. 1–19 (2). Compare a similar argument put forward by David Knowles, *Christian Monasticism* (New York: McGraw Hill, 1969), p. 12.

21 Marcel Viller, 'Le Martyre et l'ascèse', *Revue d'ascétique et de mystique* 6 (1925), pp. 105–42. One example he offers comes from Anthony Melissae, *Sententiae sive Loci Communes* II, 13 (PG 136, 1113D–1116A): 'The martyrs often attained perfection in a single moment of battle; the life of monks, a daily battle for Christ, is also martyrdom, it is not only a battle against flesh and blood, but against the principalities and powers and the masters of the world of darkness, against the spirits of evil. We sustain the struggle until the last breath...'. Cf. Pseudo-Athanasius, *Vita Syncleticae* 8 (PG 28, 1489D–1492A) where Syncletica is compared with Thecla, and the author asserts that Syncletica's sufferings were greater than her martyred counterpart.

22 For example, Cyprian, *De Habitu Virginum* 3: 'They [virgins] are the flower of the tree that is the Church, the beauty and adornment of spiritual grace, the image of God reflecting the holiness of the Lord, the most illustrious part of Christ's flock.' Hippolytus includes ascetics in the seven divine orders (*Fragmenta in Proverbia*, PL 10, 627) and Origen places virgins third in his hierarchy, following only the apostles and the martyrs (*Commentarius in Epistolam ad Romanos* 9, 1, PG 14, 1205). For a complete discussion of Origen's position on virginity, cf. Henri Crouzel, *Virginité et mariage selon Origène* (Museum Lessianum section théologique no. 58; Paris/Bruges: Desclée de Brouwer, 1963). Clement of Alexandria calls ascetics 'even more elect than the elect' (*Quis dives salvetur* 36).

23 Cf. Methodius, *Symposium*, Discourse 7, 3, 157–158, where virgins are called the legitimate brides of Christ, while all other women in the Church are concubines, young girls, or daughters; virgins are unique, elect, most honoured in Jesus' eyes. Another familiar motif in the literature of the fourth century is excessively high praise for the exceptional virgins: Macrina is called 'the common object of great boasting in our family' (Gregory of Nyssa, *Vita Macrinae* 22, 28); Eustochium is called the first among the nobles of Rome (Jerome, *Ep.* 22, 15); Melania the Elder was 'the true pride of Christians of our time' (Jerome, *Ep.* 39, 5); Melania the Younger was 'the first among the senatorial class of Romans' (*Vita Melaniae* 1), and Olympias's virtues are the object of especially abundant rhetoric (*Vita Olympiadis* 13ff.).

This unfolding ideology of virginity is highly complex, intertwining theological arguments, current philosophical ideas and a collection of contemporary rhetorical themes to produce a tightly woven image of virginity as the ideal of Christian life. The development of such an ideal was probably an inviting challenge for the writers of the early Church, since they were always treading dangerous (which is to say, potentially Gnostic) ground with the body–spirit dualism that undergirded the arguments for virginity. They avoided it by returning to the idea first expressed by Paul, that marriage was good but virginity was better; this notion became both the cornerstone for Patristic discourses on the preferability of virginity *and* the tool used against those who were thought to pursue their asceticism too rigorously, such as the Encratites attacked by John Chrysostom and the Eusthathians condemned at the Council of Gangra.[24] At the same time, the notion of sexuality was extremely narrowly defined, which is to say, heterosexual intercourse within marriage with the goal of producing children. Justin asserts, 'Formerly we took pleasure in debauchery, but now we embrace chastity alone ... If we do marry, it is absolutely only in order to raise our children, and if we renounce marriage, we keep perfect continence.' Clement of Alexandria discusses the goals of marriage, saying that the desire should be to act according to nature, which is to say, to produce children. Meanwhile, Jerome praises marriage because it produces virgins, as does Eusebius of Emesa.[25]

While the Church Fathers may have defended marriage, they were also quite zealous in conjuring images of its limitations in order to create a sharper contrast between it and the ideal of virginity. The theme of the pains of marriage is common in the Hellenistic rhetorical tradition, and it became a useful trope in the construction of the notion of virginity in the fourth-century literature. John Chrysostom found in the comparison a rich theme on which to expound in his *De Virginitate*; he devotes twenty-two chapters to the pains of marriage and how the virgin escapes them. Jealousy is an inevitable side-effect, but by no means the only disadvantage of marriage. A wealthy marriage is much more painful than a poor one: if the woman brings more property to the union, the husband must yield to the wife's authority; if the man is richer, he becomes the wife's master and she must do and suffer everything as though she were his slave. The married woman's life is full of chagrin and worry: she must concern herself with family members and their affairs, their bad luck, their loss of money, their illnesses, their accidents, their deaths. She must worry

24 1 Cor. 7.38. Cf. John Chrysostom, *De Virginitate* 1–11, 25–50; cf. also John Chrysostom, *Homilia in Matthaeum* 86, 4 (PG 58, 768) on wives leaving their husbands to practise asceticism (cited by Moulard, 132–33). Pseudo-Athanasius, *Vita Syncleticae* 77–78 (PG 28, 1531C–1534A); Camelot, 'Les traités', 279; Moulard, *Saint Jean*, 87–165; and David Amand de Mendieta, 'La virginité chez Eusèbe d'Emèse et l'ascétisme familial dans la première moitié du IVe siècle', *Revue d'histoire ecclésiastique* 50 (1955), pp. 777–820 (787–88); Karl Josef Hefele, *Histoire des conciles d'après les documents originaux* (trans. Henri Leclercq; Paris: Letouzey et Ane, 1907–1913), I: 1036–1039. The Council of Gangra was held ca. 340.

25 Justin, *Apologia* I, 14; 19 (PG 6, 347A–350A; 355B–358B); Clement of Alexandria, *Paedagogus* II, 10; cf. Musonius Rufus, 12–13. On Clement's extensive borrowing from Musonius, see Cora E. Lutz, 'Musonius Rufus, The Roman Socrates', *Yale Classical Studies* 10 (1947), pp. 3–142 (20 n. 83). On the Stoic influence on Christian writers in general concerning this point, cf. Michel Spanneut, *Le Stoicisme des pères de l'Eglise de Clément de Rome à Clément d'Alexandrie* (Patristica Sorbonensia no. 1; Paris: Seuil, 1957), pp. 259–60. Jerome, *Ep.* 22, 20; Eusebius of Emesa, *Homilia* 6, 6; 6, 17; cf. de Mendieta, 'La virginité', 788.

about her spouse's character, then over her own fertility – whether she might be sterile or, conversely, might have too many children. If she does conceive quickly, she must worry about miscarriage, about the potential death of the baby or her own death at delivery; the pains of childbirth are so torturous that they alone are capable of overshadowing all the joys of marriage. Then she dreads the possibility that her child might be malformed rather than healthy, or that she might have a girl rather than a boy. All this, without yet any mention of the problems of the child's upbringing! The fear of the death of one of the spouses and the anguish of separation round out John's rendering of the pains of marriage, a harsh and poignant account that will become the backdrop for the portrait of the ideal, virginity.[26]

John Chrysostom's description of the pains of marriage is only one of many. Gregory of Nyssa echoes many of John's observations, calling marriage the chief evil, leading to quarrels and suspicion; he invokes the authority of ancient narrators and claims that every story begins with marriage and ends in tragedy. Finally, he compares marriage with disease.[27] Jerome assumes that the arguments against marriage are well known, so that he need not bother to reiterate them, but directs Eustochium to the treatises by Tertullian, Cyprian and Ambrose on the subject.[28] Eusebius of Emesa writes about the pains of marriage as well, making many of the same arguments as John and Gregory. He concludes his poignant description with this dramatic summary:

Such are the so-called advantages which seduce so many young girls [into marriage]. They constitute a warning to wise and sensible girls. Look at these modest and prudent brides: one buries her husband while another delivers herself over to funereal lamentations, and another is crushed with grief. This one yielded to injustice, that one died before her marriage, another succumbs right in the middle of the wedding itself. Another cries for her groom, another for her children, and another is desolate at the cruelty of her husband. Here is one who cries for herself, crazed by jealousy, who increases her investigations to discover the causes of her husband's enslavement [by another woman?]. Finally, here is a mother, burdened with children: to remove illnesses and obtain medicines, she passes her nights wide awake; she sweats, she suffers, she is afraid, she torments herself. She awaits death as if it would bring to her a greater kindness than life.[29]

The virgin, by contrast, suffers with joy for Christ and escapes the many difficulties of married life.[30] The virgin, says John Chrysostom, 'is not obliged to involve herself tiresomely in the affairs of her spouse and she does not fear being abused'. Even the harshest sufferings of the virgin cannot compare to the sufferings of the married woman. 'Tell me', says Chrysostom,

---

26 John Chrysostom, *De Virginitate* 51–72. Cf. Moulard, *Saint Jean*, 201–07 for a summary of Chrysostom's thought on the subject.

27 Gregory of Nyssa, *De Virginitate* 3, esp. 3, 10.

28 Jerome, *Ep.* 22, 2; 22, 22. Note that, elsewhere, Jerome preserves a fragment of Theophrastus's *De Nuptiis*, against marriage (*Adversus Jovinianum* 1, 47; PL 23, 276–77).

29 Sufferings in childbirth: *Homiliae* 6, 4; 7, 15. Jealousy: *Homilae* 6, 4; 7, 15. Husband's reproaches and recriminations over children: *Homilae* 6, 4; 7, 16. Worries and fears inspired by husbands: *Homilae* 6, 14; 7, 15. Concern over children: *Homiliae* 6, 14; 7, 16. For a summary, cf. de Mendieta, 'La virginité', pp. 789–94. The quotation is from *Homilia* 7, 17.

30 John Chrysostom, *De Virginitate* 64.

during her entire life, does the virgin endure what the married woman endures almost every year, the one who is split apart by labor pains and wailings? For the tyranny of this suffering is such that, when divine scripture wants to represent captivity, famine, plague, and intolerable evils, it calls all these the pains of childbirth? And God imposed it on women as a chastisement and an affliction, not childbirth, I say, but childbirth with sufferings and anguish. 'For in struggle', he says, 'you will bear children'. But the virgin stands higher than this anguish or this suffering. For the one who annulled the curse of the law, annulled this curse along with it.[31]

Cyprian, earlier, used the same Genesis text (3.16) to show the liberating aspect of virginity. 'You virgins are free from this sentence,' he wrote, 'you do not fear the sorrows of women and their groans; you have no fear about the birth of children, nor is your husband your master, but your Master and Head is Christ in the likeness of and in the place of a man; your lot and conditions are the same (as that of men).'[32] This theme of virginity as liberation was common in the treatises on virginity and occurs frequently in the traditions concerning particular holy women.[33] Jerome, for example, attributes this statement to Melania the Elder, upon the death of her husband and two children: 'Lord, I will serve you more easily, since you have relieved me of such burdens.'[34]

The notion of virginity as liberation from the exigencies of earthly marriage leads into the theme of celestial marriage with Christ, as Cyprian's text quoted above suggests. The language of Christ as bridegroom is present throughout all the literature concerning virgins, along with the assertion that a vow of virginity is an irrevocable marriage contract with Jesus. Gregory of Nyssa brings together many of the images associated with this brand of 'spiritual marriage' in his *De Virginitate*. There he speaks of the marriage of the virgin with God as the authentic archetype for all marriage, a marriage in which God is preferred over all others. He uses eros-language throughout the text, and it would appear that he understands virginity to be a spiritual version of sexual love. To yield to passion is to commit adultery against the celestial bridegroom; virginity demands the mistrust of all flesh. Gregory even carries the notion of fertility into the spiritual realm: virgins possess a special spiritual fecundity and, as imitators of Mary, become themselves mothers of Christ. There is, in addition, a special and practical advantage to this spiritual fertility: it is the one way in which women can conceive without being dependent upon the will of men.[35]

Gregory was not the only writer to systematize this collection of ideas in this way, but the notion of the virgin as the bride of Christ is present from the earliest Patristic writings.[36] Tertullian uses the idea to undergird his argument that virgins

31 John Chrysostom, *De Virginitate* 59, 65.

32 Cyprian, *De Habitu Virginum* 22; translation from Michael Andrew Fahey, *Cyprian and the Bible: A Study in Third-Century Exegesis* (Beiträge zur Geschichte der biblischen Hermeneutik, 9; Tübingen: Mohr, 1971), p. 59.

33 Camelot, 'Les traités', p. 281; Gregory of Nyssa, *De Virginitate* 3, 8; Eusebius of Emesa, *Homilae* 6, 5; 6, 16; 7, 18 (cf. de Mendieta, 'La virginité', pp. 794–97).

34 Jerome, *Ep.* 39, 5.

35 Gregory of Nyssa, *De Virginitate*, Aubineau introduction, 193–204; 2, 2; 3, 3, 8; 4, 7; 14, 3; 15, 1; 16, 1–2; 20, 1 and 3–4; 23, 6.

36 On the Virgin as bride, see, for example, Augustine, *De Sancta Virginitate* 56 (PL 40, 428); Methodius, *Symposium*, Discourse 6, 5, 145; 7, 3, 157; Eusebius of Emesa, *Homilia* 6, 16; 6, 18. On Jesus as bridegroom: Pseudo-Athanasius, *Vita Syncleticae* 92 (PG 28, 1543C–1546A); Gregory of Nyssa, *De Virginitate* 3, 8; 15, 1; 16, 1; 20, 4; Jerome, *Ep.* 22, 2; *Acts of Thomas* 4ff., 6–7, 124.

ought to be veiled; since a modest wife never goes out without a veil, virgins, who are brides of Christ, should all the more so wear veils.[37] The rite of *velatio* (veiling) later committed the virgin to an irrevocable and mystical marriage with Christ,[38] and violation of the tie was considered sacrilegious adultery.[39] In the fourth century, imperial law reinforced this ecclesiastical proscription.[40] The virgin-bride should do the will of the bridegroom, repress her senses through asceticism in order to gain access to the heavenly bridal chamber, and guard her body, spirit and soul for Christ, her spouse.[41]

The erotic language that surrounds descriptions of the virgin's encounter with Christ is rather striking. The metaphor of marriage leads to a kind of spiritualized sexuality:

> Ever let the privacy of your chamber guard you; ever let the Bridegroom sport with you within. Do you pray? You speak to the Bridegroom. Do you read? He speaks to you. When sleep overtakes you He will come behind and put His hand through the hole of the door, and your heart shall be moved for Him; and you will awake and rise up and say: 'I am sick with love'. Then He will reply: 'A garden inclosed is my sister, my spouse; a spring shut up, a fountain sealed'.[42]

This motif of eroticism and erotic substitution is present in the earliest narratives concerning women's asceticism, the *Apocryphal Acts of the Apostles*, and it continues as an important theme, especially in the lives of holy women.[43] Macrina, on her deathbed, is filled with 'that divine and pure love (ἔρως) of the invisible bride-

---

37 Tertullian, *De Virginum Velandis* 16 (PL 2, 911).

38 Henri Leclercq, 'Vierge, Virginité', in Fernand Cabrol and Henri Leclercq (eds), *Dictionnaire d'archéologie chrétienne et de liturgie* (Paris: Letouzey et Ane, 1953), II, cols. 3102ff. For a complete discussion of the rites associated with the consecration of virgins, cf. René Metz, *La consécration des vierges dans l'Eglise romaine*; *Etudes d'histoire de la liturgie* (Paris: Presses Universitaires de France, 1954). For virginity as an eternal, indissoluable marriage with Christ, cf. Augustine, *De Sancta Virginitate* 8; 11 (PL 40, 400, 401); Ambrose, *De Virginibus* 1, 5, 22 (PL 16, 195); Gregory of Nazianzus, *Exhortatio ad virgines* 1–6 (PG 37, 637ff.).

39 This theme is very common in literature on 'fallen' virgins; cf. Basil, *Ep.* 46, 2; Jerome, *Ep.* 22, 13; *Vita Olympiadis* 17; John Chrysostom, *De non Iterando Coniugio* 3; Eusebius of Emesa, *Homilia* 7, 26; Cyprian, *De Habitu Virginum* 20. Cf. also Michel Aubineau, 'Les écrits de Saint Athanase sur le virginité', *Revue d'ascétique et de mystique* 31 (1955), pp. 140–73 (155), and canon 19 of the Council of Ancyra (314 CE): 'All those who have consecrated their virginity and who have violated their promise ought to be considered bigamists' (Hefele, *Histoire* I: 321f.).

40 Leclercq, 'Vierge', 310ff.; *Codex Theodosianus* IX, 25.

41 Athanasius, *De Virginitate* 2 (PG 28, 253B–D), 24 (PG 28, 279C–282A); Pseudo-Athanasius, *Vita Syncleticae* 9 (PG 28, 1491A–B); Jerome, *Ep.* 22, 25; John Chrysostom, *Ep.* 8.3; *Vita Melaniae* 42. Conversely, false virgins do not deserve entry into the bridal chamber: John Cassian, *Conference* 22, 6. Also Basil, *Ep.* 46, 3; Methodius, *Symposium*, Discourse 5, 4, 116; *Vita Melaniae* 42; Athenagoras, *Legatio* 33. On the virgin's body as an empty tomb to be filled by the spirit, cf. Jerome, *Ep.* 22, 23; Eusebius of Emesa, *Homilia* 6, 18 and elsewhere (cf. de Mendieta, 'La virginité', pp. 782–83); Crouzel, *Virginité et mariage*, pp. 46–49.

42 Jerome, *Ep.* 22, 25; cf. also Jerome, *Ep.* 22, 17, which acknowledges the difficulty of the human spirit renouncing love, but carnal love ought to be replaced by another desire: the virgin ought to be able to say, 'During the night, in my bed, I sought him who loved my spirit.'

43 Kraemer, 'The Conversion of Women', p. 303; *Acts of Paul and Thecla* 18–19; *Acts of Thomas* 116, 117; *Acts of Philip* 120; *Acts of Thomas* 4ff., 6–7, 124.

groom', and she hastens toward her lover. Olympias imitates the lovers (ἐραστής) of Christ, burning with ardour, and John Chrysostom's lessons are said to light the fire of divine love (θεῖος ἔρως) in the virgins of Olympias's convent. It is recounted that Melania the Younger was in love with Christ from her youth and wounded by divine love.[44]

Accompanying this erotic language, as with Gregory's systematized notion of spiritual marriage, is the idea of spiritual fecundity. The image is an old one, found in Philo's description of the Therapeutrides, then in early writers on the fertility of the Church and finally, fertility becomes a characteristic of virginity itself.[45] Methodius, for example, speaks of the virgins who receive the pure and fertile seed of doctrine as though they were brides.[46] Others describe the engendering of the son of God in the spirit of the virgin, thus making it possible for her to imitate Mary.[47]

The underside of these metaphors of spiritualized marriage and sexuality is a persistent suspicion of the flesh and its passions, a suspicion not solely Christian in origin but found throughout the Stoic philosophical tradition that influenced much Christian thinking about virginity.[48] The Stoic system is based on the precept that passion and reason are natural adversaries and that the goal of human life should be to become λογικός and ἀπαθής, reasonable/logical and without passion; to do so is to live life in accordance with nature.[49] Clement of Alexandria, one of the Church Fathers particularly influenced by Stoicism, based his notion of sin on this Stoic idea; for Clement, sin was defined as the passion of the spirit against nature.[50] The tyranny of sensation and the passions as an obstacle to the pathway to the Christian ideal is a common notion in early Christian writings, especially from the third century on, and especially in the writings on virginity and continence. Evagrius Ponticus describes a chain whose links are sensation leading to desire which leads to pleasure; the goal of Christian perfection must be to wipe out sensation in order to break the menacing chain.[51] Saint Syncletica, in her attempts to achieve perfection, closed off her senses to everything except the Bridegroom.[52] Eusebius of Emesa preaches:

44 Gregory of Nyssa, *Vita Macrinae* 22, *Vita Olympiadis* 5; 6; 8; *Vita Melaniae* 1; 32.

45 Philo, *De Vita Contemplativa* 68: 'Eager to have her [wisdom] for their life mate they have spurned the pleasures of the body and desire no mortal offspring but those immortal children which only the soul that is dear to God can bring to the birth unaided because the Father has sown in her spiritual rays enabling her to behold the verities of wisdom.' Cf. also *Legum allegoriae* 3, 180–81 and *De cherubim* 42, 42, 48f. for similar imagery. Cyprian, *De Habitu Virginum* 3; Methodius, *Symposium*, Discourse 3, 8, 70–71; 75 (Church as the receptacle of the fertile seed of doctrine); Discourse 8, 11,197 (the virile/potent logos). Cf. also Crouzel, *Virginité et mariage*, pp. 15–44, on Origen's development of the notion of the mystical union of the Church and Christ. Also cf. Ambrose, *De Virginibus* 1, 5, 31 (PL 16, 197); Augustine, *De Sancta virginitate* 2, 5, 6, 12 (PL 40, 397; 401).

46 Methodius, *Symposium*, Discourse 3, 7, 74.

47 Ambrose, *De Virginibus* 1, 3, 6, 11, 30 (PL 16, 191f., 197); Augustine, *De Sancta Virginitate* 2, 3, 5, 6, 7 (PL 40, 397). For general discussion, cf. Bourassa, 'Excellence de la virginité', pp. 30–33.

48 Cf. Spanneut, *Le Stoicisme*, *passim*. See also Max Pohlenz, *Die Stoa: Geschichte einer geistigen Bewegung* (Göttingen: Vandenhoeck and Ruprecht, 1948–1949), I: 400–61 on the relationship between Stoicism and Christianity until the Pelagian controversy, and 433–36 on asceticism in particular.

49 Spanneut, pp. 232–35, 241–42; Pohlenz, I: 116–118.

50 Spanneut, *passim*; Lutz, p. 20, .n. 83; Clement of Alexandria, *Paedagogus* I, 6, 1.

51 Evagrius Ponticus, *Capita Practica ad Anatolium* (PG 40, 1243–1246C).

52 Pseudo-Athanasius, *Vita Syncleticae* 9 (PG 28, 1492).

Among the virgins whom the ardent desire of God has touched, lust is dead, passion killed. Nailed to the cross with its vices and desires, the body is like a stranger to them; it does not feel what you feel, it is no longer of the same nature as your body. The resolution of virginity has transported it to heaven; the human nature of the virgin is not long on earth with you.[53]

In the spiritual marriage described by Gregory of Nyssa, to yield to the passions is to commit adultery against God and the very nature of spiritual marriage is the distrust of everything carnal.[54]

The philosophical ideal that Gregory outlines in his biography of Macrina includes liberation from the passions (ἀπάθεια) as one of its characteristics. At the tragic and unexpected death of her brother Naucratius, Macrina uses reason (λογισμός) against passion (πάθος) to overcome her grief, and thereby becomes her mother's instructor in the Stoic virtue, courage (ἀνδρεία).[55] One character-istic of the ascetic community created by Macrina at Annisa was the absence of passion; having liberated themselves from passion, these virgins were above human nature. Macrina, just before her death, so achieved the goal of ἀπάθεια that she became an angel in human form, with no affinity with the flesh.[56] This ἀπάθεια, born out of devotion to Christ, should be so complete that the virgin lives an everyday death.[57]

In Gregory's biography of Macrina, the equation of pathos and femininity is made explicit.[58] The connection may be Stoic in origin, as Seneca opens his dialogue, *De Constantia Sapientis*, with a comparison of Stoics and other philosophers, using the metaphor of sexual difference: '*Stoici, virilem ingressi viam*' ('Stoics, advancing along the manly way').[59] The idea is common in early Christian writers, and it provides an important metaphor for Philo as well.[60] Porphyry's well-known letter to Marcella provides an example from contemporaneous non-Christian writings of the connection between femininity and corruptible bodiliness:

Therefore … do not preoccupy yourself with the body, do not see yourself as a woman, since I no longer hold you as such. Flee in the spirit everything feminine (θηλυνομένων) as if you had a male body that enveloped [you]. For from a virgin spirit and a virgin mind

---

53 Eusebius of Emesa, *Homilia* 7, 13 (de Mendieta, 'La virginité', 784).

54 Gregory of Nyssa, *De Virginitate* 16, 1–2; 20, 3.

55 Gregory of Nyssa, *Vita Macrinae* 10; on the virtue of ἀνδρεία among women specifically, see below. John Chrysostom advised Olympias that she conquer her passions and sufferings through reason, *Ep.* 3, 1b.

56 Gregory of Nyssa, *Vita Macrinae* 11; 22. For ἀπάθεια as a goal beyond mastery of the passions, cf. John Chrysostom, *Ep.* 8, 5a–b. For this goal as part of the model for the Stoic sage, cf. Seneca, *De Constantia Sapientis* III.

57 *Vita Melaniae* 12. Cf. also Jerome, *Ep.* 22. 17, which advises Eustochium to seek out for company only those virgins who are thin and pale through repression of their bodily passions, those who say lovingly, 'I want to die [dissolve myself] to be with Christ.'

58 Gregory of Nyssa, *Vita Macrinae* 10. Origen makes the same equation; cf. Crouzel, *Virginité et mariage*, 135–39.

59 Seneca, *De Constantia Sapientis* I, 1.

60 Richard A. Baer, *Philo's Use of the Categories Male and Female* (Arbeit zur Literatur und Geschichte des hellenistischen Judentums, 3; Leiden: Brill, 1970).

the most blessed things are born; from the intact is born the incorruptible; but that to which the body gives birth, all the gods called polluted.[61]

Many of the ascetic women whose stories remain are considered laudable because they escaped the bonds of their feminine nature: thus, Olympias and Melania are both called ἡ ἄνθρωπος (the [feminine article] hu/man [generic, masculine noun]). Gregory says of Macrina at the beginning of her story: 'A woman is the starting-point of the narrative, if indeed a woman; for I do not know if it is proper to name her who is above nature out of [the terms] of nature.' Likewise, John Chrysostom is said to have responded to a question concerning Olympias by saying, 'Don't say "woman" but "what a man!" because this is a man, despite her physical appearance.'[62] In addition, in one of the few sayings attributed to women in the monastic tradition, Mother Sara says of herself, 'I am a woman by nature but not in reason.'[63] Athanasius advises virgins to abandon feminine mentality because women who please God will be elevated to male ranks.[64]

The idea of virgins transcending or rising above nature is a point at which Stoicism and Christianity part ways, though in the case of the Christian ideal, nature is apparently not meant in the sense of the nature–reason equation but rather as that which has to do with the material, female realm. John Chrysostom understands virginity as a struggle against the tyranny of nature as does Melania the Younger's biographer. Eusebius of Emesa portrays the Christian ideal as that which negates or transcends nature and calls fallen virgins those who 'fall to the level of nature'.[65] Jerome is alone among the Church Fathers in seeing virginity itself as the natural state, though here he seems to be using the term 'natural' as part of the nature–reason equation, since he makes the point in the context of arguing that sexuality itself is the product of the fall.[66]

The notion of ascetic women evading their female nature arises in an interesting narrative motif that appears early in the tradition and remains a controversial sign of female renunciation and spirituality well into the ninth century – the motif of women cutting their hair or disguising themselves as monks.[67] Thecla, who remains

61 Porphyry, *Ad Marcellam/Lettre à Marcella* (text established and French trans. Edouard des Places; Paris: Société d'Edition 'Belles Lettres', 1982), p. 33. For the same use of θηλυνομένων, cf. Porphyry, *De Abstentia* IV, 20 in Porphyrii, *Opuscula Selecta* (ed. Augustus Nauck; Leipzig: Teubner, 1886), 262, 1. 25. Cf. Methodius, *Symposium*, Discourse 8, 13, 205: '… make your soul male…'.

62 *Vita Olympiadis* 3; Palladius, *Historia Lausiaca* 9 (on Melania); Gregory of Nyssa, *Vita Macrinae* 1; Palladius, *Dialogus de vita S. Ioannis Chrysostomi* (PG 47, 56).

63 PG 65, 420D. The same theme occurs also in Gregory of Nyssa, *De Virginitate* 20, 4 and *Vita Melaniae* 39.

64 Athanasius, *De Virginitate* 10–12 (PG 28, 261C–266B).

65 John Chrysostom, *Ep.* 8, 6d; *Vita Melaniae* 12, Eusebius of Emesa, *Homilia* 7, 6; 7, 8 (cf. de Mendieta, 'La virginité', pp. 780–81; 819).

66 Jerome, *Ep.* 22, 19. Cf. John Chrysostom, *De Virginitate* 14 and elsewhere; cf. Grillet, 142, n. 3; Gregory of Nyssa, *De Virginitate* 4; Crouzel, *Virginité et mariage*, p. 26. By contrast, note that Augustine claimed that Adam and Eve had physical needs even in paradise: *De Nuptiis* I, 9, 24 (PL 44, 418–19; 427–28).

67 Evelyne Patlagean, 'L'histoire de la femme deguisée en moine et l'évolution de la saintéte féminine à Byzance', *Studi Medievali*, 3d. ser., 17 (1976), pp. 597–623; J. Anson, 'The Female Transvestite in Early Monasticism: Origin and Development of a Motif', *Viator: Medieval and Renaissance Studies* 5 (1974), pp. 1–32; Moine, 'Melaniana', pp. 72–73.

the model of virginity for generations of ascetic women,[68] both cuts her hair and wears men's clothing in the *Acts of Paul and Thecla* while, in other *Apocryphal Acts*, Mygdonia cuts her hair and Charitine wears men's clothing.[69] Syncletica is said to cut her hair as a sign of her renunciation of the world.[70] Transvestism among virgins is said to be accompanied by loss of female bodily characteristics, and to be followed by the negation of sexuality altogether:

> But there is more: the fundamental negation of femininity, where the physical spoiling is a manifestation of the spirit's evasion of its native condition. Our texts often express themselves in this regard in images which are quite explicit. ... 'Her breasts were not like the breasts of other women', we read about Hilaria. 'On account of her ascetic practices they were withered; and she was not subjected to the illness of women, for God had ordained it that way': the symbol remains clear under physiological evidence. The withered breasts, 'like dead leaves', reveal, when Anastasia or Hilaria was shrouded, at once their femininity and the accomplishment of their asceticism. The body of Apollonaria became 'like the exterior of a turtle', but Christ wanted to render to her 'the honor of the crown of the holy fathers', and to show her 'virile virtue' [ἀνδρεία]. The transvestite woman passes for a eunuch.[71]

Despite their function as a sign of renunciation and holiness,[72] transvestism and hair cutting were not always lauded as a practice demonstrating piety. Jerome warns Eustochium against women who dress as men, and the Council of Gangra in the mid-fourth century condemned ascetic women who, as a part of their religious renunciation, cut their hair and wore men's clothing.[73]

One last theme pertaining to the cultural construction of virginity remains to be examined: the notion of courage borrowed from Stoicism, ἀνδρεία.[74] The term is associated with virgins from very early on in the tradition; one of Hermas's similitudes in the *Shepherd* includes a description of virgins whose delicacy was contrasted with their ἀνδρεία.[75] The term is most often used in relation to particular

---

68 Pseudo-Athanasius, *Vita Syncleticae* 8 (PG 28, 1489D–1492A), where Syncletica is compared to Thecla. Gregory of Nyssa, *Vita Macrinae* 2, describes Macrina's mother's dream of Thecla on the eve of Macrina's birth; Thecla was Macrina's secret name. Thecla appears as a model often: Jerome, *Ep.* 22, 41; *Vita Olympiadis* 1; Ambrose, *De Virginibus* 2, 3 (PL 16, 212); Methodius, *Symposium*, Discourse 8, 1, 170; 8, 17, 232; 11, 282. For additional examples, cf. Maraval's introduction, p. 146, n. 2.

69 *Acts of Paul and Thecla* 25; *Acts of Thomas* 114; *Acts of Philip* 44.

70 Pseudo-Athanasius, *Vita Syncleticae* 11 (PG 28, 1491D–1494A).

71 Patlagean, 'L'histoire', pp. 605–6 (my translation).

72 Cf. also de Medieta, 'La virginité', pp. 809–11, where Didymus and Theodora exchange clothes in Theodora's prison cell in order to save her virginity, and Jerome, *Ep.*1, 14, where a woman saves her virtue by wearing men's clothes.

73 Jerome, *Ep.* 22, 27; Canon 13: 'If a woman, in the name of asceticism, changes her garment, and rather than the garment customary for women, puts on a man's garment, let it be anathema.' (Hefele, *Histoire* I: 1038); Canon 17: 'If a woman, in the name of asceticism, cuts her hair, which God gave her as a reminder of her subjugation, as a release of the commandment of subjugation, let it be anathema' (Hefele I: 1040).

74 Clark, 'Ascetic Renunciation', p. 245, n. 38; Elizabeth A. Clark, *Jerome, Chrysostom and Friends: Essays and Translations* (New York: Edwin Mellen, 1979), pp. 15, 19, 55–56; Rouselle, *Porneia*, p. 237.

75 Hermas, *Pastor* 79, 5 = *Sim.* 9, 2, 5.

exceptional women: Macrina teaches her mother patience and ἀνδρεία; John Chrysostom speaks many times of the ἀνδρεία of Olympias, and the word also appears once in her biography, and Paulinus describes Melania the Elder's ἀνδρεία on the occasion of her son's death. Palladius describes all of the virgins of whom he will speak as possessing ἀνδρεία, and there is a chapter of the *Historia Lausiaca* dedicated particularly to γυναίκες ἀνδρεῖαι.[76] The important question here is the nuance of this word, ἀνδρεία, which refers to one of the Stoic virtues, and which is also related to the Greek root, ἀνήρ, meaning 'man/male'. Are women who are designated by this term being called 'manly'? Musonius Rufus discusses in two of his discourses, first whether women should study philosophy[77] and second, whether daughters should receive the same education as sons. In the first discourse, Musonius states that women have the same inclination as men toward virtue, and in the second, he asserts that women are endowed with ἀνδρεία as well as men; if it appears that ἀνδρεία is absent from women, it is only for lack of use and practice, and not for lack of the attribute.[78] Cora Lutz, in her edition and translation of Musonius's writings, argues that Musonius goes to great lengths to defend the use of the word ἀνδρεία in reference to women, not simply out of rhetorical zeal, but because the word actually means 'manliness'. She points out, further, that Plutarch's treatise *On the Bravery of Women* avoids the term, replacing it with the more general ἀρετή.[79] Whether this argument alone is strong enough to support the assertion that ἀνδρεία, when attributed to women, means 'manliness' is not clear; what *is* clear, nevertheless, is that the nuance is present in the word, even if it is not its only meaning.

This brings to a close the overview of the *idea* of virginity and asceticism as it can be deduced from the sources which exist. It is a complex notion, weighted by both theological concerns and contemporary philosophical notions, and it is not easily synthesized. Marital and sexual metaphors are found alongside demands for the absolute renunciation of sexuality and feminine nature. Virginity is called liberation from the physical exigencies of life as a woman (marriage, sexuality, childbirth); it is also called another kind of marriage, a bond where sexuality is spiritualized, where the virgin gives birth to virtue or to Christ himself, where loyalty to the Bridegroom must be absolute. The feminine has no place in this virginal order; it is explicitly banished, along with passion, materiality and the body itself.

What did this banishment mean? How did women experience it, and why might they have chosen it? The next two sections will try to answer these questions.

Women's Experience of Virginity

Virginity and asceticism, though probably not institutionalized completely until much later, were part of Christian practice from very early on. Clement of Rome makes an allusion in his first-century letter to the Corinthians to those who practise chastity, and

---

76 Gregory of Nyssa, *Vita Macrinae* 10; John Chrysostom, *Ep.* 3, 1; 11, 1; 12, 1 (twice); 16, 1 (twice); *Vita Olympiadis* 15; Paulinus, *Ep.* 45, 2; 3; Palladius, *Historia Lausiaca*, Preamble (Butler, 3–4), p. 41.

77 Musonius Rufus, 3, 4, *Reliquae* (ed. O. Hense; Leipzig: Teubner, 1905), 8–19, 38–43; Lutz 40, 42–49.

78 Musonius Rufus, 4 (Hense, 15, 11. 17ff.; Lutz, 44, 11. 33ff.).

79 Lutz, 44, note on 1. 22.

Ignatius sends a special greeting to virgins in his letter to the Smyrneans which dates from the first decade of the second century.[80] Galen's mention of the Christians, in the second half of the second century, focuses specifically on their practice of chastity, and the virginity of Christians became a common apologetic theme in second and third-century writings.[81] The *Apocryphal Acts of the Apostles*, as noted in the previous section, attest to the importance of asceticism in the spirituality of second and third-century women. Cyprian's third-century *De Habitu Virginum* already suggests some kind of recognized category of virgins within the Church, and perhaps some form of consecration by which a virgin becomes a member of such a group.[82]

The evidence for women's asceticism becomes a bit less fragmentary with the rise of monasticism, the origins of which are traditionally placed at 307 with Pachomius's founding of a coenobitic community of monks in Egypt.[83] The tradition retains the story of Pachomius's sister, Maria, who came to visit her brother at his desert monastery. He refused to see her, but offered to build her a hut outside so that she might follow the ascetic life as well. She agreed and became the leader of one of the two women's monasteries that remained, along with nine men's monasteries, after Pachomius's death. The nuns in these first convents followed a strict form of asceticism which differed from that of Pachomian monks only in the matter of dress.[84] From these early beginnings, monasticism flourished, with evidence of communities of virgins in other parts of

---

80 Clement of Rome, *Epistola 1 ad Corinthios* 38, 2; Ignatius, *Epistola ad Smyrnaeos* 13, 1; cf. also n. 11 above for other references from the Apostolic Fathers.

81 Galen, *De Sententiis Politicae Platonicae*, in *De Placitis Hippocratis et Platonis* (ed. Iwanus Mueller; Leipzig: Teubner, 1874); Justin, *Apologia* I, 14, 29; Tertullian, *Apologia* 9, 19; Minucius Felix, *Octavius, passim*.

82 Cyprian, *De Habitu Virginum* 4, 24. For an excellent study of the development of the practice of consecration of virgins, see Metz, *La consécration*. In his discussion of the early centuries, he concludes that, while third-century texts do not rule out the practice of public vow-taking, they also do not provide enough evidence to prove its existence (p. 66). He locates the institution of public vow-taking and the establishment of an actual order of virgins in the fourth century (pp. 74–76).

83 Butler, *The Lausaic History* I: 206, n. 2 argues that the 307 date is extrapolated from the Arabic version of the Pachomian life, a version which is not authoritative; he places the founding of the first monastery between 315 and 320. For general histories of monasticism in the early years, cf. Mary Bateson, 'Origin and Early History of Double Monasteries', *Transactions of the Royal Historical Society*, n.s. 13 (London: Longmans and Green, 1899); Derwas J. Chitty, *The Desert a City: An Introduction to the Study of Egyptian and Palestinian Monasticism under the Christian Empire* (Oxford: Blackwell, 1966); Jean Decarreaux, *Monks and Civilization: From the Barbarian Invasions to the Reign of Charlemagne* (trans. Charlotte Haldane; Garden City, NY: Doubleday, 1964); Karl Suso Frank, *Grundzüge der Geschichte des christlichen Mönchtums* (Darmstadt: Wissenschaftliche Buchgesellschaft, 1975); Karl Heussi, *Der Ursprung des Mönchtums* (Tübingen: Mohr, 1936); Knowles, *Christian Monasticism*; Henri Leclercq, 'Cénobitisme', in Fernand Cabrol and Henri Leclercq (eds), *Dictionnaire d'archéologie chrétienne et de liturgie* (Paris: Letouzey et Ane, 1925), II, 2, cols. 3047–3248; Philip Rousseau, *Ascetics, Authority and the Church in the Age of Jerome and Cassian* (Oxford: Oxford University Press, 1978); I. Gregory Smith, *Christian Monasticism from the Fourth to the Ninth Centuries of the Christian Era* (London: Innes, 1892); F.C. Woodhouse, *Monasticism Ancient and Modern* (London: Gardner, Darton, 1896).

84 Palladius, *Historia Lausiaca* 33. Maria's leadership is also mentioned in Athanasius's *Vita S. Antonii* 3: 54 (PG 26, 844; 921); Bateson, 'Origin', p. 139.

Egypt and in Palestine, Asia Minor, Syria, Rome and other parts of Italy.[85] By the beginning of the fifth century, Theodoret reports virgins living in large communities everywhere, Palestine, Egypt, Asia, Pontus (the northeastern-most corner of Asia Minor) and Europe.[86]

Monastic life was not the only way that women pursued their commitment to virginity, however. Before the formation of such communities, virgins lived with their parents or with a small number of other virgins still in the world, albeit somewhat withdrawn from it.[87] The anonymous Greek homily from the fourth century published by Amand and Moons presupposes a situation in which the virgin remained in her parents' home.[88] Eusebius of Emesa's two homilies on virginity make no mention whatsoever of communities of virgins and, in fact, explicitly require a virgin to stay at home unless her family abandons her, in which case she is permitted to live with another virgin. The practice of 'home monasticism' was also common among the aristocratic women of Rome in the fourth century.[89]

There is also evidence from a variety of sources for women living continently with their husbands in marriage, apparently without suspicion.[90] However, when virgins lived with continent men, as they did in large numbers throughout the early Church,[91] the practice came to be challenged and condemned by Church Fathers and councils alike. The earliest condemnation of *virgines subintroductae*, as the women were called, came in 268 at the Council of Antioch and was followed by restrictive canons produced in 300 at Elvira, in 317 at Ancyra and

85 *Historia Monachorum in Aegypto* 5, 5–6, cites an incalculable number of monks and virgins in Oxyrhychus, with the bishop there claiming that he oversaw ten thousand monks and twenty thousand virgins. Gregory of Nazianzus, *Oratio* 43 (*in laudem Basili magni*) 60 (PG 36, 578) claims Basil founded a monastery of virgins in Palestine; for Paula and Eustochium's three communities in Bethlehem, cf. Jerome, *Epp.* 66, 108; for Melania's community in Jerusalem, cf. *Vita Melaniae* 41; Palladius, *Historia Lausiaca* 59, 67; Etheria, *Peregrinatio* 23; *Vita Olympiadis* 6. Cf. also A.-J. Festugière, *Antioche paienne et chrétienne* (Paris: de Boccard, 1959), *passim*; Ph. Schmitz, 'La première communautéde vierges à Rome', *Revue Benedictine* 38 (1926), pp. 189–95; Leclercq, 'Cénobetisme', cols. 3181ff.

86 Theodoret, *Religiosa Historia* 30 (PG 82, 1493). Cf. also Metz, *La consécration*, pp. 81–87, for a discussion of the earliest communities of virgins.

87 Metz, *La consécration*, 81 and elsewhere; Aubineau, 'Les écrits de Saint Athanase', p. 140.

88 David Amand and Matthew-Charles Moons, 'Une curieuse homilie grecque inédite sur la virginité adressé aux pères de famille', *Revue Bénédictine* 63 (1953), pp. 18–69, 211–38.

89 Eusebius of Emesa, *Homilia* 6, 22; cf. de Mendieta, 'La virginité', pp. 799–803, who sees these homilies as strong evidence for familial asceticism in the Greek east during the middle (330–350) of the fourth century; Clark, 'Ascetic Renunciation'; Yarbrough 'Christianization'.

90 *Acts of Thomas* 14, 15; Methodius, *Symposium*, Discourse 9, 4, 252; John Chrysostom, *Ad Viduam Iuniorem* 2; Socrates, *Historia Ecclesiastica* 4, 23 (PG 67, 510ff.); Sozomenes, *Historia Ecclesiastica* 1, 14 (PG 67, 899ff.); *Historia Monachorum in Aegypto* 14, 3; 22, 1–2; Palladius, *Historia Lausiaca* 8; 41; cf. also Rouselle, *Porneia*, p. 235.

91 Hefele, *Histoire* I: 201, translator's n. 2: 'This custom was widespread in the whole church in antiquity; we encounter it in Syria, Persia, Africa, Spain, Gaul, everywhere.' For more general discussion of the practice, see Hans Achelis, *Virgines Subintroductae: Ein Beitrag zum VII. Kapitel des I. Korintherbriefs* (Leipzig: Hinrichs, 1902), and more recently, Clark, *Jerome, Chrysostom, and Friends*.

in 325 at Niceae.[92] Basil and Cyprian both wrote epistles against the practice, and Jerome mentions 'those women who appear to be, but are not, virgins' several times. The author of the two Pseudo-Clementine epistles to virgins, dating from the fourth century, also condemns *subintroductae*, as do Eusebius of Emesa, Gregory of Nyssa and Gregory of Nazianzus.[93] But none of these condemnations is as rhetorically rich as those produced by John Chrysostom in his two pastoral letters against the practice of cohabitation of virgins and continent brothers.[94] All of these attempts to proscribe the practice reinforce the conclusion that it was a practice in which many virgins (and brothers) adhered. Whether virgins broke their vows of chastity in living with men, as some Church leaders claimed, cannot be ascertained from the evidence. Yet it is clear that women found it a desirable arrangement in which they continued to participate at least well into the seventh century.[95]

The evidence for the ages of women devoting their chastity to God varies, though many appear to have done so early in life. Palladius tells of Talis, a woman who followed the ascetic life for eighty years, of Taor, who was a virgin for sixty years, and another virgin, unnamed, who was ascetic for sixty years as well. Macrina was twelve when she decided to remain a virgin; Olympias was widowed at nineteen and refused to remarry; Blesilla, Paula's daughter and Eustochium's older sister, began her ascetic life at her widowhood at twenty; Melania the Elder, widowed at twenty-two, pursued asceticism, and her granddaughter, Melania the Younger, renounced the world at twenty, after seven years of marriage.[96] Such early marriages and widowhoods were quite common in the Roman period, as marriage, within the aristocracy at least, was the standard method of sealing pacts between families and assuring that a legitimate heir existed for the passing on of property. The marriage

---

92 Clark, *Jerome, Chrysostom, and Friends*; cf. also Eusebius, *Historia Ecclesiastica* 7, 30, 12. Hefele, *Histoire* I: 236: Canon 27: bishops and other clerics may cohabit only with their own sisters or daughters and only if these women are virgins and have been consecrated to God. Hefele, I: 321f. Canon 19: virgins are prohibited from living like sisters with brothers. Hefele, I: 536ff. Canon 3: bishops, priests, deacons and all other members of the clergy are prohibited from having a συνεισάκτος live with them unless she is the clergyman's mother, sister, aunt, or someone who escapes all suspicion.

93 Basil, *Ep.* 55; Cyprian, *Ep.* 4; Jerome, *Ep.* 22, 15; cf. also *Ep.* 22, 14 and *Ep.* 117. Pseudo-Clement, *Epistolae 1–2 ad Virgines* (PG 1, 379–452); for dating, see Aimé Puech, *Histoire de la littérature grecque chrétienne depuis les origines jusqu'à la fin du IVe siècle* (3 vols; Paris: Société d'Edition 'Belles Lettres', 1928–1930), II, p. 44. Eusebius of Emesa, *Homiliae* 6, 13; 7, 20–21. Gregory of Nyssa, *De Virginitate* 23. Gregory of Nazianzus, *Epigrammata* 10–20 (PG 38, 86ff.).

94 John Chrysostom, *Adversus eos qui apud de habent subintroductas virgines* (PG 47, 495–514); *Quod regulares feminae viris cohabitare non debeant* (PG 47, 513–52); ET: Clark, *Jerome, Chrysostom, and Friends*.

95 R. Kugelman and F. X. Murphy, 'Virgines Subintroductae', *New Catholic Encyclopedia* (New York: McGraw Hill, 1967), vol. XIV, p. 698.

96 Palladius, *Historia Lausiaca*, 46, 56, 59–61; Gregory of Nyssa, *Vita Macrinae*, Maraval's introduction, p. 45; John Chrysostom, *Ep.* 8, 5c; *Vita Olympiadis* 2–3. Jerome, *Ep.* 39, 1; Palladius, *Vita Melaniae*, 8. Cf. Moine, 'Melaniana', p. 65, for a challenge to Melania the Elder's age, on the basis of the unreliability of Palladius's dating.

often occurred between an older man and a young girl, sometimes younger than twelve.[97]

Despite the fact that girls were considered ready for marriage at such a young age, they were by no means thought to be capable of making decisions for themselves, and the decision to renounce the world and to guard one's virginity was not often met with encouragement from parents and other family members. Often the parents were concerned to assure the continuation of their line, as was the case with Syncletica and Melania the Younger. Macrina also faced opposition when, at the death of her fiancé, she decided to remain a virgin. John Chrysostom speaks of the fact that Olympias scandalized many people by her practice of asceticism, and her biography tells of the emperor confiscating her wealth because she refused to remarry after being widowed at nineteen. The problem of parental opposition provoked much rhetoric on the part of the Church Fathers. Paulinus of Nola describes Melania the Elder's struggle to embrace asceticism after the deaths of her husband and two of her three children:

> Many were her skirmishes down to the very elements in this warfare against the vengeful dragon ... For the whole force of her noble relatives, armed to restrain her, attempted to change her proposal and to obstruct her passage.[98]

Ambrose argues that girls can choose, by law, the men they want; Why should they not be able to choose God? Jerome speaks of family members' attempts to impede girls from becoming virgins, and implores, 'Mother, why are you distressed because your daughter wants to be the bride, not of a soldier, but of a king himself? She has brought you a big advantage: you have become the mother-in-law of God.'[99]

The decision to remain a virgin and to renounce marriage and the world did provide some virgins with an opportunity to pursue intellectual and spiritual activities that would otherwise have been unavailable to them. Especially among educated aristocratic women who wished to pursue a life of study, the life of ascetic renunciation was the only institutionally established means of pursuing intellectual work. Jerome praises the abilities of Blesilla, who knew Greek and Hebrew and rivalled her mother

---

97 M. Durry, 'Le mariage des filles impubères dans la Rome antique', *Revue internationale des droites de l'antiquité*, 3d ser. 2 (1955), pp. 262–73; cf. also Danielle Gourevitch, *Le mal d'être femme: La femme et la médicine dans la Rome antique* (Paris: Société d'Edition 'Belles Lettres', 1984), pp. 109–11; Rouselle, *Porneia*, p. 122; M. K. Hopkins, 'The Age of Roman Girls at Marriage', *Population Studies* 18 (1965), pp. 309–27; Evelyne Patlagean, *Recherches sur les pauvres et al pauvreté dans l'empire roman d'orient (IV–VIIe siècles)* (Civilisations et Sociétés, 48; Mouton: Ecole des Hautes Etudes en Sciences Sociales, 1977), pp. 343–51. Cyrille Vogel, 'Facere cum virginia (-o) sua(-o)annos ... L'âge des époux chrétiens au moment de contracter mariage d'après les inscriptions paléochrétiennes', *Revue de droit canonique* 16 (1966), pp. 355–66, discusses the age of marriage for Christians based on grave inscriptions; the median age resulting from this data is nineteen years for women. Cf. article for the details of the research.

98 Pseudo-Athanasius, *Vita Syncleticae* 7 (PG 28, 1489); *Vita Melaniae* 1; Gregory of Nyssa, *Vita Macrinae* 4–5; John Chrysostom, *Ep.* 8, 5c; *Vita Olympiadis* 4. Quotation from Paulinus of Nola, *Ep.* 29, 10 (trans. Francis X. Murphy), 'Melania the Elder: A Biographical Note', *Traditio* 5 (1947), p. 65.

99 Ambrose, *De Virginibus* 1, 10, 58 (PL 16, 205); Jerome, *Ep.* 22, 23, 25. For more discussion of parental opposition, cf. Yarbrough, 'Christianization', pp. 154–57; also cf. John Chrysostom, *Adverus Oppugnatores Vitae Monasticae* (PG 47, 318–86).

in the study and chanting of psalms. Melania the Younger rigorously pursued her life of study, and her biographer reports that many women from the senatorial class and other highly placed people came to her to discuss points of theology. Macrina, as noted before, is credited by Gregory of Nyssa with being her brother Basil's spiritual teacher; she was also the teacher of her mother and another brother, Peter, and was the leader of the home monastic community at Annisa. Palladius lauds Melania the Elder and Olympias for their studiousness and their roles as teachers, and Olympias was also an influential leader of a monastery of women in Antioch. Other ascetic women also pursued the leadership of women's communities, notably Paula and Eustochium in Bethlehem and Melania the Younger in Jerusalem.[100]

For affluent women, a life of asceticism and virginity also meant not total renunciation of their wealth, but paradoxically, control over it. Cyprian, in the third century, does not require the group of virgins to whom he writes to give up their wealth, but to be generous with it. The women of the Roman aristocracy pursued the genteel form of home asceticism without renouncing their wealth, though diverting it from the standard route of inheritance and thereby so disrupting the system of capital exchange within their class that eventually legislation was passed which prohibited such drainage of aristocratic holdings.[101]

For the most part, little is known about the financial details of much early ascetic life, aside from the sponsorship of monasteries by aristocratic Christians. Certainly, not every community of virgins possessed such sponsorship, and furthermore, the majority of virgins were not wealthy women. Ascetic life was by definition, of course, quite spartan (the genteel asceticism of certain Roman matrons notwithstanding), and the value placed on manual labour in many communities[102] may have been significant enough to produce the necessities for a group of virgins. In addition, evidence from fourth-century Egypt provides a few hints of other possibilities. Three papyrus documents in particular, two letters and a contract, attest to the fact that Christian women pursued business dealings, perhaps to support themselves.[103] The letters involve a community of 'sisters' which appears to be involved in a business providing commercial items to other groups of 'sisters'; the letters include a rather eclectic list of objects and discussion of payment. The letters do not provide a clear indication of the nature of this group of 'sisters', whether they are consecrated virgins, how many they are, how they live. The letters do suggest, however, a strong – and otherwise unattested – possibility that a group of (ascetic?) Christian women were in business to support themselves, perhaps as a community. The contract documents the fact that two nuns have rented a piece of land to a Jewish man. Otherwise, it

---

100 Jerome, *Ep.* 39; *Vita Melaniae* 23; 27; 54. Gregory of Nyssa, *Vita Macrinae* 6; 10; 12; 16. Palladius, *Historia Lausiaca* 55; 56. Butler's original text has Silvania here rather than Melania, but C.H. Turner corrected this reading in his article 'The Lausiac History of Palladius', *JTS* 6 (1905), pp. 352–54. Butler acknowledged the correction the following year, in his 'Chronicle', *JTS* 7 (1906), p. 309. *Vita Olympiadis* 6; Jerome, *Epp.* 66, 108; *Vita Melaniae* 41.

101 Cyprian, *De Habitu Virginum*, 11; Clark, 'Ascetic Renunciation', pp. 241–42; cf. also Rouselle, *Porneia*, p. 177, who notes as well that before 320 those who chose celibacy over marriage had no claim to their inheritances.

102 Gregory of Nyssa, *Vita Macrinae*, Maraval's introduction, pp. 48–49.

103 A.M. Emmett, 'Female Ascetics in the Greek Papyri', *Jahrbuch der österreichischen Byzantinistik* 32 (1982), pp. 507–15.

leaves open questions about the women's background, how they came to acquire this land, where they live. But what is striking about these documents is that they provide evidence for activity among ascetic women – business dealings that may well have been the means of support for these women – otherwise unattested by the evidence for ascetic women in the first centuries of the Church. While the documents provide very little concrete information, and while their uniqueness makes conclusions difficult, they are nevertheless an important reminder that women's asceticism is not fully described or explained by the evidence traditionally preserved as the history of the Church.

Women's material experience of asceticism was diverse. Living at home, continently with husbands or religious men, in communities of virgins, ascetic women pursued their spiritual commitment in widely varying activities, including study, manual labour, and perhaps also commercial involvements. In doing so, they also avoided the conventional duties and potential dangers of marriage and motherhood. What did this renunciation, in practice and coloured by the ideology which gave it form, mean for women and their sexuality?

The Meaning of Virginity for Women's Sexuality

The problem of interpretation remains, and it is a difficult one because the evidence is fragmentary, and because it suggests at best a paradoxical reading. Others have demonstrated ably how asceticism and virginity may well have appeared as liberating options to women living in a culture that offered them few alternatives beyond the conventions (and potential dangers) of marriage and motherhood. Kraemer, for example, argues this way about that asceticism described in the *Apocryphal Acts of the Apostles*:

> The conversion stories of the *Apocryphal Acts of the Apostles* reveal elements of the attraction which ascetic Christianity may have held for certain women in the Greco-Roman world – either women who found the traditional roles of wife and mother inadequate measures of their worth, or women who could not participate in the rewards guaranteed by adherence to those standards – socially marginal women, widows, or barren women. Although the *Acts of the Apostles* are replete with conversion accounts of men, the renunciation of sexuality and socio-sexual roles, as we have seen, had far greater implications for women than it did for men. Religious systems which legitimize the rejection of established socio-sexual standards, as did ascetic Christianity, are likely to attract large numbers of discontented and marginal women and to propound standards of worth and redemption more consonant with their circumstances.[104]

Clark and Ruether demonstrate that asceticism provided the aristocratic women of the fourth century with otherwise unavailable opportunities to pursue study and to act as administrators and spiritual leaders of their communities. Rouselle argues that women's contribution to the development and spread of Christianity had more to

---

104 Kraemer, 'The Conversion of Women', pp. 306–7; cf. also Davies, *The Revolt*, pp. 112–14, who argues, somewhat differently, that conversion to Christianity (as described in the *Apocryphal Acts*) permitted women to exempt themselves from sexual duties and to leave marriages where sexual continence was not possible.

do with the material and social freedom made possible under asceticism than with spiritual fervour.[105]

These twentieth-century scholars are not the first to have asserted the 'feminism' of the ascetic life. In an 1896 study probably influenced by the contemporary idea of a mother-age which preceded patriarchy, Lina Eckenstein describes the attraction of monasticism for early Christian women:

> For a time when contacts with Christianity brought with it the possibility of monastic settlements, the love of domestic life had not penetrated so deeply, nor were its conditions so uniformly favorable, but that many women were ready to break away from it. Reminiscences of an independence belonging to them in the past, coupled with the desire for leadership, made many women loathe to conform to life inside the family as wives and mothers under conditions formulated by men. Tendencies surviving from an earlier period, and still unsubdued, made the advantages of married life weigh light in the balance against a loss of liberty. To conceive the force of these tendencies is to gain an insight into the elements which the convent forthwith absorbs.[106]

It seems fairly clear that ascetic renunciation did offer women in the early Church an alternative to the conventions of marriage and motherhood, and thus a kind of control over their sexuality. In marriage, a woman could not deny access to her body to her husband, and, much as she might wish to control her fertility, contraception and abortion, while apparently widely practised, remained unreliable and often dangerous.[107] In this sense, asceticism, despite its harsh demands, may well have seemed attractive to many women. Yet it is not at all clear that the ideology of virginity was not as domesticating and circumscribing of women's sexuality as the ideology of marriage. Furthermore, the demands of self-renunciation had far greater implications – not only physically and socially, but culturally – for women than for

105 Clark, 'Ascetic Renunciation'; Ruether, 'Mothers of the Church', esp. pp. 93–94; Rouselle, *Porneia*, p. 227.

106 Lina Eckenstein, *Women Under Monasticism* (Cambridge, UK: Cambridge University Press, 1896), p. 3. Eckenstein also writes: 'For the convent accepted the dislike women felt to domestic subjection and countenanced them in their refusal to undertake the duties of married life. It offered an escape from the tyranny of the family, but it did so on condition of such a sacrifice of personal independence, as in the outside world more and more involved the loss of good repute. On the face of it, a greater contrast than that between the loose woman and the nun is hard to conceive; and yet they have this in common, that they are both the outcome of the refusal among womankind to accept married relations on the basis of the subjection imposed by the father-age' (p. 5).

107 M.K. Hopkins, 'Contraception in the Roman Empire', *Comparative Studies in Society and History* 8 (1965/66), pp. 124–51; Norman Himes, *A Medical History of Contraception* (2nd edn; New York: Schocken, 1970), ch. 4; Gourevitch, *La mal*, pp. 195–216; Marie-Thérèse Fontanille, *Avortement et contraception dans la médecine gréco-romaine* (Paris: Searle Laboratories, 1977). Part of the difficulty lay in medical misconceptions concerning female anatomy and fertility; cf. Aline Rouselle, 'Observation féminine et idéologie masculine: le corps de la femme d'après les médicins grecs', *Annales: Economies, Sociétés, Civilisations* 35 (1980), pp. 1089–1115. On Christian attitudes toward contraception and abortion, see Clement of Alexandria, *Paedagogus* II, 10 (96.1); Jerome, *Ep.* 22, 13 (which describes fallen virgins who inadvertently commit suicide by taking abortives which are poisonous); Crouzel, *Virginité et mariage*, pp. 80–81; R.M. Roberge, 'L'avortement dans le pensée chrétienne des premiers siècles', *Collection d'Etudes Anciennes* 7 (1977), pp. 83–90.

men because of the structure of the ideas of virginity, sexuality and femininity in relation to theological ideas about redemption.

Women's sexuality, historically, has been appropriated as a tool of men's power, a sign in the masculinist system of communication, a commodity in the system of exchange.[108] The institution of marriage arose as part of that system of exchange, and in the Roman world a girl's body was the token that sealed agreements between families, her virginity being the measure of her value. Thus, Plutarch writes of the Romans' practice of marrying their daughters off at an early age: 'But the Romans give them [their daughters] away at twelve and even younger; for thus the body and the moral character [of the girl] might be clean and untouched for her husband.'[109] In the realm of religious virginity, women's sexuality functioned in a similar way as a token offered to God as a sign of renunciation; the virgin's body belonged to the celestial Bridegroom, conceptually, in the same way that it would have to his earthly counterpart. I am not suggesting that the experience of marriage and virginity was identical; rather, I am arguing that women's sexuality was being used structurally in the same way, that the underlying idea of women's sexuality was the same in the social world and the religious realm. The religious system adopted the reigning idea of women's sexuality as token of exchange and reinforced it by investing it with theological significance. This fact would not be especially significant, except for the way in which sexuality becomes the hingepin for the whole system of asceticism. The renunciation of sexuality and sexual nature is a unique demand, given the meaning that is assigned sexuality by the culture. For women, their sexuality is synonymous with their identity in this cultural order; to demand its negation is to make a far more profound demand for alienation and renunciation of self than any demand for continence on the part of men. Thus Jerome's glorification, quoted above, of the virgins who say, 'I want to die [dissolve myself] to be with Christ', becomes a haunting reminder of what was culturally at stake in the movement toward virginity; self-dissolution has no counterpart in the culture of continence.

This does not mean that every virgin's experience of asceticism and renunciation was an experience of conscious alienation. It does mean that, to the extent to which external conceptualizations shape experience, the practice of virginity was given its contours and its tone by the idea of women's sexuality as a token of exchange in a masculine system, whether that system be social or religious. This becomes clear in two sets of evidence concerning virgins: first, the imagery of marriage which provides a structure for the virgin's relationship with Jesus, including the idea that fallen virgins are adulteresses; and, second, in a small but significant corner of the tradition concerning virgins – those who committed suicide when confronted with rape.

It is not possible to tell how frequently virgins were confronted by this threat of violence; the *Historia Monachorum in Aegypto* speaks of a virgin of God being raped by brigands, and the isolation of eremitic women in the desert probably made them the victims of assaults more often than is recorded. Macrina's mother is said to

---

108 This observation has been prevalent in much contemporary feminist theory, but originates with Claude Levi-Strauss, *Elementary Structures of Kinship* (rev. ed.; trans. J.H. Bell; eds J.R. von Sturmer and R. Needham; Boston: Beacon, 1969).

109 Plutarch, *Vita Numa* 26, 2.

have wanted to remain a virgin, but married to obtain protection because she feared abduction and rape. Jerome, in his letter to Eustochium, uses the tragic example of the results of Dinah's having gone out to exhort Eustochium (and other virgins) to remain indoors.[110]

In the literature on virginity itself, it is Eusebius of Emesa who raises the theme by incorporating three edifying tales of virgins into his *Homilia* 6; two of these stories – of Pelagia, and of Bernice and Prosdoce – result in the suicides of the virgins to escape rape; the third, concerning Theodora,[111] tells of the virgin's escape from prison (and the concomitant threat of rape) by trading clothes with Didymus, a fellow Christian who sneaked into her cell to save her and her virginity. The virgins are hailed as fine examples, who would die at their own hand rather than suffer the loss of their virginity. The horror of the threat of rape, as portrayed by Eusebius and others, is not the violence or the outrageousness of the attack, but the fact that it renders the virgins' bodies damaged goods, no longer eligible for the celestial bridal chamber. The problem was significant enough that the Church Fathers went on to debate whether a virgin had sinned in committing suicide under such circumstances; John Chrysostom concludes that the virgins had not sinned because of their sacrifice, and Ambrose says that their faith suppresses their crime. Augustine, however, asserts that flight from sin is not a sufficient motive for suicide in this case, because 'the sin of others does not stain'.[112]

It is not unimportant that, along with assigning women's sexuality and virginity this commodity-value, the ideology of virginity adopts the familiar idea of the equation of femininity and passion, both of which must be repressed, even negated. Virgins were exhorted to abandon their female nature and to pursue reason and ἀνδρεία, whose nuance of 'manliness' cannot be wholly discounted. The demand to renounce passion is therefore much more poignant when applied to women because passion itself has been located in the idea of female selfhood. The construction of the feminine as passion means that women, the embodiment or the cultural representation of the feminine, are erased by that repression of passion. Therefore, for a woman to participate in the institution that calls for the negation of the feminine is, on one level, for her to participate in a profound self-abnegation, self-denial, even self-destruction.

The result of this inquiry produces a rather bleak picture of women's experience of both marriage and virginity in late antiquity, since both experiences were framed by a constraining ideology that constructed women's sexuality as an object of value to be traded – whether in the social marketplace or in the spiritual trading ground. The practical experiences of marriage and virginity were obviously different, and for this reason, virginity must have offered a significant alternative to many women. Nevertheless, the ideology of virginity did not challenge that of the surrounding culture, but rather adopted it and added to it a theological dimension, producing perhaps an even

---

110 *Historia Monachorum in Aegypto* 14, 5; Gregory of Nyssa, *Vita Macrinae* 2; Maraval's introduction, p. 145, n. 4 documents a certain frequency of such abductions during the period; Jerome, *Ep.* 22, 25.

111 Eusebius of Emesa, *Homilia* 6, 25–28; cf. Eusebius of Caesarea, *Historia Ecclesiastica* 7, 12, 3–4.

112 John Chrysostom, *Homilia in S. Pelagiam* (PG 50, 579–84); *Homilia in SS. Bernicen et Producen* (PG 50, 629–40); Ambrose, *De Virginibus* 3, 7 (PL 16, 229–32); Augustine, *De Civitate Dei* 1, 26 (PL 41, 39–40).

more restrictive and coercive system. Virginity offered then an opportunity to avoid certain constraints and real sufferings while extracting a profound price, not only the abdication of sexuality through the denial of passions but a far more poignant price on the level of cultural meaning, that of identity and self. Unfortunately, because their testimony is conspicuously absent, whether that cost was a worthwhile one for the women who paid it is something which will never be known.

Afterword

I published 'Virginity and its Meaning for Women's Sexuality in Early Christianity' over twenty years ago. The essay was a revision of a seminar paper I had written for a course, 'Women in Early Christianity', taught by Professor Bernadette Brooten at the Claremont Graduate School in the early 1980s. Needless to say, there has been a tremendous amount of work done on the topic of early Christian women's asceticisms and monasticisms since my article appeared in print. In addition, many approaches and themes that we now take for granted in the fields of early Christianity and ancient studies – gender studies, the history of sexuality, critical cultural studies of the body, and so on – had barely arrived on the scene in the early 1980s; insights from these arenas of knowledge have radically transformed what we know about and how we think about the ascetic impulse, for both women and men. Rather than attempting to edit or revise the essay in light of all of this scholarly labour, here I simply offer readers suggestions for further reading should they wish to find critical supplements to the arguments and evidence I put forward in this essay two decades ago.

Sources in Translation

Brock, Sebastian, and Susan Ashbrook Harvey (eds), *Holy Women of the Syrian Orient* (Berkeley: University of California Press, 1987).

Peterson, Joan M. (ed.), *Handmaids of the Lord: Contemporary Descriptions of Feminine Asceticism in the First Six Christian Centuries* (Kalamazoo, MI: Cistercian Publications, 1996).

Talbot, Alice-Mary (ed.), *Holy Women of Byzantium: Ten Saints' Lives in English Translation* (Byzantine saints' Lives in Translation 1; Washington, DC: Dumbarton Oaks Library and Collection, 1996).

Valantasis, Richard (ed.), *Religions of Late Antiquity in Practice*, (Princeton Readings in Religion; Princeton, NJ: Princeton University Press, 2000).

Ward, Benedicta, *The Harlots of the Desert: A Study of Repentance in Early Monastic Sources* (Kalamazoo, MI: Cistercian Publications, 1987).

Wimbush, Vincent L. (ed.), *Ascetic Behavior in Greco-Roman Antiquity: A Source-book* (Minneapolis, MN: Fortress Press, 1990).

Theoretical Studies of Asceticism

Harpham, Geoffrey Galt, *The Ascetic Imperative in Culture and Criticism* (Chicago: University of Chicago Press, 1987).

— 'Ascetics, Aesthetics, and the Management of Desire', in Susan L. Mizruchi (ed.), *Religion and Cultural Studies* (Princeton, NJ: Princeton University Press, 2001), pp. 95–109.

Martin, Luther H., Huck Gutman, and Patrick H. Hutton (eds), *Technologies of the Self: A Seminar with Michel Foucault* (Amherst: University of Massachusetts Press, 1988).

Valantasis, Richard, 'Constructions of Power in Asceticism', *JAAR* 63 (1995), pp. 775–821.

General Studies and Conference Proceedings

Brown, Peter, *The Body and Society: Men, Women and Sexual Renunciation in Early Christianity* (Lectures in the history of Religions, 13; New York: Columbia University Press, 1988).

Clark, Elizabeth A., *Reading Renunciation: Asceticism and Scripture in Early Christianity* (Princeton, NJ: Princeton University Press, 1999).

Elm, Susanna, *'Virgins of God': The Making of Asceticism in Late Antiquity* (New York: Oxford University Press, 1994).

Francis, James A., *Subversive Virtue: Asceticism and Authority in the Second-Century Pagan World* (University Park: Pennsylvania State University Press, 1995).

Levine, Amy-Jill (ed.), *A Feminist Companion to the New Testament Apocrypha* (London: Continuum, 2006).

Martin, Dale B., and Patricia Cox Millers (eds), *The Cultural Turn in Late Ancient Studies: Gender, Asceticism, and Historiography* (Durham, NC: Duke University Press, 2005).

Rousselle, Aline, *Porneia: De la maîtrise du corps à la privation sensorielle IIe-IVe siècles de l'ère chrétienne* (Paris: PUF, 1983; English translation: *Porneia: On Desire and the Body in Antiquity*; trans. by Felicia Pheasant; Oxford: Basil Blackwell, 1988).

Shaw, Teresa M., *The Burden of the Flesh: Fasting and Sexuality in Early Christianity* (Minneapolis, MN: Fortress Press, 1998).

Vaage, Leif E., and Vincent L. Wimbush (eds), *Asceticism and the New Testament* (New York: Routledge, 1999).

Wimbush, Vincent L. (ed.), *Discursive Formations, Ascetic Piety and the Interpretation of Early Christian Literature, Semeia* 57 & 58 (1992).

Wimbush, Vincent L., and Richard Valantasis (eds), *Asceticism* (New York: Oxford University Press, 1995).

History of Sexuality/Gender in Antiquity

Castelli, Elizabeth A., and Daniel Boyarin (eds), *Sexuality in Late Antiquity*, Special issue of the *Journal of the History of Sexuality* 10.3–4 (2001).

Cohen, David, and Richard Saller, 'Foucault on Sexuality in Greco-Roman Antiquity', in Jan Goldstein (ed.), *Foucault and the Writing of History* (Oxford: Blackwell, 1994), pp. 35–59.

Foucault, Michel, *The Care of the Self: History of Sexuality III* (New York: Vintage Books, 1986).

Foucault, Michel, *The Use of Pleasure: The History of Sexuality II* (New York: Vintage Books, 1985).

Halperin, David M., John J. Winkler, and Froma I. Zeitlin (eds), *Before Sexuality: The Construction of Erotic Experience in the Ancient Greek World* (Princeton, NJ: Princeton University Press, 1990).

Hawley, Richard, and Barbara Levick (eds), *Women in Antiquity: New Assessments* (New York: Routledge, 1995).

James, Liz (ed.), *Women, Men and Eunuchs: Gender in Byzantium* (New York: Routledge, 1997).

Larmour, David H. J., Paul Allen Miller, and Charles Platter (eds), *Rethinking Sexuality: Foucault and Classical Antiquity* (Princeton, NJ: Princeton University Press, 1997).

Staples, Ariadne, *From Good Goddess to Vestal Virgins: Sex and Category in Roman Religion* (New York: Routledge, 1998).

Egyptian Asceticism

Brakke, David, *Demons and the Making of the Monk: Spiritual Combat in Early Christianity* (Cambridge, MA: Harvard University Press, 2006).

Burton-Christie, Douglas, *The Word in the Desert: Scripture and the Quest for Holiness in Early Christian Monasticism* (New York: Oxford University Press, 1993).

Frank, Georgia, *The Memory of the Eyes: Pilgrims to Living Saints in Christian Late Antiquity* (Berkeley: University of California Press, 2000).

Goehring, James E., *Ascetics, Society, and the Desert: Studies in Egyptian Monasticism* (Harrisburg, PA: Trinity Press International, 1999).

Harmless, William, *Desert Christians: An Introduction to the Literature of Early Monasticism* (New York: Oxford University Press, 2004).

Krawiec, Rebecca, *Shenoute and the Women of the White Monastery: Egyptian Monasticism in Late Antiquity* (New York: Oxford University Press, 2002).

Miller, Patricia Cox, 'Desert Asceticism and "The Body from Nowhere"', *JECS* 2 (1994), pp. 137–53.

Wilfong, Terry G., 'Reading the Disjointed Body in Coptic: From Physical Modification to Textual Fragmentation', in Dominic Montserrat (ed.), *Changing Bodies, Changing Meanings: Studies on the Human Body in Antiquity* (New York: Routledge, 1997), pp. 116–36.

Feminist Studies of Asceticism

Burrus, Virginia, *The Sex Lives of Saints: An Erotics of Ancient Hagiography* (Philadelphia: University of Pennsylvania Press, 2004).

Burrus, Virginia, 'Word and Flesh: The Bodies and Sexuality of Ascetic Women in Christian Antiquity', *JFSR* 10.1 (1994), pp. 27–51.

Cameron, Averil, 'Desert Mothers: Women Ascetics in Early Christian Egypt', in E. Puttick et al. (eds), *Women as Teachers and Disciples in Traditional and New Religions* (Lewiston, NY: Edwin Mellen Press, 1993), pp. 11–24.

— 'Early Christianity and the Discourse of Desire', in Léonie J. Archer, Susan Fischler and Maria Wyke (eds), *Women in Ancient Societies: An Illusion of the Night* (New York: Routledge, 1994), pp. 152–68.

— 'Redrawing the Map: Early Christian Territory after Foucault', *JRS* 76 (1986), pp. 266–71.

Cameron, Averil, 'Virginity as Metaphor: Women and the Rhetoric of Early Christianity', in *eadem* (ed.), *History as Text: The Writing of Ancient History* (London: Duckworth, 1989), pp. 171–205.

Castelli, Elizabeth A., '"I Will Make Mary Male": Pieties of the Body and Gender Transformation of Christian Women in Late Antiquity', in Julia Epstein and Kristina Straub (eds), *Body Guards: The Cultural Contexts of Gender Ambiguity* (New York: Routledge, 1991), pp. 29–49.

Clark, Elizabeth A., *Ascetic Piety and Women's Faith: Essays on Late Ancient Christianity* (Studies in Women and Religion, 20; New York: Edwin Mellen Press, 1986).

— 'Foucault, the Fathers, and Sex', *JAAR* 56 (1986), pp. 619–41.

— 'Patrons, Not Priests: Gender and Power in Late Ancient Christianity', *Gender and History* 2 (1990), pp. 253–73.

— 'Sex, Shame, and Rhetoric: En-gendering Early Christian Ethics', *JAAR* 59 (1991), pp. 221–45.

— 'Theory and Practice in Late Ancient Asceticism: Jerome, Chrysostom, and Augustine', *JFSR* 5.2 (1989), pp. 25–46.

Constantinou, Stavroula, *Female Corporeal Performances: Reading the Body in Byzantine Passions and Lives of Holy Women* (Acta Universitatis Upsaliensis Studie Byzantina Upsaliensia, 9; Uppsala: Uppsala University Press, 2005).

Cooper, Kate, *The Virgin and the Bride: Idealized Womanhood in Late Antiquity* (Cambridge, MA: Harvard University Press, 1996).

Corrington, Gail Paterson, 'Anorexia, Asceticism, and Autonomy: Self-Control as Liberation and Transcendence', *JFSR* 2.2 (1986), pp. 51–61.

— 'The "Divine Woman"? Propaganda and the Power of Celibacy in the New Testament Apocrypha: A Reconsideration', *Anglican Theological Review* 70 (1988), pp. 207–20.

Feichteinger, Barbara, *Apostolae Apostolorum: Frauenaskese als Befreiung und Zwang bei Hieronymous* (Frankfurt am Main: Peter Lang, 1995).

Harrison, Nonna Verna, 'The Feminine Man in Late Antique Ascetic Piety', *Union Seminary Quarterly Review* 48.3–4 (1994), pp. 49–71.

MacDonald, Margaret Y., *Early Christian Women and Pagan Opinion: The Power of the Hysterical Woman* (New York: Cambridge University Press, 1996).

Matthews, Shelly, 'Thinking of Thecla: Issues in Feminist Historiography', *JFSR* 17.2 (2001), pp. 39–55.

Sivan, Hagith, 'On Hymens and Holiness in Late Antiquity: Opposition to Aristocratic Female Asceticism at Rome', *Jahrbuch für Antike und Christentum* 36 (1993), pp. 81–93.

Tilley, Maureen A., 'The Ascetic Body and the (Un)making of the World of the Martyr', *JAAR* 59 (1991), pp. 467–79.

Studies of Traditions of Individual Saints

Albrecht, Ruth, *Das Leben der heiligen Makrina auf dem Hintergrund der Thekla-Traditionen* (Göttingen: Vandenhoeck & Ruprecht, 1986).

Burrus, Virginia, 'Reading Agnes: The Rhetoric of Gender in Ambrose and Prudentius', *JECS* 3 (1995), pp. 25–46.

Castelli, Elizabeth A., 'Mortifying the Body, Curing the Soul: Beyond Ascetic Dualisms in *The Life of St. Syncletica'*, *differences: a Journal of Feminist Cultural Studies* 4.2 (1992), pp. 134–53.

Davis, Stephen J., *The Cult of Saint Thecla: A Tradition of Women's Piety in Late Antiquity* (New York: Oxford University Press, 2001).

Poe, Gary R., 'Spirituality of Fourth and Fifth-Century Eastern Female Asceticism as Reflected in the Life of Saint Syncletica' (Ph.D. diss., Southern Baptist Theological Seminary, 1995).

Studies of Individual Authors

Buell, Denise K., *Making Christians: Clement of Alexandria and the Rhetoric of Legitimacy* (Princeton, NJ: Princeton University Press, 1999).

Hunter, David G., 'The Language of Desire: Clement of Alexandria's Transformation of Ascetic Discourse', *Semeia* 57 (1992), pp. 95–111.

— 'Resistance to the Virginal Ideal in Late-Fourth-Century Rome: The Case of Jovinian', *Theological Studies* 48 (1987), pp. 45–64.

Kraemer, Ross S., 'Monastic Jewish Women in Greco-Roman Egypt: Philo of Alexandria on the Therapeutae and Therapeutrides', *Signs* 14 (1989), pp. 342–60.

Leyerle, Blake, *Theatrical Shows and Ascetic Lives: John Chrysostom's Attack on Spiritual Marriage* (Berkeley: University of California Press, 2001).

Miller, Patricia Cox, 'The Blazing Body: Ascetic Desire in Jerome's Letter to Eustochium', *JECS* 1 (1993), pp. 21–45.

Shaw, Teresa M., 'Creation, Virginity, and Diet in Fourth-Century Christianity: Basil of Ancyra's *On the True Purity of Virginity*', in Maria Wyke (ed.), *Gender and the Body in the Ancient Mediterranean* (Malden, MA: Blackwell, 1998), pp. 155–72.

Ideology, History and the Construction of 'Woman' in Late Ancient Christianity[*]

Elizabeth A. Clark

'... and ain't I a woman?'

Sojourner Truth

I

When in 1851 the black abolitionist Sojourner Truth turned her rhetorical fire against a Protestant clergyman who had ridiculed the campaign for women's suffrage on the grounds that females were helpless and weak, she was not (we may assume) impelled by the debates over 'essentialism' that have unsettled feminist theory for the past decade and more.[1] Nonetheless, the question 'What is "woman"?' was posed far earlier than Sojourner Truth's impassioned speech; indeed, it predates the Patristic era, which is here our proper concern. Moreover, Sojourner Truth's clerical opponent also stood in a long tradition of Christian males whose selective reading of biblical texts, buttressed by a misogynistic inheritance from antiquity, was designed to create 'good [female] subjects' who work 'all by themselves', freely submitting to their inferior status.[2] Such, of course, are the signs of ideology's success. On the signs of failure, I shall later remark.

[*] First published in *JECS*, 2.2 (1994), pp. 155–84. Reprinted with permission. I would especially like to thank for their assistance my colleagues Dale Martin, Kenneth Surin and Annabel Wharton; members of the North Carolina Research Group on Medieval and Early Modern Women; Keith Hopkins; Elizabeth Struthers Malbon; Roger Bagnall; former Duke graduate students Gail Hammer, Kelly Jo Jarrett, Craig Phillips, Kathy Rudy and Randall Styers; and two anonymous readers for the *Journal of Early Christian Studies*.

1 The speech reads in part: 'The man over there says women need to be helped into carriages and lifted over ditches, and to have the best place everywhere. Nobody ever helps me into carriages and over puddles, or gives me the best place – and ain't I a woman? ... Look at my arm! I have ploughed and planted and gathered into barns, and no man could head me – and ain't I a woman? I could work as much and eat as much as a man – when I could get it – and bear the lash as well! And ain't I a woman? I have born thirteen children, and seen most of 'em sold into slavery, and when I cried out with my mother's grief, none but Jesus heard me – and ain't I a woman?' E.C. Stanton, S.B. Anthony and M.J. Gage (eds), *The History of Woman Suffrage* (6 vols.; Rochester, NY, 1881; repr., Salem, NH: Ayer Company, 1985), 1, pp. 115–17. See the discussion of these famous lines (which 'evoke the themes of the suffering servant in order to claim the status of humanity for the shockingly inappropriate/d figure of New World black womanhood') in Donna Haraway, 'Ecce Homo, Ain't (Arn't) I a Woman, and Inappropriate/d Others: The Human in a Post-Humanist Landscape', in Judith Butler and Joan W. Scott (eds), *Feminists Theorize the Political* (New York and London: Routledge, 1992), pp. 86–100 (91).

2 See Louis Althusser's discussion of religious ideology in 'Ideology and Ideological State Apparatuses (Notes Towards an Investigation)', in *idem, Lenin and Philosophy and Other Essays* (trans. Ben Brewster; New York: Monthly Review Press, 1971), pp. 127–86 (181–82).

I shall first discuss the meaning and the mechanisms of ideology as explicated by several modern commentators, before illustrating the operations of an ideology of gender with examples drawn from the writings of the Church Fathers. A third section of the paper suggests some features of the Fathers' social location and the religious apparatus that produced these ideological markers. Last, I shall offer a brief caveat regarding the triumph of an ideology of gender in Patristic literature: some early Christian women – without the help of Gramsci and other theoreticians – could use the hegemonic discourse to their own advantage.

Even within Marx's own writings, the concept of ideology received different formulations, and the emphases developed by his successors have served to complicate further its definition.[3] Does, for example, 'ideology' imply a distinction between 'truth' and 'falsehood' (i.e., 'ideology')?[4] If so, does the commentator believe himself or herself to stand 'outside ideology'? Whence did this privileged epistemological position derive? By contrast, those who claim that 'ideology' is *not* to be equated with 'falsehood' often argue that we are *all* 'in ideology', that there is no way of stepping 'out' of it.[5] But if we are *all* 'in ideology', then the concept surely cannot be as strongly tied to a *particular* class position as some have held:[6] the term would rather function descriptively as a synonym for 'worldview', thus potentially muting the concept's implied critique of power relations. Nonetheless, a middle position has developed in socialist thought since the time of Marx, in which it is alleged that different social classes have their own, varied ideologies; the analyst can, for example, distinguish between a subordinate and a dominant

3 See Michèle Barrett, *The Politics of Truth: From Marx to Foucault* (Stanford, CA: Stanford University Press, 1991), esp. pp. 1–17; Jorge Larrain, *Marxism and Ideology* (Atlantic Highlands, NJ: Humanities Press, 1983); Bhikhu Parekh, *Marx's Theory of Ideology* (Baltimore, MD and London: Johns Hopkins University Press, 1982). As Larrain points out (*Marxism*, p. 54), consistency in defining the concept was not assisted by the fact that the first two generations of Marxist thinkers did not have access to Marx's *The German Ideology*, which was published only in 1923 [Karl Marx, *The German Ideology*, in Karl Marx and Frederick Engels, *Collected Works* (trans. Richard Dixon, et al.; 50 vols; New York: International Publishers, 1976.)]

4 On the view of ideology as 'pre-scientific error', see Larrain, *Marxism*, p. 30; Barrett, *Politics*, p. 109. For a critique, see Michel Foucault, *Power/Knowledge: Selected Interviews and Other Writings, 1972–1977* (ed. and trans. Colin Gordon; New York: Pantheon Books, 1980), p. 118, and discussion in Barrett, *Politics*, p. 123.

5 See Larrain, *Marxism*, pp. 205, 223, 228, especially his discussion of Althusser's view that ideology is 'necessary' to a society, that it serves as 'social cement', in effect (pp. 226–27). This interpretation bears some resemblance to Geertz's and Ricoeur's understandings of ideology as integrative: see George H. Taylor's introduction to Paul Ricoeur, *Lectures on Ideology and Utopia* (New York: Columbia University Press, 1986), p. ix–xxxvi (xix), although Althusser no doubt gives a different evaluation of the 'benefits' of such 'integration'. For Antonio Gramsci, there is a certain 'psychological' validity in ideologies which serve as tools for the organization of masses of humans (*Selections From the Prison Notebooks* [ed. and trans. Quintin Hoare and Geoffrey Nowell Smith; New York: International Publishers, 1971], pp. 376–77).

6 Some commentators argue that it is misunderstanding of Marx to think that social class (rather than the concealment of contradiction) was the defining characteristic of ideology in the first place (see Larrain, *Marxism*, p. 29 for discussion).

ideology.[7] Here, an attempt is made to rescue the critical edge of the concept while conceding that not only the upper classes have – or exist in – 'ideology'.

A helpful contribution to this debate has been Fredric Jameson's suggestion that ideologies might profitably be viewed as 'strategies of containment'. Rejecting the association of ideology with 'false consciousness', Jameson points rather to such characteristic features as 'structural limitation and ideological closure', features that he concedes can also serve to critique forms of Marxism.[8] 'Strategies of containment', 'structural limitation', 'ideological closure': these concepts will prove especially useful for an analysis of the Fathers' ideology of gender.

More recently, Michèle Barrett has argued that 'new social groups' (by which she means primarily women, people of colour, and native residents of post-colonialist countries) should prompt theoreticians to discard concepts of ideology that are based on economic class alone.[9] When her critique is joined to the Althusserian programme that rejects a simple model of economic determinism and assigns more productive force to such superstructural apparatuses as law, education and religion,[10] the way is open for the construction of a less rigidly deterministic model than is frequently associated with a Marxist notion of ideology. Yet over against those who neutralize the concept of ideology in ways that blur the structures of domination at work,[11] I prefer to keep the notion of power at the forefront.

From the numerous recent discussions of ideology, I extract two definitions that I think are useful for my purposes. The first is supplied by Anthony Giddens: ideology, he writes, is 'the mode in which forms of signification are incorporated within systems of domination so as to sanction their continuance'.[12] The second is from John B. Thompson, for whom ideology designates 'the ways in which meaning serves, in particular circumstances, to establish and sustain relations of power which

---

7 See the discussions in Larrain, *Marxism*, pp. 46, 88, 233; Parekh, *Marx's Theory*, pp. 33, 48; and Barrett, *Politics*, p. 21.

8 Fredric Jameson, *The Political Unconscious: Narrative as a Socially Symbolic Act* (Ithaca, NY: Cornell University Press, 1981), pp. 52–53.

9 Barrett, *Politics*, pp. 32–33, 158–59.

10 For Althusser's discussion, see his 'Ideology and Ideological State Apparatuses', esp. pp. 141–57. Indeed, Althusser so privileges the realm of superstructure that he can write: '... in History, these instances, the superstructures, etc. – are never seen to step respectfully aside when their work is done or, when the Time comes, as his pure phenomena, to scatter before His Majesty the Economy as he strides along the royal road of the Dialectic. From the first moment to the last, the lonely hour of the "last instance" never comes' ('Contradiction and Overdetermination: Notes for an Investigation', in *idem, For Marx* [trans. Ben Brewster; London and New York: Verso, 1990], pp. 86–128 (113)). Also see Gramsci's discussion of Marx's comment that 'a popular conviction often has the same energy as a material force...' (*Selections from the Prison Notebooks*, p. 377).

11 Singled out by Larrain as one of the most significant fates of the concept of 'ideology' after Marx: *Marxism*, p. 88. Sometimes referred to as a more 'positive' view of ideology, the developments are linked to Lenin and then Lukács.

12 Anthony Giddens, 'Four Theses on Ideology', *Canadian Journal of Political and Social Theory/ Revue canadienne de théorie politique et sociale,* 7 (1983), pp. 18–21 (19).

are systematically asymmetrical'; it is 'meaning in the service of power'.[13] These definitions, in my judgement, have the advantage over many others in stressing power and power differentials, on the one hand, and the role of discursive formations in shaping the construction of the self, on the other – points often passed over by earlier theorists, who shied away from the Marxist tone of 'domination' and remained blissfully ignorant of structuralist and post-structuralist analysis. In addition, both Giddens and Thompson eschew definitions which simplistically pit 'truth' versus 'falsehood', thus implying that the theorist has a firm stand *outside* ideology by which to distinguish it from 'science'.[14] Nonetheless, most recent commentators, as political Leftists, tend to mean by the word ideology 'the ideology of the dominant classes', which to them necessarily cries out for critique.

Developing themes broached by Louis Althusser several decades ago,[15] recent analysts of ideology who are informed by post-structuralist theory affirm that 'the subject' created by ideology is not a unitary consciousness, but is multiple and always exists in a process of construction. This recognition, as John Frow puts it, leaves space for 'the possible discontinuity between positions occupied within the economic, political and symbolic orders',[16] and thus acknowledges the likelihood of 'uneven developments' among an individual's social, economic, educational, legal (and so on) statuses.[17] This last point provides an important theoretical tool for analysis of notable Christian women in late antiquity who suffered from such 'uneven developments', from 'status dissonance': to this issue I shall return.

To unpack the central characteristics of ideology and to indicate their primary literary components is my first task. Commentators agree that a central function of

---

13 John B. Thompson, *Ideology and Modern Culture: Critical Theory in the Era of Mass Communication* (Stanford, CA: Stanford University Press, 1990), p. 7. Both Giddens's and Thompson's definitions seem to me to be more adequate than those of Michèle Barrett, who tends to underplay (at least in her definitions) the 'power' aspect of ideology's work: 'discursive and significatory mechanisms that may occlude, legitimate, naturalise or universalize in a variety of different ways but can all be said to mystify' – although Barrett's concern to lower 'the epistemological profile of the concept of ideology, while broadening its practical applicability' (*Politics*, p. 167) is welcome.

14 Sometimes thought to be a problem in the early Althusser of *For Marx*. See discussion in Giddens, 'Four Theses', p. 19; John Frow, *Marxism and Literary History* (Cambridge, MA: Harvard University Press, 1986), pp. 26–29, 51; Bruce Robbins, 'The Politics of Theory', *Social Text*, 18 (1987/88), pp. 3–18 (15). For a different construction of Althusser's understanding of 'science', see Terry Eagleton, *Ideology: An Introduction* (London and New York: Verso, 1991), p. 139. For a recent critique of these points, see Nancy C.M. Hartsock, 'Louis Althusser's Structural Marxism: Political Clarity and Theoretical Distortions', *Rethinking Marxism* 4 (1991), pp. 10–40.

15 Althusser abandoned the rigid Marxist notion that the material 'base' entirely determines the cultural 'superstructure', allowing that religious, legal (etc.) systems also work on the economic. See Althusser, 'Ideology', pp. 134–36, 141–48.

16 Frow, *Marxism*, p. 76; see also Rosalind Coward and John Ellis, *Language and Materialism: Developments in Semiology and the Theory of the Subject* (London: Routledge & Kegan Paul, 1977), pp. 7, 68.

17 The term is usually employed by Marxist writers focusing on the economy: see the following references in Althusser's *For Marx*, pp. 200–1, 210, 212, 250; also see his essay, 'Est-il simple d'être Marxiste en philosophie?', *La Pensée*, 183 (1975), pp. 3–31 (17). The phrase seems appropriate in a wider context to suggest the divergence of statuses for one individual, perhaps analogous to 'status dissonance'.

ideology is to 'fix' representations of the self,[18] to constitute 'concrete individuals as subjects'.[19] The 'fixing' of the self operates through various mechanisms, for example, through stereotyping, claimed by Roland Barthes as ideology's central mode of operation.[20] Indeed, stereotyping will prove to be one of the Church Fathers' most frequently employed strategies for the symbolic construction of 'woman'.[21]

Moreover – and related to stereotyping – ideology naturalizes and universalizes its subjects, ignoring the 'historical sedimentation'[22] that undergirds the present state of affairs. Ideology thus functions to obscure the notion that ideas and beliefs are particular and local, situated in specific times, places and groups;[23] to the contrary, it encourages the view that our society's values *have* no history, but are eternal and 'natural'.[24] Situations that have come about through human construction are thus rationalized and legitimated as conforming to timeless truth. According to Marx, the ideologist turns the consequences of society into the consequences of nature.[25]

Paradoxically, while ideology collapses history into 'the natural', it still directs its subjects to contemplate ideals of the past rather than to envision a different future. Traditional symbols and values are upheld in one arena – for example, gender – while other aspects of the social, economic or political orders change. Closing the gap between the past and the present by privileging the past is thus one of the conservative operations of ideology.[26] As medievalist Brian Stock argues, this approach to history is basically 'theological': the alleged rationality of the past is pitted against the chaotic irrationality of the present.[27] Nowhere in Patristic literature are such tendencies more evident than in the Church Fathers' exhortations to and

18 Coward and Ellis, *Language*, p. 2. Their discussion owes much to Lacan throughout; see especially p. 7 and ch. 6.

19 Althusser, 'Ideology', p. 171.

20 Roland Barthes, *The Pleasure of the Text* (trans. R. Miller; New York: Hill and Wang/Farrar, Straus and Giroux, 1975), p. 40, discussed in Coward and Ellis, *Language*, p. 54.

21 On 'symbolic construction', see Thompson, *Ideology*, p. 60.

22 The phrase is from Gayatri Spivak's discussion of ideology in 'The Politics of Interpretation', in W.J.T. Mitchell (ed.), *The Politics of Interpretation* (Chicago and London: University of Chicago Press, 1983), pp. 347–66 (347).

23 See Eagleton, *Ideology*, p. 59. His list of ideology's functions: '*unifying, action-oriented, rationalizing, legitimating, universalizing* and *naturalizing*' (p. 45).

24 Thompson, *Studies in the Theory of Ideology* (Berkeley and Los Angeles: University of California Press, 1984), p. 131, citing C. Lefort; also see Parekh, *Marx's Theory*, pp. 36, 49, 136. For a discussion of this 'naturalizing' aspect of ideology as 'the pre-constructed' ('what everyone knows'), see Michel Pêcheux, *Language, Semantics and Ideology* (trans. Harbans Nagpal; New York: St. Martin's Press, 1982; French original, 1975), pp. 115–16, 121.

25 Marx, *The German Ideology* 2.1B; cf 1.1.1.4; 1.1.22 in Marx and Engels, *Collected Works*, 5, pp. 479, 36, 39.

26 Thompson, *Ideology*, p. 41; *idem, Studies*, p. 186. Also relevant is Karl Mannheim's comment: 'It is no accident that whereas all progressive groups regard the idea as coming before the deed, for the conservative … the idea of an historical reality becomes visible only subsequently, when the world has already assumed a fixed form' [*Ideology and Utopia: An Introduction to the Sociology of Knowledge* (trans. L. Wirth and E. Shils; New York: Harcourt, Brace & Co., 1946), p. 208].

27 Brian Stock, *Listening for the Text: On the Uses of the Past* (Baltimore, MD and London: Johns Hopkins University Press, 1990), p. 84. One could complain that this use of the word 'theological' is overly pejorative: after all, theologically inspired visions have sometimes stimulated progressive social change.

chastisement of women, based on nostalgia for the ideals of a bygone era rather than on the laws and customs pertaining to women in their *own* day.

Moreover, commentators on ideological literature claim that certain types of writing and signification are especially adept at conveying these effects. Thus myth, which in Roland Barthes's phrase 'transforms history into nature',[28] is a prime suspect. According to some literary theorists, a second candidate, perhaps born out of mythic writing,[29] is narrative, for narrative, they claim, works in tandem with the 'backward-looking' orientation of ideology to serve as the carrier of conservative values. It is perhaps no coincidence that the narratives from which such critics derive their examples were those that developed in bourgeois society during the eighteenth and nineteenth centuries, and which through their authors' imaginative constructions suggested that the values of such society were universal and natural. In this approach to narrative, the focus is on the stories of the past told by the dominant classes, which 'create a sense of belonging to a community and to a history which transcends the experience of conflict, difference and division'; such stories, in John Thompson's words, 'justify the exercise of power by those who possess it' and 'serve to reconcile others to the fact that they do not'.[30] Since the coherence, integrity and closure that narrative projects upon its depiction of life is purely 'imaginary',[31] in Hayden White's phrase, it functions to promote a 'mythical view of reality'.[32] White further claims that history-writing of the narrative type is likewise implicated, for the notions of continuity, wholeness and individuality – the 'essentialized self' – that mark historical narrative as much as novelistic narrative are the very qualities which construct subjects who will be the law-abiding and self-regulating citizens that our society demands.[33] Adopting Althusser's definition of ideology for his own critique of narrative historiography, White argues that in narrative, individuals are taught to live 'an imaginary relation to their real condi-

---

28 Roland Barthes, *Mythologies* (trans. Annette Lavers; New York: Noonday Press/Farrar, Straus and Giroux, 1972), p. 129; cf. Coward and Ellis, *Language*, p. 29.

29 Roland Barthes, 'The Discourse of History', trans. Stephen Bann, in E.S. Shaffer (ed.), *Comparative Criticism: A Yearbook* (25 vols.; Cambridge, UK: Cambridge University Press, 1981), 3, pp. 3–20 (18).

30 Thompson, *Ideology*, pp. 61–62; *idem*, *Studies*, p. 11. Commentators on ideology tend to view narrative much less positively than do contemporary theologians and philosophers who stress the valuable role of narrative in creating community: from the standpoint of ideological critiques, that 'community' is precisely founded on exclusion. Although many feminists might argue that narrative is not necessarily a conservative genre and that it can serve progressive ends, commentators on ideology are more apt to stress the reactionary workings of narrative, no doubt because narratives are usually constructed by those who control cultural meaning.

31 Hayden White, 'The Value of Narrativity in the Representation of Reality', *Critical Inquiry*, 7 (1980), pp. 5–27 (27).

32 Hayden White, *The Content of the Form: Narrative Discourse and Historical Representation* (Baltimore, MD and London: Johns Hopkins University Press, 1987), p. ix; *idem*, 'The Historical Text as Literary Artifact', in R.H. Canary and H. Kozicki (eds), *The Writing of History: Literary Form and Historical Understanding* (Madison: University of Wisconsin Press, 1978), pp. 41–62 (48–49), 61.

33 Hayden White, 'Droysen's *Historik*: Historical Writing as a Bourgeois Science', in *idem*, *Content*, pp. 83–103 (87).

tions of existence'.[34] Commentators such as White and Barthes, who hold this view of narrative, would deem it no accident that Patristic writers turn largely to biblical myths and historical narratives to create models of submission for female audiences.[35]

Yet other literary theorists and feminist commentators would question both the characteristics here ascribed to narrative and their allegedly conservative function. The tendency to associate the literary inscription of ideology with purely formal categories such as representation, narrative closure and the centred subject, Jameson comments, 'brackets the historical situations in which texts are effective and insists that ideological positions can be identified by the identification of inner-textual or purely formal features', as if the latter 'always and everywhere bear the same ideological charge'. Such a formalist approach (which Jameson associates with a type of French theory that emanated from *Tel quel* and *Screen*, and, in another mode, from Derrida) is simply 'ahistorical'.[36] Feminists would here join Jameson to claim that narrations can embody utopian impulses as well as (negative) 'ideological' ones.[37] On this alternative assessment of narrative – to which I shall return in my discussion of the Fathers' construction of an ideology of gender – narratives are necessary for situating one's analysis within a larger historical context;[38] in Jameson's words, 'the unity of a single great collective story' is important for understanding the cultural past, its polemics and its 'vital claims upon us'.[39] Feminist theorists such as Nancy Fraser and Linda J. Nicholson would add that although grand metanarratives inattentive to temporal and cultural specificity should be discarded, feminists indeed *need* 'large historical narratives' that detail the particularity of sexism across diverse times and societies.[40] Presumably feminist theorists would agree that narrative can be used not only to open up the past and connect it with the present, but to sketch a vision of the future: here, narrative acquires a potentially utopian function. Given the varying political functions of narrative, it will be of interest to note how frequently the Church Fathers deploy narrative to restrict women's activities in their own day, to offer 'strategies of containment'.

---

34 Althusser, 'Ideology', p. 162; White, *Content*, p. x. See also Michel de Certeau's attack on narrative that produces a 'textual globalization' for the unscientific discipline of historiography: 'History, Science and Fiction', in *idem*, *Heterologies: Discourse on the Other* (trans. Brian Massumi; Theory and History of Literature, 17; Minneapolis: University of Minnesota Press, 1986), pp. 199–221 (219).

35 According to Hayden White, narrative itself carries with it a moralizing message ('Value', pp. 18, 26).

36 Jameson, *Political Unconscious*, p. 283 n. 2.

37 Feminist science fiction is sometimes noted as particularly adept in conveying feminist utopian effects. I thank former Duke graduate student Kathy Rudy for this reminder.

38 Steven Best and Douglas Kellner, *Postmodern Theory: Critical Investigations* (New York: Guilford Press, 1991), p. 186.

39 Jameson, *Political Unconscious*, p. 19. The 'single great collective story' for Jameson is, of course, Marxism, whose master theme is 'the collective struggle to wrest a realm of Freedom from a realm of Necessity' (p. 19).

40 Nancy Fraser and Linda J. Nicholson, 'Social Criticism without Philosophy: An Encounter between Feminism and Postmodernism', in Linda J. Nicholson (ed.), *Feminism/Postmodernism* (New York and London: Routledge, 1990), pp. 19–38 (34), cf. p. 22 on Lyotard's critique of meta-narratives.

The assistance that myth and narrative sometimes lend to impressing ideological meaning on their audiences is joined by a particular literary device that can be adeptly manipulated to express ideological meaning: intertextual reading and writing practices, in which one text is 'read' in light of other explicitly or implicitly suggested texts, and in which both text and intertext are transformed by their new positioning.[41] Originally explored by literary theorists in relation to the realist novel,[42] intertextuality is sometimes claimed as a technique that contributes to making the story seem 'natural' – that is, its effect is ideological.[43]

Investigating ancient Jewish texts, Daniel Boyarin in his book *Intertextuality and the Reading of Midrash* has explained the function of intertextual interpretation in these words:

> Intertextuality is, in a sense, the way that history, understood as cultural and ideological change and conflict, records itself within textuality. As the text is the transformation of a signifying system and of a signifying practice, it embodies the more or less untransformed detritus of the previous system. These fragments of the previous system and the fissures they create on the surface of the text reveal conflictual dynamics which led to the present textual system.[44]

Intertextual exegesis is especially apt to be employed when an ancient text has been granted sacred status – and hence must be retained as Scripture – but contemporary commentators feel called to 'read' it so that it addresses the concerns of their own day rather than those of the text's authors: texts that were unrelated, or worse, in conflict, are now harmonized into a new, unified system of meaning. The 'fissures' that the critic's eye spots belie the apparent smooth surface of the new text at hand, in which the 'detritus' of the old system has been patched together with the new. In this sense, intertextual writing and reading practices could be seen as a form of interpretation pure and simple, if with Jameson we define interpretation as 'the rewriting or restructuration of a prior historical or ideological *subtext*, it always being understood that the "subtext" is not immediately present as such ... but must rather always be (re)constructed after the fact'.[45] Although intertextual writing practices do not *necessarily* signal

---

41 Frow, *Marxism*, p. 157.

42 See, e.g., M.M. Bakhtin, *The Dialogic Imagination: Four Essays* (ed. M. Holquist; trans. C. Emerson and M. Holquist; Austin: University of Texas Press, 1981); Julia Kristeva, *Le Texte du roman: Approche sémiologique d'une structure discursive transformationnelle* (Approaches to Semiotics, 6; The Hague and Paris: Mouton, 1970), pp. 69–70; *idem*, *La Révolution du language poétique: L'Avant-Garde à la fin du XIXᵉ siècle: Lautréamont et Mallarmé* (Paris: Editions du Seuil, 1974), pp. 59–60. Kristeva was fascinated by Bakhtin's understanding of the 'literary word' as an 'intersection of textual surfaces'; in her opinion, he was the first to see that 'any text is constructed as a mosaic of quotations; any text is the absorption and transformation of another'. Language thus carries social and political messages: 'History and morality are written and read within the infra-structure of texts', she claims ('Word, Dialogue and Novel', in Toril Moi [ed.], *The Kristeva Reader* [New York: Columbia University Press, 1986], pp. 36, 37; original English translation in Kristeva's *Desire in Language* [1980]) pp. 36–41.

43 Coward and Ellis, *Language*, p. 52; Frow, *Marxism*, pp. 101–102, 125, 155–57.

44 Daniel Boyarin, *Intertextuality and the Reading of Midrash* (Bloomington and Indianapolis: Indiana University Press, 1990), p. 94.

45 Jameson, *Political Unconscious*, p. 81.

the conveyance of a conservative message, the Church Fathers, we shall see, construct a restrictive message for women of their era via some ingenious inter-textual reading and writing practices: here, 'strategies of containment' operate through intertextuality.

Given these strong workings of ideology, the critic's task will be to show how 'seemingly politically innocent objects, forms of subjectivity, actions, and events' are the effects of power and authority,[46] that is, the task is to 'de-naturalize' and 're-historicize' what the ideological operations have produced.[47] The would-be unmasker of ideology must attend to 'the constructed nature of the "real"'[48] and to the conditions under which that construction took place. By what Althusser calls a 'symptomatic reading', she must look to the gaps and absences in the text, read what in effect is 'illegible', note how the answers given by a writer do not correspond to the questions he posed.[49] By interpretive practices such as these, the critic interrogates 'the implicit narratives, grammars, and rhetorics that reproduce and reinforce forms of power and authority'.[50] Thus she explores the use of symbolic forms in creating and sustaining relations of domination.[51]

II

My exploration of the ideology of gender in the Church Fathers will proceed by first examining the characteristics of ideology as set forth in the previous section (stere-otyping, universalizing, naturalizing and the appeal of the past); then I shall turn to the literary forms and devices that offered 'strategies of containment' through which the Fathers attempted to define female subjectivity.

Examples of the stereotyping, universalizing and naturalizing of 'woman' in Patristic literature are so manifest that a few should suffice to remind us of their prevalence. Examining the literary corpus of Jerome, for example, the reader learns that the stereotypic trait of 'woman is her weakness', sometimes aligned with 'softness of soul'[52] or 'fickle-mindedness'[53] – yet Jerome can resort to

---

46 Michael J. Shapiro, *The Politics of Representation: Writing Practices in Biography, Photography, and Political Analysis* (Madison: University of Wisconsin Press, 1988), p. 21.

47 Shapiro, *Politics*, p. 51. Here, Althusser's claim that Marx was the founder of the 'science' of history is striking; see his essay, 'Philosophy as a Revolutionary Weapon', in *Lenin*, p. 15.

48 Shapiro, *Politics*, p. 24.

49 Louis Althusser, 'From *Capital* to Marx's Philosophy', in *idem* and E. Balibar, *Reading 'Capital'* (London and New York: Verso, 1979), pp. 11–70 (28). See also Shapiro, *Politics*, p. 22; Frow, *Marxism*, pp. 24–25. Rosemary Hennessy defines 'symptomatic reading' as 'a practice which makes sense of the gaps in narrative coherence as signs of the dis-ease that infects the social imaginary'; a practice that 'draws out the unnaturalness of the text and makes visible another logic haunting its surface' (*Materialist Feminism and the Politics of Discourse* [New York and London: Routledge, 1993], pp. xvii, 93).

50 Shapiro, *Politics*, p. 54.

51 Thompson, *Ideology*, p. 85.

52 Jerome, *hom. 42 on Ps. 127/128* (CCL 78.265); *Nah.* (on Nahum 3.13–17) (CCL 76A.569); *Is. 2* (on Is. 3.16) (CCL 73.55).

53 Jerome, *ep.* 130.17 (CSEL 56.197–98): here used as a reason why ascetic women should live in community. That Jerome's stress on women's 'weakness' is an ancient notion that also can be found

the *topos* of 'feminine weakness' to produce a variety of ideological effects. Sometimes he appeals to 'female weakness' to deter women from embarking on actions that would lure them toward pleasures too difficult to resist – warnings against second marriage, for example, or against a widow's appearing in public surrounded by handsome male servants.[54] At other times, the 'weakness' characteristic of the sex serves to highlight the exemplary labours a few 'token' women were able to perform *despite* their inherent disability: Paula and Eustochium's monastic life in Palestine is a case-in-point.[55] Moreover, the *topos* of female weakness can be used as a shaming device for males, as when Jerome mocks those men, would-be Christian teachers but deficient in Aristotle and Cicero, who dare to enter the company only of the uneducated and of 'weak women'.[56] Or, finally (and contradictorily), he can praise a member of the 'weaker sex' who has 'overcome the world' (i.e., given up sexual relations), using his encomium on the feminine 'weakness' to shame the matron's recalcitrant husband.[57] It is instructive how the same stereotype can thus serve very differing ends for Jerome: yet even when the intent is to compliment, the praise is delivered via the denigration of women-in-general.

In the writings of John Chrysostom, stereotyping of female characteristics appears especially in his warnings to men to eschew either first or second marriage, where Chrysostom calls women wicked, false, insulting, garrulous, irrational and given to drink – 'all the vices dear to the sex'.[58] But nothing surpasses Chrysostom's rhetorical catalogue of female characteristics that will be impressed upon the soul of any ascetic man who dares to take up residence with a female ascetic in 'spiritual marriage'. The women, he writes, 'render them [the men] softer, more hot-headed, shameful, mindless, irascible, insolent, importunate, ignoble, crude, servile, niggardly, reckless, nonsensical, and, to sum it up, the women take all their corrupting feminine customs and stamp them into the souls of these men'.[59] To be sure, none of Jerome's or Chrysostom's *special* female friends, such as Paula or Olympias, shared these characteristics – but they were not, it seems, 'woman'.[60] They alone of their sex escape this negative stereotyping.

'Naturalizing' and 'universalizing' are two additional mechanisms of ideology, and the naturalizing and universalizing of 'woman' is likewise abundantly evident

---

in Roman law is stressed by Anita Arjava, 'Jerome and Women', *Arctos: Acta Philologica Fennica* 23 (1989), pp. 5–18 (8–9); Joëlle Beaucamp, 'Le Vocabulaire de la faiblesse feminine dans les texts juridiques romains du IIIe au IVe siècle', *Revue historique du droit français et étranger* 54 (1976), pp. 485–508, and Suzanne Dixon, '*Infirmitas sexus*: Womanly Weakness in Roman Law', *Tijdschrift voor Rechtsgeschidenis/Revue d'Histoire du Droit/The Legal History Review* 52 (1984), pp. 343–71.

54 Jerome, *ep.* 54.13 (CSEL 54.479).
55 Jerome, *ep.* 66.13 (CSEL 54.664).
56 Jerome, *ep.* 50.1; 5 (CSEL 54.388–89, 393–94).
57 Jerome, *ep.* 122.4 (CSEL 56.70).
58 John Chrysostom, *laud. Max.* 2 (PG 51. 227); cf. Chrysostom, *virg.* 40.1 (SC 125.232).
59 John Chrysostom, *subintr.* 10 (PG 47.510).
60 Hence, the frequent claim that they ceased to be 'women': see the discussion in Elizabeth A. Clark, 'Friendship Between the Sexes: Classical Theory and Christian Practice', in *eadem, Jerome, Chrysostom, and Friends: Essays and Translations* (Women and Religion, 2; New York and Toronto: Edwin Mellen Press, 1979), pp. 35–106 (54–57).

in the writings of the Church Fathers. The varied uses of the word 'nature' in patristic literature have often been remarked: from serving as a synonym for 'God'[61] to designating bodily necessities such as food,[62] from naming the limit for acceptable sexual expression[63] to designating a girl's arrival at puberty,[64] from indicating 'our common humanity'[65] to expressing women's weakness and delicacy,[66] from signalling the sexual impulse itself[67] to (paradoxically) representing virginity (the 'natural' condition of humanity)[68] – and supplying the leading moral argument against homosexuality,[69] bestiality,[70] long hair on men,[71] cosmetics,[72] women appearing without head coverings,[73] adultery[74] and non-vaginal forms of heterosexual intercourse.[75] As this catalogue suggests, matters concerning sex and gender are by far the dominant category within which appeals to 'nature' are made by the Church Fathers. In addition, women's subjection to men as a 'natural' phenomenon (i.e., instituted from the time of creation, by God's command) is also a common theme,[76] although the alternative construction, that women were subjected to men only *after* the first sin, sits by its side in Patristic writings.[77] The primary consistency in these appeals to 'nature' lies in the use of the *topos* as a controlling device for sex and gender issues.[78]

As for the universalizing tendency of ideology, nowhere is this more obvious in Patristic literature than in the amalgamation of all women to 'woman' and the identification of 'woman' with Eve. Since Scriptural verses themselves (namely, 1 Tim. 2.11–15) hold Eve to be the 'reason' for the limitation of women's activities and sphere of authority, the motif of 'woman as Eve' was thought to come with apostolic

---

61 Tertullian, *cult. fem.* 1.8.1 (CCL 1.350); John Chrysostom, *hom. 26 1 Cor.* 4 (PG 61.217).

62 E.g., John Chrysostom, *hom. 19 1 Cor.* 4 (PG 61.535).

63 Tertullian, *pud.* 4. 5 (CCL 2.1287).

64 E.g., Tertullian, *virg.* 11.1–4 (CCL 2. 1220–21).

65 E.g., John Chrysostom, *hom. 6 Matt.* 8 (PG 57.72) (here the phrase is *koinon genos*); *hom. 48 Matt.* 3 (PG 58.490).

66 E.g., John Chrysostom, *hom. 8 Matt.* 4 (PG 57.87); *hom. 55 Matt.* 6 (PG 58.548).

67 E.g., John Chrysostom, *virg.* 19.1 (SC 125.156); *hom. 2 Eph.* 3 (PG 62.20); Jerome, *ep.* 54.9 (CSEL 54.475).

68 Jerome, *ep.* 22.19 (CSEL, 54.169); Gregory of Nyssa, *virg.* 12.2 (SC 119.400).

69 E.g., John Chrysostom, *hom. 42 Gen.* 5 (PG 54.391); *hom. 4 Rom.* 1 (PG 60.417); *oppugn.* 3.8 (PG 47.360–61).

70 E.g., John Chrysostom, *hom. 9 Rom.* 4 (PG 60.472).

71 John Chrysostom, *educ. lib.* 16 (B.K. Exarchos [ed.], *Johannes Chrysostomos, Uber Hoffart und Kindererziehung* [München: Max Hueber Verlag, 1955], pp. 42–43).

72 E.g., John Chrysostom, *hom. 18 1 Cor.* 3 (PG 61.148); Jerome, *ep.* 38.3 (CSEL 54.291).

73 E.g., John Chrysostom, *hom. 26 1 Cor.* 4 (PG 61.217–18).

74 John Chrysostom, *hom. 3 Tit.* 4 (PG 62.682).

75 Augustine, *nupt.* 2.20.35 (CSEL 42.289); *bon. coniug.* 11.12 (CSEL 41.203–4).

76 E.g., John Chrysostom, *hom. 10 Col.* 1 (PG 62.365–66); *hom. 26 1 Cor.* 4 (PG 61.215); *hom. 9 1 Tim.* 1 (PG 62.544).

77 E.g. John Chrysostom, *serm. 5 Gen.* 1; 3 (PG 54.599, 602); *hom. 26 1 Cor.* 2 (PG 61.215); *hom. 9 1 Tim.* 1 (PG 62.544).

78 For a discussion of the use of the word 'nature' in some roughly contemporary secular literature, see John J. Winkler's analysis in *The Constraints of Desire: The Anthropology of Sex and Gender in Ancient Greece* (New York: Routledge, 1990), esp. pp. 17–22, 38–44, 217–20.

sanction. Although numerous Church Fathers and ecclesiastical documents use the identification of women with Eve as the justification for women's submission to men and for their exclusion from the priesthood and public teaching offices,[79] perhaps none is so vociferous as Tertullian. Informing his female audience why they should wear 'garments of penitence', Tertullian declaims:

> *You* are the Devil's gateway; *you* are the unsealer of that tree; *you* are the first foresaker of that divine law; *you* are the one who persuaded him whom the Devil was not brave enough to approach; *you* so lightly crushed the image of God, the man Adam; because of *your* punishment, that is, death, even the Son of God had to die. And you think to adorn yourself beyond your 'tunics of skins' (Gen. 3.21)?[80]

Stereotyping, naturalizing, universalizing – three common ideological mechanisms through which the Church Fathers constructed 'woman'.

Perhaps less well explored than these familiar motifs are the uses of history by which the Fathers attempted to mould women's behaviour in their own day, how they sought to 'fix' the subjectivity of contemporary women by an appeal to the past: here, their construction of a Christian narrative is most often directed toward 'strategies of containment'. Nonetheless, their project suffers from a certain incoherence, since their appeal to examples from yesteryear lacks a consistent approach to 'salvation history' into which these examples could be inserted. The ideological function of their appeals to history is betrayed by their indecision as to whether *Heilsgeschichte* – which in many other circumstances they would read as a message of liberation – should so be understood when the topic is 'woman'. Several problems beset the larger historiographical enterprise: Could a progressive view of revelation that assumes an upward development from the realm of 'the old' ('Law') to that of 'the new' ('Grace') be squared with the belief that each Scriptural verse – 'old' as well as 'new' – was equally sacred and meaningful? Was the trajectory of revelation upward, or simply 'flat'? And where should the Church of the present be placed? Had it been even more gloriously endowed with grace than the apostolic era, or had it suffered a downward slide from its primitive lustre? Was 'woman' to remain a constant in a history that itself evolved either 'upward' or 'downward'? Did the appeal to history work its ideological function by closing the gap between past and present – or did the appeal itself ironically serve to widen the gulf?

Although typology and allegory were two common ways in which the Fathers resolved the problem of interpreting the Old Testament in relation to the New so that the validity of *both* Testaments was upheld, when they sought biblical inspiration for directing female behaviour in their *own* era, they were not much interested in either

---

79 See discussion of Chrysostom's argument in Elizabeth A. Clark, 'Devil's Gateway and Bride of Christ: Women in the Early Christian World', in *eadem*, *Ascetic Piety and Women's Faith: Essays on Late Ancient Christianity* (Women and Religion, 20; Lewiston, NY and Queenston, Ont.: Edwin Mellen Press, 1986), pp. 23–60 (31–32); for references to the patristic texts on the subject, see Roger Gryson, *The Ministry of Women in the Early Church* (trans. J. Laporte and M.L. Hall; Collegeville, MN: Liturgical Press, 1976). For a lively recent discussion, see Karen Jo Torjesen, *When Women Were Priests: Women's Leadership in the Early Church and the Scandal of their Subordination in the Rise of Christianity* (San Francisco, CA: HarperSanFrancisco, 1993).

80 Tertullian, *cult. fem.* 1.1.2 (CCL 1.343).

typology or allegory: they wanted stories about 'real' women for their hortatory and moralizing projects.[81] Insofar as they read Genesis 1–3 as 'history', they received extra assistance – from Eve – in their quest for 'real' negative exemplars. Yet their approach to history was not motivated by antiquarian interests, for even when they appealed to sections of the Bible usually classified as historical writings, their very project – the chastisement and moral uplift of women – militated against a strictly historical reading. In their hands, the biblical stories acquired a certain timelessness, that is, they took on features of myth. As John Frow has expressed it in writing of the literary canon, once a text becomes part of a canon that must speak meaningfully to daily life in a different era, it is 'removed from its real historical time to be situated in a time of habitual repetition', an 'ideal nontime'.[82] And here, once more, we find ourselves in the realm of ideology: history is (paradoxically) erased on the very occasion that it is appealed to. The 'history of women' has been flattened to the 'myth of woman'.

This approach to history in the Church Fathers we might label, with Brian Stock, 'traditionalistic', by which he means 'the self-conscious affirmation of traditional norms' selected from the past 'to serve present needs'.[83] Thus the Fathers call up examples from the Greek and Roman past as models for Christian women's behaviour: Lucretia and Dido are put to the service of Christian chastity and monogamy.[84] Patristic writers liked to recall the 'good old days' of Greece and Rome when women were under stricter control of their fathers and husbands. Then, women stayed at home, spun, and were submissive to their husbands. Thus the Fathers align themselves with the distant legal and social past of Greece and Rome, not with the legal and social 'present' of women's lives in their own era.[85] Their rhetorical appeals to the glories of past tradition were noticeably out of step with the actual legal condition of women in their own era – women who could, for example, retain their own property separate from their husband's, serve as guardians to their children,

---

81 Douglas Burton-Christie has also noted the appeal to exemplary characters of Scripture as 'the primary means through which the Bible entered and affected the imaginations of those who took up life in the desert' (*The Word in the Desert: Scripture and the Quest for Holiness in Early Christian Monasticism* [New York and Oxford: Oxford University Press, 1993], p. 167).

82 Frow, *Marxism*, pp. 101, 230.

83 Stock, *Listening*, p. 164, contrasted with 'traditional action', defined as 'the habitual pursuit of inherited norms of conduct, which are taken to be society's norm'.

84 Tertullian, *mon.* 17.2 (CCL 2.1252); *cast.* 13.3 (CCL 2.1034–35); Jerome, *Iou.* 1, 43; 46; 49 (PL 23.286, 287–88, 294); *ep.* 79.7 (CSEL 55.96).

85 Jerome, *ep.* 107.10 (CSEL 55.3). In *ep.* 121.6 (CSEL 56.22), Jerome has high praise for Xenophon's *Oeconomicus*, which contains traditional household regulations. For Augustine, see *ep.* 262 to Ecdicia (CSEL 57.621–31). For Augustine's picture of his own mother's wifely submission, see *conf.* 9.9.19–22 (CCL 27.145–47). Judith Evans-Grubbs notes that Augustine's close tie to his mother may represent a 'continuity with the pre-Christian Roman past', in which close relations between mothers and adult sons appear to have been common (Review of Suzanne Dixon's *The Roman Mother*, in *Classical Philology* 85 [1990], pp. 333–38 [338]). The hearkening back to 'the good old days' is characteristic of (pagan) Latin moralists and satire writers: see Judith Evans-Grubbs, *Law and Family in Late Antiquity: The Emperor Constantine's Legislation on Marriage* (Oxford: Oxford University Press, 1995), ch. 2.

and initiate divorce.[86] The Fathers' appeals can be better understood, however, if we contemplate the lack of success churchmen had experienced in making law their *own* stands against divorce or a husband's sexual straying:[87] the force of rhetorical

86 For discussions of the changes in Roman law pertaining to women by late antiquity, see especially Percy Ellwood Corbett, *The Roman Law of Marriage* (Oxford: Clarendon Press, 1930); Jane F. Gardner, *Women in Roman Law and Society* (Bloomington: Indiana University Press, 1986); Susan Treggiari, *Roman Marriage: Iusti Coniuges from the Time of Cicero to the Time of Ulpian* (Oxford and New York: Clarendon Press, 1991), *passim*; Jean Gaudemet, 'Tendances nouvelles de la legislation familiale au IVe siècle', in *Transformations et conflicts au IVe siècle ap. J.-C.* (Colloque organisé par la Fédération Internationale des Études Classiques, Bordeaux, 7. au 12. septembre 1970; Antiquitas 1, 29; Bonn: Rudolf Habelt Verlag, 1978), pp. 187–207; Richard P. Saller, '*Familia, Domus*, and the Roman Conception of the Family', *Phoenix* 38 (1984), pp. 336–55, esp. 338–40; Yan Thomas, 'The Division of the Sexes in Roman Law', in P.S. Pantel (ed.), *A History of Women: From Ancient Goddesses to Christian Saints* (trans. A. Goldhammer; Cambridge, MA and London: Belknap Press of Harvard University Press, 1992), pp. 83–137; Jill Harries, '"Treasure in Heaven": Property and Influence Among Senators of Late Rome', in Elizabeth M. Craik (ed.), *Marriage and Property* (Aberdeen, UK: Aberdeen University Press, 1991), pp. 54–70; Suzanne Dixon, 'The Marriage Alliance in the Roman Elite', *Journal of Family History* 10 (1985), pp. 353–78; Beryl Rawson, 'The Roman Family', and J.A. Crook, 'Women in Roman Succession', in Beryl Rawson (ed.), *The Family in Ancient Rome: New Perspectives* (Ithaca, NY: Cornell University Press, 1986), pp. 1–57, 58–82; Philippe Antoine, *Le Mariage: Droit canonique et coutumes africaines* (Théologique Historique, 90; Paris: Beauchesne, 1992), chs 1–2 (on engagements). The various essays of Jean Gaudemet on marriage are collected in his *Sociétés et mariage* (Recherches institutionnelles, 5; Strasbourg: Cerdic-Publications, 1980), esp. pp. 46–103, 116–39; and Antti Arjava, *Women and Law in Late Antiquity* (New York: Oxford University Press, 1996). Although Arjava reads Jerome, *ep.* 147.11 and John Chrysostom, *virg.* 52.3 to mean that husbands in their time may have been reclaiming the ancient legal right summarily to kill a wife and her lover caught in the sex act (*Women and Law*, ch. 2, 2), it seems to me that such expressions (in the absence of any legal evidence to support Arjava's claim) betoken these Fathers' rhetorical appeal to a past in which husbands had more power over their wives. For a summary of developments as they affect the notion of 'consent' to marriage, see Elizabeth A. Clark, '"Adam's Only Companion": Augustine and the Early Christian Debate on Marriage', *Rech. Aug.* 21 (1986), pp. 139–62, esp. pp. 158–61, with numerous references to Roman marriage law. For a discussion of the ideological nature of texts pertaining to adultery, see Amy Richlin, 'Approaches to the Sources on Adultery at Rome', in Helene P. Foley (ed.), *Reflections of Women in Antiquity* (New York, London and Paris: Gordon and Breach Science Publishers, 1981), pp. 379–404. The conflict between state need and Christian ideology regarding women is well noted by Judith Evans-Grubbs in her essay, 'The Good, the Bad, and the Holy: Women in Late Roman Law', presented at the annual meeting of the American Philological Association, December 29, 1993.

87 On the Fathers' lack of success in influencing imperial law on such points, see Arjava, *Women and the Law*, chs 2 and 3, and 'Divorce in Later Roman Law', *Arctos: Acta Philologica Fennica* 22 (1988), pp. 5–21; Hans Julius Wolff, 'Doctrinal Trends in Post-classical Roman Marriage Law', *Zeitschrift der Savigny-Stiftung für Rechtsgeschichte, Romanistische Abteilung* 67 (1950), pp. 261–319, esp. pp. 268, 276, 278–79, 296–98, 311, 318–19; Treggiari, *Roman Marriage*, pp. 319, 463–64; and Roger S. Bagnall, 'Church, State and Divorce in Late Roman Egypt', in K.-L. Selig and R. Somerville (eds), *Florilegium Columbianum: Essays in Honor of P.O. Kristeller* (New York: Columbia University Press, 1987), pp. 41–61. The degree to which legislative changes by Constantine do or do not reflect his religious sentiment is carefully examined by Judith Evans-Grubbs in her essay, 'Constantine and Imperial Legislation on the Family', in Jill Harries and Ian Wood (eds), *The Theodosian Code: Studies in the Imperial Law of Late Antiquity* (London: Duckworth, 1993), pp. 120–42.

exhortation was necessarily their major weapon in the enforcement of what they considered Christian values, since they lacked actual legal sanctions for their views.

But more than the recollection of the pagan past, the Fathers liked to summon examples from the ranks of *biblical* women for the eyes and ears of their female audiences. Thus we find frequent appeals to Rebecca[88] and Sarah,[89] to Prisca,[90] Mary and Martha.[91] Nonetheless, the question remained: into which narrative trajectory should they be placed? Was there an upward sweep from the Old Testament to the Christian era, in which the shocking behaviour of the Hebrew forefathers and foremothers was explained (away) as belonging to 'different times'? Thus Methodius in *The Banquet* has one of his female symposiasts describe how God had allowed incest in the early days of the human race, which had later been prohibited by the Mosaic law; next polygamy, formerly permitted, was forbidden. Eventually came an attack on the previously tolerated adultery ... and finally, the Christian era bloomed, in which continence and virginity reigned supreme. According to Methodius, God like a skillful pedagogue had educated the human race in morality by stages, from the time that humans were allowed to 'frolic like calves', through their student days, to full maturity.[92]

Yet even if the trajectory of *Heilsgeschichte* were upward, where should it stop? Should it continue to soar beyond the New Testament to the Church Fathers' own time?[93] Although such an approach supplied a useful shaming device for contemporary men ('how much better "weak women" of our day are than you!'), it lacked rhetorical leverage for the chastisement of contemporary *women*, who might foolishly imagine that they excelled all biblical characters in virtue. Perhaps it was better to stop the moral ascent with the New Testament, claiming only that grace had devolved more fully on women there than in the Hebrew past.[94] For if grace were allowed to flourish too fulsomely after the New Testament period, the Fathers might lose the ground for their critique of Montanist women, who prophesied and claimed to receive revelations in accordance with Jesus' promise that the Paraclete would soon bring fuller truth (Jn 14.26; 15.26).[95]

Given such interpretive perils, perhaps more rhetorical force against contemporary women's behaviour could be derived from adopting a 'downhill' trajectory for women after the New Testament era. By this means, the greater dissoluteness – mysteriously unexplained – of women in the Church Fathers' own time could serve to rationalize the curtailment of women's earlier freedoms. In this scenario, women of the Bible could be raised up as models of a virtue and chastity that were sadly lacking in the

---

88 Tertullian, *virg.* 11.3 (CCL 2.1220–21; *Or.* 22.10 (CCL 1.271); John Chrysostom, *laud Max.* 6 (PG 51.235); *hom. 48 Gen.* 5–6 (PG 54.441–43); *hom. 50 Gen.* 1 (PG 54.448).
89 John Chrysostom, *hom. 32 Gen.* 5–6 (PG 53.300); *hom. 41 Gen.* 5 (PG 53.381–82).
90 John Chrysostom, *hom. 1 Rom. 16.3* 3 (PG 51.191–92).
91 John Chrysostom, *hom. 62 Joh.* 3 (PG 59.345).
92 Methodius, *symp.* 1.2.16–18 (GCS 27.9).
93 E.g., John Chrysostom, *hom. 13 Eph.* 4 (PG 62.99).
94 John Chrysostom, *hom. 5 Acta* 2 (PG 60.51–2).
95 Jerome, *ep.* 41.4 (CSEL 54.314). Tertullian came to favour the New Prophecy: *mon.* 14.4; 6 (CCL 2.1249, 1250).

present. Thus although Rebecca, as depicted in the book of Genesis, could move at will in public space and interact with men without endangering her purity,[96] and although New Testament women could travel with men, perform ministries, and even be called 'apostles',[97] none of these possibilities now obtained, due to the negative 'slide' that Christian women had suffered.

Still another historical trajectory was proposed by the ascetic writers of the later fourth and fifth centuries. According to this narrative, human life had begun on a virginal 'high' in the Garden of Eden, but had plunged to the abyss with the institution of sexual intercourse and marriage. Humans had gradually risen from the swamp of carnal concerns and desires to reclaim, in the Church Fathers' day, the virginal Paradise: this epic tale of defeat and recovery held much appeal to writers such as Jerome, Chrysostom and Gregory of Nyssa.[98] On this 'ascetic trajectory', Genesis 1 and 2 exemplified the lofty chastity of the later Christian era, while the behaviour of most Old Testament characters was at best explained as a sign of the human weakness that God had graciously tolerated in the shadowy era after the first sin and before Christ's advent.[99] Of course, this strategy ran the risk of denigrating Old Testament ethics, which carried with it the charge of Manicheanism, as Jerome learned to his distress.[100]

Thus all possible historical scenarios entailed some explicit or implicit difficulty. In consequence, it is not surprising that the Fathers' appeal to female exemplars from the Bible remains uncoordinated with any consistent trajectory that *Heilsgeschichte* was imagined to have followed: any metanarrative that stressed the liberating effects of Christianity ran up against the Fathers' perceived need to construct 'strategies of containment' for women. It is not just that this incoherence is found among the *various* Church Fathers, nor that it is exhibited from treatise to treatise in a single Patristic writer's corpus: the incoherence is apparent in one and the same treatise. A case-in-point is Tertullian's *De monogamia*, which begins with a denial that monogamy is a novel idea propagated by the New Prophecy, since it is found not just in the New Testament but in the Old as well.[101] Yet Tertullian then switches in mid-stream seemingly to reverse his argument: from chapter seven on, he posits that there really *was* a 'difference of times' between the two Testaments, the Old allowing sexual behaviour no longer acceptable to Christians.[102] None of us, I think, would

96 John Chrysostom, *laud. Max* 7 (PG 51.236); not to speak of her physical strength in leaping on camels and carrying water jugs (*hom. 48 Gen.* 6 [PG 54.443]).

97 John Chrysostom, *hom. 73 Matt.* 3–4 (PG 57.677–78); *hom. 31 Rom.* 2 (PG 60.669–70). Chrysostom is exceptional among the Church Fathers in allowing Junia of Rom. 16.7 to be a woman; he even grants her apostolic status. See Bernadette Brooten, '"Junia ... Outstanding among the Apostles" (Rom 16.7)', in L. and A. Swidler (eds), *Women Priests: A Catholic Commentary on the Vatican Declaration* (New York: Paulist Press, 1977), pp. 141–44.

98 Jerome, *Iou.* 1.4; 16; 2.15 (PL 23.255, 245–46, 319–21); John Chrysostom, *virg.* 14.3; 17.1–3 (SC 125.140, 150–52); Gregory of Nyssa, *virg.* 13.1 (SC 119.422).

99 E.g., John Chrysostom, *hom. in 1 Cor. 7.39* 2 (PG 51.219–20); *virg.* 41.1 (SC 125.236).

100 Jerome, *Iou.* 1.3 (PL 23.223); *ep.* 49 (48)2 (CSEL 54.352). Compare with the ethics of the anonymous, presumably Pelagian, author of *De castitate*, for whom Old Testament sexual ethics are not worthy of defence; here, a very sharp breach is registered between behaviour allowable under the Old Law and the New: *cast.* 11.2; 12.2–4 (PLS 1.1490, 1491).

101 Tertullian, *mon.* 2-6 (CCL 2.1229–37).

102 Tertullian, *mon.* 7 (CCL 2.1237–39).

accuse Tertullian of intellectual dullness: the example rather signals how the appeal to the past by the Fathers is polemical, rhetorical and moral[103] – and in these cases, it serves as a regulatory device for women of the present.

If these were the workings of the Fathers' appeal to 'history', how did they attempt to construct female subjectivity through appeals to certain literary forms and techniques? Given the ideological cast of the Fathers' approach to 'the woman question', their turn to the grand biblical narratives and myths – and their reading of them in a decidedly conservative way – is not surprising: stories, according to some analysts of ideology, are often its effective carriers. Thus it is to the historical narratives, to books such as Job and Song of Songs (read as embodying stories), and to the mythic material of Genesis 1–11 that the Fathers turn over and again. Moreover, the examples they lift therefrom are often themselves elaborated in story form, ancient narratives being encapsulated in contemporary ones, such as sermons constructed along 'story' lines. Homilies of this type were surely one of the most successful ways to address women, since they were preached to congregations; longer commentaries and treatises designed to be read, in contrast, would have found a largely, although not exclusively, male audience.[104]

In the Fathers' sermonic narrations of biblical tales, all Christians are bound into a seamless history that runs from the Garden of Eden to the present: they are 'one people of God'. But this account is somewhat deceptive, since the Church Fathers, after all, had constructed their *own* master narrative by appropriating the Jews' sacred history from them, so that all of the Hebrew Scriptures could (and should) be read as a 'Christian' document. Moreover, although tales of women as well as men comprise the narrative of 'the unity of God's people' (as Gal. 3.28 proclaims) this narrative was not run in a liberatory direction such as contemporary feminist exegetes might press: for the Fathers, there was a notable discrepancy between the male components of that 'people', who could preach, publicly teach and offer the sacraments, and the female members who could not. The unity of all Christians in the allegedly common history that the sermonic narrative proposes is sharply called into question by the recognition of its selective application. Salvation history, if not differentially salvific for men and for women, was differentially elaborated: 'Christian freedom' meant something different for women than for men. The universalizing effect of the Christian master narrative thus concealed the subaltern status of many of its characters.

That the appeal to female inferiority and 'danger' also received a ready hand from the literary device of intertextual writing is suggested by a variety of Patristic sources. A few examples will here suffice to show how it assisted the Fathers in their construction of an ideology of gender. Take the explication of the opening chapters of Genesis. John Chrysostom, in his *Sermons on Genesis*, reads the creation and 'Fall'

---

103 See de Certeau, 'History', p. 220, on how history is essentially an 'ethical' discipline; also see White, 'Value', pp. 18, 27, on the moralizing quality of narrative history.

104 Several of Jerome's longer commentaries are dedicated to women; one presumes he thought that they might read them. To Paula are dedicated his own commentaries on Ephesians, Philemon, Titus, Galatians, Micah, Nahum, Zephaniah and Haggai, plus his translation of Origen's *Commentary on Luke*; to Marcella (and Pammachius) he dedicates the *Commentary on Daniel*. For a discussion of Jerome's dedications of treatises to various friends, see Elizabeth A. Clark, *The Origenist Controversy: The Cultural Construction of an Early Christian Debate* (Princeton, NJ: Princeton University Press, 1992), ch. 1.

stories with the help of 1 Corinthians 11 as an intertext. The Genesis 1 account of the first man and woman as created 'in the image of God' is here 'corrected' through 1 Corinthians 11, in which only males enjoy the blessing of 'God's image'. Why is this so?, Chrysostom asks. And he answers: because 'the image of God' means 'authority', and only males possess this quality; like God in the heavens, so the male on earth has no superior and rules over all beings (including woman). She, on the other hand, is called in 1 Corinthians 11 – though not in Genesis 1 – 'the glory of man' because she is under his authority.[105] Thus the force of the creation of both sexes 'in God's image' is mitigated to send a message of female inferiority.

Elsewhere, in his longer *Homilies on Genesis*, Chrysostom also employs 1 Corinthians 11 as the intertext for Genesis 1–3, but here, it is Paul's designation of man as the 'head' and woman as the 'body' that provides the correct interpretation of these chapters. Thus for Chrysostom, man was the 'head' at the time of creation. This 'natural' hierarchy was upset by the first sin, when the 'body' (Eve) did not obey her 'head' (Adam); rather, he was allured by the 'body' and put himself in submission to her.[106] Read with the help of 1 Corinthians 11, Genesis 1–3 conveys the message that sexual hierarchy was given at creation as 'natural', but was disturbed by the first sin. Yet Chrysostom brings more than 1 Corinthians 11 to his interpretation: various motifs from the Pastoral Epistles and other late New Testament books are introduced to reinforce the point that the 'oneness' of the first couple consisted not just in being 'head' and 'body'; 'head' and 'body' are elided with 'teacher and disciple, ruler and subject'.[107] For Chrysostom's exegesis in this homily as well, the intertext supplies the theme of female inferiority and submission that then governs the interpretation of the stories of creation and 'Fall'.

The past master of intertextual interpretation in later Latin Christianity was doubtless Jerome. Two illustrations from his writings will suggest how he creates meaning, more specifically, how via intertextual interpretation he 'raises the stakes' for asceticism. The *Adversus Jovinianum* 1, 7 provides an instructive example. According to Jerome – who here exegetes 1 Corinthians 7 – when Paul in that chapter advises his male audience that it is 'better for a man not to touch a woman', the passage should be read in light of verses from Proverbs 6, 7 and 9 that warn young men against dangerous women who 'touch', 'preying upon' their lives, and causing them to lose their understanding. The view that Jerome here argues – that if 'touching' isn't good, then it is necessarily bad – becomes a misogynistic message of the dangers that women pose to men.[108] Paul's advice regarding male restraint is thus lent different colouration by the insertion of an explicit message about 'female danger'.

Likewise in *Epistle* 123 to a Gallic widow, Geruchia, Jerome cleverly revises the message of 1 Timothy 5 that young widows should remarry: this advice, not at all to Jerome's taste, is explained away with the help of two intertexts that 'constrain' the text of 1 Timothy 5. First, Jerome reminds Geruchia (and other readers) that Noah's ark (a figure for the Church) contains unclean animals as well as clean ones (Gen. 7.2–3): she can still be called a Christian if she remarries, but only an 'unclean'

---

105 John Chrysostom, *serm. 2 Gen.* 2 (PG 54.589); cf. *hom. 7 de statuis* 2 (PG 49.93).
106 John Chrysostom, *hom. 17 Gen.* 4 (PG 53.139).
107 John Chrysostom, *hom. 12 Col.* 5 (PG 62.388).
108 Jerome, *Iou.* 1.7 (PL 23.228–29); he appears to borrow the argument from Tertullian, *mon.* 3.

one. Next, he summons up the Parable of the Sower, accompanied by his own famous interpretation in which the 100-fold, 60-fold and 30-fold harvests (virginity, widowhood and a single marriage) leave no room for countenancing remarriage if a Christian wishes to be present at the 'harvest'. For Jerome, second marriage is better represented as 'the weeds among the thorns'.[109] By interlarding his exegesis of 1 Timothy 5 with such passages, Jerome seeks to ensure that his readers comprehend the lowly status of second marriage. The carnal 'detritus' (in Boyarin's phrase) of the Pastoral Epistles is here reconfigured for the new message of female asceticism: texts have not been discarded, but rather given their proper interpretation – an interpretation that again betrays the Fathers' 'strategies of containment' regarding women's sexual and marital activity.

Thus in three ways related to literary forms and technique – through intertextual reading strategies, through the appeal to biblical narratives and myths, and through encoding these stories in narratives of their own – the Fathers helped to promote the ideology of 'woman' that would prevail through the centuries to come.

III

Theorists of ideology challenge historians to uncover the conditions that prompted the production of such interpretations, that is, to 'denaturalize' and 're-historicize' the conditions that produced ideologies of gender such as we have been considering. Some notable efforts have already been made to ferret out the contexts of early Christian writings by such New Testament scholars as Jouette Bassler and Elisabeth Schüssler Fiorenza, who engage in a kind of Althusserian 'symptomatic reading' by noting the gaps, by attending to what might seem 'illegible', in the text. Bassler and Schüssler Fiorenza have thus offered illuminating suggestions regarding (for example) the social situations that perhaps produced the messages of female subservience that mark the Pastoral Epistles: 'false teachers' were making significant inroads in wooing women to their camp and allowing them more freedom and opportunity for leadership than did the church represented by 'the Pastor'.[110] A similar explanation has been offered as one reason for Catholic writers' slander of the Gnostics: they wished to use the different treatment of women in their own group and among (at least some) Gnostics as a marker to differentiate 'us' from 'them'.[111]

For the period of the late fourth and early fifth centuries, from which I have drawn most of my evidence, I have elsewhere argued for the following scenario regarding the relative prevalence of women in literature composed by ascetically inclined writers: with the conversion of the Roman aristocracy, women of vast wealth and exalted social status not only embraced Christianity, they embraced a rigorous asceticism that impelled them to renounce their fortunes for charitable and

109 Jerome, *ep*. 123.8 (CSEL 56.81–82).

110 Jouette Bassler, 'The Widows' Tale: A Fresh Look at 1 Tim. 5.2–16', *JBL*, 103 (1984), pp. 23–41. For interesting comments on the importation of hierarchy from the patriarchal household, and of the values of the patronage system, into the Church, see Elisabeth Schüssler Fiorenza, *In Memory of Her: A Feminist Theological Reconstruction of Christian Origins* (New York: Crossroad, 1983), ch. 8.

111 See discussion in Clark, 'Devil's Gateway', pp. 33–37.

religious causes. The Church became a primary outlet for female patronage, just at the moment when some older avenues of patronage were closing to aristocratic women, in part due to shifts in patronage arrangements: local benefaction tended to give way to the linkage between patronage and the holding of high governmental offices which were, of course, closed to women.[112] The almost-unimaginable wealth of some of these aristocrats-turned-ascetics (recall that a conservative estimate of Melania the Younger's annual income – not her entire fortune, to be sure – could have supported 29,000 persons for a year[113]) was enthusiastically accepted by the Church, which with the expansion of Christianity in the post-Constantinian era and with the burgeoning ascetic movement, needed extensive income for its charity and construction operations.

The ambivalence that these women occasioned for Church Fathers such as Jerome and Chrysostom was, I posit, considerable; here were humans of the highest virtue, self-control and intelligence, whose incredible generosity made possible their own monastic and ecclesiastical operations: yet Olympias, Paula, Marcella and the others were most clearly 'women'. *Could they be 'women' without being 'woman'?* The gender bias that renders them unequal is a most telling expression of 'uneven development' among these women whose economic, social and educational positions would have suggested no such disability. The 'status dissonance' they suffer is linked solely to their sex and to no other factor.

Moreover, the Church Fathers' *own* social location should be noted in relation to that of the women to whom they directed their exhortations and correspondence: for the most part – Ambrose excepted – it was not of the aristocratic status occupied by the two Melanias, Marcella, Olympias and others. John Chrysostom's father was, in all likelihood, merely a 'high grade civil servant'.[114] Jerome's family lived in a town in the Dalmation hinterlands,[115] a fact that in itself sets his family's 'society' apart

---

112 Elizabeth A. Clark, 'Patrons Not Priests; Gender and Power in Late Ancient Christianity', *Gender and History* 2 (1990), pp. 253–73 (254–61), esp. pp. 256–58.

113 *Vita Melaniae Junioris* 15 (Latin): text in M. del Tindaro Rampolla (ed.), *Santa Melania Giuniore, senatrice romana: documenti contemporei e note* (Roma: Tipografia Vaticana, 1905), p. 11. The Greek version attributes this amount to her husband's income (SC 90.156–58). The calculations are based on the costs of supporting the poor at subsistence level, given what we know of late ancient wages and prices. See Roger S. Bagnall, *Currency and Inflation in Fourth Century Egypt* (Bulletin of the American Society of Papyrologists, Supplement 5; Chico, CA: Scholars Press, 1985), especially the prices and salaries listed on pp. 61–72; Richard Duncan-Jones, *The Economy of the Roman Empire, Quantitative Studies* (Cambridge, UK: Cambridge University Press, 1974), pp. 4–5; *idem*, 'Costs, Outlays and Summae Honoriae from Roman Africa', *Papers of the British School at Rome* 30 (1962), pp. 47–115 (75), who emphasizes the difficulties of calculating purchasing power that corresponds to modern price structures. For a survey, see A.H.M. Jones, *The Later Roman Empire, 284–602: A Social, Economic and Administrative Survey* (Norman: University of Oklahoma Press, 1964), pp. 1. 438–48; on prices of clothing, pp. 2. 848–50. A contemporary discussion of grain equivalents, food requirements and basic consumption needs is provided by Colin Clark and Margaret Haswell, *Economics and Subsistence Agriculture* (4th edn; London: Macmillan, 1970), esp. chs 1, 4, 11. I thank Keith Hopkins for assistance with these details.

114 A.H.M. Jones, 'St John Chrysostom's Parentage and Education', *HTR* 46 (1954), pp. 171–73 (171).

115 Jerome, *vir. ill.* 135 (PL 23.697–98). For the relatively undistinguished situation of late ancient Dalmatia, see J.J. Wilkes, *Dalmatia* (Cambridge, MA: Harvard University Press, 1969), esp. pp. 271, 333–36, 417, 419.

from that of the Roman senatorial aristocracy; moreover, Jerome, even with Paula's assistance, did not have sufficient funds to build monasteries for men and women in Bethlehem when they first settled there.[116] Augustine's father was apparently a minor official in Thagaste, a small and not very distinguished city in Roman Africa;[117] when Augustine rose to the bishopric of Hippo Regius, he came to control church property worth twenty times his own patrimony.[118] Thus although Chrysostom, Jerome and Augustine cannot be said to have come from poverty, their families' social and economic statuses were no match for those of the women on whom they came to depend: their own social location, by virtue of family background, is noticeably lower. It is tempting to speculate whether their attempts to rein women in under the control of male ecclesiastics and monastic leaders do not relate in part to their own lower social and economic status – now bolstered by the positions of authority they had come to occupy by virtue of their intellectual (and 'political') achievements.

It is perhaps the Church Fathers' emotional and financial dependence on such women – recall that Olympias almost singlehandedly supported the operations of the Constantinople Church during Chrysostom's episcopate[119] – coupled with their misogynistic constructions of 'woman' that gives an unpleasant edge to their diatribes against rich women. Thus Chrysostom reminds men that if they pick wealthy brides, they will have many woes – as he simultaneously tries to impress upon any women who came into marriage with fortunes equal to their husbands' that the 'law of obedience' causes any presumed equality to vanish.[120] The woman who has her own money, he claims, sets up her own will and becomes a 'wild beast', failing to exhibit desirable wifely submission.[121] In a most telling merger of the financial with the sexual, Chrysostom interprets the 'becoming one (flesh)' text of Ephesians 5 to mean that brides should deposit their money in their husbands' coffers[122] – a stunning example of the social conservatism exhibited by the Fathers on gender issues, for both law and custom in the Roman Empire had for several centuries (since the decline of *manus* marriage) supported the separation of the wife's and the husband's property.[123] Jerome's theoretical approach to rich women takes a rather different tack: that they are prone to fall into heresy, being much courted by heretical leaders who know where to find their sustenance.[124] Likewise, women who attempt to dispose of their own property without their husband's consent become the targets of Patristic

---

116 Jerome, *ep.* 108.14 (CSEL 55.325).

117 See Peter Brown, *Augustine of Hippo: A Biography* (Berkeley and Los Angeles: University of California Press, 1969), pp. 20–22.

118 Augustine, *ep.* 126.7 (CSEL 44.13).

119 *Vita Olympiadis* 5; 13 (SC 13bis.416–18, 435); Palladius, *v. Chrys.* 61, P.R. Coleman-Norton (ed.), (Cambridge, UK: Cambridge University Press, 1928), pp. 110–11.

120 John Chrysostom, *virg.* 53–55 (SC 125.298–304).

121 John Chrysostom, *hom. 59 Acta* 4 (PG 60.344).

122 John Chrysostom, *hom. 20 Eph.* 9 (PG 62.148). The nineteenth-century sexual metaphor of 'spending' here seems replaced by one of 'saving'.

123 See, for example, Gardner, *Women in Roman Law*, pp. 68–77.

124 Jerome, *ep.* 75.3 (CSEL 55.36).

wrath,[125] even though legally their property was separate from their husband's.[126] The ideal, it appears, was for a committed virgin or widow to donate her entire substance to the Church and like Althusser's 'good subject', willingly submit herself to the control of ecclesiastical authority.

Although the Church Fathers overwhelmingly appeal to the divine will, to the order of creation and to 'nature' to justify unequal treatment of a significant portion of their Christian flock, there are occasional – very occasional – lapses in their argumentation that stand against their rhetorical appeal to female disability. Thus although Chrysostom calls women of his own day 'weak', he acknowledges that the 'weakness' results not just from a fault of their 'nature', but from their upbringings: they have been improperly educated and encouraged to lead indolent lives.[127] Likewise, he can abandon the *topos* of 'woman as temptress' long enough to suggest that it is not women's beauty that is at fault in the arousal of lust, but the unchaste eyes of men. 'We should not accuse the objects, but ourselves and our own sluggishness', he intones,[128] in a view far more in keeping with his belief that wrongdoing is 'up to us' and is not be blamed on our 'nature'.[129]

Jerome's writings also provide instances that work against his more usual ideological appeal to 'the natural'. For example, when discussing the marital and sexual habits of various peoples in his treatise *Against Jovinian*, he offhandedly observes that differing ethnic groups take for a 'law of nature' that which is simply the practice most familiar to them[130] – but not for a minute does Jerome concede that this dictum applies to his *own* views on marital and sexual arrangements! In a similar vein, Augustine notes that people have difficulty understanding how their *own* modes of life appear 'sinful to people of other nations and times'[131] – but he does not, any more than does Jerome, apply this observation to his *own* notions concerning women and sexual relations. Here we have striking examples of Althusser's argument that those who are 'in ideology' always believe that they themselves stand outside it.[132] One wonders how different the history of Christianity might have been if writers such as Chrysostom and Jerome had probed further the 'constructedness' of their own views on women and sexuality, if they had allowed insights such as I have just noted to guide their gender politics. It is worth noting, however, that such moments, which could have spurred a trenchant critique of the Fathers' own ideology of gender, seem *not* to have been stimulated by theological reflection on universal human sinfulness: although in other times and places, a biblically or theologically motivated call to self-repentance might have prompted such critiques, in these instances, the

---

125 Augustine, *ep.* 262.4; 5; 7; 8 (CSEL 57.624–25, 626–27).

126 On the separation of husbands' and wives' property in later Roman law, see especially the works listed by Gardner, Dixon and Treggiari in note 86 above.

127 John Chrysostom, *hom. 29 Heb.* 3 (PG 63.206).

128 John Chrysostom, *hom. 15 de statuis* 3 (PG 49.158); cf. *hom. 7 2 Cor.* 6 (PG 61.450–51).

129 See discussion in Elizabeth A. Clark, 'The Virginal *Politeia* and Plato's *Republic*: John Chrysostom on Women and the Sexual Relation', in *eadem*, *Jerome*, pp. 3–4, with references.

130 Jerome, *Iou.* 2.7 (PL 23.308).

131 Augustine, *doct. chr.* 2.14.22 (CCL 32.91).

132 Althusser, 'Ideology', p. 175.

counter-arguments appear to stem simply from the Fathers' observation of the varying 'ways of the world'. Such observations thus provided no theological leverage for an overarching critique of gender ideology.

IV

Theorists of ideology currently debate whether there is at present, or has been anytime during the recent past, a 'dominant ideology'[133] – that is, an ideological consensus among a majority of a population that is perpetrated by the class(es) in power and accepted by those whom they dominate. Yet even the sceptics[134] (those who *don't* believe there is a 'dominant ideology' in the present) sometimes claim that in the distant past there was one, variously described as lying in 'the pre-capitalist historical period'[135] or, more narrowly, in the 'feudal era'.[136] According to these commentators, the name of this 'dominant ideology' of the past is – as one might expect – Christianity. The untestability of the thesis renders it dubious. But more: the little we know about the actual women who were represented in Patristic writings makes us question whether the ideological stance of the Fathers entirely won the day. Although we have no body of literature by early Christian women which could be used to compare with that of the Fathers, we can infer even from the representations of these women by male writers that the gender ideology described in this paper did not result in their total silencing. For one important lesson that women historians have learned in the past decades – and without the explicit assistance of theorists of ideology – is how women and other subject populations manage to find small openings for their own projects and expressions of value:[137] in this case, how women even 'within ideology' used the Patristic discourse to gain positions of monastic leadership and access to education and to travel. Although Church Fathers such as Jerome and Chrysostom, through stereotyping, naturalizing and universalizing, present an unattractive picture of 'woman', they encouraged the actual women they esteemed to pursue lives of study and extra-domestic activity, and left us portraits of them that suggest the Patristic ideology of 'womanhood' had been to some degree subverted from within, by the women themselves. Probably it is too much to see in ancient Christian women's manipulation of the system an emerging form of consciousness. Yet if such small moments of subversion had been more systematically registered by the Fathers and connected to their occasional reflections on the 'constructedness' of all human argumentation, a somewhat different rhetoric regarding women might have dominated the discourse of late ancient Christianity. Still, it is worth noting that the triumph of the Fathers' gender ideology was not complete.

133 Althusser, 'Ideology', p. 175.

134 See Eagleton, *Ideology*, pp. 35–36, 56; Giddens, 'Four Theses', p. 20 (where the integrating effect on society is questioned); Raymond Williams, *Marxism and Literature* (Oxford: Oxford University Press, 1971), p. 132, discussed in Eagleton, *Ideology*, p. 47.

135 Althusser, 'Ideology', p. 151.

136 Frow, *Marxism*, p. 63; also see Eagleton, *Ideology*, p. 154.

137 For a discussion of the formation of counter-hegemonic discourses, and the difficulty of Althusser's notion of 'interpellation' to provide space for 'subversive agency', see Hennessy, *Materialist Feminism*, pp. 75, 92–93.

For as Sojourner Truth and other women in 1851 learned, even the dominant ideology can be manipulated: when her opponent claimed that women should not be accorded equal rights with men because 'Christ was a man', her retort – entirely orthodox from a Christian perspective – might provide the grounds for a counter ideology: 'Where did your Christ come from? From God and a woman! Man had nothing to do with him!'[138]

---

138 In Stanton et al., *History*, 1.116.

THE PENTATEUCH OR PLATO: TWO COMPETING PARADIGMS OF CHRISTIAN SEXUAL MORALITY IN THE SECOND CENTURY CE

KATHY L. GACA

Alexandrian Christians in the second century CE witnessed a fascinating disputation about the human sexual mores that God is thought to have designed and mandated for people to follow.[1] The main participants were a little-known philosopher named Epiphanes and the much more famous Clement of Alexandria, both of whom draw upon Greek biblical and Christian Platonist tenets. Epiphanes is associated with the Gnostic Carpocratians,[2] while Clement is a voice of what would later crystallize into the orthodox tradition of Church Fathers. Epiphanes, whose argument appears in his now-fragmentary treatise *On Justice*, supports the idea of God as represented in Plato's dialogues, and he also advocates the communal sexual norms in the *Republic* which he thinks the Platonic God endorses. Clement, by contrast, replies in the *Stromateis* by supporting the biblical notion of God and the patriarchal norms of marriage found in the Greek Pentateuch and the Pauline Epistles.

The disputation between Epiphanes and Clement pertains directly to feminist inquiries into the origins of Christianity. It reveals that Christian Platonists such as Clement, who went on to be considered relatively orthodox from an emergent Church perspective, largely had to disavow the more equitable potential of sexual communalism in their Platonic heritage. Instead of this ideal, they staunchly advocated the marital sexual mores of the Pentateuch and Paul. Those Christian Platonists who remained loyal to Plato's communal sexual principles were ridiculed and silenced by supporters of biblical sexual mores, regardless of the strengths of Plato's argument. When Epiphanes overtly argued that biblical sexual mores ought to be set aside to attain justice for all, he was grossly caricatured as a libidinous heretic. Thus the Christian Platonist legacy that informs Church orthodoxy involved a debate that led

---

1 Many thanks to A.-J. Levine for her helpful comments and suggestions.

2 It remains worthwhile to refer to Epiphanes as a Gnostic. Though polymorphous, Gnosticism as a historical phenomenon does indeed reflect an 'acute Hellenization of Christianity', as Harnack notes (for which see Karen L. King, *What is Gnosticism?* [Cambridge, MA: Harvard University Press, 2003], pp. 67–70), as well as 'protest exegesis' as described by Michael A. Williams, *Rethinking 'Gnosticism': An Argument for Dismantling a Dubious Category* (Princeton, NJ: Princeton University Press, 1999), p. 57. As shown here, Epiphanes exemplifies Hellenizing protest exegesis in his acute Platonization of Christian notions of God and God's sexual and social plans for mortals to follow. For the little that is known about the life of Epiphanes and his ostensible connection with the libertine Carpocratians, see H. Chadwick, *Alexandrian Christianity* (London: SCM Press, 1954), pp. 25–29; F. Bolgiani, 'La polemica di Clemente Alessandrino contro gli gnostici libertine nel III libro degli Stromati', *SMSR* 38 (1967), pp. 94–99, and the introductory remarks on Epiphanes in Arland J. Hultgren and Steven A. Haggmark, *The Earliest Christian Heretics: Readings from Their Opponents* (Minneapolis, MN: Fortress Press, 1996). Note also the still valuable entries on Epiphanes in DHGE (by A. Torhoudt) and by G. Salmon in W. Smith and H. Wace (eds), *The Dictionary of Christian Biography* (London: J. Murray, 1880).

to the rejection of the sexual norms promoted by Plato in favour of those attributed to Moses in the decalogue.

As will become clear in due course below, Epiphanes's sexual principles show promise of being equitable in some respects and thus are worth knowing for ethical and historical reasons. A desire for social justice for women and men alike moves him to offer his critique of biblical patriarchy. His principles are also of interest because the transitional social period in which he lived gave them a chance of succeeding. Epiphanes advocated Plato's communal sexual mores at a time when Christianity was still a counter-cultural movement partly shaped by communal social ideals. Among Christians of the second century it still remained a live question whether or not Christianity as a social order would become predominantly communal, which is in accordance with some apostolic norms, and perhaps even equitable as well, as Epiphanes argues. Before the fourth century, when Christianity became more fully absorbed into the ancient status quo of 'man and wife' marriage and child-rearing, the Christian social question was not whether communal principles were desirable, but just how far such principles should be taken. According to the Book of Acts, for example, Jesus' first followers showed strong sympathy for communalism and practised it in earnest. In a passage that would warm Plato's heart, 'They held everything in common' (Acts 2.42–45).[3] Further, the disciples of Jesus learned that they should go and give all they had so as to share it with the poor rather than keeping their material goods to themselves.[4] The apostolic ideal of equitable sharing on a communal basis did not die out with first-generation Christians, for Christian monastic orders later developed partly as a receptive response to this teaching. This ideal is consonant with Plato's desire to curtail acquisitiveness in his hypothetical cities so as to diminish the gulf that separates the rich from the poor. In the second century, then, Epiphanes's Christian Platonist social programme was not hopelessly unrealistic and utopian, for the force of ancient patriarchal traditions had not yet shaped Christians to live predominantly in family units with 'the husband as head of the wife' (Eph. 5.23), in which father knows best.

Even though Christian patriarchal mores have strong biblical support in Eph. 5.22–24 and elsewhere, and eventually succeeded to become the dominant Christian social mode, Christianity in the time of Epiphanes did not yet uniformly reflect a familial status quo. The communal Christian social order was not yet relegated to sexually segregated and celibate monasteries and convents on the margins of the

---

3 A passage in the earlier strata of the Jewish Sibylline Oracles sympathizes with communal values to the extent advocated in Acts and presents it as God's plan: 'The Heavenly One distributed the earth in common to all' (3.247). A later Christian passage in this work bears a similar sentiment but transposes the communal ideal to life after the resurrection. In this paradise, 'life and wealth will be common to all, and the earth will be equally shared by all, not divided by walls or fences' (8.205–7). See J. Geffcken, *Die oracula sibyllina*, (*GCS* 8, Leipzig: J. C. Hinrichs, 1902). Epiphanes's extension of communal ideals to include communal sexual practices, however, is nowhere supported in the Sibylline Oracles or Acts. Plato's *Republic* 5 is his source and precedent for making this extension. On communalism in early Christianity, see too D. Dawson, *Cities of the Gods: Communist Utopias in Greek Thought* (New York: Oxford University Press, 1992), pp. 258–63, and Brian J. Capper, 'Community of Goods in the Early Jerusalem Church', *ANRW* 26.2 (1995), pp. 1731–74.

4 Mt. 19:21, and see too Origen, *In Matt* 15.14, where Origen attributes the same teaching to the Gospel according to the Hebrews (in evangelio quodam, quod dicitur secundum Hebraeos).

Christian family as the fundamental social unit. Thus, Epiphanes was reasonably well positioned to put Plato's dream of sexual communalism into Christian practice.

Points of Substantive Agreement between Epiphanes and Clement

Epiphanes and Clement, despite their differences in theology and sexual morality, concur on some religious and social norms that form shared terms of their disputation. First, they both assume that there is a God and that God is a singular masculine being. Epiphanes and Clement follow Greek biblical and philosophical traditions, which predominantly conceptualize and describe God or θεός with the singular number, masculine grammatical gender and other masculine traits, such as identifying him as a father. They accordingly do not consider God as feminine, androgynous, or above gender, nor do they imagine God as a polytheistic many. They vest divine authority in a paternal male figure.

Second, Clement and Epiphanes agree that God is the teleological creator and maker of the world, not an aloof entity in the manner of Aristotle's unmoved mover. In their understanding God has designed and created the world, human beings and society by a plan that mortals can and should learn to follow. God also observes and monitors how well his plan is being carried out. From their perspective, mortals in relation to God are rather like employees in relation to the founder and chief executive officer of a corporation with a top-down hierarchy of power. They must follow the founder's general plan for the company, abide by his specific rules, and suffer a penalty if they are negligent or disobey. Clement and Epiphanes do not consider alternatives that are eminently viable today, such as that the world might not have been created by or through any divine entity, or that even were it so created, it need not have been done for any particular ends with which human beings are to comply and which God continues to oversee. Rather, they are both concerned to interpret God's plan properly.

Third, Clement and Epiphanes both agree that God's plan involves a social programme for mortals to follow. Central to their programmes is what Plato calls 'the first law' for determining the degree of justice a society accords its members, that is, the pattern of sexual mores by which the people should abide. Epiphanes and Clement insightfully recognize that sexual structures are a pivotal first law of social and moral order. Sexual rules shape and perpetuate rules of kinship, inheritance customs and related broader patterns of wealth distribution. Sexual mores are likewise integral to core values a society has, such as whether it idealizes the family in the conventional sense of one man per wife as mother of his children. This in turn influences myriad other ethical questions. If, for example, God's sexual plan is taken to be predominantly heterosexual and family oriented with a male head of the household, then unwed mothers, gays, lesbians and single persons are allowed but marginalized in the ensuing social order. But if God's blueprint is seen to be exclusively heterosexual and family oriented, then persons with non-compliant sex lives are an affront to the blueprint followers. Sexual regulations therefore play a crucial role in shaping a society and its degree of social justice. Epiphanes and Clement, like Plato, regard a society's sexual principles as the pre-eminent law, the first item on God's agenda for mortals.

Clement and Epiphanes, despite their shared assumptions about God, his creation and his plan, differ in the sexual norms that they each think are divinely ordained. These differences derive from whether their one true masculine God the father and creator is the biblical God, as he is for Clement, or the Platonic God, as he is for Epiphanes.

Whose God? Which Sexual Mores?

Epiphanes is an ardent communalist in his sexual and social principles. He strongly supports Plato's arguments in the *Republic* in favour of a communal society and against the more conventional tradition of patriarchal marriage and family mores. In fact, he regards Plato's communal social theory as God's plan, which he indicates by attributing it to God as conceptualized in Plato's writings. God, Epiphanes maintains, has ordained that human beings must live by the principle of 'communal sharing on an equitable basis (κοινωνία μετ' ἰσότητος)'. Societies that transgress this principle are contrary to God's will and for this reason are unjust. Epiphanes appeals directly to Plato's *Republic* in support of this position. Laws and customs, Epiphanes states, are unjust if they lead people to regard persons and goods as property to be owned individually as 'that which is mine (τὸ ἐμόν)' and 'that which is yours (τὸ σόν)' (*Strom.* 3.6–7). This point strongly reflects Plato's claim in the *Republic* that the human distinction between 'that which is mine' and 'that which is not mine (τὸ ἐμὸν καὶ τὸ οὐκ ἐμόν)' is the root of social injustice (*Rep.* 462c3–5, 464c5–e2). Human beings must abandon their desires to acquire persons and goods of their own if they are ever going to establish an equitable society.

As the first step toward enacting this ideal plan, Epiphanes emphasizes that men in particular must renounce the 'to each his own' principle of owning individual wives as property and instead practise communal sexual mores (*Strom.* 3.8). Epiphanes thus supports Plato's key argument that the custom of each man taking and having a wife of his own is the most problematic type of ownership and that therefore it needs to be eliminated first. Only then may a society deactivate the vices of divisive acquisitiveness and the uneven distribution of wealth. Epiphanes hopes that other Christians will similarly see the merit of Plato's argument and adopt it as God's plan so as to strengthen their commitment to the communal and just society. In the one brief fragment we have from *On Justice*, however, Epiphanes does not himself further explicate the Platonic arguments that he supports. For this we have to turn to Plato and look at the communal social theory he has to offer.

Plato thinks that human beings are born with inherently excessive appetitive desires, such as the desires for food, drink and sexual activity. By his diagnosis, societies inevitably become corrupt and appetitively inflamed when men have too much wealth at their disposal, on which their families' and their own desires may feed and proliferate. The only reliable cure for this ingrained human problem is a communal sexual and social order. Persons are virtuous when they exercise and restrain their sexual and other appetites in a 'necessary and salutary' way, and they are wicked when they let their appetites run to excess, as it is the appetites' proclivity to do (*Rep.* 558d9–e1, 559c3–4). 'Goodness (ἀρετή) is the outcome for those who conduct themselves well in relation to their threefold need and appetite [for eating, drinking and sexual activity], and the opposite is true for those who conduct themselves badly in relation to them' (*Laws* 782d10–e3). The sexual and other appetites are necessary and healthful to the extent that persons cannot avoid them and that they benefit physically from them. 'The appetites that we cannot deflect and that are healthy when acted on are rightly called necessary for us' (*Rep.* 558d9–e1). Thus, when people are appetitively virtuous, they eat, drink and engage in sexual activity strictly in a controlled manner that is beneficial to themselves and society at large (*Laws* 784e5–85a3). People and society become corrupt, however, when they let the appetites get their way, succumb to immoderate gratification, and thereby do harm to themselves and others. In order to curtail appetitive desires, people must liberate themselves from two core social habits. They must abandon customs of private ownership of persons and property, and they must reduce the amount of things they buy and sell strictly to a healthy minimum. Only in this way, Plato thinks, will people successfully restrict their appetitive desires in a beneficial way.

Rampant physical desires also stimulate and rule over numerous sensuous and acquisitive desires of other kinds according to Plato, and these have broader social repercussions. The sexual appetite of Plato's tyrannical man provides a good, though extreme, illustration of this point. This man's sexual appetite not only produces his desires for love affairs, it also provokes him to sponsor elaborate drinking parties to promote erotic trysts, to steal from his own parents and neighbours, and even to loot temples so as to indulge these desires in a spendthrift way (*Rep.* 573b6–74e1). Further, a man dominated by sexual passion is likely to commit murder as a crime of passion (*Rep.* 571d1–2). Even worse are the effects of such desires when manifested by the lower classes: the hoi polloi 'are always looking down, bent toward the ground. They feast, stuffing themselves and copulating. Out of excessive desire for such things they kick and butt with horns and hoofs of iron, and kill one another due to their insatiability' (*Rep.* 586a6–b6). The proliferation of acquisitive desires on a broader social scale goes beyond individual crimes of passion and leads to chronic wars of conquest and famine (*Rep.* 373b2–74a2). Plato therefore believes that the three physical appetites, unless held in check by reason, are at the root of social ills insofar as they stimulate other unchecked desires and acquisitive violence. If individuals only ate and drank moderately and minded the necessary limits of sexual activity, the proliferation of other rampant desires would not occur and society would be at peace.

Historically speaking, living men or legendary male personages in antiquity such as Alexander or Agamemnon fit Plato's paradigm of the appetitively dominated agent of violence and conquest more readily than female personages or women do. Plato's own examples of such behaviour are masculine as well, such as the tyrannical man in the *Republic*. Nonetheless, he portrays rampant desire as though it were a universal human problem for men and women alike.

To cure the acquisitive licence that ruins the city, Plato disallows private ownership, unrestricted consumption and the unregulated exchange of goods.[5] In place of this breeding ground for appetitive excess, he would implement instead a Pythagorean-inspired communalism. This kind of communalism works in a voluntary cooperative spirit, such as seen among Jesus' disciples in Acts, in which 'friends hold goods in common (κοινὰ τὰ φίλων)' (*Rep.* 424a1–2, 449c4–5). A cooperatively communal society is thus Plato's plan to restrain the appetites and acquisitive desires in order to promote the greater social good.

The first kinds of property that Plato would free from men's individual ownership are women and their physical capacities for reproduction and nurture. Women gain first priority because reproductive sexual mores are central to Plato's first sexual law of social order. If this primary law mandates, as Athenian society did in his day, that men own wives and daughters – wives as household managers and mothers of their children, and daughters to be exchanged in marriage to other men – then to Plato's mind the society is bound to be unjust and feverish. Communalizing the women eliminates such acquisitive customs because it severs sexual desire from possessiveness and consumerism, helps restrict sexual activity to the beneficial degree, and yields other advantages. First, the communal pooling of women and reproductive labour removes kinship-based factionalism and competition for wealth in the city. As Plato sees it, a city must strive to be politically unified and psychologically holistic (*Rep.* 462c10–d3), because 'there is no greater evil than the fragmented city' (*Rep.* 462a9–b3). Traditional procreation within marriage, however, hinders civic unity and motivates families and clans to vie with one another to acquire wealth for their own households at each other's expense (*Rep.* 462b4–c5, 464c5–e2). Families and clans, preoccupied with their own material prosperity, tend to neglect and may even contribute to suffering in the city outside of the biologically related circle that claims their primary loyalty and identity (*Rep.* 462a9–e3).[6] Plato's communal pooling of reproductive labour and his child-rearing reforms would dismantle the acquisitive

---

5 According to Plato, untrammelled buying and selling in a marketplace is inherently deleterious because it helps breed appetitive excess and violence. Even if a city begins with material simplicity and restraint, it ends up feverishly unrestrained when its inhabitants are left to their own devices to 'buy and sell, [using] the marketplace and coinage as a means of exchange' (*Rep.* 371b4–10, 372e2–3). This is the case, he maintains, because there are no checks on what people may want to acquire, own and consume for themselves and their families. Rather, excess is encouraged as though it were economic growth and prosperity, and this eventually unleashes a mob of related desires rather than keeping them properly subdued. Consequently, the initially restrained city 'will not satisfy'. Its inhabitants will aggressively exceed the bounds of necessary appetition, demand more luxury goods, and thereby make their once healthy community feverish (*Rep.* 373a1–8). In such a diseased city, happiness is materialistic and property-oriented. 'Men think they will be happy by owning land, big fine houses, fine furnishings, … gold, silver, and all other such things … and they spend money as they wish, such as giving it to mistresses' (*Rep.* 419a4–9, 420a4–6). My study supplements Susan Moller Okin, 'Philosopher Queens and Private Wives: Plato on Women and the Family', *Philosophy and Public Affairs* 6 (1977), pp. 345–69.

6 Reproduction of kin also leads to a problem of divided loyalty between family and city. If, for example, a city goes to war, male citizens face conflicting civic and kinship obligations – to fight for their country and possibly get killed or do whatever possible to remain alive so as to provide support for their ageing kin. On the kinship duty of γηροβοσκία, see, for example, Laws 930e3–32d8. Plato's communal procreative reform would unify the city by eliminating this kind of conflicting allegiance.

bastions of kinship groups so as to produce a genuinely collective civic body guided by appetitive restraint.

Second, the communal pooling of women, Plato further suggests, is also of great benefit to women themselves. It frees them from being overly burdened by family-oriented acquisitiveness and household maintenance, and through this freedom they are much better positioned to help shape a holistic and unified city. When women are privately managed as wives, mothers and daughters, the ensuing social order runs on the assumption that a married couple's desires for their own children, house, household purchases and domestic maintenance are basic subsistence needs rather than acquisitive wants. A wife embedded in this appetitive system belongs to a particular man and is the mother of his children. This woman is habituated to want her family's comforts foremost even if the cost of such comforts, including her physical energy, could be better spent on community projects that matter to everyone, such as helping to keep a city safe and healthy or contributing to a community's creative and intellectual life. Her daily tasks inefficiently replicate the so-called 'women's work' of neighbouring wives and mothers house by house in a repetitive choreography. In this way they are all left with less time and initiative for more collective social pursuits.

This problem that Plato notes becomes even more apparent the more consumer-oriented the society becomes. Then the women have bigger houses, more furnishings, and so on, whose upkeep is the responsibility of the wife, regardless of whether she owns female slaves or hires maids. Plato explains this argument by analogy with female guard dogs. If female dogs, like Athenian women, were restricted to feminine roles such as tending the pups and cleaning the den, then the pack as a whole would not be as well off as it is. The female dogs would not, for instance, go hunting as they do along with the male dogs to help meet the entire pack's need for sustenance (*Rep.* 451d4–52a1). This would be especially true if the den kept getting needlessly bigger and more elaborate due to acquisitive canine visions of the good life.

Women's energy would not be so drained in a society that communally pooled its child-rearing and other traditionally domestic work. Plato's communal reforms would promote greater social restraint overall because he does away with the separate households that lead to the unnecessary replication and proliferation of appetitive demands. Women are then freed along with the men to shape a holistic and unified city, rather than remaining pawns to the human passions for ownership.

Plato is optimistic in the *Republic* that his communal proposals are feasible and practical. His reforms would be put into place and work successfully, so long as philosophers become kings and their subjects are collectively raised and educated by the principle that 'friends hold goods in common (κοινὰ τὰ φίλων)'.[7]

Sexual communalism remains an elite practice in the *Republic*, however, restricted as it is to the guardian class and not extended to other groups in the city.[8] Despite this narrow application of communal sexual mores, the principle itself poses a direct challenge to any social theory that privileges private ownership of goods and persons and favours family values over the common welfare.

In the *Laws*, Plato reaffirms and broadens his conviction that communal repro-

---

7 *Rep.* 423e4–24a2, 457b7–58b7, 473a1–e5.
8 *Rep.* 423e6–24b1, 449c2–5, 450c1–5, 451b9–c7, 457b7–c1, 457c10–d3.

duction and child-rearing are the best way to create a society. If he could, Plato in his last years would extend these reforms to all citizens, not only to the elite class of the *Republic*. 'No one will ever posit a more correct or better definition [of the ideal city] in its preeminence toward human virtue than one in which the private ownership of women, children, and all other goods is everywhere and by every means eliminated from human life' (*Laws* 739b8–e1). Nonetheless, Plato by this time is resigned to the weaker position that such reform is not possible on a pragmatic level. Only 'gods or children of gods dwell happily in the fully communal city' (*Laws* 739d6–e1), but mere mortals are apparently incapable of such enlightenment. Plato's later surrender to familial norms in the *Laws* is unsurprising given the reactionary flood of resistance and ridicule that swamped his communal sexual proposals,[9] just as a similar flood would later swamp Epiphanes's Platonic proposals for the children of God. In the *Laws*, accordingly, Plato aims only to encourage restraint on the acquisition of wealth and private property within the more traditional Greek customs of marriage, procreation and the family. These new and improved customs are second-rate in his view (*Laws* 739e4), for they leave in place the appetitive breeding ground he thinks should be uprooted, the individual male ownership of women, their wombs, and children in the family.

Epiphanes, moved by Plato's thoughtful arguments for grounding the social good in communal sexual practices, hopes further to augment Christian communalism on the model of the *Republic*. He seeks to break down the distinction between 'mine' and 'yours' in order to achieve the city of 'communal sharing on an equitable basis (κοινωνία μετ' ἰσότητος)'. To build this city of sharing, Christians must communalize the women first, and the rest of social justice will follow.

As Epiphanes plainly sees, the sexual regulations of the Pentateuch are at odds with the *Republic*. The biblical tenth commandment supports the male ownership of individual wives and their wombs. By prohibiting each man from coveting his neighbour's wife, it implicitly authorizes each man in the community to have a wife who is exclusively his own. This rule is diametrically opposed to the city of communal sharing. Epiphanes accordingly challenges the Pentateuch for presenting its marital sexual regulations as though they were God's sacred and inviolable word. The tenth commandment, 'You shall not covet your neighbour's wife', cannot genuinely represent God's position. The one true God of Plato objects to the private male ownership of women and their reproductive capacities, as exemplified by Christian procreative monogamy. Instead God mandates communal sexual relations. Epiphanes consequently finds this commandment 'quite ludicrous (γελοιότερον)' (*Strom.* 3.9). Especially foolish, he thinks, is the misguided idea that God formulated this rule, given its opposition to God's plan in the *Republic*. Epiphanes attacks the biblical tenth commandment as he does because he feared that Christians were

---

9 The image of the flood is Plato's, *Rep.* 457b7–d5. Plato's peers so mocked his preference for a communal society that he found it impossible to persuade them even that it might be a good idea for citizens habitually to eat outside the family at a common table (*Laws* 781b6–c2). A prominent lampoon of communal sexual mores, which may or may not be directed explicitly at Plato, appears in Aristophanes's *Ecclesiazousae*, on which see R.G. Ussher's edition (Oxford: Clarendon Press, 1973), pp. xiv–xx. Aristotle gives a more earnest argument against Plato's communal society, *Pol.* 1263a22–64a1.

poised to heed it and turn their backs on the communal heritage that he sought to strengthen by Plato's model.[10]

Epiphanes boldly links the Christian norm of patriarchal marriage to the Pauline notion of biblical law making sin manifest in the world. Sin 'entered (παρεισελθεῖν)' the world, Epiphanes contends, ever since people first decided that it was a God-given right that a man 'who has taken one woman into marriage should keep her as his own' (*Strom.* 3.8). From this marital practice have flowed other vices that Plato deplores and similarly links to paired marriage, such as greed, the wasted labour of women's domestic work, and the narrow-minded favouring of familial loyalties over the collective good. Epiphanes completely reverses the Pauline views about biblical law and marriage. According to Paul, the biblical law of God is good, and it 'entered (παρεισῆλθεν)' the world in order to make people aware of their inclination to sin against God's regulations (Rom. 5.20, 7.7–11). One especially dangerous sin, as Paul sees it, is for sexually active members of the Lord's people to deviate from confining their sexual practices within the bounds of the decalogue norm of marriage. As he expressly states, among Christians who decide to lead sexually active lives, 'Each man must have his own wife and each wife her own husband' (1 Cor. 7.2). Any other pattern of sexual activity involves extra-marital sexual fornication, which Christians must unconditionally 'fear and shun' lest they provoke God's wrath (1 Cor. 6.18, 10.8–9, cf. Rom. 1.18, 1.26–27).

According to Epiphanes, by contrast, the 'law (νόμος)' of men taking wives 'entered (παρεισελθεῖν)' the world as original sin (*Strom.* 3.7), and this practice has corrupted society ever since. Epiphanes's way of describing 'the entry' of primary sin and its progeny uses Pauline phrasing for a twofold purpose: to demote Paul's ideas about sin, biblical law and marriage, and to promote Plato's communal ideas. He offers this strikingly anti-biblical and anti-Pauline notion of the law that entered the world to make sin manifest on the basis of his Platonic conviction that the biblical type of marriage pattern is the root of all social evil. This sort of marriage sharply deviates from the genuinely desirable plan in *Republic* 5 and makes it unattainable. Hence for Epiphanes societies built on the 'man and wife' rule are sinful, corrupt and illegitimate, not worthwhile and genuinely lawful, as the Pentateuch would have it, even if only as a prophylactic against sexual fornication, as Paul maintains. Epiphanes pointedly appropriates Paul's notion of the law entering to reveal sin in the world so as to give greater emotive force to his Platonic conviction.

Clement contends that Epiphanes's position is shockingly immoral and outrageous. In Clement's view, the biblical God alone is the one true God. Given this tenet, God's sexual blueprint for the good society cannot possibly be revealed anywhere other than in the decalogue and the other parts of the Pentateuch, the pastoral letters and Paul. He thus finds it extremely dangerous for Epiphanes to argue in a Platonic vein that Christians must be sexually communal in order to bring about a just society. Rather, Epiphanes teaches a doctrine of rampant sexual fornication and adultery by advocating Plato's arguments in favour of sexual and social communalism, and

---

10 Epiphanes does not consider Luke's or Paul's interest in celibate communitarianism because in his view, as informed by Plato, it is neither possible nor desirable to quell the sexual appetite altogether. The only advisable aspiration is to curb this appetite within necessary and beneficial limits.

he thereby tempts Christians to worship the false god Aphrodite (*Strom.* 3.10). Moreover, Epiphanes 'fights against God' as portrayed in the Bible, and hence he disqualifies himself from Christianity (*Strom.* 3.9). Clement demonizes Epiphanes's – and Plato's – conception of the ideal society because, like Paul, he thinks fearsome dangers lurk in any social pattern that allows the sexually active to deviate from the biblical paradigm and its primary norm of each man having his own wife. If sexually active Christians break the tenth commandment, then their community becomes defiled by these acts of sexual fornication and adultery, and thereby it elicits God's anger. Epiphanes's envisioned social order not only transgresses these sexual regulations, it would overthrow them altogether. Hence for Clement, Epiphanes's Platonic principles of sexual and social communalism are a cardinal example of 'religiously alien ideas that are opposed to the truth' (*Strom.* 3.80). Orthodox Church Fathers must strenuously fight against such ideas so that the marital sexual limit of the biblical paradigm prevails. Only through preserving this plan of God do Christians remain securely protected by God rather than destroyed for their sexual disobedience.

Clement refuses to attack Plato, even though he vituperatively denigrates his opponent's Platonic argument in favour of the sexually communal society. Instead he accuses Epiphanes of misreading Plato's *Republic*. Clement boldly denies that Plato ever supported the communalization of women for reproductive and other purposes that Epiphanes advocates in the name of Plato and God. Instead the unmarried women in *Republic* 5 are a 'community (κοινωνία)' strictly in the sense that they are available as a collective of eligible prospective wives until men marry them individually, just as seats in a theatre are collectively available until each person in the audience claims one. Once each man takes his pick for a wife, the woman he selects belongs to him alone (*Strom.* 3.10). Clement drastically changes the contents of *Republic* 5 in this manner because he thinks Plato's ideas are consistent with the Pentateuch, so much so that he regards Plato as an obedient disciple of Moses (*Paed.* 2.90). Plato, in this persona as Moses' student, could never have argued for sexual reforms that would nullify those of his teacher and Moses' God. Rather, Plato favours the biblical sexual paradigm. Clement tries to make his own worse reading of *Republic* 5 appear the better because orthodox Christian Platonism needs to be consistent with the Pentateuch.

The outcome of Epiphanes and Clement's disputation is clear from contemporary Christian practices. Christian family values, which have been defined conservatively for a long time, are grounded in the biblical sexual dictates that Clement supported, not in Plato's. Epiphanes's Platonic sexual paradigm failed to influence significantly the path of Christianity. At most it remained a counter-cultural alternative. Still, the disputation is extremely valuable because of the ethical questions that Plato and Epiphanes raise about traditional marriage, owning private property and raising children within a strictly two-parent and heterosexual household, where mothers individually still must do much of the domestic and child-rearing labour, and in so doing replicate one another's tasks household by household.

Conclusion

Epiphanes's Platonic argument in favour of sexual and social communalism was reasonably well positioned to become influential in early Christian society. His book *On Justice* was 'much talked about' in Alexandrian circles (*Strom.* 3.9), not only for its notoriety, but because it tried to extend and strengthen the communal and equitable tendencies that were undeniably in place in early Christianity, even if only as fragile shoots in the societal weed-bed of dominance and inequality in antiquity. Epiphanes imparted greater intellectual force to these tendencies by linking them with Plato's arguments for social justice through communal appetitive restraint.[11] Nonetheless, Epiphanes's paradigm came to be caricatured as grossly libidinous by Clement, despite the fact that his Platonic plan for social reform is expressly anti-libidinous in its aims.[12] Epiphanes was trying to give practices of early Christian communalism a more solid social foundation by communalizing sexual mores as well, in the image of Plato's ideal. Epiphanes was motivated to argue expressly against the sinful law of 'man and wife' marriage as he did largely because he was alarmed that Christian advocates of biblically grounded sexual norms were pressuring sexually active Christians to adopt this form of marriage, reproduce within its social parameters, and thereby maintain the anti-communal status quo of the family and property divisions as usual.

As far as Clement was concerned, however, the burgeoning Christian Church needed to be protected as Christ's monogamous bride (*Strom.* 3.80) from the promiscuity of Platonic social theory and its communal sexual practices. Thus he attacks Epiphanes's arguments as though they were merely a den of iniquity. Epiphanes and Plato, however, give thoughtful reasons for regarding Clement's biblically based marriage system as a den of sacred inequity that remains with us today.[13] This is

11 Epiphanes was an early (but hardly the only) Christian who attempted to link communal sexual and social practices. In the nineteenth century, to name but one of several examples, the Christian Oneida community in upstate New York practiced communal sexual relations and thought that such sexual mores provided the appropriate basis for their utopian religious community. Exclusive monogamy, by contrast, was deemed impure. This social experiment lasted approximately thirty years, until it succumbed to external pressures, for which see S. Klaw, *Without Sin: The Life and Death of the Oneida Community* (New York: Allen Lane, 1993).

12 This caricature is taken to be true by H. Chadwick in his expressed opinion of Epiphanes, which is strongly influenced by Clement. Chadwick dismisses *On Justice* as 'merely … the scribblings of an intelligent but nasty-minded adolescent of somewhat pornographic tendencies' (Alexandrian Christianity, p. 25). A. Erskine (*The Hellenistic Stoa* [Ithaca, NY: Cornell University Press, 1990], pp. 112–16) and D. Dawson (*Cities of the Gods*, pp. 264–67) are the first to begin interpreting Epiphanes's argument in a dispassionate way. Erskine offers the speculative yet interesting argument that Epiphanes's communal ideals are partly indebted to early Stoic thought as well.

13 Clement is interested in some Platonic and other philosophical ideas, but only provided that they do not conflict with his conception of the truth or right way, which includes upholding biblical sexual mores. When Clement sees a conflict between biblical and philosophical principles, as he does with Platonic communalism in Epiphanes's argument, then he is as hostile as Tatian or Tertullian toward such 'pagan' ideas. On Clement's position that only some ideas in Greek philosophy can be safely adapted for Christian purposes, see E. de Faye, *Clément d'Alexandrie. Étude sur les rapports du christianisme et de la philosophie grecque au IIe siècle* (Paris: Ernest Leroux, 2d edn, 1906), pp. 192–200, and more recently C. Stead, *Philosophy in Christian Antiquity* (New York: Cambridge University Press, 1994), pp. 84–85.

not to champion Plato's alternative, as Epiphanes does, for this alternative as well arguably has the anti-feminist overtones of making women rather like a herd to be held, impregnated, worked and thus, as it were, 'milked' in common by the men in the community. Making women seem an aggregate collective held in common by adult males is a weakness in Plato's notion of communalism, especially as presented in *Republic* 5. Nonetheless, Epiphanes's Platonic challenge to the Christian turn toward biblically grounded 'man and wife' sexual norms remains valuable for its insights into the unfairness and inefficient replication of women's work that devolves from men keeping women as their private property in the household.

Mater Ecclesia AND *Fons Aeterna*: THE CHURCH AND HER WOMB IN ANCIENT CHRISTIAN TRADITION

ROBIN M. JENSEN

The conversation between Jesus and Nicodemus concerning the requirement that a person be 'born again' (γεννηθῆναι) in order 'to see the kingdom of God' (Jn 3.1–10) had both symbolic and practical implications for the ritual of baptism in the early Church. Although Jesus repudiated Nicodemus's sardonic queries – 'How can anyone be born after having grown old? Can one enter a second time into the mother's womb and be born? (patiently explaining that he meant a spiritual and not a physical birth) – ancient Christians instituted a practice that ritually enacted this miracle of new birth. In this ritual, the Church was the spiritual mother – at once both fecund and virginal – from whose impregnated womb (a baptismal font) her children emerged.

Christian baptism almost certainly arose out of Jewish purificatory practices and, at least according to the accounts of John the Baptist's washings in the synoptic Gospels, originally signified a person's repentance and cleansing from sin, not regeneration or renewal. However, some time before the compilation of John's Gospel, baptism had already come to denote the end of one life and beginning of another (cf. Rom. 6.3–6, Mk 10.38 and parallels) – a death and rebirth that ritually united recipients with Christ's death, burial and resurrection. The next generation developed this idea, in particular referring to a salvation through the water (or washing) of rebirth (διὰ λουτροῦ παλιγγενεσίας, Tit. 3.5). Through the next four centuries, the Christian ceremony of initiation enacted both death and rebirth in varying but concrete ways. Candidates were stripped and anointed, dunked, and emerged from a mother's watery 'womb' to begin life anew.[1]

This symbolism of death and renewal or rebirth had parallels in non-Christian religious and philosophical concepts as well as in the initiatory practices of certain Greco-Roman mystery cults, some of which also incorporated cleansing into their ordeal of identity transformation through death and rebirth.[2] The term παλιγγενεσία that occurs in the Letter of Titus also appears in Stoic descriptions of restoration after destruction.[3] It refers as well to the transmigration of souls in

---

1 This article concentrates only on the symbolism of birth, which is not to say that other symbols are not also associated with baptism, such as cleansing, death (including martyrdom) and illumination. See my forthcoming book, *The Signs and Symbols of Baptism in the Early Church* (Peabody, MA: Hendrickson Press).

2 For example, the cults of Demeter (Apuleius, *Met.* 11.23) and of Isis (Aristophanes, *Nub.* 497). See Thomas M. Finn, *From Death to Rebirth: Ritual and Conversion in Antiquity* (Mahwah, NJ: Paulist Press, 1997), pp. 74–77; and J. Ysebaert, *Greek Baptismal Terminology* (Nijmegen: Dekker and Van de Vegt, 1962), pp. 89–119.

3 Ysebaert, *Greek Baptismal Terminology*, lists several examples including some in the works of Philo, *Aet. mun.*

several ancient systems, including Orphism and Pythagoreanism.[4] The Christian inclusion of these ideas into its baptismal theology need not signal a simple appropriation from pagan tradition, however. Nicodemus's queries suggest the potent possibilities for language, action and visual expression which the early Church found irresistible. It is as if Jesus' rebuke of Nicodemus ironically encouraged the shaping of a symbolic but sensible experience of rebirth rather than militating against it.

The Church – the figurative birthing mother in the resulting baptismal ritual – is never merely an abstract personification or metaphor. A survey of early documents shows her to be a robust, central and heroic figure. Even more than her eventual prototype, the Virgin Mary, the Church unites opposing feminine virtues. She is at once mother and virgin, faithful consort and chaste daughter. Sexually receptive and generative she is perpetually intact and immaculate. She is the Mother of all Christians (a title later attributed to Mary) and beloved Bride of Christ (cf. Eph. 5.22–25). Her prolific womb is the source of life, her parturition is painless and unending, and her breasts are infinitely lactating. These qualities effectively make her the Christian personification of fertility and maternity although without actually making her an autonomous and otherwise active goddess.

The following summary of selected and chronologically organized second-through fifth-century documentary, liturgical and material evidence focuses on baptism as a ritualized act of rebirth from this mother's womb. This collection not only demonstrates the extent of such imagery in the early Church, it also delineates the way the imagery functions in different kinds of theological discourse (e.g., apologetic, polemical, homiletical, catechetical and exegetical). Whatever purpose they serve, the many depictions of Mother Church and her font-womb are remarkable for their vivid and compelling use of feminine, maternal and sexual imagery. The social and religious significance of this symbolism for the construction of gender roles and its impact on the religious imagination of the early Church, as well as on the lives of actual women and men (then and now), warrant further consideration.

We must ask whether this imagery values the potential fertility and generativity of real women's bodies, or rather if it demonstrates a transfer of value from the human to the institutional sphere – a sphere that was largely managed and defined by men. Early Christian writers continually emphasized that Mother Church's spiritual procreation was vastly better than that of a human, biological mother (whose parturition they often described in highly derogatory language). On the other hand, that this imagery was present at all has some implications for the continuing place and power of a female, maternal figure, albeit an externally constructed and controlled one. The children born to her are (at least theoretically) equally loved siblings, with identical claim to the family's inheritance; the image is thus arguably a way of countering elitist divisions in the community and promoting the sense of the Church as a birthing and nurturing institution.

---

4 See Ysebaert, *Greek Baptismal Terminology*, pp. 95–107. One example is from Plutarch, *Mor.* 379–80.

Baptism as Generation from Mother Church in Justin and Irenaeus

Jesus' dialogue with Nicodemus is cited by Justin Martyr (ca. 160) in one of the earliest explanations of baptism, directed especially to outsiders. Describing how candidates are brought to a place of water for the purpose of their regeneration, Justin paraphrases Jn 3.3: 'Unless you be born again, you shall not enter into the Kingdom of Heaven'.[5] Noting the obvious objection, he adds that the act of regeneration (ἀναγεννήσεως) means being cleansed from sin, not being reborn from a mother's womb (here citing Isa. 1.16–20). Interestingly, Justin returns to the theme of birthing by pointing out that we do not remember our 'first birth' that came about of necessity and in ignorance from 'fluid seed (ὑπᾶς στορᾶς) through the mutual union of our parents'. The second birth – or regeneration – is consequently one of choice and knowledge, which is why it also may be called 'illumination'. Thus Justin maintains that baptism is a kind of birth, but he elaborates the distinction that Jesus made between birth from flesh and birth from Spirit. Such regeneration actually requires no mother figure, and Justin never mentions one. Nevertheless, identifying the Church as the mother of those twice-born children soon becomes a hallmark of early Christian thought.[6]

Perhaps the earliest and most developed example of this move is found in Irenaeus's treatise *Against Heresies* (ca. 175). In an effort to establish the validating authority of the community's tradition (thereby countering the claims of heretics), Irenaeus describes the Church as the repository of the 'waters of life'. By means of these waters, she is 'the entrance to life', while all others are 'thieves and robbers'.[7] Wherever the Church is, there is the Spirit of God and vice versa. On this account, he argues, those who are not in the Church are lost. They 'defraud themselves of life through their perverse opinions and infamous behaviour' and are neither 'nourished into life by the mother's breasts (*mammillis matris*), nor obtain that shining fountain (*nitidum fontem*) issuing forth from the body of Christ'.[8] These deceived ones cause this mother to grieve. She bewails them their false 'invented mother' whom they erroneously believe to be beyond the Pleroma or the knowledge of God. That they imagine a different mother, one begotten without a father (thus a defective female begotten from a female), is only a sign of their corruption.[9]

---

5 Justin Martyr, *1 Apol.* 61.

6 An old but thorough study of the material may be found in Joseph C. Plumpe, *Mater Ecclesia: An Inquiry into the Concept of the Church as Mother in Early Christianity* (Washington, DC: Catholic University Press, 1943). Other useful works that discuss the theme of the Church as mother include Walter Bedard, *The Symbolism of the Baptismal Font in Early Christian Thought* (Washington, DC: Catholic University Press, 1951), pp. 17–36 and Timoteo José M. Orfrasio, S.J, *The Baptismal Font: A Study of Patristic and Liturgical Texts* (Ph.D. diss.; Rome: Pontificio Instituto Liturgico, 1990), pp. 80–98. Both works have good summaries of key documents on this subject.

7 Irenaeus, *Haer.* 3.4.1. Plumpe, *Mater Ecclesia*, pp. 35–37, convincingly argues that the earliest evidence of the title Virgin Mother (παρθένος μήτηρ) used for the Church is found in the account of the *Passion of the Martyrs of Lyons and Vienne*, which he believes to have been written by Irenaeus.

8 *Haer*, 3.24.1 (all translations by the author unless otherwise noted). Also note the Church's 'nourishing bosom' in 5.20.2.

9 *Haer*. 3.25.5–6, cf. also 1.5.6. By their 'mother' Irenaeus means Sophia, whom (according to Irenaeus) Gnostics believed was begotten without a father, and for this reason (he argues) she can give birth only to crude and shapeless abortions.

In another section of his long treatise, Irenaeus advances a concept that becomes key to subsequent discussion of the Church's unique motherhood. Here he speaks not only of the Church as the one who enlivens and nourishes the faithful, but he specifically describes her as a *virgin* mother whose regenerative act is a pure, spiritual one. In this respect it is modelled by the Virgin Mary's conception of Christ, and thus one virgin mother becomes the type of the other. Speaking here of the Church (and not about Mary) he asks: 'By what means should someone escape from the generation of death, if not by means of a new generation, given miraculously and unexpectedly by God as a sign of salvation – that is the regeneration through faith from a virgin (*ex Virgine per fidem regenerationem*)?'[10] A few paragraphs later, however, he clearly means Mary's womb (*vulva*) when he refers to that 'pure womb that regenerates humanity unto God, which God himself made pure'.[11]

Although Irenaeus's parallel between these two virgin mothers becomes a central motif later on, his more overt parallel is between Mary and Eve. Mary's regenerative ability comes, of course, from her obedience. In this she contrasts with the disobedient Eve, also a virgin (prior to her fall).[12] One virgin mother becomes the source of life (salvation) and reverses the consequences (i.e., death) of the other's error.[13] One mother (bearing a single child) thus redeems the act of the other (the mother of all living) and becomes her advocate.[14] Meanwhile, standing in the background of this comparison of the two mothers is a third – the Church – through whom Mary's gift is extended to all humanity. Eve may be the mother of all mortals and Mary the mother of salvation, but the Church is the mother of all the faithful. Soon *her* womb comes to be portrayed as purified by God in order to regenerate humanity. The transitions should be noted, however. One mother has sexual intercourse, conceives and gives birth to children; the next has no sexual intercourse and yet conceives and gives birth; the third has no intercourse and gives birth, but that birth is spiritual (i.e., 'from above') rather than physical. Here may be seen an increasing distinction between human biological procreation and ecclesial conception at birth.

Mother Church's Children in North African Polemic: Tertullian, Cyprian, Optatus and Augustine

The image of the Mother Church having a baptismal font for a womb was particularly resonant in Roman North African theology, identity and practice. One famous tomb mosaic, from Tabarka on the northern coast of present-day Tunisia, illustrates the centrality of the Church as mother in the imagination of African Christians (Fig. 1). African theologians perceived the miraculously fertile *Mater Ecclesia* as both the source of salvation and the nurturer of faith. In strikingly graphic terms, they describe the Church's womb as filled with the power of generativity and her embrace a refuge for the elect. To

---

10 *Haer.* 4.33.4, here the text appears to speak of the Church, not of Mary, as the Virgin Mother.
11 *Haer.* 4.33.11.
12 Irenaeus argues that Eve and Adam had no sexual intercourse in Paradise, as they were not yet adults, *Haer.* 3.22.4.
13 *Haer.* 3.22.4.
14 *Haer.* 3.22.4. See also *Haer.* 5.19.1.

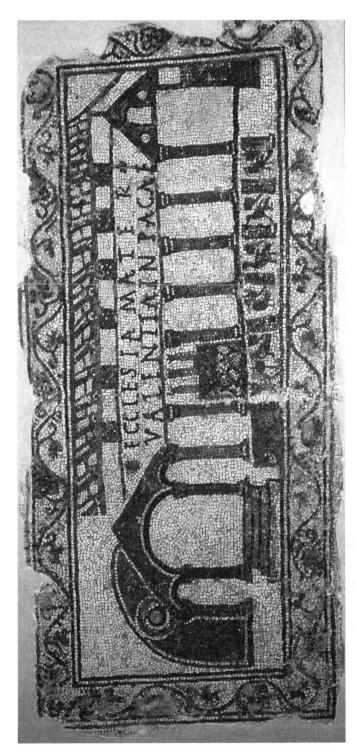

Figure 1. Tomb Mosaic from Tabarka, Tunisia

them, baptism in water ritually demonstrated the Church's fecundity as well as her welcome and protection. Other mothers were either infertile or their children illegitimate.

Tertullian, in his treatise *On Baptism* (ca. 200), specifically contrasts the lustrations of the pagans with Christian baptism. Those 'gentiles' lie to themselves about their barren 'widowed water' (*viduis aquis*),[15] whereas the Holy Spirit is able to penetrate and inhabit (*penetrare et insidere*) the water of baptism through which it conceives the power of sanctification (*sanctificare concepit*).[16] Tertullian refers here to the Spirit's presence at creation, as it is born upon the water and imparts holiness easily because of the water's permeability (*per substantiae subtilitatem*, cf. Gen. 1.1). By referring to his pagan contemporaries' ritual water as 'widowed', Tertullian may mean to imply that the gods themselves are dead, or he may be playing on the idea that wombs of elderly women (like the rituals of those cults) are, in fact, 'dried up'. Thus the efficacy of baptism's cleansing is due to this water's particular receptivity and fertility. Tertullian's use of procreative imagery for the Spirit over the water seems intentional here, but he never expressly identifies the font as a womb.

At the end of his treatise, Tertullian shifts from metaphors of penetration and conception to domestic and familial imagery. As the newly baptized emerge from that sacred washing of new birth (*novi natalis*), they joined together as siblings dwelling in their mother's house (*apud matrem cum fratribus*).[17] Here they petitioned their common father (*petite de patre*) for added spiritual gifts. The mother (Church) thus signifies the safe space in which the children may gather to ask the father for what they need. In this treatise on prayer, Tertullian explains that when the faithful address God as 'Father' in the first clause of the Lord's Prayer, they recognize their mother (the Church), by which they come to know both Son and Father and recognize their filial obligation and relationship.[18]

This domestic imagery, in particular the filial relationship of all the baptized, was a crucial concept in North African ecclesiology. Christians, sharing the same mother (and father), possessed a familial bond that superseded all other relationships. Separating oneself from the Church was equivalent to leaving one's family and losing the identity, protection and inheritance the family structure guaranteed. The necessity of this sacred bond is one of Cyprian's main themes, and he appeals to the image of Mother Church to contend that schismatics not only placed themselves outside of the Church's promise of salvation but became her enemy. Thus baptism apart from the one (true) communion, in 'spurious and unhallowed water', was ineffective since for Cyprian the water of Mother Church was, like her, faithful and unpolluted. Respecting that pure and holy mother was understood in the commandment to honour one's parents. Furthermore, baptism apart from the Church was tantamount to cursing one's mother – a sin punishable by death (Mt. 15.4).[19]

Cyprian's treatise *On the Unity of the Catholic Church* (ca. 252) expands this position. Using analogies from nature he depicts a barely transformed earth goddess:

---

15 Tertullian, *Bapt.* 5.2.
16 *Bapt.* 4.4.
17 *Bapt.* 20.5.
18 *Or.* 2.
19 Cyprian, *Ep.* 73.

She spreads her branches in generous growth over all the earth, she extends her abundant streams ever further; yet one is the head-spring, one the source, one the mother who is prolific in her offspring, generation after generation: of her womb are we born (*illius fetu nascimur*), of her milk are we fed (*illius lacte nutrimur*), of her Spirit our souls draw their life-breath.[20]

In the next paragraph, Cyprian describes this fecund and nurturing mother as also inviolate, chaste and modest. She has only one home (*domus*) and one bedroom (*cubiculum*). Other mothers (e.g., rival Christian sects) are therefore adulterous, and their offspring (e.g., those baptized by these sects) are bastards; they cannot be heirs to the salvation that comes only to legitimate children: 'You cannot have God for your father if you have not the Church for your mother.'[21]

Since the problem of division in the community was a continuing and particular plague of the North African Church in the fourth and fifth centuries, it is not surprising that similar maternal language and analogies reappear in the polemical writings of Cyprian's successors. Optatus of Milevis and Augustine of Hippo both countered the claims of the competing Donatist sects, but because they dissented from Cyprian's position that baptism outside the communion was invalid, they transformed the imagery to suit their arguments. The mother remained chaste and singular, but her womb was seen as sanctifying in itself, even if her children wandered away from the family. She remained mother to her disinherited offspring.

Optatus outlines this argument in his writings against the Donatist bishop Parmenian of Carthage (d. 391/2). Parmenian, holding Cyprian's view of the Church, claimed efficacy for his communion alone and enjoined rebaptism for any coming in from outside. By contrast, Optatus claims that all offspring of the Church's generative womb are legitimate, even if they leave the fold. They may lose their inheritance, but never their identity. All Christians are conceived through the mingling of heavenly and spiritual seeds (*ubi miscentur caelestia et spiritualia semina*), which produces a regeneration of nature. This is why all regard God as their father and the Church as their mother. An unworthy minister of the sacrament cannot harm it, since the gifts belong to the womb (*viscera*) of the bride, and are not to be confused with her ornaments or dowry.[22] Because of this fundamental identity, family bonds can be strained but never entirely severed. Even when siblings refuse to make peace, they remain kin to one another: 'For you cannot but be brothers (*fratres*), when one Mother Church brought you forth from the same sacramental womb (*quos isdem sacramentorum visceribus una mater ecclesia genuit*).'[23]

Augustine, like Optatus, accepts the validity of the baptisms of children 'born' outside the catholic communion, but he offers an interesting elaboration on the issue of legitimate and illegitimate maternity. In his treatise *On Baptism, Against the Donatists* (ca. 402–3), he cites the examples of children born to both slaves and wives in the Old Testament. Augustine notes that children born to both kinds of women were legitimate so long as they shared a common father. Nevertheless, those children born to slave women need to be peacefully joined to the lawful wives of

---

20 Cyprian, *Unit. Eccl.* 5, also 19, 23. Cf. Cyprian, *Laps.* 2, 9.
21 *Unit. Eccl.* 6: *Habere iam non potest Deum patrem qui ecclesiam non habet matrem.*
22 Optatus, *Bapt. cont. Don.* 2.10.
23 *Bapt. cont. Don.* 4.2.

their father to receive their inheritance, just as Ishmael needed to be joined to Sarah (cf. Gal. 4.22). Those born within the family, of the womb of the mother herself, who then neglected her grace, by contrast, were like Esau, who despised his birthright (Gen. 25.34).[24] Thus, Augustine argues, while different wombs may bring forth children, so long as those children are sooner or later joined to the true wife, they shall receive their promised inheritance. Nor (*contra* Cyprian) are the children of these mothers to be viewed as the offspring of an adulterous union.[25]

The Church's Womb in Augustine's Catechetical Sermons

Augustine frequently refers to the imagery of the maternal Church with a font for a womb in a non-polemical context, in particular when he addresses catechumens preparing for baptism. In a sermon on the Lord's Prayer, given about the time that candidates received baptism, he explains why Christians address God as 'Our Father'. Saying these words for the first time indicates that those preparing for their baptism are beginning to have God for a father, like children conceived but not yet brought forth from the womb: 'You will certainly have him as such, when you have been born – although even now, before you are born, you have already been conceived by his seed (*illius semine concepti estis*), to be duly brought forth from the womb of the Church (*utero ecclesiae*), so to say, in the font.'[26]

In another sermon, delivered to catechumens as they were about to be given the creed, he takes up the section that confesses faith in the holy Church. Personifying the Church as 'true Mother' and 'true consort of the bridegroom' (*mater nostra vera, vera illius sponsi coniunx*), Augustine claims that she deserves honour because she whom the Lord found a whore he made a virgin (*meretricem invenit, virginem fecit*). Echoing Irenaeus's parallels, he contrasts Eve, whose virginity was extinguished by the seduction of the serpent, with the Church, whose fidelity is the sign of her restored chastity. Anticipating a question, he interjects: 'You're going to say to me, perhaps, "If she is a virgin, how does she give birth to children? Or if she doesn't bear children, how is it we give in our names to be born of her womb (*visceribus nasceremur*)?" I answer: She is both virgin and she gives birth. She imitates Mary, who gave birth to the Lord.'[27]

Augustine refers to the Church's womb as *uterus* and as *viscera*. These two terms turn up again in another sermon, this one addressed to the candidates or 'seekers' (*competentes*) as gestating fetuses. Urging them to make it to their full term lest they be 'aborted', he employs vivid birthing language: 'Look at the womb of Mother Church (*uterus matris ecclesiae*), look at her giving birth to you, groaning in her labour, to bring you forth into the light of faith (cf. Rom. 8.22–23). Do not agitate her maternal womb (*viscera*) with your impatience, and thus constrict the passage to your delivery.'[28] In another place, explaining why these persons are called *compe-*

---

24 Augustine, *Bapt. Don.* 1.10. 14.

25 Augustine, *Bapt Don.* 4.17: *Nec adultera est aqua in baptism haereticorum.*

26 Augustine, *Serm.* 56, in Edmund Hill (ed. and trans.), *Sermons, (51–94) on the Old Testament* (O.P. Series edited by John E. Rotelle; Brooklyn, NY: New City Press, 1991), III/3, p. 97.

27 *Serm.* 213, Hill III/6, p. 145.

28 *Serm.* 216.7.

tentes prior to their baptism, he says that they are called that because they agitate in their mother's womb, they are struggling to be born. Once born (baptized), they will be called infants (*infantes*).[29]

Augustine directed many of his Easter week sermons to these infants. No matter how old they are according to the flesh, he reminds them that they are newly 'born of God' (*ex Deo nati sunt*). Using yet another expression, he identifies their mother's womb (*vulva matris*) with the water of baptism (*aqua baptismatis*).[30] They are the offspring of a virgin mother, 'washed clean in the bath of lenience (*lavraco indulgentiae*)' and 'watered from the fountain of wisdom (*irrigati fonte sapientia*)'.[31] Their second birth is not like their first, a 'birth in misery' (*nativitas misera*) from the mingling of the blood and flesh of male and female, but rather from God with the Church (*nativitas ex Deo et ecclesia*).[32] In the first week after their baptism, the neophytes were allowed to join the clergy in the chancel – their 'cradle' (*cunabulum*) during the eucharist.[33]

The Virginal Church's Parturition in Fourth-Century Catechetical Discourse: Ambrose of Milan, John Chrysostom, Cyril of Jerusalem and Theodore of Mopsuestia

Universally popular in African theology and polemical discussion, this imagery of insemination, conception, gestation and birth also occurred in other parts of the early Christian world. The great catechetical writings of the fourth century similarly incorporated images of the Church as a virgin mother with an exceptionally fertile womb (the baptismal font) – a mother who remains a '*virgo intacta*' even in childbirth. As such, not only is the Virgin Mary her prototype, but she in turn is the personified ideal for consecrated virgins whose own procreativity was a spiritual, rather than a fleshly one. The Church's conception of children was not the result of a sexual union or the reception of male semen, but the reception of a divine seed, through the power of the Holy Spirit, invoked and mingled with the water in the font. The mother's role was essentially that of vessel, although birth from her womb imparted particular (and salvific) identity, and her shelter offered both protection and sustenance.

Among these fourth-century catechists was Ambrose of Milan (who baptized Augustine). In his exegesis of the Gospel of Luke, Ambrose regards the Virgin Mary as a type of the Church, the one who could give birth without pain and without losing her virginity. Like this mother, the Church is also simultaneously spotless and married (*immaculata sed nupta*); she conceives by the Spirit (*concepit de Spiritu*) and gives birth without groaning (*sine gemitu*).[34] In his treatise *On Virginity*, he elabo-

---

29 *Serm.* 228.1.
30 *Serm.* 119.4.
31 *Serm.* 223.1.
32 *Serm.* 121.4. One may want to compare the sermon of Augustine's contemporary Quodvultdeus of Carthage on the conception of the catechumens. See *Sym ad Cat.* 1, in which he explains to the catechumens that they have been conceived in the womb of the Church by the sign of the cross. In *Ad Cat serm. alius*, Quodvultdeus echoes Irenaeus's parallels between Mary's virginal conception and the Church's, contrasting both with Eve's conception and childbearing in sin, sorrow and pain.
33 *Serm.* 253.1.
34 Ambrose, *Exp. Luc.* 2.7.

rates, extolling the Church in dialectical language as 'immaculate in intercourse' (*immaculate coitu*), 'fertile in childbirth' (*fecunda partu*), 'virgin by her chastity' (*virgo est castitate*), 'mother by her having children' (*mater est prole*). Again, he emphasizes that her motherhood results not from impregnation by a man, but by being filled with the Spirit. She gives birth without suffering (*parit non cum dolore membrorum*), but rather with the rejoicing of angels. She nourishes her children, not by the milk produced by her body (*nutrit non corporis lacte*), but by the teaching of the Apostle. She is a virgin in her sacraments and a mother to her people. She has no husband, but does have a bridegroom – the Word of God is her eternal spouse.[35]

In his conclusion to his lectures to the newly baptized (ca. 390), Ambrose is perhaps most eloquent on the subject of the virginal Church's parturition of her children. Recalling Nicodemus's question (Jn 3.4), he explains that the second birth contradicts the order of nature, just as Mary's conception of Jesus did. Just as Mary's impregnation was not by human sexual intercourse but rather from receiving the Holy Spirit into her womb (*in utero accepit*), so also the font conceives by the descent of the Spirit into it in order to produce 'the generation of truth' (*veritatem generationis*).[36] In one other place, Ambrose associates the nudity of the baptized ones with the nakedness of birth as well as death (*nudus es natus, nudus moriturus es*).[37]

In one of his post-baptismal lectures to neophytes (ca. 395), John Chrysostom tells the newly born Christians that they are the 'joy of their mother' (the Church). He describes her happiness as she sees her children surrounding her and is glad that she herself is like a fertile field producing a lush, spiritual crop. Speaking to the neonates, he contrasts spiritual with fleshly gestation: 'Consider my beloved, the excess of her love. See how many children this spiritual mother has brought forth suddenly and in a single night. But we must not be surprised, spiritual child-bearing is such that it needs neither time nor a period of months.'[38]

This comparison between spiritual and fleshly childbirth is even more vividly drawn in John's homily on Jn 3.6, Jesus' telling Nicodemus that what is born from the flesh is flesh, but what is born from the Spirit is spirit. In this context, however, John seems to eliminate the mother (but not the womb) from that second birth altogether:

> There is no longer a mother, or pangs, or sleep, or coming together and embracings of bodies; henceforth all the fabric of our nature is framed above, of the Holy Spirit and water. The water is employed, being made the birth to him who is born; what the womb is to the embryo, the water is to the believer (ὅπερ γὰρ ἐστιν ἡ μήτρα τῷ ἐμβρύῳ τοῦτο τῷ πιστῷ τὸ ὕδωρ).[39]

Although he speaks frequently of the imagery of death and rebirth at baptism, Cyril of Jerusalem makes only one direct reference to the maternity of the Church

---

35 Ambrose, *Virg.* 1.6.31.

36 Ambrose, *Myst.* 9.5. See also *Sac.* 3.2 on the use of the word 'regeneration', but here in reference to resurrection rather than to rebirth.

37 Ambrose, *In Ps 61 Ennarr.* 32.

38 John Chrysostom, *Bapt Inst.* 4.1, in *St. John Chrysostom: Baptismal Instructions* (trans. P. Harkins; ACW, 31; New York: Newman Press, 1963), p. 66

39 John Chrysostom, *Hom. Jo.* 26.1, *NPNF*[1] 14.90.

in his catechetical lectures (ca. 348).[40] Toward the end, when he affirms that the Church is mother of all and spouse of Jesus Christ, he draws a triumphalistic picture of the Church as the figure of the heavenly Jerusalem, free and the mother of all 'who once barren now has many children'.[41] Similarly, his only allusion to the font in a maternal sense appears in his second mystagogical lecture (ca. 387) where he explains to the newly baptized how they had been mystically joined to Christ's death and resurrection (Rom. 6.3–4). Here he refers to the water of the font as both tomb and mother, as those undergoing baptism had to die first in order to be reborn.[42]

Like Ambrose and John, Theodore of Mopsuestia cites the story of Jesus and Nicodemus in his catechetical writing, but specifically in reference to the consecration of the font in the baptismal ritual. In his third baptismal homily (ca. 390) Theodore, interpreting Jesus' distinction between fleshly and spiritual birth, argues that as in a human birth, the mother's womb receives a seed, so too in baptism the womb (the font) also receives a seed, but one of a different kind, one that is delivered by the power of God and is received in the sanctified water. He specifies that this takes place by certain words and actions of the bishop who presides over the ceremony: 'asking God to let the grace of the Holy Spirit come upon the water and make it capable of begetting this awesome birth, making it a womb for sacramental birth'.[43] So, in his view, the one entering the font is like a fertilized embryo being placed into the womb. Formed by God's hand, the seed is transformed from mortal to immortal, from corruptible to incorruptible (cf. 1 Cor. 15.53–54).

Theodore returns to the theme of birth when he explains the particular significance of the neophytes' first eucharist. Wrapped in their 'swaddling clothes' (by which he means the 'bands of instruction' but might also imply their white baptismal garments) the 'infants' receive necessary nourishment in order to preserve the life they just received. They get their first taste of a kind of food 'wonderful beyond description' (the consecrated bread and wine), that will sustain them until their resurrection, when they shall no longer need it.[44]

From these catechetical writings, scholars have attempted to reconstruct the actual ritual of baptism as it was practised by the churches these different writers represent. Certain actions undoubtedly reinforced and actually embodied the symbolism of rebirth. The consecration of the water was equated with its insemination by the Holy Spirit or by God the Father.[45] The nakedness of the neophytes as they emerge from the

---

40 The font also seen as a tomb is attested in all four of the famous fourth-century catechetical writers. See Cyril of Jerusalem, *Myst.* 2.4; Ambrose, *Sac.* 3.1.1; John Chrysostom, *Hom. Jo.* 25.2, *Hom. Col.* 6.

41 Cyril of Jerusalem, *Cat.* 18.26.

42 Cyril of Jerusalem, *Myst.* 2.4.

43 Theodore, *Bapt. Hom.* 3.9, Edward Yarnold, S.J. (trans.), *The Awe-Inspiring Rites of Initiation*, 2nd edn (Collegeville, MN: Liturgical Press, 1994), p. 185. See also 3.2–5.

44 Theodore, *Bapt. Hom.* 4.105.

45 The practice of dipping the paschal candle into the water at the Easter Vigil is still part of the ritual of consecration in many places. See for example the late medieval English Sarum Rite. This act, intended to symbolize the presence of the risen Christ in the rite, is clearly also a representation of 'spiritual insemination'.

water symbolized the nakedness of babies emerging from the birth canal.[46] The first eucharist, which included a drink of sweetened milk, represented the nourishment offered by the mother to her children (cf. Heb. 5.12).[47] Finally, as we have seen, the newly baptized were referred to as infants and considered themselves siblings together in their mother's home – a place where they addressed God as Father.

Exhortations to the Font in the Poetry of the Latin West

The metaphors of birthing as applied to baptism gained much more popularity in the West in the late fourth and early fifth centuries. Zeno of Verona (ca. 370) perhaps represents a zenith in poetic use of the regenerative and nourishing mother figure in his invitations to the baptismal font. These invitations may have once been part of a single exhortatory sermon, but they are scattered among a collection of disparate homilies. Taken together, they provide a kind of catalogue of maternal references. For example, in his 'first invitation' Zeno describes the eternal font as inviting and warm. He contrasts human fleshly birth accompanied by groaning, travail and sordid rags (*pannis sordidis*) with a joyful, blessed heavenly generation, and babies nourished in filthy cradles (*foetidis cunis*) with those fed at fragrant altar rails.[48] In another (Invitation 3) he describes the sweet squalling (*dulcis vagitus*) of the infants as they emerge from the one womb (*uno de ventre*) and gather together as nurslings.[49]

Echoing the African theory of sibling relationship established through baptism, Zeno claims that differences in age, gender, nationality, race, or condition of life are erased when candidates 'fly to the font, to the sweet womb of the ever-virgin mother' (*fontanum simper virginis matris dulcem ad uterum convolate*). All are joined in the one body.[50] A new people is forged in the 'milky liquid of the genital font' (*lacteum genitalis fontis ad laticem*).[51]

A quarter-century later, Paulinus of Nola (409–413) produced a poetic inscription for the baptistery built between two basilicas by his friend Sulpicious Severus at Primulacum. In this text, Paulinus revisits these familiar themes, but he adds evocative procreative imagery along with a tone of nobility:

> Here the font that begets restored souls
> > Brings forth living water by divine light.
> The Holy Spirit decends from heaven into this river
> > And marries the water in the sacred, heavenly font.
> The water conceives God and from the fertile fluid

---

46 Nakedness at baptism is well attested and seems to have been applied to both men and women. Some of the literary evidence includes Hippolytus, *Trad. ap.* 21.3.5, 11; Cyril of Jerusalem, *Myst.* 2.2 (where it represents Christ's nakedness on the cross as well as Adam and Eve in Paradise, naked and unashamed); Theodore, *Bapt. Hom.* 3.2 (Adam); John Chrysostom, *Bapt. Inst.* 11.28 (Adam and Eve in Paradise); John the Deacon, *Ep. ad Sen.* 6.

47 Milk and honey as first foods are also mentioned by Augustine (see above); Hippolytus, *Trad. Ap.* 22.3–4, John the Deacon, *Ad Sen.* 12; Tertullian, *Adv. Marc.* 1.14.3; and Jerome, *Adv. Lucif.* 8. Also see *Brev. Hippo* 23 (the proceedings of the Council of Hippo in 393).

48 Zeno, *Tract.* 1.32 (Invitation 1).

49 *Tract.* 2.28 (Invitation 3).

50 *Tract.* 33 (Invitation 4).

51 *Tract.* 37 (Invitation 7).

Gives birth to a sacred progeny from an eternal seed.
Miraculous is God's compassion; the sinner is plunged into the flow
    And emerges from the water justified.
This one, undergoing a blessed death and birth
    Dying to earthly things and being born to eternal things.
Guilt is lost, but life returns; the old Adam perishes,
    And the new is born for the eternal kingdom.[52]

A little further on in his poem, Paulinus refers to the towers of the twin basilicas as like the two breasts of the Mother Church, who joyfully receives the newborn children brought forth in her water (in the single baptistery found between those breasts). One breast represents the Old Law, the other the New. From the baptistery/womb between them the priest delivers newborn children – baby lambs whom he leads to the altar and feeds with the bread of salvation.[53]

Paulinus's actual inscription did not survive in stone, but a text very much like it is still visible on one of the most important early baptismal monuments, the baptistery belonging to the basilica of St. John Lateran in Rome. The original building constructed by Constantine I in the early fourth century was renovated under Pope Sixtus in the mid fifth. The new design, an octagon surmounted by a dome, housed a large centralized font surrounded by an ambulatory created by eight porphyry columns topped with an octagonal architrave. On each of the horizontal blocks of this architrave a line of text appears, forming the verses of a dedicatory inscription (Fig. 2):

Here, born from fruitful seed is a sacred tribe to be consecrate, citizens,
    Which the Spirit draws from fertile waters.
Plunge, sinner, to be purified in the flow
    Whom it receives old, the water makes new.
No differences exist among those who are reborn,
    Whom one font, one Spirit, one faith makes one.
By virginal delivery, Mother Church bears children in the stream,
    Whom she conceives by the breath of God.
If you wish to be innocent, be purified in this bath,
    Whether you are burdened with your first ancestor's sin or your own.
This is the fountain of life, which washes the whole world,
    Having its origin in Christ's wound.

---

52 Paulinus, *Ep*. 32. 5. The Latin text reads (from Bedard, *Symbolism*, pp. 43–44):
Hic reparandarum generator fons animarum
Vivum divino lumine flumen agit.
Sanctus in hunc caelo descendit Spiritus amnem
Caelestique sacras fonte maritat aquas;
Concepit unda Deum sanctamque liquoribus almis
Edit ab aeterno semine progeniem.
Mira Dei pietas: peccator mergitur undis,
Mox easdem emergit justificatus aqua.
Sic homo et occasu felici functus et ortu
Terrenis moritur, perpetuis oritur.
Culpa perit, sed vita redit; vetus interit Adam,
Et novus aeternis nascitur imperiis.
    53 Paulinus, *Ep*. 32.5.

Figure 2. Octagonal architrave inscription, St. John Latevan Basilica, Rome

Reborn ones, by this font hope for the kingdom of heaven,
    The blessed life does not admit those born only once.
Neither the number of your sins, nor their gravity should frighten you,
    The one born in this river will be holy.[54]

Based on similarities with certain of his writings, this inscription is generally assumed to have been authored by Leo I while he was a deacon under Sixtus III. Many of its themes or images are reiterated in sermons that Leo preached after becoming Bishop of Rome.[55] For example, in a Christmas sermon Leo reminded his listeners that they had all participated in the birth of Christ through their baptism:

> Each person partakes of this spiritual origin in regeneration, and to every one reborn, the baptismal water is an image of a virginal womb (*instar est uteri virginalis*); for the same Holy Spirit fills the font who filled the Virgin, so that the sin, nullified by that sacred conception, might be removed by this mystical washing.[56]

In a sermon delivered during Lent, he uses the language of a new race (*gens*), adopted as God's children, who are brought in through the fecundity of the virgin Church.[57] In a homily on Christ's passion, Leo speaks of an 'innumerable multitude of children' born to the unpolluted Church (*incontaminatam ecclesiam*), fertilized by the Holy Spirit and brought to life in baptism.[58]

In various ways, then, early documents extol the Church by using the figure of a virgin mother, parallel to Mary, also a virgin mother and her perfect type.[59] The

---

54 The renovation of the baptistery under Sixtus is noted in the *Lib. Pont.* (46.7, Sixtus III). The Latin is as follows:
Gens sacranda polis hic semine nascitur almo,
Quam fecundatis Spiritus edit aquis.
Mergere, peccator sacro purgande fluento,
Quem veterem accipiet, proferet unda novum.
Nulla renascentum est distantia, quos facit unum
Unus fons, unus Spiritus, una fides.
Virgineo faetu genitrix ecclesia natos,
Quos spirante Deo concepit, amne parit.
Insons esse volens isto mundare lavacro,
Seu patrio premeris crimine seu proprio.
Fons hic est vitae, qui totum diluit orbem,
Sumens de Christi vulnere principium.
Caelorum regnum sperate, hoc fonte renati,
Non recipit felix vita semel genitos.
Nec numerus quenquam sclerum nec forma suorum terreat,
Hoc natus flumine sanctus erit.

55 For the now standard argument see F. J. Dölger, 'Die Inschrift im Baptisterium S. Giovanni in Fonte an der Lateranensischen Basilika aus der Zeit Xystus III (432–440) und die Symbolik des Taufbrunnens bei Leo dem Grossen', *JAC* 2 (1930), pp. 252–57.

56 Leo, *Serm.* 24.3, trans. *NPNF*, ser. 2, 12, 135.

57 Leo, *Serm.* 49.3. See also *Serm.* 24.3, which speaks of the spiritual origins of a new people through the water of baptism.

58 Leo, *Serm.* 63.6.

59 Many other documents survive that express these ideas. See the works of Bedard and Orfrasio, as well as author's forthcoming work, *The Signs and Symbols of Baptism in the Early Church.*

Church too conceives without sexual intercourse and delivers without labour pains, physical discharge or harm to her body. Unlike Mary, however, the Church's fertility is infinite. She brings forth innumerable children, earning her the title Mother of All Christians (a title significantly close to Eve's). But she is not like earthly women, since her fecundity results either from the descent of the Holy Spirit upon her watery womb (the font) or by its insemination by God the Father himself. The Church is at once faithful spouse, chaste bride and prolific mother. Because all her children are generated from the seed of a common Father, they are equally heirs to the promise of salvation. Once delivered, she nurtures her children and keeps them safe from sin and death so long as they are in her embrace.

That the Church should be conceptualized as a mother is consistent with a general ancient (and modern) tendency to personify institutions, cities, nations and virtues as feminine figures. Biblical literature, furthermore, is filled with the prototype of the mother, equated with Israel, Jerusalem, or the Church (cf. Isa. 54; Gal. 4.22). Given this, the early Church's use of such poetic language, metaphor and allegory is not necessarily surprising. What does call our attention is the use of sexual and birthing imagery, which points to the centrality of an archetypal image of fertility and nurturance – an image that was later applied to the Virgin Mary as she came to be depicted nursing the infant Jesus and, as the 'mother of mercies', sheltering her children. In addition, this image functions as a unitive force. Mothers, more than fathers, assure that siblings are related to one another, that they belong to the same family. Sharing this institutional, ecclesial mother gives unrelated individuals a bond that surpasses ordinary citizenship.

Finally, we see that in early Christian literature, the sexual and procreative metaphors are concentrated on this allegorized figure, especially with reference to the rite of baptism, where the imagery is concentrated and extremely potent. A religion with an immaculate virgin mother at the centre of its narrative, and one that places a high value on sexual renunciation, finds its fertile mother goddess nonetheless – but one whose value as a symbol for women is at least ambiguous. Like her sister Mary, the Church must achieve the humanly impossible – be both mother and virgin. Furthermore, this mother's procreative organ is openly discussed and displayed; her womb (baptismal font) filled, consecrated and delivered of children over and over again. She is an active participant in human regeneration, but her fecundity and nurturance are undeniably dependent upon male agency.[60]

The Font as Womb: An Architectural Example

The preceding textual evidence demonstrates the importance in antiquity of the image of Church as mother with a font for a womb. As we have seen, several aspects of the ancient baptismal ritual itself embodied this concept, including the nakedness of candidates as they entered and emerged from the font. Perhaps even more concrete than certain words or actions were a few of those ancient fonts, designed to represent a mother's womb.

Historians of Christian architecture have noted that early baptismal fonts came in a wide variety of shapes, sizes and relative placement to the main hall. And while

---

60 See the even more negative conclusion of Jill Raitt, 'The *Vagina Dentata* and the *Immaculatus Uterus Divini Fontis*', *JAAR*, 48 (1980), pp. 415–31.

one of the earliest known (the font in the house church of Dura Europos) was rectangular, perhaps in order to suggest the shape of a tomb, other early shapes included octagonal (as in Ambrose's basilica in Milan), hexagonal, cruciform, polylobed and round (e.g., the original font built at St John Lateran and the late fourth-century font in the baptistery of S. Giovanni in Naples; see Fig. 3). Those round shapes may have been meant to correspond to the mother's womb.[61]

One very well preserved font appears to have been designed to symbolize the Church's maternal organs even more concretely. Copied from a fourth-century original, this fifth-century model has been painstakingly restored in the ruins of the ancient north African city of Sufetula (modern day Sbeitla in Tunisia).[62] Found in the centre of a small room attached to the eastern apse of the main hall of what must have been the Catholic cathedral, the elongated and undulating shape of the font looks much like a woman's vulva (Fig. 4). Candidates would enter from one direction (presumably the west) and stand in the well of the font to be baptized. Emerging, then, from the Mother Church's vagina, they would climb out on the opposite side (the east) and present themselves, wet and naked, as new-born babies, ready to join their new siblings and perhaps to receive a symbolic swallow of sweetened milk along with wine and bread at the altar rail.

61 On the subject of baptismal fonts in antiquity see J.G. Davies, *The Architectural Setting of Baptism* (London: Barrie and Rockliff, 1962); A. Grabar, *Le baptistère paléochrétien* (Mulhouse: Centre de culture chretienne, 1980); A. Khatchatrian, *Origine et typologie des baptistères paléochrétiens* (Mulhouse: Centre de culture chrétienne, 1982); and the author's forthcoming work, *Living Water: Iconography and Architecture of Early Christian Baptism* (Leiden: Brill).

62 See a discussion of this site and its font in Noël Duval and Françoise Baratte, *Les ruines de Sufetula, Sbeïtla* (Tunis: Société Tunisienne de Diffusion, 1973), pp. 56–59. Contemporary fonts are (more and more) being designed for full immersion, but are rarely designed to suggest the shape of a womb and even less of the mother Church's vulva. Rather, modern baptistery plans tend to have tub, cruciform, or octoganal shapes to suggest the baptizand's cleansing, participation in Christ's death and resurrection, or the eighth day of the new creation. See S. Anita Stauffer, *On Baptismal Fonts: Ancient and Modern* (Nottingham: Grove Books, 1994); and Regina Kuehn, *A Place for Baptism* (Chicago: Liturgical Training Publications, 1992).

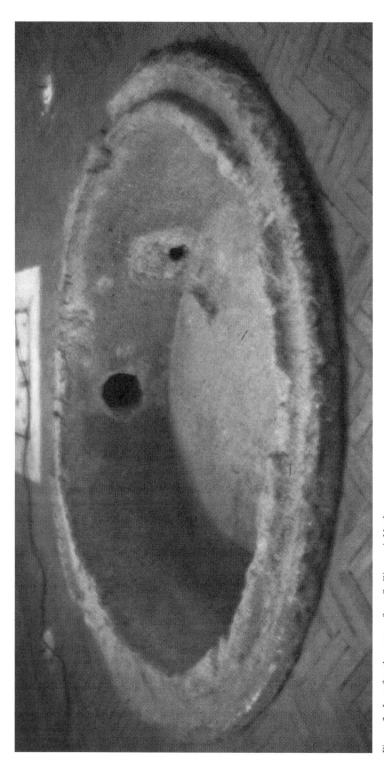

Figure 3. Late fourth-century font, S. Giovanni, Naples

Figure 4. Fifth-century font, Sufetula (modern-day Sbeitla), Tunisia

WHEN IS A TEXT ABOUT A WOMAN A TEXT ABOUT A WOMAN?: THE CASES OF ASENETH AND PERPETUA[1]

ROSS S. KRAEMER

Authors of divers ethnic identity and religious proclivity, including Jews and eventually Christians, suffuse Hellenistic and Roman literature with narratives about women. Such works range from Judith, Susanna and the expanded Greek Esther in those ancient Jewish writings usually classed as 'apocrypha' or deuterocanonical,[2] to Apuleius's *Metamorphoses* and various Hellenistic novels such as Chariton's *Chareas and Callirhoe*,[3] to Livy's account of the importation of the Bacchanalian rites to Rome, to the Christian *Acts of Thecla*, martyrdom accounts in Eusebius, and 'biographies' of exemplary Christian women by Jerome and others.[4] None of these writings is known to have been authored by women. Some, like Apuleius's *Metamorphoses* or Jerome's encomia are *known* to have been authored by men; many are anonymous, like Judith, Susanna and the *Acts of Thecla*.[5] One section of an otherwise anonymous work, the so-called 'diary' portion of the *Martyrdom of Perpetua*, claims female authorship.

With the resurgence of the second wave of feminism[6] in the last third of the twentieth century, these texts became the focus of intensive study and debate.[7] Of particular concern was the question of what, if anything, they tell us about actual women in the ancient Mediterranean. Hypothetically, stories that appear to be about a woman, or women, may be about any number of things. They may be about

1 This article draws on two prior publications, Ross Shepard Kraemer, *When Aseneth Met Joseph: A Late Antique Tale of the Biblical Patriarch and his Egyptian Wife, Revisited* (New York and Oxford: Oxford University Press, 1998), especially ch. 7, 'Why is Aseneth a Woman? The Use and Significance of Gender in the Aseneth Stories', and Ross S. Kraemer and Shira L. Lander, 'Perpetua and Felicitas', in Philip Esler (ed.), *The Early Christian World* (London: Routledge, 2000), vol. 2, pp. 1048–68.

2 On which see generally Lawrence A. Wills, *The Jewish Novel in the Ancient World* (Ithaca, NY and London: Cornell University Press, 1995).

3 Collected and translated in B. P. Reardon (ed.), *Collected Ancient Greek Novels* (Berkeley and Los Angeles, CA and London: University of California Press, 1989).

4 Selections of many of these, in translation, together with introductions and bibliography, may be found in Ross Shepard Kraemer (ed.), *Women's Religions in the Greco-Roman World: A Sourcebook* (New York: Oxford University Press, 2004).

5 For Tertullian's claim to know the author of *Thecla*, see below, p. 167; see also Kraemer, *Women's Religions*, pp. 259–61.

6 The first feminist 'wave' refers to activism and thought from the mid nineteenth century through 1920, culminating in the passage of the nineteenth amendment to the US Constitution, granting women the right to vote. Although technically the second 'wave' begins after 1920, feminist thought and activism became much more significant in the period following WWII, with the publication of works such as Simone de Beauvoir's *The Second Sex* (*Le Deuxième Sexe,* Paris: Gallimard, 1949) and Betty Friedan's *The Feminine Mystique* (New York: Norton, 1963).

7 For bibliography, see Kraemer, *Women's Religions*.

historical individuals, or they may be fictionalized accounts of the experiences of real women, although not necessarily of any one particular woman. Alternatively, stories about women may be allegories whereby one or more female characters represent something other than real women, the soul for instance, or the people of Israel, or the Church.

These are by no means the only possibilities. Stories seemingly about women may rather reflect competing ancient constructions of gender, that is, to offer a somewhat coarsely grained definition, the meanings that cultures ascribe to the categories male and female, meanings that are neither fixed nor uniform but are themselves human constructions and therefore variable.[8] In such stories, women characters may serve a variety of functions. They may represent their authors' ideal women (who may have little connection to real women, ordinary or otherwise). Moreover, as some recent studies suggest, they may function as stand-ins for male authors and readers, an heuristic device by which ancient men explored concerns about identity and gender.[9] These alternatives are not mutually exclusive: many stories may be an amalgamation of two or more of these, or perhaps about none. To a feminist historian with a particular interest in reconstructing and theorizing the so-called 'religious' practices and ideas of women in the ancient Mediterranean,[10] these texts are both alluring and aggravating. They are alluring for their richness of representation, and they are aggravating for their resistance to categorization and their refusal to yield reliable, verifiable answers to the questions such historians wish to ask of them.

These issues may be explored in more depth by considering two particular ancient narratives about women. The first is a relatively obscure work conventionally called

8 Definitions of gender and of gender construction are themselves quite fraught and highly contested. The extensive literature on the subject is beyond the scope of this note, but readers unacquainted with these discussions might find helpful Joan W. Scott, 'Gender: A Useful Category of Historical Analysis', *American Historical Review* 91 (1986), pp. 1053–75; Daniel Boyarin, 'Gender', in Mark C. Taylor (ed.), *Critical Terms for Religious Studies* (Chicago: University of Chicago Press, 1998), pp. 117–35, and Elizabeth A. Castelli (ed.), *Women, Gender, Religion: A Reader* (New York: Palgrave, 2001).

9 See, e.g., Kate Cooper, *The Virgin and the Bride. Idealized Womanhood in Late Antiquity* (Cambridge, MA: Harvard University Press, 1996); Elizabeth A. Clark, 'The Lady Vanishes: Dilemmas of a Feminist Historian after the Linguistic Turn', *CH*, 67.1 (1998), pp. 1–31; *eadem*, 'Ideology, History and the Construction of "Woman" in Late Ancient Christianity', *JECS*, 2.2 (1994), pp. 155–84, *eadem*, 'Holy Women, Holy Words: Early Christian Women, Social History, and the Linguistic Turn', *JECS*, 6.3 (1998), pp. 413–30; *eadem*, 'Rewriting Early Christian History: Augustine's Representation of Monica', in J. W. Drijvers and J. W. Watt (eds), *Portraits of Spiritual Authority* (Leiden: E.J. Brill, 1999), pp. 3–23. For another instance questioning the historicity of persons in ancient texts, see Daniel Boyarin, *Carnal Israel: Reading Sex in Talmudic Culture* (Berkeley: University of California Press, 1993), p. 11, who says of Rabbinic texts: 'Many critics have realized that these texts are essentially literary, that is fictional, accounts about men (and occasionally) women who probably lived but functioned primarily as signifiers of values within the culture, as exempla.'

10 By theorizing, I mean here the formulation and testing of explanatory models. For a helpful discussion of some of these issues, see Russell T. McCutcheon, '"My Theory of the Brontosaurus...": Postmodernism and "Theory" of Religion', in his *Critics Not Caretakers: Redescribing the Public Study of Religion* (Albany: State University of New York Press, 2001), pp. 3–23, esp. p. 111. I use the term 'religious' in quotation marks because too often readers assume both that the terms 'religion' or 'religious' naturally refer to certain things, and that the categories themselves describe human behaviours and ideas that are wholly different from other human behaviours and ideas.

Joseph and Aseneth, although I prefer to call it simply *Aseneth*, after its female protagonist.[11] The second text is the somewhat better known *Martyrdom of Saints Perpetua and Felicitas*.[12]

Aseneth

Most scholarly works characterize *Aseneth* as a Jewish text written in Greek sometime between about 100 BCE and 135 CE, probably in Alexandria or perhaps elsewhere in Egypt. In my view, *Aseneth* is more likely to have been composed in the third or perhaps even the fourth century CE, anywhere from the land of Israel itself to neighbouring Syria to Asia Minor, by an author or authors whose religious identity – Jewish or Christian – is difficult to determine. Composed, probably, in Greek, it was subsequently translated into Syriac, Latin and Armenian.[13] Extant are both a shorter and a longer version of the story, with some significant differences: in my view the shorter text is earlier, and the summary below is taken from that version.[14]

The story appears to take its cue from the brief notice in Gen. 41.45 that Pharaoh, the ruler of Egypt, rewarded the biblical Joseph for his wise interpretation of dreams by giving him, among other things, a bride named Asenath, daughter of a priest of On. It opens at the beginning of the seven years of plenty, as Joseph, now Pharaoh's second-in-command, travels Egypt to collect grain against the forthcoming famine. He comes to Heliopolis, the City of the Sun, where Aseneth lives with her father, Pentephres, her unnamed mother, and a large household of servants. Aseneth is a beautiful virgin of eighteen who lives in a high tower within the family compound.

Learning of Joseph's imminent arrival, Pentephres calls his dutiful daughter and proposes that she marry Joseph. But Aseneth, refusing, recounts local gossip that Joseph is an abandoned son who, sold into slavery, had sex with his master's wife. He is therefore obviously an unsuitable husband. This scene clearly alludes to Genesis 37–39, particularly 39.6–20, where the unnamed wife of Potiphar, Joseph's owner, attempts unsuccessfully to seduce the Hebrew slave and, when she fails, accuses him of attempted rape. In light of her story, Potiphar throws Joseph into prison.

Upon first seeing Joseph, Aseneth is thunderstruck. Riding a gold chariot drawn by four snow-white horses with gold bridles, Joseph is the very image of Helios, and

---

11 Greek texts in M. Philonenko, *Joseph et Aseneth: Introduction, texte critique, traduction, et notes* (Studia Post Biblica; Leiden: E. J. Brill, 1968); Christoph Burchard (ed.), *Joseph und Aseneth* (Pseudepigrapha Veteris Testamenti Graece, 5; Leiden and Boston: E.J. Brill, 2003); introduction, bibliography and substantial English translation in Kraemer, *Women's Religions*, pp. 308–27. See also Kraemer, *When Aseneth Met Joseph*; Marinus de Jonge, *Pseudepigrapha of the Old Testament as Part of Christian Literature: The Case of the Testaments of the Twelve Patriarchs and the Greek Life of Adam and Eve* (Leiden and Boston: E.J. Brill, 2003), pp. 58–62.

12 Text and English translation in H. Musurillo (ed.), *Acts of the Christian Martyrs* (Oxford: The Clarendon Press, 1972), pp. 106–31; text and French translation in Jacqueline Amat (ed.), *Passion de Perpétue et de Félicité suivi des Acts: Introduction, Texte Critique, Traduction, Commentaire et Index* (SC, 417; Paris: Les Éditions du Cerf, 1996); for introduction, bibliography and Musurillo's translation, see also Kraemer, *Women's Religions*, pp. 356–68.

13 For extensive discussion of these issues, see Kraemer, *When Aseneth Met Joseph*; also de Jonge, *Pseudepigrapha*, pp. 58–62.

14 My translation in Kraemer, *Women's Religions*, is based on the shorter text but contains some of the more significant passages from the longer text.

this is precisely what Aseneth, watching from her tower, calls him. Noticing her at the window and fearing that she, like all the Egyptian women, will be overcome by their desire for him (another allusion to – and exaggeration of – Genesis 39), Joseph asks Pentephres to send her away. Pentephres explains that Aseneth is his daughter and a pure virgin, so Joseph consents to meet her. But when Aseneth moves to kiss him chastely, Joseph holds her off with his hand against her chest and then makes a long speech. Witnessing Aseneth break into tears, he relents somewhat, and he prays to God that she may receive life and blessing. The virgin flees to her rooms, renounces idolatry, throws all her idols out the window, and rids herself of a wardrobe of clothing embroidered with idolatrous images. After seven days of lying face down in ashes and sackcloth, fasting, weeping and repenting, Aseneth confesses her sins to the God of Joseph and prays for forgiveness.

As she finishes, the morning star rises in the east, the heavens split apart, and a luminous angelic being with the form and face of Joseph descends to Aseneth's chamber. He tells her that the Lord has heard her confession and that Joseph's earlier prayer for her will be fulfilled. He further announces that she will become Joseph's bride. Overjoyed, Aseneth throws herself at the angel's feet and offers to prepare him a table of bread and wine. The angel requests that she also bring a honeycomb, which she finds, miraculously but conveniently, in an inside chamber. He tells her that the honey of the comb is angelic food that confers immortality on all who consume it.

Next, the angel shows Aseneth an astonishing mystery in which snow-white bees with purple wings and gold diadems rise up from the honeycomb and entwine her from head to toe. At the angel's commands, they all fall down dead and then rise up and fly away to the courtyard of her tower. Finally, the angel ascends to heaven in a fiery chariot. Shortly thereafter, Aseneth and Joseph marry and have two sons, Manasseh and Ephraim.

Though the story could end here, both the shorter and longer versions contain an appendix of sorts that chronicles the events of the seven years of famine. When Joseph departs to distribute grain, Pharaoh's son, who had previously sought to marry Aseneth, attempts to abduct her; he is aided by two of Joseph's brothers. In good romantic form, the plot is foiled not only by Joseph's other, virtuous brothers but also by the miraculous intervention of God, invoked by Aseneth.

No study of *Aseneth* takes it to be an historical account of a late second-millennium BCE marriage. But it might be read as a thinly veiled portrait of elite life in the author's time. The portrait of the daughter raised in the seclusion of her elite father's high tower, of familial relationships, clothing, food, household arrangements, etc., all might reflect realia. Aseneth's acceptance of Joseph's God and her transformation into an acceptable Jewish wife become for this approach best understood as fictionalized accounts of conversion experiences and rituals undergone by actual proselytes to Judaism.[15] In my initial published work on the text, I took precisely such a stance.[16]

---

15 See e.g., Randall A. Chesnutt, *From Death to Life: Conversion in Joseph and Aseneth* (JSPSup, 16; Sheffield, UK: Sheffield Academic Press, 1995); Howard C. Kee, 'The Socio-Cultural Setting of Joseph and Aseneth', *NTS*, 29 (1983), pp. 394–413.

16 Ross Shepard Kraemer, *Her Share of the Blessings: Women's Religions Among Pagans, Jews and Christians in the Greco-Roman World* (New York: Oxford University Press, 1992), pp. 110–12.

Other scholars read *Aseneth* allegorically. Some late nineteenth-century studies, written when the texts were first 'rediscovered', saw the work as a Christian allegory of the Soul.[17] A fairly recent study explores the figure of Aseneth as an allegory of an alternate Temple to the God of Israel in Hellenistic Egyptian Leontopolis.[18] Although I think that *Aseneth* may, in fact, intentionally utilize some allegorical components (particularly in its repeated association of the heroine with divine Wisdom), I am doubtful that allegory is its central driving force. While Christian readers in fourth and fifth-century Syria did read the story of Joseph and Aseneth in Genesis as an allegory of the relationship between Christ and the Gentile church, this fact does not enable us to gauge anything about the intentions of the author(s) who committed *Aseneth* to the versions we now have.[19] Despite numerous theoretical discussions that deny to authorial intentionality any role in determining the 'meaning' of a text, for the purposes of historical reconstruction, authorial intention is not entirely irrelevant.[20]

Increasingly persuasive in my view are those studies that read late Hellenistic and early Christian romances in which female protagonists play central roles as reflective of debates about gender construction.[21] An excellent example of such an approach may be found in A.-J. Levine's reading of the Deuterocanonical Book of Tobit as a tale in which the proper subjugation and domiciling of women serve as the vehicle to express and resolve anxiety about the conditions of diaspora.[22] In Levine's analysis, the story of Sarah and her eventual husband, Tobias, becomes the medium for discussion of the larger question of how Jews in the diaspora can flourish. Levine argues that by exaggerating various representations of difference, of boundaries and definitions, and then resolving them, Tobit symbolically restores order to a potentially disordered diaspora existence, an order that is further guaranteed by adherence to certain social practices and norms. While elements of Tobit might reflect actual social experience, the narrative is not, in Levine's reading, primarily a story of how marriages are made. Instead, she writes,

> [w]omen properly domiciled in an endogamous relationship become the means by which the threat of the diaspora is eliminated. ... territorial relations are displaced onto gender relations. ...[23]

17 P. Batiffol, 'Le Livre de la Prière d'Aseneth', in *idem* (ed.), *Studia patristica: Ètudes d'ancienne littérature chrétienne* 1–2 (Paris: Leroux, 1889–90), pp. 1–115.

18 Gideon Bohak, *Joseph and Aseneth and the Temple of Leontopolis* (EJL, 10; Atlanta: Scholars Press, 1996).

19 See Kraemer, *When Aseneth Met Joseph*, pp. 245–85.

20 For a helpful discussion of these issues, see Elizabeth A. Clark, *History, Theory, Text: Historians and the Linguistic Turn* (Cambridge, MA: Harvard University Press, 2004), especially ch. 7 ('Texts and Contexts').

21 See above, n. 8, although the degree to which the work of Cooper, Clark and others shifts the focus from women's history to men's history continues to concern me. For a nicely self-conscious discussion of the potential problems, see David A. Halperin, 'Why Is Diotima a Woman?', in D. Halperin, J. Winkler and F. Zeitlin (eds), *Before Sexuality: The Construction of Erotic Experience in the Ancient Greek World* (Princeton, NJ: Princeton University Press, 1990), pp. 257–308 (esp. 294–98).

22 A.-J. Levine, 'Diaspora as Metaphor: Bodies and Boundaries in the Book of Tobit', in Andrew Overman and R.S. Maclennan (eds), *Diaspora Jews and Judaism: Essays in Honor of, and in Dialogue with, A. Thomas Kraabel* (South Florida Studies in Judaism; Atlanta: Scholars Press, 1992), pp. 105–17.

23 Levine, 'Diaspora as Metaphor', p. 105.

By constraining women's roles, by using women as tokens of exchange to preserve economic and kinship ties, by depicting them as the cause as well as the locus of despair, and by removing them from direct contact with heaven, the Jewish male has brought order to his diaspora existence. In captivity, he can assert his freedom and his self-identity by depicting the other as in captivity to him. With boundaries redefined in relation to as well as upon bodies, Tobit's family is more stable than the world of the exile. ...[24]

Certainly, the motif of self and other dominates *Aseneth*. Paramount among the aspects of Aseneth's transformation is her change from a foreign (Egyptian) idolater, wholly unsuitable as a wife for a man who reveres God, to the opposite: a reverent woman who renounces all her former idolatry and worships only the same God. *Aseneth* may be seen as a narrative of transformation from the other to the self, viewed from the perspective of the author(s), who here clearly identifies with the household and community of Joseph.

Aseneth's otherness has many dimensions: she worships Egyptian gods, wears emblems of her idolatry on her clothing and jewellery, and eats food unacceptable to 'Hebrews'. Her otherness is epitomized in that early scene where Aseneth attempts to kiss Joseph, and he – holding her off physically – responds:

It is not appropriate for a man who reveres God (θεοσεβὴς ἀνήρ), who blesses the living God with his mouth and eats the blessed bread of life and drinks the blessed cup of immortality and is anointed with the blessed ointment of incorruptibility, to kiss a foreign woman, one who blesses dead and deaf idols with her mouth and eats the bread of strangling from their table and drinks the cup of ambush from their libations and is anointed with the ointment of perdition. But a man who reveres God (θεοσεβὴς ἀνήρ) will kiss his mother, and his sister who is of his own tribe and family, and his wife who shares his bed, those women who with their mouths bless the living God. Similarly, also it is not appropriate for a woman who reveres God (θεοσεβὴς γυνή) to kiss a strange man, because such is an abomination before God. (*Aseneth* 8.5–7)

In this passage, self and other are clearly differentiated with respect to food, worship and physical contact, both sexual and filial.

In the subsequent representation of Aseneth's transformation, gender looms large. First, it is the other, the Egyptian, who is in this narrative represented by a woman, while the self, the one who reveres God, is represented by a man.[25] One might argue that this representational pattern is simply a consequence of the tale told in Genesis. Alternatively, the story of Joseph and Aseneth may have received such extensive articulation precisely (though certainly not only) because it offers the opportunity to elaborate upon the transformation of a woman. The choice of a woman as the exemplar of one transformed (or even 'converted'), most familiar in the biblical story of Ruth, may reflect an idea of woman as a more natural exemplar of the other and therefore as a better candidate for transformation. The ideal transformation narrative, then, may well be one that utilizes gender as a central component of difference. Both Joseph and Aseneth are described in language that is sometimes significantly gender-specific. Joseph is a man strong (or powerful) in wisdom and knowledge (ἀνὴρ δυνατὸς ἐν

---

24 Levine, 'Diaspora as Metaphor', p. 117.

25 The primary signifiers of identity in the text are θεοσεβής (for Joseph, his brothers and his community), and 'Egyptians'. See Kraemer, *When Aseneth Met Joseph*, pp. 272–73.

σοφία καὶ ἐπιστήμη). He is called σώφρων, wise, temperate, reasonable: one of the cardinal virtues of the Greek (male) philosopher. (Σωφροσύνη is also applied to women, but usually with different connotations, primarily of chastity.)

In contrast to Joseph's wisdom and self-control (manifest *inter alia* in his ability to resist foreign women), Aseneth is miserable and foolish (ἄφρων καὶ θρασεῖα). Her initial failure to perceive the truth about Joseph and her acceptance of the false Egyptian gossip exemplify her ignorance, a stereotypical trait of women in ancient sources. Aseneth exemplifies the most negative aspects of ancient constructions of the feminine, while Joseph exemplifies virtuous masculinity (a phrase that is technically redundant).

Aseneth's transformation utilizes gender in yet another, central way. In her initial state, Aseneth is not only a woman but also, in several respects, the wrong sort of woman. Although Aseneth is early on said 'in all things [to resemble] the daughters of the Hebrews',[26] not only does she lack the virtues of the Israelite matriarchs, she is initially arrogant, unsubmissive and disdainful of men. After her transformation, Aseneth epitomizes the good woman: she is submissive, willing if necessary to be servile, appropriately affectionate toward men, the ideal daughter, wife and, soon, mother. This transformation may point to a particular characterization of the other which classifies 'their' women as not properly submissive and as not conforming to appropriate gender categories, whereas 'our' women are and do.

Particularly susceptible to gender analysis is Aseneth's professed desire to become enslaved to Joseph (a reversal, perhaps, of the Israelite enslavement to Egyptians). The transformed Aseneth prays not for marriage to Joseph, but for (another form of?) permanent subservience. (The portions set in boldface represent the readings of the longer version; those in parentheses represent wording found only in the shorter.)

> Deliver me to [Joseph] as a servant (παιδίσκη) **and slave (δούλη)**, (that) **and I** (may) **will make his bed and** wash his feet and wait on him (διακονήσω) **and be a slave (δούλη) to him** and serve as his slave (δουλεύσω) for all the rest of my life.[27]

This concern for subservience is an integral part of narratives depicting encounters between humans and angelic or other divine beings, such as Dan. 8.17–19, 10.9 or Judges 13. Since the human assuming the status of slave or servant is male in most other examples of such encounters, it might appear that Aseneth's desire to subordinate herself to Joseph has no particular gendered significance. But on the contrary, it is precisely the construction of feminine gender as subordinate and submissive that is at work in all of this imagery. Before the masculine God or angel or other divine emanation, petitioners are as women and as slaves, whose status itself incorporates an element of gender differentiation. For in their relation to their owners, slaves, too, assumed the role of women in relation to men. For a woman, then, the acquisition of wisdom appears to include recognition and acceptance of her subordinate status.

During Aseneth's encounter with Joseph's angelic double, gender is also an explicit element.[28] Instructed by the angel[29] to change out of her mourning clothes, wash her

---

26 *Aseneth* 1.7. This phrase is actually reconstructed from divers manuscripts: for some discussion, see Kraemer, *When Aseneth Met Joseph*, pp. 44–45, n. 16 and Burchard, *Joseph und Aseneth*, pp. 74–75.

27 *Aseneth* 13.12 (shorter): 13.15 (longer).

28 *Aseneth* 15.1.

29 *Aseneth* 15.1.

face in living water (ὕδατι ζῶντι), and dress in pristine garments,[30] Aseneth not only follows but adds to the angelic instructions: she covers her head with a beautiful veil. The angel remarks immediately: 'Lift off the veil from your head, because today you are a holy virgin, and your head is as a young man's.'[31] Aseneth complies, and nothing further is said about the veil. After the angel departs, Aseneth will again veil her head.

The angel's words signal that Aseneth's transformation includes at least a temporary change in her gender identity. One possibility is that the author intended the scene to signify Aseneth's androgyny, which characterizes the status of initiates in many religious traditions. If so, this verse presumes a social system in which Aseneth's veil symbolizes her gender (and probably also her place within the social hierarchy), whereas the absence of the veil symbolizes her distancing from her gender and her (temporary) removal from that same hierarchy. We may also have here a more specific allusion to the state of the primordial being in Gen. 1.26–27, understood to have been initially without gender distinction.[32]

> Then God said, 'Let us make humankind in our image, according to our likeness...'
> So God created humankind in his image, in the image of God he created them, male and female he created them.[33]

Alternatively, the author may have intended to signify Aseneth's transformation into masculinity. Numerous writers, from the Jewish philosopher Philo of Alexandria to various Christian authors such as Paul to the Neoplatonic Porphyry, utilize the metaphor of becoming male as a stage in the salvation of the soul, which is feminine in Greek (ἡ ψυχή). Porphyry's exhortation to his wife, Marcella, is particularly instructive:

> [d]o not be overly concerned about whether your body is male or female; do not regard yourself as a woman, Marcella, for I did not devote myself to you as such. Flee from every effeminate element of the soul as if you are clothed in a male body. For the most blessed offspring come from virginal soul and unmated Intelligence.[34]

Paul's tortuous argument about women's headcoverings in 1 Corinthians is explicitly supported by his exegesis of Genesis 1–3. In 1 Cor. 11.7, he interprets Gen.

---

30 *Aseneth* 14.12–13.

31 Νεανίσκος. The ordinary meaning of this term is as translated. But in some instances, it appears to have an angelic connotation: it is the word used in Mk 16.5 for the being encountered by the women who come to Jesus' now-empty tomb (who in Mt. 28.2 is an angel of the Lord [ἄγγελος κυρίου] and in Lk. 24.4, two men [ἄνδρες δύο]). It is not impossible to read this passage as saying that today, Aseneth's head is as that of an angelic being, which is consistent with other aspects of the transformation scene. Still, the language remains gendered as masculine.

32 See, e.g., Wayne Meeks, 'The Image of the Androgyne: Some Uses of a Symbol in Earliest Christianity', *HR* 13.3 (1974), pp. 185–89.

33 Translation from the NRSV, which notes that in Hebrew, the text literally reads, 'in the image of God he created *him*, male and female he created them'.

34 *Letter to Marcella* 33, in Kathleen O'Brien Wicker, *Porphyry the Philosopher to Marcella, Text and Translation with Introduction and Notes* (SBLTT, 28; Atlanta: Scholars Press, 1987). Porphyry appears to share some of Philo's hierarchical ranking of irrational feminine soul, rational male soul, virginal soul. The last phrase is reminiscent of Philo's statement about the Therapeutrides's preference for spiritual children in *On The Contemplative Life*, 68–69, which itself has resonances with the work of Plato (see, *inter alia*, Halperin, 'Why is Diotima a Woman?').

1.26–27 with Gen. 2.21–25 to argue: 'For a man ought not to have his head veiled/covered, since he is the image and reflection/glory [δόξα] of God; but woman is the reflection/glory [δόξα] of man.' For Paul, creation establishes a divine hierarchy of God–man–woman, which he believed had to be preserved in human social relationships. If the author of this passage in *Aseneth* held similar concepts, we might infer that because Aseneth's head is on the day of her angelophany like that of a young man, it is inappropriate for her to cover her head. For the moment, at least, Aseneth stands in a human–divine hierarchy as though she were male and as the direct image of the divine, as the primordial *adam* (ἄνθρωπος, the term regularly used in *Aseneth* for Joseph's angelic double) in Gen. 1.26–27 was the direct image or glory of God and perhaps also androgynous.

At the very least then, the tale of Aseneth evidences particular ancient constructions of gender, most notably one in which biology and gender are not necessarily coterminous. Such a construction had important practical ramifications for constraints on women: in the writings of Philo of Alexandria, this construction is linked to his account of elite women who are said to live as full members of a monastic contemplative enclave on the shores of Lake Mareotis;[35] among followers of Christ in mid first-century CE Corinth, it appears to be central to their claims to charismatic authority; in the letter of Porphyry to Marcella quoted above, it is what enables her to practise the philosophical life.

Aseneth *and Ancient Social Reality*

Aseneth's portrait of ancient social life *is* generally consistent with what we know from numerous other sources. Elite, aristocratic families did live in large houses in relative luxury, with retinues of servants and slaves, and they did own massive country estates. Daughters of such families were likely to be raised in relative seclusion, with dedicated female companions; the daughters were also likely to be married at age eighteen, if not before, in marriages arranged by their families. Yet contemporary literary theorists caution us that details of verisimilitude may not be what they seem: rather than affording us direct access to the underlying social realia of the author, they function to create a persuasive narrative world that inclines us to accept the author's rhetoric. Studies on the relationship between Greek novels and social reality also caution us about seeking too close a correspondence between the details of the text and the social reality of the author(s) and intended audience(s). Numerous details, such as Aseneth's residence in a high tower, seem more consistent with folktales and popular narratives, including not only Greek romances, but also

---

35 On the Therapeutics and Philo's *On the Contemplative Life*, see Kraemer, *Women's Religions*, pp. 28–31, with extensive introduction and bibliography. As my careful phrasing implies, however, I have become more sceptical about the likelihood that Philo's account of the female and male Therapeutics describes actual persons and social practices, as I develop in a project in progress. In this view, I thus differ somewhat from the detailed, interesting recent study by Joan E. Taylor, *Jewish Women Philosophers in First-Century Alexandria: Philo's 'Therapeutae' Reconsidered* (Oxford: Oxford University Press, 2003), and I have considerable interest in the arguments of Troels Engberg-Pedersen, 'Philo's *De Vita Contemplativa* as a Philosopher's Dream', *JSJ* 30 (1999), pp. 40–64.

late antique Christian narratives and martyrologies (that may themselves be indebted to the genre of Greek novels).[36]

Brigitte Egger's analysis of the representation of women and marriage in Greek novels affords additional insight into this question. Focusing specifically on the presentation of private marriage law in ancient romances, Egger shows that Greek novelists utilize not the realities of marital law and practice as can be reconstructed from existing legal and historical sources, but rather draw upon 'a combination of old and new legal assumptions, literary allusions and contemporary practice'.[37] She demonstrates that although Greek novelists do not always archaize in their representation of social reality, when they do archaize, they inevitably 'impose upon their women limitations and incapacities that did not exist in the same degree for their intended contemporary readers'.[38] In particular, the construction of marital law in the Greek novels represents a regression from the advances of Hellenistic law, which gave women considerably greater autonomy in comparison to earlier Athenian regulation.[39] 'The fabrication of femininity, as endorsed by the texts, is conventional and archaizing as compared to contemporary reality.'[40]

The resultant 'disabling' of women in these texts is accomplished subtly.[41] Modern readers have been struck by the novels' apparent characterization of women as unusually powerful and predominant in comparison to the representation of women in much other ancient literature. While Egger agrees that women predominate in these narratives, she finds the heroines of Greek romance 'immensely emotionally powerful and erotically ravishing', but otherwise 'restricted and disempowered ... The price paid for women's erotic centrality is their social containment in the realms of law and marriage, among others.'[42]

Together with my earlier consideration of gender construction, Egger's observations suggest that the representation of women in Hellenistic novels is far from straightforward, and it points to the authors' underlying efforts to construct femininity in ways that hint at social conflict over women's roles. If Egger is correct that Greek fiction constructs women as more constrained than they actually were, and marital law as more consonant with those constraints than it actually was, we may surmise that these stories are to some degree polemical: simultaneously, they wish for such a reality and present it as attractive and desirable.

Egger's observations about the presentation of both women and marriage in Greek novels are generally true for *Aseneth* as well. The heroine is presented as

---

36 The (probably) Byzantine *Martyrdoms* of St. Christine and St. Irene also feature heroines who live in a high tower, although there is some possibility of dependence between these stories and *Aseneth*. The text may be found in A. Wirth, *Danae in christlichen Legenden* (Prague: F. Tempsky, 1892), pp. 103–11; that of Irene in Medea Norsa, 'Martirio Di Santa Christina', *Studi italiani di filologia classica* 19 (1912), pp. 316–27.

37 Brigitte Egger, 'Women and Marriage in the Greek Novels: The Boundaries of Romance', in James Tatum (ed.), *The Search for the Ancient Novel* (Baltimore, MD and London: Johns Hopkins University Press, 1994), pp. 260–80 (271).

38 Egger, 'Marriage', p. 271.

39 Egger, 'Marriage', pp. 266–69.

40 Egger, 'Marriage', p. 271.

41 Egger, 'Marriage', p. 271.

42 Egger, 'Marriage', pp. 272–73.

both emotional and erotic. Just as Hellenistic novels tend to portray women as constrained socially and legally as well as to minimize the representation of women as autonomous, so, too, when Aseneth attempts to act autonomously (for instance, by refusing her father's suggestion that she marry Joseph), the text's condemnation of that autonomy is readily apparent. Conversely, Aseneth's eventual conformity to appropriate gender roles is praised and affirmed, and her rewards are precisely those of Greek romance, namely legitimate marriage, legitimate male heirs and familial acceptance.

All this, then, calls for scepticism about the utility of ancient fiction as unqualified evidence for the social practices of the authors and audiences, even more so with ancient fiction such as *Aseneth* whose authorship, date and provenance cannot be determined independently from the clues in the text itself. In fact, whenever it was composed, *Aseneth* was already a story about a past far distant from, and probably idealized by, its authors and audiences. The story's extensive dependence on biblical and related traditions for its construction of that idealized past leads to the conclusion that it says little specific about the lives and experiences of 'real' persons in the author(s)' own times and places.[43] The representation of women, or construction(s) of gender, in *Aseneth* (which differ significantly in the shorter and longer versions) are at best of modest use for reconstructing the realities of women's lives and the range of constructions of gender prevalent when the texts were initially composed and redacted.[44] Furthermore, these textual representations of reality are likely to be ideological: while seeming to 'describe' a particular reality, the story in fact takes a stance on that reality. Whether, though, *Aseneth* is a model to emulate or a cautionary tale may well have depended on the perspective of subsequent audiences.

The Martyrdom of Perpetua

A second text that has received extensive attention among scholars of both early Christianity and the later Roman empire is the *Passio Sanctarum Perpetuae et Felicitatis*, or *The Martyrdom of Saints Perpetua and Felicitas*. Set in Roman North Africa in the early third century and extant in Latin and Greek, the *Passio* narrates the martyrdom of Vibia Perpetua, Felicitas and three men, all five young recent converts to Christianity. The opening and closing portions of the *Passio* are written in the third-person, narrating the circumstances of the catechumens' arrest (sections 1–2) and the gruesome details of their death in the Roman arena (14–21). What distinguishes the *Passio* from numerous other ancient martyrdom narratives is that it claims to incorporate the first-person narratives of both Perpetua (sections 3–10) and Saturus, one of the young men (11–13). If this claim is correct, Perpetua's portion of the *Passio* would be the earliest known writing by a Christian woman.

For a feminist historian, the *Passio* would seem to be nothing short of a goldmine. The so-called 'diary' portion of the martyrdom contains a rich

---

43 See Kraemer, *When Aseneth Met Joseph*, pp. 19–88.

44 Kraemer, *When Aseneth Met Joseph*, pp. 191–224; see also Angela Standhartinger, *Das Frauenbild im Judentum der hellenistischen Zeit. Ein Beitrag anhand von 'Joseph & Aseneth'* (Leiden: E.J. Brill, 1995).

description of four visions that Perpetua has while awaiting death, in addition to a detailed account of her conflicts with her Roman father, her concerns for her infant son, and her leadership role in negotiating with the Roman officials on behalf of the prisoners. In the last several decades, numerous scholars, accepting the narrator's claim, have mined both the diary and the martyrdom narrative for a wealth of historical details.[45] Although I have been somewhat cautious, I, too, have drawn on the text as evidence for ancient Christian debates about leadership and gender, among other issues.[46]

Several years ago, while working on a co-authored brief 'biography' of Perpetua,[47] my then-doctoral student Shira Lander and I recognized some serious difficulties with the view that Perpetua wrote the central portion of the *Passio*, and even, perhaps, with the historicity of the martyrdom itself. Writing something in someone else's name, whether understood as intentional fraud or pious fiction, is a widespread practice in the ancient world.[48] The same Christian writer who provides our earliest attestation to the story (although not necessarily the text) of Perpetua, the North African Tertullian (late second–early third centuries CE) himself denounces an anonymous presbyter in Asia Minor who, he says, forged the story of Paul and Thecla.[49] (Whether Tertullian is here correct is irrelevant.[50]) The editor's claim that Perpetua (and Saturus) wrote the prison narrative in her own hand does not insure its authenticity for the modern scholar. The same assertion occurs, for instance, not only in several undisputed Pauline letters (1 Cor. 16.21; Gal. 6.11; and Phlm. 19) but in

---

45 E.g. Brent Shaw, 'The Passion of Perpetua', *Past and Present* 139 (1993), pp. 3–45, but see now Jan N. Bremmer, 'Perpetua and Her Diary: Authenticity, Family and Visions', in Walter Ameling (ed.), *Märtyrer und Märtyrerakten* (Stuttgart: Franz Steiner Verlag, 2002), pp. 77–120, who considers our views excessively sceptical. For additional bibliography, see Kraemer, *Women's Religions*, pp. 357–58.

46 Kraemer, *Her Share of the Blessings*, pp. 159–65.

47 Above, n. 1.

48 For discussion of the general question, see Bruce M. Metzger, 'Literary Forgeries and Canonical Pseudepigraphy', *JBL*, 91.1 (1972), pp. 3–24; Martin Rist, 'Pseudepigaphy and the Early Christians', in David E. Aune (ed.), *Studies in New Testament and Early Christian Literature*: *Essays in Honor of Allen P. Wikgren* (Leiden: E.J. Brill, 1972), pp. 75–91; Moshe J. Bernstein, 'Pseudepigraphy in the Qumran Scrolls: Categories and Functions', in Esther Glickler Chazon, Michael E. Stone, and Avital Pinnick (eds), *Pseudepigraphic Perspectives: The Apocrypha and Pseudepigrapha in Light of the Dead Sea Scrolls: Proceedings of the International Symposium of the Orion Center for the Study of the Dead Sea Scrolls and Associated Literature, 12–14 January, 1997* (Leiden: E.J. Brill, 1999), pp. 1–26; Marc Bregman, 'Pseudepigraphy in Rabbinic Literature', in Chazon et al. (eds), *Pseudepigraphic Perspectives*, pp. 27–41; see also J.A. Farrer, *Literary Forgeries* (New York: Longmans, Green and Co., 1907); Wolfgang Speyer, *Die literarische Fälschung im heidnischen und christlichen Altertum: Ein Versuch ihrer Deutung* (Munich: C.H. Beck, 1971).

49 For an English translation of the *Acts of (Paul and) Thecla*, see Kraemer, *Women's Religions*, pp. 297–307; for a feminist commentary with helpful bibliography, see Sheila McGinn, 'Perpetua', in Elizabeth Schüssler Fiorenza (ed.), *Searching the Scriptures: A Feminist Commentary* (New York: Crossroad, 1994), vol. 2, pp. 800–28. For an important analysis of recent debates about Thecla, see Shelly Matthews, 'Thinking of Thecla: Issues in Feminist Historiography', *JFSR*, 17.2 (2002), pp. 39–57. My present research project also entails a substantial re-consideration of *Thecla*.

50 Tertullian, *De Baptismo* 17.5. For discussion and bibliography, see Kraemer, *Women's Religions*, pp. 260–61.

letters now thought by many to be pseudonymous (e.g., Col. 4.18 and 2 Thess. 3.17, where the author's insistence on this point seems particularly telling).

Recently, Thomas Heffernan has critiqued the characterization of the prison narrative as a diary and questioned the authenticity of Perpetua's section on philological grounds.[51] Heffernan proposes instead that the prison narrative is a mediated account from one of Perpetua's visitors, to whom she revealed her dreams and the circumstances of her imprisonment.[52]

Contemporary claims about the authenticity of the prison narrative often appeal to the controversial notion of a particular and discernible female rhetoric.[53] Characterized as emotional, personal, fragmented and colloquial, the style of Perpetua's account is thought to prove the trustworthiness of the editor's claim. Even if the diary is somehow associated with 'female' style, it still seems highly plausible that such a style is purposefully constructed by an ancient author to appear as a (female) martyr's diary.

In reality, the essentialist claim that women in antiquity dependably wrote in a distinctive and detectable form and voice collapses in view of ancient sources.[54] Pliny the Younger, for instance, expresses his doubts that the wife of his friend Pompeius Saturninus could be the author of certain letters ascribed to her. Their style, he says, is reminiscent of 'Plautus or Terence being read in prose'.[55] Either, he argues, his friend's wife did not write them, or she learned how to write in male rhetorical style from her husband, something he ultimately concedes is possible. Implicit in Pliny's judgement may well be a notion of a distinctive female writing style, to which, however, these letters do not conform. The point is not that ancient male writers adhered to the notion of such a style; it is that works written in such a style need not point to women writers. Whether or not a woman could be trained to write 'like a man', it is demonstrable that a man could write 'like a woman', that is, in a voice recognizable as female. Numerous playwrights and novelists construct not only female characters but their speeches and letters as well, and in so doing they appeal to assumptions about gendered language similar to Pliny's. In his novel *Chaereas and Callirhoe*, Chariton has Callirhoe write a letter, which he has, of

51 Thomas Heffernan, 'Philology and Authorship in the *Passio Sanctarum Perpetuae et Felicitatis*', *Traditio: Studies in Ancient and Medieval History, Thought, and Religion* 50 (1995), pp. 315–25. Heffernan nevertheless retains the historicity of Perpetua, her detention and her visions. See also P. Habermehl, *Perpetua und der Ägypter oder Bilder des Bösen im frühen afrikanischen Christentum. Ein Versuch zur Passio Sanctarum Perpetuae et Felicitatis* (Berlin: Akademie Verlag, 1992), pp. 241–48, who raises concerns but ultimately does not resolve the question of the diary's authenticity.

52 Heffernan, 'Philology', pp. 323–24.

53 See, e.g., Peter Dronke, *Women Writers of the Middle Ages: A Critical Study of Texts from Perpetua († 203) to Marguerite Porete († 1310)* (Cambridge, UK: Cambridge University Press, 1984), pp. 1–17; Elizabeth A. Petroff, *Medieval Women's Visionary Literature* (New York: Oxford University Press, 1986), p. 63; Shaw, 'Perpetua', p. 19.

54 See, e.g., Mary R. Lefkowitz, 'Did Ancient Women Write Novels?', in Amy-Jill Levine (ed.), *'Women Like This': New Perspectives on Jewish Women in the Greco-Roman World* (EJL, 1; Atlanta: Scholars Press, 1991), pp. 199–219.

55 Pliny, *Ep.* 1.16.6, in Elaine Fantham, Helene Peet Foley, Natalie Boymel Kampen, Sarah B. Pomeroy and H. Alan Shapiro, *Women in the Classical World* (New York: Oxford University Press, 1994), p. 349.

course, composed himself. Like Paul, Callirhoe writes in the letter, 'this letter is written in my own hand'.[56] Additional evidence may be found in the intriguing but generally ignored pseudepigraphic correspondence between one Mary of Cassabola and Ignatius of Antioch.[57] Both letters are clearly written by the same author, so either a woman has written in both male and female voices, or a man has done so. In either case, our dilemma is apparent, if its solution is not. Thus, attempts to verify the authenticity of Perpetua's narrative on gendered stylistic grounds prove troubling. Furthermore, the similarity of the section to other autobiographical narratives that are considered authentic but heavily edited and rewritten should give us pause about identifying stylistic features as a sign of authenticity rather than as self-consciously constructed rhetorical devices.

Another aspect of the *Passio* contributes to our concerns about its composition, namely, the startling degree to which its specifics conform to a prophecy in Joel 2.28–29, which occurs in slightly different form in Acts 2.17–18. It is possible, indeed perhaps tempting, to read the *Passio* in its present form as a narrative dramatization of the passage, which it quotes:

> For in the last [literally newest] days, says the Lord, I will pour out my spirit over all flesh and their sons and daughters will prophesy; and I will pour my spirit over my male servants and female servants (*servos et ancillas meas*) and the young shall see visions and the old shall dream dreams. (1.4)

Many elements of the *Passio* conform closely to the prophecy. As the prologue makes clear, the events of the *Passio* take place in these 'newest' days (1.1–3). The outpouring of the divine Spirit over all flesh may be depicted in the catechumens as a whole, or even in the larger phenomenon of conversion to Christianity which they may represent. Perpetua and probably Saturus demonstrate the prophesying daughters and sons (the vision of Saturus comes after those of Perpetua). The extraordinary emphasis on Perpetua's role as a daughter, primarily through her relationship with her father, coheres exceedingly well with the characterization of the female prophets as daughters.

While Acts 2.18 predicts that the servants will also prophesy, Joel limits this activity to the sons and daughters, as does the citation in the *Passio*. And not surprisingly, none of the slaves prophesies. They appear only to receive the Spirit, most notably perhaps in the response to their prayers for the pregnant Felicitas's early delivery and probably also in their baptism. Their very presence in the story enhances the conformity of the *Passio* to the biblical verses. Apart from her description in the opening as the *conserva* ('co-slave') of Revocatus, there is no reason to think that Felicitas is a slave.[58] The characterization of Felicitas and Revocatus as *conservi*,

---

56 *Chaereas and Callirhoe* 8.3 in Reardon (ed.), *Collected Ancient Greek Novels*, p. 116.

57 In Kraemer, *Women's Religions*, pp. 375–77; see also Ross S. Kraemer, 'Women's Authorship of Jewish and Christian Literature in the Greco-Roman Period', in Levine (ed.), *'Women Like This'*, pp. 221–42 (236–39).

58 For the thesis that she was not, see M. Poirier, 'Note sur la Passio Sanctarum Perpetuae et Felicitatis: Félicité était-elle vraiment l'esclave de Perpetué?', in Frank M. Cross (ed.), *Studia Patristica* 10.1 (1970), pp. 306–9. Neither Augustine nor Ps. Augustine nor Quodvultdeus describes Felicitas as a slave.

construed as co-slaves, enhances the correspondence of the prophecy and the *Passio*, which requires examples of slaves who receive the Spirit if not also who prophesy.

At several points, the redactor emphasizes both the youth of the catechumens as a whole and that of Perpetua in particular. They are described as *adolescentes* (2.1), while she is twenty-two (2.3) and still called *puella* (20.1–2). The attention to her age and the emphasis on her visions cohere with the prediction of the young seeing visions.

While it is unlikely that the *entire* martyrdom of Perpetua is generated out of the biblical passage(s), these and other correspondences between the text and the prophecy make it quite possible that both the general outline and many of the details of the prison narrative and the remaining sections are shaped to conform to the biblical text.[59]

Against the trend of recent scholarship that generally considers the prison account of Perpetua to be authentic and accurate and the *Passio* as a whole to be a reasonably trustworthy representation of the martyrdom of Perpetua, Felicitas and their male associates, Lander and I concluded that the *Passio* is a 'representation' whose correspondence to actual persons and events cannot be determined. There may well have been an historical Perpetua, executed for her adherence to Christianity in North Africa in the early third century, but we consider unwarranted the wealth of historical 'facts' that numerous recent scholars have attempted to extract from the text, including particularly claims about accessibility to the thoughts and the subjectivity of Perpetua herself.

Faced with these difficulties (or perhaps, having never asked the same questions in the first place) some feminist scholars have retreated, or at least refrained, from the historical inquiries that marked the early phases of women's studies in antiquity. As noted earlier, some would shift our attention to the discourses of gender in the ancient world, a shift that has the effect, although unquestionably unintentional, of refocusing our attention on the study of men and masculine constructions of women and of gender.[60] They would insist that the sources do not enable us to do otherwise, and much of my discussion so far might support such a view.

Yet the situation is not entirely bleak for those who still desire to write histories of women in antiquity, rather than histories of the discourse of gender. Some important evidence for the lives and practices of women may be gleaned from non-literary sources such as inscriptions and various documents on papyrus.[61] In the study of ancient Jewish and Christian women, these materials have proved particularly significant, providing evidence for women's public lives which frequently challenges the representations of Jewish and Christian communal life in literary sources.[62]

---

59 In a manner not unlike this, James Kugel argues for the Rabbinic Joseph traditions (*In Potiphar's House: The Interpretive Life of Biblical Texts* [San Francisco, CA: Harper Collins, 1990]), and I explore with regard to the Greek tales of Joseph and Aseneth (*When Aseneth Met Joseph*, pp. 19–49). For the view that the citation of this passage represents self-conscious Montanist exegesis, see P.C. Atkinson, 'The Montanist Interpretation of Joel 2:28, 29 (LXX 3:1,2)', *SE*, Bd. 126.7 (1982), pp. 11–15.

60 See above, nn. 8 and 21.

61 For numerous examples and basic introductions, see Kraemer, *Women's Religions.*

62 See, e.g., Kraemer, *Her Share of the Blessings*, pp. 106–27; Ross S. Kraemer, 'Jewish Women in the Diaspora World of Late Antiquity', in Judith R. Baskin (ed.), *Jewish Women in Historical Perspective* (Detroit, MI: Wayne State University Press, 1998; 2nd edn), pp. 46–72; see also Lee I. Levine, 'Women in the Synagogue', in *idem*, *The Ancient Synagogue: the First Thousand Years* (New Haven, CT: Yale University Press, 2000), pp. 471–90.

The contradictions of non-literary and literary evidence are by no means limited to Jewish and Christian sources, of course. In her 2001 doctoral dissertation, Elizabeth Pollard demonstrates that whereas Roman-period literary sources such as Apuleius's *Metamorphoses* regularly depict women as the primary performers and consumers of so-called 'magical arts', this depiction is contradicted by the extensive archaeological evidence in which men are clearly the majority of the producers and consumers of spells, incantations, amulets, recipe books and the like.[63] Analyzing the spells and rituals probably performed by some real women, Pollard argues that many of these performances would have cast women in the role of 'male' actors; active, powerful, controllers of demons and gods, and that such roles conflicted with pervasive ancient gendered norms. She demonstrates that the concerns manifest in fictional, historical and legal sources cluster precisely around violations of gendered norms including such things as the subversion of the production of legitimate male heirs, boundaries between the living and the dead, and women's presence in inappro-priate space. Inversely, however, these same sources display little if any concern for women's performance of spells and rites that tended to affirm gendered hierarchies, such as spells against thieves or those intended to heal fevers and such. Pollard's work suggests that while we cannot escape the pervasive webs of gender construction in which evidence for ancient women's lives is enmeshed, we can extract both some sense of the realities of women's lives and some better understanding of how ancient, male, elite concerns about gender contribute to the construction of women's lives, and distort those lives, in literary sources.

Conclusions

Stories about women are unreliable, though not entirely unusable, sources for the actualities of women's lives and experiences in the ancient world. This same point may hold, by the way, for the realities of many men's lives and experiences as well, but it is probably more true for women. Readers alert to the many techniques utilized in the representations of women in these texts may, with care, extract some sense of ancient social and historical 'realities' beyond the 'reality' of ancient constructions of gender. Non-literary sources such as burial, donative and honorific inscriptions and papyrus documents provide some correctives, although they are not themselves immune from such problems: inscriptions, for example, routinely employ conven-tions of gender in their representations of women, identifying women in terms of their male relations, particularly husbands, and praising them for such conventional virtues as marital fidelity and maternal devotion. Still, as in the case of their attes-tation to women office-holders in synagogues and churches,[64] or their evidence for

63 Elizabeth Ann Pollard, *Magic Accusations Against Women in the Greco-Roman World* (Ph.D. diss., University of Pennsylvania, 2001).

64 Bernadette J. Brooten, *Women Leaders in the Ancient Synagogue. Inscriptional Evidence and Backgroud Issues* (BJS, 36; Chico, CA: Scholars Press, 1982); Ute E. Eisen, *Women Officeholders in Early Christianity* (trans. Linda M. Maloney; Collegeville, MN: Liturgical Press, 2000); see also Kraemer, *Her Share of the Blessings*, pp. 106–27 (on Jewish women), pp. 174–90 (on Christian women); Francine Cardman, 'Women, Ministry and Church Order in Early Christianity', in Ross Shepard Kraemer and Mary Rose D'Angelo (eds), *Women and Christian Origins* (New York and Oxford: Oxford University Press, 1999), pp. 300–29.

male and female performance of the so-called magical arts, they appear to afford us glimpses of 'real' life, and their contradictions of the portraits in literary sources continue to offer us productive avenues of exploration.[65]

65 For another recent, fascinating exploration of how these issues affect the utilization of letters of the Egyptian monastic leader, Shenoute, for the lives and experiences of women monastics in fourth and fifth-century Egypt, see Rebecca Krawiec, *Shenoute and the Women of the White Monastery: Egyptian Monasticism in Late Antiquity* (New York and Oxford: Oxford University Press, 2003).

THE PATRONAGE OF WOMEN IN EARLY CHRISTIANITY[*]

CAROLYN OSIEK

The patronage system in antiquity has been studied from numerous perspectives: cross-cultural analysis of the social construction of patronage,[1] its specific exercise in ancient Rome,[2] and its role in the early Church.[3] In all of these cases, however, the androcentric norm prevails. Despite substantial evidence of women's roles as both patrons and clients, their participation in the patronage system goes generally ignored. By giving attention to women's participation, we contribute not only to a recovery of women's history, but also to a new understanding of the social and economic life of early Christianity.

Patronage in the Early Roman Empire

Through their exchange of differently valued goods and services, patron–client relations functioned as one of the basics of ancient society. The client could expect to receive economic and political benefits, such as gifts of food, invitations to

---

[*] An earlier version of this article, 'Women Patrons in the Life of House Churches', appears in Carolyn Osiek, Margaret Y. MacDonald, with Janet Tullock, *A Woman's Place: House Churches in Earliest Christianity* (Minneapolis, MN: Fortress Press, 2005), pp. 194–219.

1 Ernest Gellner and John Waterbury (eds), *Patrons and Clients in Mediterranean Societies* (London: Duckworth, 1977); S.N. Eisenstadt and L. Roniger, *Patrons, Clients and Friends: Interpersonal Relations and the Structure of Trust in Society* (Cambridge, UK: Cambridge University Press, 1984); John H. Elliott, 'Patronage and Clientage', in Richard Rohrbaugh (ed.), *The Social Sciences and New Testament Interpretation* (Peabody, MA: Hendrickson, 1996), pp. 144–56, with extensive further bibliography.

2 Richard P. Saller, *Personal Patronage under the Early Empire* (Cambridge, UK: Cambridge University Press, 1982); Andrew Wallace-Hadrill (ed.), *Patronage in Ancient Society* (London: Routledge, 1989); Jens-Uwe Krause, *Spätantike Patronatsformen im Westen des Römischen Reiches* (Munich: C. H. Beck, 1987).

3 Beginning with the ever-insightful work of E.A. Judge, including *The Social Pattern of Christian Groups in the First Century* (London: Tyndale Press, 1960); 'The Early Christians as a Scholastic Community', *Journal of Religious History* (1960), pp. 4–15 and (1961), pp. 125–37; 'Paul as a Radical Critic of Society', *Interchange* 16 (1974), pp. 191–203; 'Cultural Conformity and Innovation in Paul: Some Clues from Contemporary Documents', *Tyndale Bulletin*, 35 (1984), pp. 3–24. Among the most influential works is Frederick W. Danker's *Benefactor: Epigraphic Study of a Graeco-Roman and New Testament Semantic Field* (St. Louis, MO: Clayton, 1982). More recently, see John K. Chow, *Patronage and Power: A Study of Social Networks in Corinth* (JSNTSup 75; Sheffield: Sheffield Academic Press, 1992); David A. deSilva, *Honor, Patronage, Kinship and Purity: Unlocking New Testament Culture* (Downers Grove, IL: InterVarsity Press, 2000). Stephan J. Joubert, 'One Form of Social Exchange or Two? "Euergetism", Patronage, and New Testament Studies', *BTB*, 31 (2001), pp. 17–25, places public/group patronage, or 'euergetism' in the Greek world and personal patronage in the Roman world. However, public and personal patronage are different aspects of the same social phenomenon; there is far less evidence in the *earlier* Greek world for personal patronage, but public patronage was common in both worlds.

dinner,[4] gifts of land, a house, or sometimes cash, low or no-interest loans, lodging in the patron's town house or villa, favourable recommendations and appointments, help with matchmaking, and bequests and inheritance.[5] In turn, the patron expected loyalty, public support, economic assistance if needed and possible, votes, and most important, public praise and presence, especially at significant times and for political advancement. Because of the asymmetry of the relations, the patronage system reinforced social inequity,[6] yet at the same time, the system did provide the weak a means of influencing the powerful.[7]

Patron–client relations tended to be informal and personal rather than fully legal, and at times they furnished a means to circumvent laws. Because of this informality, they could be entered into or abandoned more or less voluntarily, though social constraints – including the concepts of honour and shame – could limit the client's choice. Clients found themselves in a double bind: it was expected that they would publicize the generosity of their patron's *beneficia*, but the admission of having received them marked one's own lower social status.[8] A client who did not give proper praise was considered *ingratus* and unworthy of more.

Patronage systems existed in classical Greece even though there seems to have been no terminology to refer to them exactly.[9] For example, the word προστά-της, so important for understanding Rom. 16.1, applied in classical Athens to the citizen-patron required for a μέτοικος, a resident alien who, without such a social protector, would be vulnerable to exploitation. The term thus carried connotations of social inferiority/superiority, so no citizen would acknowledge having a προστά-της. Yet in the Roman period, Plutarch understands προστάτης as the equivalent of *patronus* (*Romulus* 13), not in the modern sense of, say, a 'patron of the arts', but of a socially more powerful person who defends and promotes a social inferior, who in return owes honour and loyalty.[10] The shift may be due in part to the resurgence of patronal relationships at the end of the Republic and beginning of the Empire, as the old structures yielded to new and yet uncertain ways of exercising power. Governing by an intricate balance of relationships with the elite families, the new figure of the *imperator* took on the role of receiving and granting favours on a grand scale, and thus took advantage of the power vacuum by seizing control of major power networks that had been exercised by powerful families. Augustus deepened and nurtured the patronage system, and consolidated his power, by establishing 'the inaccessibility

---

4 For the importance of this dinner invitation as symbol of patronage, see Juvenal, *Sat.* 5.12–15.

5 Peter White, '*AMICITIA* and the Profession of Poetry in Early Imperial Rome', *JRS* 68 (1978), pp. 90–92.

6 Saller, *Personal Patronage*, p. 1.

7 Saller, *Personal Patronage*, pp. 191–92.

8 Saller, *Personal Patronage*, pp. 127–28.

9 Paul Millett, 'Patronage and Its Avoidance in Classical Athens', in Wallace-Hadrill (ed.), *Patronage in Ancient Society*, pp. 15–47.

10 Millett, 'Patronage and Its Avoidance', pp. 33–34.

of the center except through personal links'. He cast himself as *pater patriae*, chief benevolent father figure of the entire Mediterranean world.[11]

While Latin patronage language contains such direct words as *patronatus*, *patronus/a*, *clientela* and *cliens*, by the early Empire this language was generally considered too abrasive to the delicate honour system, and a new set of terms was adapted into the structures of patronage: that of friendship. The semantic field of *amicitia* becomes the preferred language.[12] Because the patronage relationship was by definition asymmetrical, one could speak of *amici minores* (Pliny, *Ep.* 2.6.2), *amici pauperes* (Pliny, *Ep.* 9.30), *amici inferiores* (Seneca, *Ep. Ad Lucilium* 94.14) et al., which were all meant to be less condescending than the bald word *cliens*.[13] Seneca (*De beneficiis* 6.34.2) credits and applauds Gaius Gracchus and Livius Drusus as the first to classify their 'friends' into three categories: *amici primi* who are received in private, *amici secundi* received with others, and *numquam veri* (never trustworthy) to be received all together in one group. Some preferred the term *cultor* for one who was attempting to ingratiate him- or herself with a patron, and more commonly, the verb *colere*, which also applied to honour and reverence due to the gods, a meaning that carried over into Christian usage. With regard to artists, poets and writers, words like *patronus* and *patrocinium* are never used.[14]

The range of terms varies greatly: *amare/amor*, *sodalis*, *diligere/dilectus*, *contubernium* (more often used for a non-legal marriage), *caritas/carus*, *familiaritas/familiaris*, even *meus* and *noster*.[15] The exchange of goods and services was connoted by such terms as *meritum* and *gratia*, but primarily by *officium* and *beneficium*, originally a gesture of duty and loyalty from the inferior vs. a gesture of largesse and generosity on the part of the superior. The terms became interchangeable, as Cicero's treatise *De officiis* demonstrates.[16]

In the particular relationship between patron and freed slave the *officia* and loyalty owed to the patron, under the title of *operae* and *obsequium*, were specifically designated, not at all voluntary, and enforceable by law. There are abundant examples of both women and men in both positions, that of patron/former owner and that of freedwoman/former slave, with no gender restrictions on ownership, i.e., women could own men and vice versa. Here the terminology of patron and *libertus/a* was used, even in funerary inscriptions. The relationship was certainly not voluntary on the part of the freedperson, who often continued in what was tantamount to a slave's

---

11 Saller, *Personal Patronage*, pp. 2–3; Wallace-Hadrill, 'Patronage in Roman Society: From Republic to Empire', in *idem* (ed.), *Patronage in Ancient Society*, pp. 63–87, esp. 74, 79–81, and in that same volume, Terry Johnson and Chris Dandeker, 'Patronage: Relation and System', pp. 219–42, esp. 237–38.

12 Saller, *Personal Patronage*, pp. 11–15; P.A. Brunt, '"Amicitia" in the Late Roman Republic', *Proceedings of the Cambridge Philological Society* n.s. 11 (1965), pp. 1–20; reprinted in Robin Seager (ed.), *The Crisis of the Roman Republic: Studies in Political and Social History* (Cambridge, UK: Heffer, 1969), pp. 199–218.

13 Saller, *Personal Patronage*, p. 12; White, '*AMICITIA*', p. 81.

14 Joubert, 'One Form of Social Exchange', p. 20; White, '*AMICITIA*', p. 79; cf. Barbara K. Gold (ed.), *Literary and Artistic Patronage in Ancient Rome* (Austin: University of Texas Press, 1982).

15 White, '*AMICITIA*', pp. 80–81.

16 Saller, *Personal Patronage*, pp. 12–22.

role. Jennifer Glancy[17] cautions that the patron–client model was rather more often exploitative than beneficial in this more coercive case. Nevertheless, the terminology was used, and some of the same mutually advantageous benefits were applied.

It was possible to have more than one patron, and clients could manipulate the situation to their own advantage.[18] The famous fourth-century orator Libanius delivered at Antioch his oration against patronage (*De patrociniis vicorum*) in the context of social upheavals that were driving peasants to align themselves in clientage with powerful military patrons and so undermine the authority of aristocratic landowners. Libanus, the wealthy landowner, argues strongly that there must be only one patron: the landowner.

In addition to such examples of private patronage, the early Roman world witnessed the phenomenon of public patronage or euergetism[19] as well as an intermediate form that is important for early Christianity, patronage of a private group. While the essence of the patronage system is a relationship between socially unequal individuals, the system includes the relationship of one dominant person to groups of social inferiors, whether a professional guild, a club, a group of the poor, the devotees of a private religion, or a city. Building public facilities like fountains or baths, providing free meals to a city's needy or to its children, or holding banquets at civic celebrations are all examples of public patronage. The role of the emperor constitutes the highest form of public patronage. Building meeting houses and temples or providing economic assistance or banquets to devotees are examples of the exercise of patronage of a group. In return, the patron is named in thankful inscriptions or honoured by the erection of a statue, is seated in a place of honour at the group's formal gatherings, or is appointed to an official position (which may be honorary). Those exercises that today would be regarded as charity or social aid were based not primarily in compassion, but were driven by the patronage system's goal for the elite: honour, φιλοτιμία, φιλοδοξία.[20] As the Christian system of social aid developed, in imitation of the Jewish one, those who could give were encouraged to do so without looking for a reward, not to let the left hand know what the right hand was doing, etc., in the spirit of Mt. 6.1–4.

Women's Patronage in the Roman World

Women were deeply involved in both private and public patronage. They could attend or preside at the morning *salutatio* (Juvenal, *Sat.* 1.120–16), the early morning visit of clients to their patron's house for social exchange and sometimes the giving of gifts. Women who had the legal status *sui iuris* (that is, women not under the

---

17 Jennifer Glancy, *Slavery in Early Christianity* (Oxford: Oxford University Press, 2002), pp. 124–26.

18 Saller, 'Patronage and Friendship in Early Imperial Rome: Drawing the Distinction', in Wallace-Hadrill (ed.), *Patronage in Ancient Society*, pp. 49–62 (53–54).

19 Louis Harmand, *Le patronat sur les collectivités publiques, des origins au bas-Empire; un aspect social et politique du monde romain* (Paris: Presses Universitaires de France, 1957); A.R. Hands, *Charities and Social Aid in Greece and Rome* (Ithaca, NY: Cornell University Press, 1968); cf. Joubert, 'One Form of Social Exchange', whose attempt to draw sharp distinctions between Roman patronage and Greek euergetism is not convincing.

20 Hands, *Charities and Social Aid*, p. 49.

potestas of a man) could conduct their own transactions, though there were some legal limitations imposed. The exercise of patronage would necessitate some levels of social independence. The earlier institution of *tutela*, male guardianship requiring permission to alienate property, was mostly inactive by the Augustan age, though former owners could still exercise considerable control over the property of a *liberta*. Additional legislation was enacted that prevented women from taking on liability for the debts of others, perhaps to protect women from unscrupulous husbands.[21] As is often the case with Roman law, what was on the books was not necessarily what was done, and there may have been more exceptions than strict applications of the law.

Patronage of Individuals

All forms of reciprocal exchange between social unequals were part of the patronage system in some way. The social and political patronage of elite women can be well documented. First, women often served as patrons for other women. In one of his letters to the emperor, M. Cornelius Fronto, tutor of Marcus Aurelius, refers to his wife Cratia as the *clienta* of Domitia Lucilla, the emperor's mother. In this capacity she visited the imperial family and stayed with them, but without her husband, in Naples to celebrate her patron's birthday.[22] An otherwise unknown woman named Valatta on the British frontier writes to the commanding officer of the Vindolanda outpost, Flavius Cerialis, about a favour mediated by his wife, Sulpicia Lepidina.[23] The epitaph of Epiphania, a second or third-century benefactor and the well-travelled daughter and wife of ship owners, reports that she was generous with her wealth, motivated by *eusebeia*, especially to abandoned friends ὡς γυνὴ γυναιξί, woman to woman.[24]

While women were excluded from voting and elected office – though in the Roman province of Asia women did hold some of the highest public municipal appointments – the prohibition by no means kept them out of politics or the patronage system. It seems likely that all elite women were involved in politics at some level by reason of their family connections. The influence of powerful women in the palace and the law court through their exercise of patronage, *amicitiae muliebres*, was ever present.[25] Valerius Maximus 8.3 cites situations in which women argued their own cases in court. Though he thought this self-defence unusual, he does not imply that it was unusual for women to be involved in legal suits, either as defendants or plaintiffs.[26]

---

21 Jane F. Gardner, *Women in Roman Law and Society* (Bloomington: Indiana University Press, 1986), pp. 233–36.

22 Marcus Cornelius Fronto (trans. C. R. Haines; LCL; Cambridge, MA: Harvard University Press, 1962), 1, pp. 145–51; Edward Champlin, *Fronto and Antonine Rome* (Cambridge, MA: Harvard University Press, 1980), p. 25.

23 Alan K. Bowman and J. David Thomas (eds), *'Per Lepidinam': The Vindolanda Writing-Tablets (Tabulae Vindolandenses II)* (London: British Museum Press, 1994), no. 257 (inv. 85.117), pp. 230–31. The tablet is dated to period 3 of the fort, 97–102/3 CE.

24 *NewDocs* 2.16, pp. 55–56.

25 Champlin, *Fronto and Antonine Rome*, pp. 109, 171 n. 87; Richard A. Bauman, *Women and Politics in Ancient Rome* (London: Routledge, 1992); Suzanne Dixon, 'A Family Business: Women's Role in Patronage and Politics at Rome 80–44 B.C.', *Classica et Mediaevalia* 34 (1983), pp. 91–112, at p. 91.

26 Dixon, 'Family Business', p. 100.

The social status that enabled women to act in these ways would necessarily imply a certain independence and thus involvement in the system of reciprocal exchange.

Roscius of Ameria, later defended by Cicero in a parricide case that involved political machinations against Sulla, fled for protection in Rome to the aristocrat Caecilia Metella, not to any of her abundant male relatives or her husband, because of her *amicitia* with his deceased father. Whatever the political intricacies, it was recognized that *she* was his patron.[27]

Public imagery exalted Augustus's wife Livia as the paragon of wifely virtue, *patrona ordinis matronarum*, and upholder, with her husband, of 'family values', in spite of their utter failure to instill their values in their daughter, Julia. Livia, who had her own entourage and client loyalties, even received the Senate in her house during her widowhood. Josephus recounts her benefactions to the Herodian family, including marriage advice to Salome (*Ant.* 17.10),[28] and she earned the Senate's gratitude by saving the lives of several of its members, providing for their orphaned children, and paying their daughters' dowries. So popular was she that she was called, informally, in parallel to Augustus's title, *mater patriae*. Although upon her death the Senate voted to erect an arch in her honour, an unprecedented honour for a woman, Tiberius never allowed it to be built. Nor did he allow her informal title to become official (Dio Cassius 58.2.3).[29]

Nero's aunt Domitia had clients, and the schemer Agrippina, Nero's mother, was known to be patron for numbers of men eager for political advancement. It was she who succeeded in getting Seneca's exile rescinded (Tacitus, *Ann.* 12.8). On the death of her father Germanicus, his *clientela* passed to her as well. At one point, Nero had her residence moved from the palace to the house that had belonged to Antonia in order to prevent the crowds that arrived for the morning *salutatio* (Tacitus, *Ann.* 13.18.5). Her political enemy, Junia Silana, got two of her own male clients to charge Agrippina with inciting revolt from imperial authority in the person of Rubellius Plautus.[30]

Antonia Caenis, freedwoman of Claudius's mother Antonia, became mistress of Vespasian until her death. Dio Cassius (65.14.1–5) gives a vivid description of her patronal power and wealth: she gave in exchange for money various kinds of public offices and priesthoods, and she obtained imperial decisions and secured imperial pardons in favour of her clients. Women patrons also associated with the emperor include Poppaea Sabina with Nero, Plotina with Trajan, Marcia with Commodus and Julia Domna with Caracalla.

---

27 Dixon, 'Family Business', p. 94, with other examples.

28 Other imperial women who were benefactors to the Herodians, according to Josephus, were Antonia and Agrippina the Younger. Poppaea Sabina, wife of Nero, was also said to be mediator for Jewish causes (*Ant.* 18.143, 164; 20.135–36; 20.189–96; *Life* 13–16). In a typical patronage manoeuvre, Josephus records that at Puteoli he met an actor named Aliturus, and through him, was introduced to Poppaea. Domitia, wife of Domitian was also a personal benefactor and defender of Josephus, toward whom she was *euergetousa*, benefactor (*Life* 429). See Shelly Matthews, *First Converts: Rich Pagan Women and the Rhetoric of Mission in Early Judaism and Christianity* (Stanford, CA: Stanford University Press, 2001), pp. 30–36.

29 Bauman, *Women in Politics*, pp. 124–29. Livia's power was derivative of that of Augustus, but, like many queens and empresses, while she had it, she exercised it quite independently.

30 Bauman, *Women in Politics*, pp. 146–98.

It appears that the social patterns documented among the elite were replicated insofar as was possible by the rest of society, a sort of 'trickle-down' effect. For example, Cornelius Nepos's comment about the presence of Roman women on the dining couches at dinner parties indicates not only greater social freedom for first-century Roman and romanized women outside royal corridors, it indicates as well greater access to the corridors of informal power and greater ability to influence them (Preface, *Illustrious Lives*). Juvenal, who complains of women who not only attend mixed dinner parties but also host them and discourse on politics and literature (*Sat.* 6.434–56),[31] hints that the best way to social advancement is through some ageing wealthy woman's patronage (*Sat.* 1.39).

Before considering the involvement of non-elite women in the patronage system per se, we need to be aware of their role in economic life. The evidence from Pompeii reveals women active in a variety of businesses and trades. The 154 wax tablets in the business files of the auctioneer L. Caecilius Iucundus mention fourteen women who transacted business with him, including Umbricia Ianuaria who received 11,039 sesterces from the proceeds of a sale he had conducted for her (*CIL* 4.3440).[32] Other women lent money and, though they could not vote, supported local candidates for public office with wall graffiti like this one: 'Statia and Petronia ask you to vote for Marcus Casellius and Lucius Alfucius for aediles. May our colony always have such citizens!' (*CIL* 4.3678).[33] Many women earned income from real estate,[34] like the enterprising Julia Felix, probably a freedwoman, who owned a vast urban property in the southeast corner of Pompeii that contained a parking lot for horses and carriages, private dining rooms (one with its own fountain), baths, a swimming pool, a wine shop and more modest areas for dining – and probably for takeout as well. Her notice on the outside wall advertised for lease 'the Venus baths, fitted up for the best people, taverns, shops and second story rooms'.[35] The property is situated just across the street from the city palestra and amphitheatre. One suspects that this was *the* place to see and be seen before and after the local games or an afternoon exercising at the palestra.

Any non-elite women who had accumulated even a modest amount of wealth and connections could be active in patronage relationships. A freedwoman named Manlia T. 1. Gnome, for example, boasts on her epitaph that she had many clients (*clientes habui multos; CIL* 6.21975). Women were also patrons of their own freedmen and freedwomen. A *patronissa* whose name has been lost from the inscription is honoured on a second or third-century Roman Greek epitaph by the freedman Gaius Fulvius Eutyches.[36] The freedwoman Naevoleia Tyche erected a

---

31 See Suzanne Dixon, *Reading Roman Women: Sources, Genres and Real Life* (London: Duckworth, 2001), p. 101.

32 Roy Bowen Ward, 'Women in Pompeii: Work in Progress' (unpublished paper), pp. 10–11.

33 Other examples in Mary R. Lefkowitz and Maureen Fant (eds), *Women's Life in Greece and Rome: A Source Book in Translation* (2nd edn; Baltimore, MD: Johns Hopkins University Press, 1992), pp. 152–53.

34 For a discussion of women landowners in Hellenistic Egypt, see Sarah B. Pomeroy, *Women in Hellenistic Egypt: From Alexander to Cleopatra* (New York: Schocken Books, 1984), pp. 148–60, 171–73.

35 Translation by Ward, 'Women in Pompeii', p. 9.

36 *NewDocs* 2.19, pp. 60–61.

monumental tomb for herself, her freedman husband, Gaius Munatius Faustus and their slaves and freedmen/women at the Herculaneium Gate cemetery at Pompeii. The inscription states that Munatius was an *augustalis* (member of an important college of freedmen), and *paganus*, an official in charge of a district of the city or suburbs. Yet the ashes of Naevoleia and her husband were actually buried in another simpler monument at the Nucerian Gate, erected by the husband.[37] Whichever came first, Naevoleia decided to make the best of her wealth and to tell the world (in two places!) how important she and her husband were.

The same laws and customs applied to female as to male patrons. They set up their *libertus/a* with loans or gifts of money to start a new business, with a certain amount of legal control and the expectation of generous bequests in their former slaves' wills.[38] They provided in their funerary monument that their freedmen/women should also be buried there: *libertis libertabusque posterisque eorum*. Marriages between a *patrona* and her *libertus*, though heavily discouraged by social disapproval and even forbidden by law at some points, are not unknown (e.g., *CIL* 6.14014; 14462; 15106; 15548; 16445; 21657; 23915; 25504; 28815; 35973). Some of these were likely cases in which the *patrona* herself came from originally servile status, but at least one is not: T. Claudius Hermes in Rome commemorates his freeborn wife, Claudia, as *patrona optima* and *coniux fidelissima* (no. 15106). Alimentary and funerary foundations provided sustenance in life and burials and commemorations at death, whether in the patron's lifetime or by bequest, for members of the *familia*, that is, predominantly slaves and former slaves.[39] When Christians began to organize socially, they did many similar things; most of the burial complexes later known as catacombs began with such familial burial plots, and they were later expanded into larger systems in which the familial connection was no longer the household, but the entire church community.

Patronage of Groups

Women's patronage of unofficial groups bears directly on our understanding of their patronage in early Christianity. Euxenia, priestess of Aphrodite in Megalopolis in the Peloponnesus in the second century BCE, donated a guesthouse and a wall around the temple (*Inscriptiones graecae* 5.2.461).[40] Tation, from Kyme, daughter of Straton son of Empedon, either built or remodelled at her own expense the building and the surrounding precinct of a synagogue, for which the Jews honoured her with two traditional ways of rewarding a patron: a gold crown and a place of honour (προεδρία). The wording of the inscription ('the Jews honour her'), as well as the family names, suggests that she was not Jewish, but an outside benefactor *(CIJ* 2.738).[41] Similarly,

---

37 John R. Clarke, *Art in the Lives of Ordinary Romans* (Berkeley: University of California Press, 2003), pp. 184–85.

38 This was a bit restricted by the Papian Law of the Augustan period: *patronae* acquired more inheritance rights if they had two or three children (see Susan M. Treggiari, *Roman Marriage: Iusti Coniuges from the Time of Cicero to the Time of Ulpian* [Oxford and New York: Clarendon Press, 1991], pp. 74–75).

39 Dixon, *Reading Roman Women*, pp. 106–7.

40 Riet Van Bremen, 'Women and Wealth', in Averil Cameron and Amélie Kuhrt (eds), *Images of Women in Antiquity* (rev. edn; Detroit, MI: Wayne State University Press, 1993), pp. 223–42 (223).

41 *NewDocs* 1.69, p. 111.

Julia Severa of Acmonia in Phrygia, who held a number of distinguished priesthoods and city offices and who was a member of a family sufficiently prominent that her son entered the Senate, donated property to the local synagogue, perhaps because two of its archons were her freedmen or clients (*CIJ* 2.766; *MAMA* 6.264).[42]

Eumachia, a public priestess of Pompeii and patroness of the fullers' guild, erected at her own expense in her own name and that of her son, Numistrius Fronto, a gallery, cryptoporticus and portico for the fullers' building in a prominent place in the forum; she dedicated them herself to *concordia* and *pietas augusti*. In gratitude, the guild erected a dedicatory statue of her with inscription, a copy of which still stands behind their building at the forum in Pompeii. She also built a tomb for herself and her *familia* outside one of the city gates (*CIL* 10.810, 811, 813).[43]

Alimentary programmes for poor children were popular ways for both men and women to exercise civic patronage, and so be honoured. Crispia Restituta of Beneventum set up one such project on income from her farm in 101 CE (*ILS* 6675). Caelia Macrina set up a fund to distribute a monthly meal to one hundred boys and one hundred girls in Tarracina (*ILS* 6278*5CIL* 10.6328). Fabia Agrippina of Ostia contributed the sizable sum of one million sesterces to such a programme for one hundred girls, in memory of her mother (*CIL* 14.4450). Since officially sponsored alimentary programs favoured boys, deliberate attention to the needs of girls may have been a conscious effort on the part of women benefactors to create a balance.[44] Menodora in first-century Sillyon in Pisidia gave wheat and money to her city, including 300,000 denarii for the support of its children. She also erected a statue of her deceased son, all the donations being in his memory.[45]

Other forms of public patronage by women are also common, including in Asia Minor those connected with holding public office. The same Menodora held quite a number of public offices, including priestess of Demeter and of the imperial cult, ἱεροφάντης (a priest involved in initiations), δεκαπρῶτος (a committee of ten who supervised public revenue and collected taxes), κτίστρια (founder), δημιουργός (magistrate), and γυμνασίαρχος (superintendent and/or supplier of the palestra). She was honoured with many statues and inscriptions, as was the early second-century benefactor of Perga, Plankia Magna, who held the titles of δημιουργός and γυμνασίαρχος.[46] Vedia Marcia of late third-century Ephesus had held the title of πρύτανις, representative of the official cult of Artemis and also one of the principal

42 L. Michael White (ed.), *Social Networks in the Early Christian Environment: Issues and Methods for Social History* (Semeia 56; Atlanta: Scholars Press, 1992), pp. 18–19.

43 Cf. Roy Bowen Ward, 'The Public Priestesses of Pompeii', in Abraham J. Malherbe, Frederick W. Norris and James W. Thompson (eds), *The Early Church in its Context: Essays in Honor of Everett Ferguson* (Leiden: Brill, 1998), pp. 323–27. Eumachia's tomb outside the Nucerian Gate, which is one of the largest funerary monuments in the area, states simply her name and filiation on one side, EVMACHIA L F, and on the other side, SIBI ET SVIS, for herself and those who belong to her *familia*.

44 Dixon, *Reading Roman Women*, p. 108.

45 Van Bremen, 'Women and Wealth', p. 223.

46 Cf. Mary Taliaferro Boatwright, 'Plancia Magna of Perge: Women's Roles and Status in Roman Asia Minor', in Sarah B. Pomeroy (ed.), *Women's History and Ancient History* (Chapel Hill: University of North Carolina Press, 1991), pp. 249–72. Other female gymnasiarchs are known: L. Casarico, 'Donne ginnasiarco', *ZPE*, 48 (1982), pp. 118–122. There is even one in Egypt, and a female tax collector: *NewDocs*, 8.4, p. 49.

magistrates of the city.[47] Tata of second-century Aphrodisias bore the title of στεφανήφορος (crownbearer), as did her husband, Attalus. She, however, supplied oil for athletes, was a priestess of the imperial cult, and many times held banquets for the citizens for which she supplied dining couches and the best entertainment.[48] Such detail completely counters the older interpretation that public offices and titles when held by men were actual but when held by women were merely honorifics. Conversely, many of the titles and offices in cities, temples and synagogues were in fact honorary, but equally so for both men and women.[49]

Junia Theodora of first-century Corinth, originally from Lycia (the combination of her Latin and Greek names may indicate her Roman citizenship), provided an anchor-hold for Lycians passing through this commercially strategic city. Among the services she performed for travelling Lycians were hospitality in her own house, cultivating the friendship of the Roman authorities in their favour, and designating her heir, Sextus Iulius, who gave every sign of carrying on what she began. Her patronage was not only directly to the Lycians but also on their behalf with the political powers. The decree of the Lycian city of Telmessos speaks of her προστασία in the context of hospitality and mediation.[50] Because of her location in first-century Corinth and because of the use of the word προστασία for her activity, Junia Theodora is an important comparative figure for the work of Phoebe προστά-τις in Rom. 16.1–2.

In return for Junia Theodora's benefactions, the Lycians set up in or near Corinth (the stone was discovered nearby in secondary use), five inscriptions on a single stone dedicated to her honour from the cities she had served. The monument was set up during her lifetime, for the inscription from the federal assembly of the Lycians says that they send her a gold crown 'for the time when she will come into the presence of the gods'. A second decree of the assembly offers her not only a gold crown but also 'a portrait for her deification after her death', painted on a gilt background.

Another important civic patron from the time of Nero is Claudia Metrodora of Chios, probably also a Greek woman with Roman citizenship besides that of her native Chios. An illegitimate daughter of Claudius Calobrotus, Claudia Metrodora was adopted by another man named Skytheinos, a rare instance of the adoption of

---

47 *NewDocs*, 6.3, p. 26.

48 Ross Shepard Kraemer, *Her Share of the Blessings: Women's Religions among Pagans, Jews, and Christians in the Greco-Roman World* (New York: Oxford University Press, 1992), p. 84; *eadem* (ed.), *Women's Religions in the Greco-Roman World: A Sourcebook* (New York: Oxford University Press, 2004), p. 249. Another *stephanephora*, the first woman in her city, was Philo of Priene who, in the first century BCE erected by herself a cistern and water system (H.W. Pleket, *Epigraphica II: Texts on the Social History of the Greek World* [Leiden: Brill, 1969], p. 16 #5); James Rives, 'Civic and Religious Life', in John Bodel (ed.), *Epigraphic Evidence: Ancient History from Inscriptions* (London: Routledge, 2001), pp. 118–36 (136).

49 Tessa Rajak and David Noy, '*Archisynagogoi*: Office, Title and Social Status in the Greco-Jewish Synagogue', *JRS*, 83 (1993), pp. 75–93.

50 Roz Kearsley, 'Women in Public Life in the Roman East: Junia Theodora, Claudia Metrodora, and Phoibe, Benefactress of Paul', *Ancient Society: Resources for Teachers* 15 (1985), pp. 124–37 (124–28; translation of documents, 132–34), also in *Tyndale Bulletin* 50.2 (1999), pp. 189–211; *NewDocs*, 6.3, pp. 24–25. See the long discussion in Bruce W. Winter, *Roman Wives, Roman Widows: The Appearance of New Women and the Pauline Communities* (Grand Rapids, MI: Eerdmans, 2003), pp. 183–93.

a girl to supply an heir in a wealthy family. Like other civic patrons, she held some of the highest offices: gymnasiarch four times, ἀγωνοθέτης and στεφανήφορος, likely in exchange for public benefactions. Among them was an entire public bath complex. She also held the office of lifetime priestess of empress Livia under the title Aphrodite Livia. She was elected 'queen' of the federation of thirteen Ionian cities, a title that is probably completely honorary whenever it or 'king' occurs in this context (something like Miss Ionia?). At some point she married a man whose name is lost and lived in Ephesus, where together they carried on their civic benefactions by erecting a portico.[51]

Sergia Paullina hosted a burial society in her house in Rome (*CIL* 6.9148) and Pompeia Agrippinilla, wife of a consul, was patron of a second-century Dionysiac association near Rome; the association, boasting more than three hundred members, gratefully erected a statue to their patron and priestess (*AE* 1933.4).[52] Memmia Victoria, freeborn woman of third-century Italy, whose son was a decurion, was named 'mother' of an artisan group (*CIL* 11.5748), while Claudia, wife of a freedman from Faleri Piceni, Italy, was hailed as 'mother' of a fullers' brotherhood (*CIL* 11.5450). Six Jewish women in Italy are known to have held the title 'mother of the synagogue'.[53] Others were town benefactors for public works. The unflappable Ummidia Quadratilla, grandmother of a friend of Pliny the Younger, indulged her taste for gambling and pantomime entertainment, both carried on in her own home, to the dismay of many of her friends. Visitors had to accommodate. However, her hometown of Casinum remembered Ummidia Quadratilla differently when she died at the age of seventy-nine. There she was commemorated for her benefactions of amphitheatre, temple and theatre, a glory of the city and not an embarrassment (Pliny, *Ep.* 7.24.5; *CIL* 10.58135*ILS* 5628; *AE* 1946.174).[54]

In North Africa, Aradia Roscia Calpurnia Purgilla was acclaimed in the third century as patron of Bulla Regia (*CIL* 8.14470) and Caecilia Sexti f. Petroniana Aemiliana patron of Thuburbo Minus (*AE* 1931.42). Egnatia Certiana was hailed as a patron of Beneventum in the second or third century (*CIL* 9.1578) and Publilia Caeciliana and Publilia Numisiana at Verecunda in the third century. Laberia Hostilia Crispina is proclaimed patron of the women of Trebulae, though it is not clear why (*AE* 1964.106).[55] At Herculaneum, 40 per cent of the dedicatory statues, mostly large and in bronze and metal, are of women. They were set up alongside those of men in the theatre and the forum area, without any perceptible pattern.[56]

We are accustomed to thinking about ancient women in terms of a gender-based dichotomous and hierarchical structure. The evidence indicates, however, that women

---

51 Kearsley, 'Women in Public Life', pp. 128–30; translation of fragments of inscription, pp. 135–36.

52 Chow, *Patronage and Power*, p. 68 n. 2.

53 Evidence and discussion in Bernadette J. Brooten, *Women Leaders in the Ancient Synagogue* (BJS, 36; Chico, CA: Scholars Press, 1982), pp. 57–72.

54 Dixon, *Reading Roman Women*, p. 109 and n. 109, p. 188.

55 Harmand, *Patronat*, pp. 282, 301, 241; Dixon, *Reading Roman Women*, p. 109.

56 Giuseppina Cerulli Irelli, 'Archaeological Research in the Area of Vesuvius: Portraits from Herculaneum', in *Pompeii and the Vesuvian Landscape* (Washington, D.C.: Archaeological Institute of America and the Smithsonian Institution, 1979), pp. 16–24; Caroline Dexter, 'The Epigraphic Evidence of Pompeiian Women' (unpublished paper), p. 23 n. 18.

of sufficient social status in the Roman world exercised a great deal of freedom and power with regard to business and social activities. What made this possible? The concentration of wealth in the hands of some women and the lessening of the social controls over them through the weakening of the distinction between public and private dimensions of social life facilitated women's participation in the patronage system.[57] Another factor is that in the Roman social system, as distinct from the older Greek ways, status took precedence over gender as a marker of prestige and power. A person of higher social status and access to power could function as mediator and dispenser of favour regardless of sex, with the same expectations of reciprocity in terms of honour, praise and loyalty on the part of clients.

Christians and the World of Patronage

The social reality of networks based on informal and asymmetrical relationships underlies the relationships that created the early Christian communities, in a 'series of overlapping but not systematically related circles'.[58] Patronage underlies exchanges of hospitality, the hosting of Christian gatherings, and most relationships of persons to other persons and to groups. The kinds of things clients could expect of patrons obtained also in Christian communities: material and cash gifts, food and dinner invitations, lodging, favourable recommendations and appointments, help in matchmaking, and bequests and inheritances.

A number of questions must be asked about the function of patronage in the early church, especially with regard to hierarchy and authority. First, the Roman world loved honour, prestige, status symbols and signs of precedence. In the literature of the period, the love of honour and praise (φιλοτιμία) is the primary motive for benefactions. Would the portrait of the humiliated, crucified Jesus and Paul's proclamation of the cross and strength in weakness have any effect on this system? Paul puts a great deal of effort into changing the cultural views by language of the cross in 1 Corinthians 1 and Galatians, but his attempt to change the *content* of honour to humiliation and self-giving, after the example of Christ, succeeded only in part. The Corinthian church's schismatic tendencies suggests that the lesson was not well learned in Paul's day. The behaviour of many bishops in the better-preserved Christian records of the fourth and fifth centuries suggests that it never was. Indeed, the proclamation of the Christ raised in power and subjecting his enemies under his feet, a triumph in which the Christian believer was promised an eventual share (1 Cor. 15.24–25; Ps. 110.1), perhaps offered a more culturally compelling vision. If some texts written by women had survived from this period, we would perhaps have more information about how these changes affected women. Many women, especially the majority of non-elites, could presumably have identified more readily with the appeal to the giving up of status, since they hadn't had much initially.

Second, patronage normally presupposes an unequal relationship, because the whole point of it is access to power that the client would not otherwise have. Where do figures like Jesus and Paul fit here? Does their charismatic authority take precedence over the usually established criteria of status? And does not Paul have some

---

57 Van Bremen, 'Women and Wealth', p. 223.
58 Judge, *Social Pattern*, p. iii.

relationships in which he is alternately patron and client, e.g., founding apostle and yet accepter of financial help from those he has evangelized? There is a strong possibility that baptizing someone set up a spiritual patronal relationship: note Paul's care in delimiting whom he had baptized at Corinth (1 Cor. 1.14–16). This may also help explain later resistance to women baptizing.

Third, network theory tells us that it is not ideas but personal contacts that create the environment for joining, for continued allegiance and therefore for conversions. How did those social networks operate among the non-elites of the Roman cities who were brought into contact with Christian evangelizers?[59] Though not all networks involved patronage in a formal way, it is probable that most did at least informally: the one who brings a previous outsider into a network or social context, e.g., a group of followers of Jesus, introduced and vouched for him/her and thus held a certain position of informal authority with regard to the one introduced.

The portrayal of the social behaviour of Jesus is clearly influenced by the ideology of the patronage system. The proclamation of the Reign of God is the announcement of efficient patronage: all who approach it will receive what they ask (Mt. 7.7; cf. Heb. 4.16). The relationship is certainly asymmetrical, and it is reciprocal: loyalty and praise are expected of clients in return for favours granted. Jesus is God's authorized agent, dispensing such favours as healing, exorcizing and, above all, forgiveness of sin. The (mostly male) disciples are empowered to carry on the same work of dispensing God's patronage. The female disciples also exercise patronage in less direct ways, by evangelizing in domestic settings, and by providing material support for the group (Lk. 8.2–3). In view of the emperor's claim to be chief father figure and Pontifex Maximus, that is, major mediator between gods and inhabitants of the Empire, these claims to represent the authority of God were dangerous views.

In Paul's letters, we find a remarkable paucity of friendship terminology (only the closing greeting in 1 Cor. 16.22, which may be a quoted formula), despite efforts to portray his relationship to the communities as one along the traditional lines of the topos of friendship.[60] There is, however, an abundance of talk about χάρις – understood theologically as grace – a word whose semantic field is that of favour, graciousness, benefaction, and therefore of the asymmetrical relationship of patronage. Paul emphasizes God's χάρις, and in so doing, Paul is creating a new dimension to the patronage pattern that will be followed by Luke and others: to God be the glory, praise and honour, and therefore the patronage.[61]

It seems that at Philippi a communal collection was delivered to Paul rather than gifts from individuals (Phil. 4.16–19; God will reciprocate). J. Murphy-O'Connor suggests that this communal support was not forthcoming at Corinth, and that this was the reason for the mutual resistance between Paul and the Corinthians which emerges in both of his extant letters to them. At Corinth, it was to be personal patronage, into whose entangling alliances Paul did not wish to venture.[62]

---

59 Cf. Chow, *Patronage and Power*; White, *Social Networks*.

60 John T. Fitzgerald (ed.), *Friendship, Flattery, and Frankness of Speech: Studies on Friendship in the New Testament* (Leiden: Brill, 1996).

61 A good exposition of χάρις as language of patronage is de Silva, *Honor, Patronage, Kinship and Purity*, pp. 95–156. Elliott, 'Patronage and Clientage', p. 152, lists seventeen New Testament terms associated with patronage.

62 J. Murphy-O'Connor, *Paul: A Critical Life* (Oxford: Clarendon Press, 1996), pp. 305–7.

Paul seems not to have been able completely to avoid such entanglements at Corinth, however. The most likely reason for his baptizing Crispus, Gaius and the household of Stephanas, given that he did not see baptizing as part of his mission (1 Cor. 1.14–17), is that he perceived these individuals as prominent, as likely to sponsor his gospel to their dependents, and as viable patrons who would support him in his mission and help the church thrive.[63] Paul has set up his own patronage system, in which gratitude to him will cultivate loyalty. Stephanas hosts Paul and the whole church, the members of which are expected, as good clients, to be submissive to him (1 Cor. 16.15–16). He has also taken part in the Corinthian delegation to Paul at Ephesus.

The submission language about Stephanas and the language of respect and esteem for those who 'labour among you, who preside over you and admonish you' in 1 Thess. 5.12–13 indicates that very early the expected way to treat leadership figures was, as should be expected, with respect and submission. In return, loyal church members could anticipate receiving the benefits of clientage. What *is* surprising is that, apart from one passage in *1 Clement* (1.3) and in the long recension of Ignatius's *Philadelphians* 4, the language of submission (ὑποτάσσειν) that is so closely associated with marriage relationships and slavery in the New Testament's household codes, even though it occurs in many other contexts there including civic authority (Rom. 13:1), ceases to be used in the marital or slavery context in early Christian literature; rather, it appears in the context of the deference owed to church leaders (also in *1 Clem.* 1.3). The language of submission migrates from household to patronally and patriarchally organized church, where the male church leader is seen as analogous to a *paterfamilias* who must know how to administer his property and govern his family as prerequisite qualification to governing the church (1 Tim. 3.4, 12).

The policies of church leadership toward personal patronage of individuals and especially of groups within the church fluctuated in the following centuries. Diotrephes, the bane of the Elder in 3 John 9, is characterized as φιλοπρωτεύων, which means 'more than liking to put himself first', as the NRSV renders it: he is overbearing about his patronal claims and does not wish to acknowledge those of the Elder. Hermas criticizes the wealthy for shirking patronal duties: they get so involved in their business interests that they avoid lesser persons because they do not wish to be asked for favours (*Herm. Sim.* 9.20.2–4). Such behaviour would have been considered not only bad but stupid; it would incur the disdain not only of peers but of the Christian poor as well. Their repentance will consist in 'doing some good', namely, being generous with their riches and establishing patronage relationships. The traditional titular churches and catacombs of Rome witness to the benefactions of early patrons: nearly every instance reveals a legacy of original private ownership by a wealthy benefactor who allowed communal use of the property for gatherings and burials.[64]

Later writers under a growing church centralization are not so encouraging. The *Apostolic Tradition* of Hippolytus discourages individuals from holding charity meals

---

63 Chow, *Patronage and Power*, pp. 88–90.

64 See discussion of women's participation in family funerary rights in Janet Tulloch, 'Women Leaders in Family Funerary Banquets', in Osiek, MacDonald and Tulloch, *A Woman's Place*, pp. 164–93.

for the needy without clerical supervision.[65] Cyprian, probably like most bishops of his time, wanted to consolidate patronal power in his own office by weakening the power of wealthy members of the church. Consequently, he encouraged centralized charity and rejected the charismatic claims of martyrs to forgive sins, thereby indirectly disempowering women who were confessors or martyrs. The consolidation of charity, already evidenced by Justin and Tertullian, gradually becomes the norm for Christians to exercise their generosity. By then, there is only one major patron left: the bishop.[66] To be sure, the bishop or presbyter is still under the patronage of the wealthy, e.g., John Chrysostom of Olympias and others, Jerome of Paula, Rufinus of Melania. In the *Apocryphal Acts*, the figure of the apostle attracts social power to himself, including the affection and loyalty of significant women who renounce marriage in favour of discipleship. What we see in these examples is the Christian transformation of patronage that occurs when the factors of spiritual power and authority are introduced into it.

The Patronage of Christian Women

Among early Christian women, both personal and group patronage is evident. Women extend benefaction to individual leaders like Paul and Ignatius, and they open their houses for Christian gatherings. The evidence of women hosting house churches is clearly present in the New Testament: Mary mother of John Mark in Jerusalem (Acts 12.12), Nympha (Col. 4.15), Lydia (Acts 16.14–15, 40)[67] and Prisca with Aquila. In such context, it is likely that the gatherings were conducted in the same way as any other patronage situation, namely, with deference, respect and submission owed to the patronal figure who expected to be the centre of attention and of honour except at those times when founding apostles were present.[68]

Several more general remarks in Acts leave gaps. In Acts 17.4 and 12, Paul's preaching in Thessalonica and Beroea, respectively, results in the conversion of important men and distinguished women.[69] In both cases, as with Paul's dealings with important people in Corinth, he likely welcomed these prominent connections as opportunities to establish patronage networks whereby the less distinguished, especially their dependents, would be favourably impressed and even perhaps pressured toward conversion. The reverse is true at Acts 13.50 in Pisidian Antioch, where the leading Jews incite the leading men and distinguished women *against* the missionary preachers. Here the well-established power connections are not in Paul's favour. Given what we know about women's patronage, we need not assume in any

---

65 Charles A. Bobertz, 'The Role of Patron in the *Cena Dominica* of Hippolytus' *Apostolic Tradition*', *JTS*, 44 (1993), pp. 170–84.

66 Brian Daley, 'Position and Patronage in the Early Church: The Original Meaning of the "Primacy of Honour"', *JTS*, 44 (1993), pp. 529–53, carries the expectations of honour through episcopal relationships among the great centres in the fourth and fifth century, showing that the language of primacy and honour cannot be separated from the expectations of the patronage system.

67 On the various readings of Lydia's social status, see Matthews, *First Converts*, pp. 85–89.

68 For further discussion of the role of women hosts of house churches, see Osiek, MacDonald and Tulloch, *A Woman's Place*, esp. pp. 144–63.

69 On the *topos* of the rich female convert in many ancient religious traditions, see Matthews, *First Converts*, pp. 51–71.

of these three cases that the mention of both men and women indicates married couples.

Ignatius's letters attest to several more prominent women who must have provided patronage for the bishop, if not hosted their own house church: Tavia with her household (*Smyrn.* 13.2) and perhaps the highly placed Alke, 'a name that is dear to me', probably the same Jewish woman whose brother Niketas was later inimical to Polycarp (*Smyrn.* 13.2; *Pol.* 8.3; *Mart. Pol.* 17.2). Alke may have sacrificed some family ties for her continued support of Ignatius. *Pol.* 8.2 refers to another woman, an unnamed wife of an unnamed steward (ἐπίτροπος), or of a man called Epitropos, with her whole household and children. This must be the case of a Christian *materfamilias* with an unbelieving husband. Thus married women performed patronage roles to Christian groups independently of their husbands, just as their non-Christian counterparts did to synagogues and temples. The inclusion of the household and children in this case suggests hospitality of some kind, with the husband not objecting.[70] The absence of the woman's name, which is surprising, may be a way of protecting her or her husband from public shame by being associated with a convicted criminal – or perhaps Ignatius has forgotten her name!

And so we come to Rom. 16.1–2, where Paul refers to Phoebe as both διάκονος and προστάτις. We will not take up here the question of what a διάκονος would do in the middle of first-century Cenchrae, except to suggest that the context in Rom. 16.1–2 hints that it involves representation of one church to another, since representation or agency is one of the principal connotations of the διακονία word group.[71] A parallel may perhaps be found in two passages of Ignatius. In *Phil.* 10.1 he encourages the church to appoint (χειροτόνησαι, the term later to be the most common for clerical ordination) a διάκονος as representative (εἰς τὸ πρέσβευσαι) to the Syrian church.[72] According to *Smyrn.* 10.1 Philo and Rheus Agathopous, who accompany Ignatius (*Phil.* 11.1), were received by the Smyrnaeans as representatives of God (ὡς διάκονους θεοῦ) when they came to Philadelphia. Margaret Mitchell has shown that the officially designated envoy, in the context of epistolary conventions, was to be received in the same way as the sender would be received and is the authoritative representative of the one who sends.[73] Phoebe functions this way with regard to Paul.

The connotations of the ascription προστάτις are less of 'presider' as in a liturgical assembly, though that is not ruled out by reason of the privileged place of the patron in an assembly, than of patronal benefaction and the prestige and authority the position

---

70 But for discussion of the difficulties to husbands and wives caused by such 'mixed' marriages, see Osiek, MacDonald and Tulloch, 'Dutiful and Less Than Dutiful Wives', *A Woman's Place*, pp. 17–49.

71 'Service rendered in an intermediary capacity, *mediation, assignment*', BDAG[3], p. 230.

72 However, Ignatius also uses the term 'deacon' in a triple-tiered leadership structure, as he does in the next paragraph, saying that other churches have sent on the same mission bishops, presbyters and deacons. See William R. Schoedel, *Ignatius of Antioch: A Commentary on the Letters of Ignatius of Antioch* (Hermeneia; Philadelphia, PA: Fortress Press, 1985), pp. 213–14, 248.

73 Margaret M. Mitchell, 'New Testament Envoys in the Context of Greco-Roman Diplomatic and Epistolary Conventions: The Example of Timothy and Titus', *JBL*, 111 (1992), pp. 641–62.

entails.[74] While neither the masculine προστάτης nor the feminine προστάτις necessarily includes hospitality, this role cannot be ruled out either, by reason of the προστασία of Junia Theodora, Phoebe's Lycian contemporary in Corinth, whose role clearly includes hospitality to Lycians passing through Corinth.[75]

Some have suggested a specific strategy on Paul's part by entrusting his letter to Phoebe. Robert Jewett sees Phoebe as Paul's emissary and guarantee for his Spanish mission. Since he knows no one in Spain and there is not a sizable Jewish community there to which he could attach himself, he relies on the wealthy and influential Phoebe to pave the way in Rome and stimulate there the desire to finance his Spanish mission. The greeting list of Romans 16 is then 'a roster of potential campaign supporters ... the first stage in the recruitment process'.[76]

On the other hand, Caroline F. Whelan sees Romans 16 as intended for Ephesus, where Paul relies on Phoebe to secure his interests while he heads west. Paul relies on Phoebe's client network and at the same time introduces her to his network to reciprocate her patronage to him. She sees their relationship as 'an agreement of "equals", albeit with vastly different spheres of interest', this equality, or at least different kind of reciprocity, on some levels creating a different kind of patron–client relationship containing some kind of mutuality.[77] Whereas patronage between two near-equals, such as a senior and junior senator, was possible, from what we know of relationships in general, seldom was the concept of equality part of the equation, and almost never between men and women until the days of the Christian ascetics several centuries later. Otherwise, however, in Rom. 16.2 we have the odd case of a client, Paul, commending his patron, Phoebe. But this may be justified in the case that the patron is moving into new territory that the client already knows, as is probably the case here. Whether Romans 16 is addressed to Rome or to Ephesus, it is likely that Paul is not just commending Phoebe to a new group, but is participating in some greater plan for advancing evangelization, which Phoebe herself may have initiated.

An unusual fourth-century Christian inscription from Jerusalem commemorates a 'slave and bride of Christ' named Sophia, a deacon (διάκονος), 'the second Phoebe' (ἡ δευτέρα Φοίβη). It is doubtful that she is hailed as second Phoebe because she is a deacon, a title held by many Christian women of the period. G.H.R. Horsley proposes several parallels in which inscriptions hail men as 'new Homer', 'new Themistocles', 'new Theophanes' and 'new Dionysos', the last also applied to the emperor, Commodus and Gallienus.[78] In every case, the person so titled seems to have been a major benefactor of his own or his adoptive city. The title probably began with popular acclamation and stuck to the man's public identity. The same likely holds for Sophia because of her benefactions to the church of Jerusalem.

---

74 A mother is προστάτις for her son in an inscription of 142 BCE (probably a guardian), and another named Zmyrna is προστάτις of the god Anoubis (probably a benefactor); *NewDocs*, 4. 122, p. 243.

75 As suggested by Marco Zappella, 'A proposito di Febe PROSTATIS (Rm 16,2)', *RivB*, 37 (1989), pp. 167–71.

76 'Paul, Phoebe and the Spanish Mission', in Jacob Neusner, et al. (eds), *The Social World of Formative Christianity: Essays in Tribute of Howard Clark Kee* (Philadelphia, PA: Fortress Press, 1988), pp. 142–61 (153).

77 'Amica Pauli: The Role of Phoebe in the Early Church', *JSNT*, 49 (1993), pp. 67–85 (84).

78 *NewDocs*, 4.122, p. 241.

A few more glimpses of Christian women patrons must be mentioned. The reference to 'Chloe's people' in 1 Cor. 1.11 means that Chloe is the central person in some kind of household staff. Her 'people' are either members of her immediate household or of her extended network of clients. If they have written from Corinth to Paul in Ephesus, Chloe herself is probably not a Christian; if she were, the reference would be to 'Chloe and her people'. On the other hand, if some members of her household are in Ephesus and are reporting to Paul, it is possible that Chloe herself is a believer, at home in Corinth. A certain number of Christians in her *familia* are functioning either independently with regard to religion, which would not be unusual, or under the patronage of this woman, much as a synagogue received the patronage of Tation at Kyme or Julia Severa at Akmonia, two women patrons who were probably not Jewish.[79] Marcia, concubine of Commodus, is known to have interceded in imperial machinery for the release of a group of Christians condemned to the mines in the early third century, among them Callistus, according to his rival Hippolytus. One of the things that Hippolytus found objectionable about Callistus's policies once he became bishop of Rome is that he allowed higher-status women to marry men of lesser status, a practice always frowned upon by society at large (*Ref.* 9.12). This is likely to have meant a freeborn woman, an *ingenua*, marrying a freedman, a *libertinus*. The old objection about women patrons marrying their own freedmen may have risen once again, this time in Christian context.[80]

The evolution of the office of widow also gives glimpses into what was happening with Christian women patrons. While Acts does not explicitly call Tabitha a widow (Acts 9.36–42), she is a benefactor especially to widows, and there is no mention of her husband. By encouraging women patrons to care for needy widows so that the church does not have to carry the burden, 1 Tim. 5.16 both acknowledges the power of wealthy and influential women and suggests that they could be of service by befriending other women in need.[81] While widows are presented in many texts from 1 Timothy 5 onward as predominantly recipients of charity, the 'enrollment' to which they are subject also implies a certain status of honour. In Tertullian's Carthage the order of widows is seated with the clergy to receive petitions for a second marriage and for the ritual prostration of public penitents (*De monog.* 11.1; *De pud.* 13.7). Beginning in 1 Tim. 5.13, the traditional fear of the power of widows is raised: since they no longer link two families and are no longer under a man's direct authority, they have too much freedom and their integrity is suspect.

The long recension of Ignatius's *Philadelphians* 4 includes at the end of an extensive discussion of submission relationships an exhortation to widows not to wander about and be lacking in austerity, but to be serious like Judith and Anna. The same motif recurs in the third-century *Didascalia Apostolorum* 15 (*Apostolic*

---

79 For further discussion, see Margaret MacDonald, 'Reading Real Women through the Undisputed Letters of Paul', in Ross Shepard Kraemer and Mary Rose D'Angelo (eds), *Women and Christian Origins* (New York: Oxford University Press, 1999), pp. 199–220, at pp. 200–2.

80 On this issue, see also Osiek, MacDonald and Tulloch, 'Women as Agents of Expansion', *A Woman's Place*, pp. 220–43.

81 Some manuscripts read πιστὸς ἢ πιστή (believing man or believing woman), but the majority and better witness is that the text refers only to women.

Constitutions 3.5–11).[82] Here widows, asked about the faith, must only respond about the basics; they must leave catechesis to the qualified, for were outsiders to hear about the incarnation and passion of Christ from a woman, their response would be derision. The whole idea of women teaching or baptizing is disapproved, but the obsession, repeated several times and echoing 1 Tim. 5.13, is with widows moving from house to house. They are not to instruct, visit the sick, or lay hands on anyone without the bishop's permission.

From earlier tradition, widows are compared to the altar of God. Just as the altar stays in one place, so should they![83] The *Didascalia* mounts deliberate attempts to thwart the mutual aid system that usually functions in women's subgroups and to make widows entirely dependent on the bishop and his representatives, the deacons. Moreover, the widows are expressly told that they should not know, and may not reveal if they do know, the identity of their benefactors. The text thus suppresses the expected desire of clients to be personally connected to their patrons in favour of centralized coordination. By this time, we can see a conscious attempt by church authorities to control women's patronage as well as men's, and to break the network of personal patronage that had been the backbone of social relationships.

The patronal activity of women did not entirely disappear in this new centralized system. Wealthy women continued to be major donors to the Church, and as such to command social respect if not social power. By the fourth century, lay patronage of churches was beginning to be commemorated in stone within those structures. The patronage of these wealthy women sometimes appears in inscriptions, the only way in which their memory was preserved. Women also participated as deacons, especially but not exclusively in the East, where through the sixth century often the preferred title was διάκονος rather than διακονίσα. Male deacons were responsible for carrying out the patronage programme of the bishop. Female deacons participated in that work, especially in ministry to other women. Female deacons also contributed to churches and cities and exercised their own charitable works. The deacon/ness Matrona of fourth-century Stobi, for example, paved an exedra in fulfillment of a vow, as did the διάκονος Agrippiane a mosaic floor in Patrae, while Mary the deacon in sixth-century Archelais, Cappadocia, in keeping with the description in 1 Tim. 5.10, 'raised children, exercised hospitality, washed the feet of the saints, and distributed her bread to the needy'.[84]

---

82 See n. 79, above; Bonnie Bowman Thurston, *The Widows: A Women's Ministry in the Early Church* (Minneapolis, MN: Fortress Press, 1989), pp. 96–104.

83 Cf. Carolyn Osiek, 'The Widow as Altar: The Rise and Fall of a Symbol', *Second Century*, 3.3 (1983), pp. 159–69.

84 Texts and discussion in Ute E. Eisen, *Women Officeholders in Early Christianity: Epigraphical and Literary Studies* (trans. Linda M. Maloney; Collegeville, MN: Liturgical Press, 2000), pp. 164–67, 175–76. Matrona and Maria also in *NewDocs* 2.109 pp. 193–95; Agrippiane in Kraemer, *Women's Religions in the Greco-Roman World*, p. 259; cf. Kevin Madigan and Carolyn Osiek, *Ordained Women in the Early Church: A Documentary History* (Baltimore, MD: Johns Hopkins University Press, 2005).

Conclusion

The extent and importance of women's patronage in the Greco-Roman world and especially in early Christianity is still in need of exploration. But to catch the nuances, we need to be sensitive to the social signals, networks and hierarchical relationships inherent in ancient Mediterranean society.

While real legal and ideological differences remained, it is doubtful whether in the everyday practice of patronal relationships much difference could have been perceived between the practice of patronage among men and women, except for voting and holding elective office, and even there, other aspects of the political process are very similar. Likewise, in early Christianity there was little difference between the patronage of men and women, but the patronage function was an essential ingredient in the life of house churches. This does not mean that anywhere in the patronage system something approximating what moderns understand by equality was ever achieved. Gender hierarchy continued, but because status hierarchy was more significant in the way social relations played out, some approximation of similar status between men and women was sometimes present. In Christian groups, the interplay between spiritual power and social power created new patterns of reciprocity. Any way we look at it, though, the system became one of spiritual equity but not of social equity. Gal. 3.28 proclaims unity in access to the grace of Christ; it does not proclaim social equality, contrary to the way many modern readers want to interpret it.

The martyrs, of course, became big-time patrons, for in heaven they were now in a position to influence directly God, the ultimate dispenser of favours. From the martyrs, the understanding extended to all saints. Patronage has been absorbed into Roman Catholic spirituality from its Mediterranean base. Hence, one speaks of 'patron saints' or is devoted to a certain saint as 'patron' of a certain group of people: sailors, musicians, incurables, etc. Many Mediterranean, Asian and African cultures are consciously patronage systems. Cultures and religions that have emanated from northern Europe tend to frown on all of this, with the belief that one does not need an intermediary to access either God or justice before the law. Yet patronage continues to function everywhere, just more or less directly: in politics, academia, employment, promotion and many more areas. When patronage works well, it provides protection for the powerless by the powerful. When it does not work well, it can be a means of exploitation of the powerless by the powerful. Must it always be so?

The Virgin Charioteer and the Bride of Christ: Gender and the Passions in Late Ancient Ethics and Early Christian Writings on Virginity[*]

Teresa M. Shaw

Scholars have rightly interpreted and considered much of the literature of early Christianity within the context of the larger body of late ancient moral theory, that is, the philosophical and medical discourse on the ethical subject, the virtues and vices, and the relationship between practical or physical behaviour and the health of the soul. This essay explores some of the ways in which early Christian writings addressed to virgins (women dedicated to celibate lives) construct the nature of moral formation and the techniques required for avoidance of vice and progress in virtue. In particular, I both consider how gender imagery and categories shape the understanding of the passions or vices as they affect soul and body and show that the literature on virginity, which in many ways claims to construct an alternative to the cultural norm of femaleness, subverts as well as reinforces traditional notions of female virtue.

In order to analyse these themes in Christian texts addressing the moral formation of female virgins, it is necessary first to summarize a few of the features of ethical discourse in the first centuries of the common era. Accordingly, the first section of this essay describes briefly the terminology and imagery related to the nature of the soul, the origin of the passions, and the treatment or therapy of the passions in the authors identified with the Stoic and Platonic schools in the late ancient period. In the second section I summarize how these relate to the concepts of virtue and vice and the articulation of specifically ascetic regimens and discourse. The third section explores the relationship among gender, the language of the passions and the regimen prescribed for virtue in Christian literature. I examine three texts, dating from the fourth and fifth centuries, that share a common ascetic heritage and a focus on female asceticism in particular, in order to show how Christian ascetic instruction and theory reinterpret contemporary ethical models.

The Passions in Late Ancient Ethics

In late antiquity, ethical discourse features concern with the care of the soul and body in an intimate and interdependent relationship, and advice concerning the daily regimen and training (ἄσκησις) by which the soul's passions or vices are controlled

[*]An early version of this paper was delivered at the Society of Biblical Literature Annual Meeting, Orlando, Florida, 1998. I am grateful for feedback from respondent Hanne Sigismund Nielson and presenter David Brakke, and I am grateful to Amy-Jill Levine for her careful reading and insightful suggestions.

or suppressed and the virtues are nourished.[1] The physician Galen (ca. 129–200) as well as late Stoic writers Musonius Rufus (ca. 30–101) and Epictetus (ca. 55–135) and the middle Platonist author Plutarch (ca. 47–120) are particularly strong representatives of this focus on the therapies of soul and body. They took as a given that whatever one did to or through the body affected the condition of the soul, and that whatever happened to be the condition of one's soul would be manifest physically. Plutarch, for example, cited with approval Plato's assertion that 'there should be no movement of the body without the soul or the soul without the body', but that both should be cared for in balance as a 'well-matched team'.[2] These authors also share a conviction that virtue, like vice, is cultivated not merely by theoretical reflection but by practical training (or ἄσκησις) and daily effort. Thus they discuss the best ways to develop good habits in diet, lifestyle, daily regimen and the exercise of choice and avoidance. They recommend variously a light, dry and vegetarian diet as best for the health of the soul and maintenance of intelligence, the exercise of self-control (σωφροσύνη) and abstinence (ἐγκράτεια), moderation in sexual pleasures, and mental exercises in detachment from desire. They also advocate a therapeutic technique for controlling the passions or vices of the soul and body which involves careful observation and diagnosis of the affliction and the application of certain impulses or virtues to assist or counteract others.[3]

The Greek word for 'passion', πάθος, can also be translated as 'emotion' or 'disease', in the sense of that which is experienced or suffered. The passions (πάθη) of the soul in ancient ethical discourse include desire, sadness, anger, pleasure, grief, greed and pride. At the risk of oversimplifying, in general we can distinguish two broad strands of influential theories in late antiquity concerning the nature of the soul, its relation to the body, and the origin and treatment of the passions. Yet, as with most broad distinctions, there are numerous exceptions,

---

1 For general discussions see A.A. Long, *Hellenistic Philosophy: Stoics, Epicureans, Sceptics* (New York: Charles Scribner's Sons, 1974); *idem, Soul and Body in Stoicism* (The Center for Hermeneutical Studies in Hellenistic and Modern Culture: Colloquy, 36; Berkeley, CA: Center for Hermeneutical Studies, 1980); Wayne Meeks, *The Moral World of the First Christians* (LEC; Philadelphia, PA: The Westminster Press, 1986); Helen North, *Sophrosyne: Self-Knowledge and Self-Restraint in Greek Literature* (Cornell Studies in Classical Philology, 35; Ithaca, NY: Cornell University Press, 1966); Martha C. Nussbaum, *The Therapy of Desire: Theory and Practice in Hellenistic Ethics* (Martin Classical Lectures, n.s. 2; Princeton, NJ: Princeton University Press, 1994); Jackie Pigeaud, *La maladie de l'âme: Étude sur la relation de l'ame et du corps dans la tradition médico-philosophique antique* (Paris: Les Belles Lettres, 1981); Teresa M. Shaw, *The Burden of the Flesh: Fasting and Sexuality in Early Christianity* (Minneapolis, MN: Fortress Press, 1998), pp. 27–78.

2 Plutarch, *De tuenda sanitate praecepta* 137e (Frank Cole Babbitt [ed. and trans.], *Plutarch's Moralia* [LCL; 11 vols.; Cambridge, MA: Harvard University Press, 1928; repr., 1971], 2.292).

3 See for example Musonius Rufus, *Discourses* 5; 6; 12; 18A (Cora B. Lutz [ed.], 'Musonius Rufus: The Roman Socrates', *Yale Classical Studies* 10 [1947]: pp. 48–56; 84–88; 112–14); Epictetus, *Dissertationes* I.27.3–5; II.9.11–14; II.18.4–18; III.12; IV.1.81–113 (W. A. Oldfather [ed. and trans.], *Epictetus: The Discourses as Reported by Arrian, The Manual, and Fragments* [LCL; 2 vols; Cambridge, MA: Harvard University Press, 1966–1967], 1.170–72; 268–70; 350–54; 2.80–86; 270–82); Galen, *De cognoscendis curandisque animi morbis* (Galen, *Galeni Opera Omnia* [Leipzig: K. Knobloch, 1823–1833; repr., Hildesheim: Georg Olms, 1965], 5.1–57); C.G. Kühn [ed.], *Quod animi mores corporis temperamenta sequantur* (Kühn 4.767–822); Plutarch, *De tuenda sanitate praecepta* (Babbitt [ed.], *Plutarch's Moralia*, 2.216–92).

mutual influences and hybridizations. The strand of philosophy, medicine and ethics identified most clearly with Plato and the Platonic tradition generally argued for an incorporeal soul that was tripartite or threefold in nature. In the Platonic tradition, the rational part of the soul (τὸ λογιστικόν) is the source of rationality and reasoning power and is associated in the body with the brain. The irrational part of the soul consists of the irascible and the concupiscible (or desiring) souls. The irascible soul (τὸ θυμικόν), as its name indicates, controls the impulses of anger and courage and is seated in the heart, while the concupiscible soul (τὸ ἐπιθυμητικόν) is linked to the forces of bodily desire, eros, generation and nutrition, and is seated in the liver. In the Platonic concept of the tripartite soul, the rational soul controls and guides the parts of the irrational soul, yet the powers and passions associated with desire and anger are not necessarily evil and in fact may be useful toward the good (for example, the desire for the good and the courage to pursue and endure are associated with this part of the soul).

The Stoic strand emphasizes instead a materialist understanding of the soul as a very rarefied and fine type of corporeal spirit or πνεῦμα. The soul includes eight faculties or aspects (the five senses, the power of procreation, the voice, and the ruling principle of reason, called the ἡγεμονικόν). Neither Platonic nor Stoic psychological theory is without variation and nuance in late antiquity, yet in general Stoic thought on the passions identifies them, in contrast to the Platonic concept, not as part of the irrational soul but as poor judgements of reason or ἡγεμονικόν.[4] For example, Epictetus discusses the relationship between reason and the passion of greed:

> For when once you conceive the desire for money, if reason be applied to bring you to a realization of the evil, both the passion is stilled and our governing principle [ἡγεμονικόν] is restored to its original authority; but if you do not apply a remedy, your governing principle does not revert to its previous condition, but, on being aroused again by the corresponding external impression, it bursts into the flame of desire more quickly than it did before. And if this happens over and over again, the next stage is that a callousness results and the infirmity strengthens the avarice.[5]

Here Epictetus illustrates the idea that the passions, which originate from thought processes or beliefs ('money is good'), are like 'infirmities' or illnesses that weaken and infect the soul unless properly *rational* thoughts or beliefs ('money is not good in itself') are applied against them. Nevertheless both passions and their rational

---

4 Stoic ethical writers were not completely of one mind on the nature of passions and their relation to the rational mind. On these issues see Nussbaum, *Therapy of Desire*, pp. 366–86; John M. Rist, *Stoic Philosophy* (Cambridge, UK: Cambridge University Press, 1969), pp. 22–35; Long, 'Soul and Body in Stoicism'; Christopher Gill, 'The Emotions in Greco-Roman Philosophy', in Susanna Morton Braund and Christopher Gill (eds), *The Passions in Roman Thought and Literature* (Cambridge, UK: Cambridge University Press, 1997), pp. 5–12. On Galen and his relation to Stoic thought see James Hankinson, 'Actions and Passions: Affection, Emotion, and Moral Self-Management in Galen's Philosophical Psychology', in Jacques Brunschwig and Martha C. Nussbaum (eds), *Passions and Perceptions: Studies in Hellenistic Philosophy of Mind* (Cambridge, UK: Cambridge University Press, 1993), pp. 184–222.

5 Epictetus, *Dissertationes* II.18.8–10 (trans. Oldfather, I.351–53).

remedy originate in the working of the reasoning principle, and not, as in the classic Platonic formula, in the soul's distinct rational and irrational parts.

While both Platonic and Stoic ethical theorists argue that the passions should be dominated by reason and rationality, and this becomes the ascetic project in both schools, their different understandings of the nature of the passions imply as well two distinguishable *goals* of that ἄσκησις. If the passions are associated with the natural working of the soul, then the goal is to control the passions with rationality and guide them to their proper, positive use. Yet if the passions are associated with poor judgement and faulty reason, the goal becomes complete freedom from passion (ἀπάθεια) in the exercise of reason. The first approach is typified by the Platonic image of the rational soul as the chariot driver who controls two strong and spirited 'horses', representing the irascible and desiring souls. Just as the charioteer's job is to control the horses so as to guide them to their proper use and harmonious function, so also the rational mind controls the impulsive and energized parts of the irrational soul for the purpose of their harmonious function in service to the rational soul.[6] We see this approach also in passion therapists' advice to use the passions carefully in the pursuit of virtue or to apply one passion as an instrument to aid or repress another. The passions, properly directed, have good and therapeutic use in the service to the soul. For example, Plutarch argues that anger can, when properly controlled, sustain courage,[7] and Galen suggests that anger is useful for the repression of desire.[8]

The second approach, which emphasizes ἀπάθεια as a goal of the virtuous life, views the passions less as impulses or even emotions and more as diseases of the soul that corrupt judgement. Hence in the 'classic' Stoic formulation the health of the soul is restored by the elimination of its πάθη.[9] The tension between these two visions of the goal of ethical formation and ascetic effort continues in late antiquity, yet many Christian and non-Christian authors exhibit a willingness to use the imagery, argumentation and psychological models from both traditions as needed. This in itself points to a certain amount of fluidity or eclecticism with the language of ethical formation. Galen the philosopher-physician, for example, identifies himself much more intentionally with the Platonic tradition concerning the soul, yet he admits that he cannot embrace certain concepts distinctive to that tradition such as the soul's incorporeality. And in his treatise 'On the Passions and Errors of the Soul', he makes use of concepts of passions as diseases of the soul as well as arguments that passions can be controlled and properly directed, even employed in the cultivation of virtue.[10] Moreover, he defies easy and singular

6 See also Plato, *Phaedrus* 246a–b; 253c–254c (Harold North Fowler [ed. and trans.], *Plato: Euthyphro, Apology, Crito, Phaedo, Phaedrus* [LCL; 12 vols Cambridge, MA: Harvard University Press, 1966], pp. 470, 1. 494–98).

7 Plutarch, *De virtute morali* 451e (W. C. Hembold [ed. and trans.], *Plutarch's Moralia* [LCL; Cambridge, MA: Harvard University Press, 1939; repr., 2000], 6.80).

8 Galen, *De cog. cur. animi morbis* 6 (Kühn, 5.26–27).

9 See the discussion in Rist, *Stoic Philosophy*, pp. 26–27.

10 See *De cog. cur. animi morbis* 3; 6; 7 (Kühn 5.7–14; 26–30; 35). English translations: Paul W. Harkins, *Galen: On the Passions and Errors of the Soul* (Columbus: Ohio State University Press, 1963); P.N. Singer (trans.), 'The Affections and Errors of the Soul', in *Galen: Selected Works* (The World's Classics; Oxford: Oxford University Press, 1997), pp. 100–49. See also the discussion in Hankinson, 'Actions and Passions', pp. 184–222.

categorization by distinguishing between 'passions' that arise from irrational power and 'errors' (τὰ ἁμαρτήματα) that originate in false judgement or opinion. He writes, 'as everybody knows, there are passions of the soul: anger, wrath, fear, sadness, envy, and excessive desire. In my opinion excessive haste in loving or hating anything is also a passion. I believe the saying "moderation is best" is right, as nothing that happens immoderately is good.'[11] Errors of the soul, on the other hand, are most often made possible by 'excessive love of the self, conceit of wisdom, false pretense, or ambition'.[12] Thus by the first centuries of the common era ethical and psychological theories as well as the therapeutic discussions of passions and their cures have a long history and a highly developed vocabulary and methodology, and demonstrate a willingness to borrow and adapt in ways that did not necessarily respect strict ideological borders.

Ἄσκησις *and Virtue*

Characteristic of the literature and moral theories of late antiquity is the popularity of lists or catalogues of vices, virtues and passions of the soul. Intertwined with discussions and advice concerning the passions, moral theorists and passion therapists also delineate particular vices (κακίαι) and virtues (ἀρεταί) of the soul. For some authors the lists of virtues and vices became formulaic, as the language of virtue and vice became part of the familiar discourse of Christian and non-Christian ethics. The Stoic tradition, for example, identifies four principle virtues: rationality (φρόνησις), courage or manliness (ἀνδρεία), justice (δικαιοσύνη) and self-control or temperance (σωφροσύνη). As counterparts there are four principle vices (irrationality, cowardice, injustice and licentiousness) and four principle passions (sadness, fear, desire and pleasure). Similarly, Galen reveals the breadth of shared interest in the topic when he writes that '*as everybody knows*, there are passions of the soul'.[13]

The cultivation of moral virtue and happiness as well as the management of passions such as anger or pleasure are popular subjects in moral theory and instruction. For example, Plutarch returns repeatedly to the themes of virtue and vice and to questions not only of how one might develop and maintain virtue, but also how one knows if one is even making progress in virtue.[14] Galen, who was fascinated by the workings of emotion and the interdependence of emotional and physical health, writes at length of the need for therapeutic guidance in one's efforts to control passions, and in particular of the struggle with anger, that most powerful,

---

11 *De cog. cur. animi morbis*, 1; 3 (Kühn, 5.2–3; 7–8). The term here translated as anger, θυμός, is associated more with the irascible part of the soul and, as noted above, could have in the Platonic tradition positive as well as negative expression. Some translators thus opt for the more neutral term 'spirit'. The word translated 'wrath' is ὀργή, a more immediately negative emotion. In this passage Galen appears to give both θυμός and ὀργή negative connotations (see Singer, *Galen: Selected Works*, pp. 412–13).

12 *De cog. cur. animi morbis*, 2; 3 (Kühn, 5.3–8).

13 *De cog. cur. animi morbis*, 3 (Kühn 5.7), emphasis mine.

14 See for example *Quomodo quis suos in virtute sentiat profectus* 75a–86a (Frank Cole Babbitt, [ed. and trans.], *Plutarch's Moralia* [LCL; 11 vols; Cambridge, MA: Harvard University Press, 1927; repr., 2000], 1.400–56); *De virtute et vitio* 100b–101e (Babbitt, 2.94–100); *An virtus doceri possit* 439a–440c; *De virtute morali* 440d–452d; and *De cohibenda ira* 452e–464d (Hembold, 6.4–158).

dangerous and ambiguously valued emotion.[15] And the writings of Musonius and Epictetus represent just the sort of advice and guidance that Galen recommends for the one who wants to be rid of negative habits and to train for virtue.

The notion that one is able to 'train' for virtue lies at the junction of ancient psychology, medicine and ethics.[16] In late ancient authors such as Galen, Musonius, Epictetus and Plutarch, we find a shared expectation that with an intentional and rigorous training or asceticism (from ἄσκησις), one improves the health of the soul and cultivates virtue. This training involves observing a certain lifestyle, diet and physical regimen characterized by renunciation or ἐγκράτεια (itself a companion virtue to σωφροσύνη)[17] and a rigorous commitment to the therapeutic observation and control of the passions. Epictetus reminds his students that repeated behaviours strengthen both bad and good habits, which is why philosophers recommend not simply learning about what is advantageous or dangerous but actually training, practising and carefully observing moral progress. Thus the one who is battling anger should count the number of days without an outburst, and the man resisting sexual desire should make a mental note if he looks at a woman without lust.[18] Musonius, who is more of an advocate of physical ascetic exercises than Epictetus, recommends specific renunciations in sexual relations, diet, clothing and personal appearance, and in general advocates an acceptance of hardship (πόνος) as necessary for cultivating virtue.[19] The passion therapists of late antiquity thus understood that the health of the soul and the control of irrational passion could only be achieved through a combination of mental exercises, self-examination, moral guidance and physical renunciations.

In discussions of virtue and the passions and related vices, gender becomes a factor both in explicit considerations of the differences between male and female virtue and in the use of gendered bodily images and metaphors. Distinctions of virtues particularly suited to either female or male subjects, as well as debate on the question of whether males and females could be equal in terms of virtue, already have a long history in the late ancient period. For example, Helen North demonstrates that σωφροσύνη is associated throughout Greek and Roman literature in particular with the virtuous woman. In drama, moral discourse, oratory and general advice the virtuous woman displays her σωφροσύνη by her decorum, knowing how to hold her tongue, sexual fidelity and honour, obedience, restraint in moving about, and chastity (in some late ancient writers σωφροσύνη is nearly synonymous with sexual chastity). While men also cultivate σωφροσύνη – expressed through public self-mastery and self-knowledge, moderation and resistance to uncontrolled passion and ambition – the term takes on a distinct nuance as the *virtus feminarum*.[20]

---

15 See *De cog. cur. animi morbis.* (Kühn, 5.1–57); Hankinson, 'Actions and Passions', pp. 206–8.

16 See Hijmans' observation that for Epictetus 'ἄσκησις to virtue' was possible (B. L. Hijmans, Ἄσκησις: *Notes on Epictetus' Educational System* [Wijsgerige Teksten en Studies, 2; Assen: Van Gorcum, 1959], p. 64).

17 See North, *Sophrosyne*, e.g., p. 219.

18 Epictetus, *Dissertationes* II.9.11–14; II. 18.12–18 (Oldfather, 1.268–70; 352–54).

19 Musonius, *Discourses, passim*, especially *Discourses* 6; 7; 12; 18A; 18B; 19; 20; 21 (Lutz, 'Musonius Rufus', pp. 52–56, 56–58, 84–88, 112–14, 116–20, 120–22, 124–26, 128).

20 North, *Sophrosyne, passim*; see also Kate Cooper, *The Virgin and the Bride: Idealized Womanhood in Late Antiquity* (Cambridge, MA: Harvard University Press, 1996), esp. pp. 45–67.

In similar fashion, ἀνδρεία (courage or, more literally, manliness) becomes, not surprisingly, the 'manly' virtue, encompassing not only the general characteristics of action, courage and spirit but also the aspects of human behaviour identified with masculinity. North shows that the tension between σωφροσύνη and ἀνδρεία is one of the 'persistent themes' of ancient literature: as much as action and courage are valued, they must be controlled by the soundness of mind and intentional restraint represented by the virtue of σωφροσύνη. North notes that the 'perfect symbol' for this tension and balance is the Platonic charioteer guiding the spirited horses and protecting them 'from the assaults of appetites and passion but at the same time making use of their motive power to reach goals unattainable without them'.[21] By their association with gendered expectations for virtue (expectations that could be applied to either male or female subjects), as well as by their dominance and close association in ethical writing, the concepts of σωφροσύνη and ἀνδρεία play key roles in Christian ascetic discourse.

Ancient authors further disagree about whether males and females could equally attain virtue. Musonius Rufus alludes to this debate in his treatises 'That Women Should Study Philosophy' and 'Should Daughters Receive the Same Education as Sons?' He argues that women and men have the same faculties of reason, the same senses and the same bodily parts. Moreover, he argues that 'there are not some virtues for men, others for women', but women as well as men should cultivate rationality, self-control, justice and manliness or courage. For example, he observes that 'it is good for a woman to be self-controlled; and in the same way it is good for a man. For indeed the laws punish the adulterer and the partner in adultery equally'. Likewise, he writes,

> Perhaps someone would say that manliness [ἀνδρεία] only applies to men. But this is not the case. For woman also should be manly, and the best woman should be free from cowardice, in order that she is bowed down neither by pain nor by fear. Otherwise, how will she be self-controlled, if someone, by creating fear or by inflicting pain, could force her to endure some disgrace?[22]

Here Musonius suggests that manliness serves a woman by protecting her honour and avoiding disgraceful attack (e.g., torture or sexual assault). Thus although Musonius acknowledges an equality in virtue, his argument is qualified by the fact that his practical examples of female virtue focus on the household, marriage and the guarding of σωφροσύνη.[23] Indeed, while Musonius's arguments for equality in virtue, philosophical training and education for women, and the value of marriage may strike readers as 'modern' or at least as representative of a change in late ancient social outlook, David Cohen and Richard Saller caution that Musonius, Plutarch and their contemporaries who praise marriage and 'a certain reciprocity in marriage' do so without challenging more fundamental social expectations of gender hierarchy and women's subordination.[24]

---

21 North, *Sophrosyne*, pp. ix–x.

22 Musonius Rufus, *Discourse* 4 (Lutz, 'Musonius Rufus', p. 44).

23 Musonius Rufus, *Discourses* 3–4 (Lutz, 'Musonius Rufus', pp. 38–49).

24 David Cohen and Richard Saller, 'Foucault on Sexuality in Greco-Roman Antiquity', in Jan Goldstein (ed.), *Foucault and the Writing of History* (Oxford: Basil Blackwell, 1994), pp. 35–60 (36, 49–55).

In Musonius as in other ethical writers, the 'ideal ethical subject that they construct is simply masculine'.[25] That is, the female as ethical subject is constructed as opposite to, in tension or harmony with, or similar and even equal to, a male norm. The male remains the generic in relation to which the female is measured or qualified.[26] Yet as we have seen in Musonius's description of the woman who cultivates ἀνδρεία in large part to protect her σωφροσύνη, male or female images can be applied to either sex in the rhetoric of virtue and ethical construction. Here is where thinking about gender, virtue and vice in antiquity becomes tricky and not a little paradoxical. Just as a woman exercising ἀνδρεία is masculinized while ultimately demonstrating female virtue, so also a man cultivating σωφροσύνη (which is one of the keys to proper civic authority) to counter, for example, the impulse to anger, is in one sense feminized while ultimately demonstrating male self-mastery.[27] Maud Gleason and others have examined the ways in which ancient rhetoric employs malleable or even fluid categories of masculine and feminine to portray character, whether to condemn or to praise. The public and rhetorical display or construction of gender becomes a standard feature in late ancient literature, ethical theory, polemic, medicine, physiognomy and – in early Christian literature – hagiography and heresiology.[28]

The Soul and the Passions in Ascetic Literature

While the models and language of late ancient ascetic and ethical theory continue and are further shaped within early Christian literature, they are particularly developed, often systematically, in Christian ascetic discourse. During the fourth century there was a dramatic rise in the number of texts that praise and regulate the life of virgins, that is, women who dedicated themselves to Christ through sexual chastity and ascetic discipline. These texts could be in the form of regulations and advice addressed to virgins living at home with their families or in organized communities, or could be written for wider audiences in order to praise individual holy women or the ideal of virginity in general. They build their arguments on the foundation of many of the commonplaces of Hellenistic ethical theory, especially the understanding of the dynamic relationship between body and soul. They also continue images of masculine and feminine strengths and weaknesses familiar from much Greco-Roman literature, philosophy, medicine and oratory. Indeed, marital and familial advice, such as that found in Musonius or Plutarch, is translated (if subverted) to the arena of the virgin's lifestyle, not simply regarding her fidelity to

25 David Brakke, 'The Passions and the Social Construction of Masculinity', paper delivered at the Society of Biblical Literature Annual Meeting (Orlando, Florida, 1998), pp. 2–3. I am grateful to David Brakke for sharing the paper with me.

26 On this see also Thomas Laqueur, *Making Sex: Body and Gender from the Greeks to Freud* (Cambridge, MA: Harvard University Press, 1990), pp. 22, 34–35.

27 Brakke, 'Passions and the Social Construction of Masculinity', p. 13.

28 Studies of these themes are too numerous to include a complete list, but see for example Maud Gleason, *Making Men: Sophists and Self-Presentation in Ancient Rome* (Princeton, NJ: Princeton University Press, 1995); Virginia Burrus, 'The Heretical Woman as Symbol in Alexander, Athanasius, Epiphanius, and Jerome', *HTR* 84 (1991), pp. 229–48; *eadem*, *The Making of a Heretic: Gender, Authority, and the Priscillianist Controversy* (The Transformation of the Classical Heritage; Berkeley: University of California Press, 1995).

Christ the heavenly bridegroom but more generally regarding her daily activities, personal associations, bodily decorum, the passions and the cultivation of virtue.[29]

Christian ascetic writers in general, like their non-Christian philosophical and medical counterparts, make use of a complex and interrelated variety of gendered images, metaphors and categories in their presentation of passion, virtue and vice. Strong masculine language about the control, conquering, or slaying of the passions exists along with feminized representations of the soul or body as vulnerable to invasion, penetration and defilement by passionate thoughts or sensations. Borrowing Plato's influential image, some authors portray the female or male ascetic practitioner in the masculine role of the strong, athletic and wise charioteer who dominates, guides and subdues the body and physical passions like obedient horses. Thus in a fourth-century treatise on female virginity, Basil of Ancyra observes that the virgin controls her sense of taste just as she would control a powerful horse, by placing the '[horse's] bit' of rationality in its metaphorical mouth,[30] and by firmly controlling her whole body so that it neither disobediently skips away with too much energy nor falls down from weakness on the road to virtue.[31]

Basil and other ascetic advocates also portray both male and female practitioners in masculine imagery as wrestlers, athletes and warriors struggling for victory, as in a famous bit of rhetorical flair by which John Chrysostom describes young ascetic girls whose devotion to Christ and ascetic renunciations are so great that they are like 'noble athletes' and 'champions', shaming the men in Chrysostom's audience by running swiftly past them and leaving them in their dust.[32] One of the most common rhetorical elements of the discourse on female virginity is the exhortation to 'manliness' (ἀνδρεία), and authors praise female ascetic subjects for their manly endurance, mentality and courage.[33] For example, the ascetic chronicler Palladius describes Melania the Elder as a 'man of God',[34] and the biographer of her granddaughter Melania the Younger praises her 'manly deeds' and notes that she had a 'masculine mentality'.[35]

That such masculine ideals occupy a prominent place in texts for and about women is not surprising. Christian ethical writers agreed with many of their non-Christian contemporaries and predecessors that male and female were equal in the arena of virtue. For example, Clement of Alexandria (ca. 150–215), who was influenced on this topic especially by Stoic thinkers such as Musonius, asserts that just as there is only one virtue for both male and female, so also there is 'one σωφροσύνη, one shame (αἰδώς)'. In fact, for both the man and the woman wishing to pursue this virtue there is one moral guide in the pedagogue (Christ the Logos), one common

---

29 See Cooper, *Virgin and the Bride*.

30 Basil of Ancyra, *De vera virginitatis integritate* 5 (PG 30.680A–B).

31 Basil of Ancyra, *De vera virginitatis integritate* 5; 8 (PG 30.680A–B; 684C–685B).

32 John Chrysostom, *Homiliae in Epistula ad Ephesios* 13.3–4 (PG 62.97–99).

33 See for example John Chrysostom, *Homiliae in Epistula ad Ephesios* 13.3–4 (PG 62.97–99); Gregory of Nyssa, *De vita Macrinae* 10; 14 (Pierre Marval [ed.], *Grégoire de Nysse: Vie de Saint Macrine*, [SC 178 Paris: Éditions du Cerf, 1971], 172; 188–90,; *Vita Melaniae Junioris*) prologue; 12; 39 (Denys Gorce [ed.], *Vie de Sante Mélanie* [SC 90; Paris: Éditions du Cerf, 1962], 126; 150; 200–2); Basil of Ancyra, *De virg.* 18; 51 (PG 30.708B; 772B–C).

34 Palladius, *Historia Lausiaca* 9 (Cuthbert Butler [ed.], *The Lausiac History of Palladius* [2 vols; Texts and Studies 6/1–2; Cambridge, UK: Cambridge University Press, 1898 and 1904], 2.29).

35 *Vita Melaniae Junioris,* prologue; 39 (Gorce, pp. 126, 202).

salvation and one 'way of life'.[36] Yet our interpretation of Christian ascetic discourse is complicated by the fact that it combines images of female virility and masculinized virtue with images and interpretations of a feminized soul, body and ethical subject into a montage of gendered models which defies any clear perception of the ascetic lifestyles and goals of men and women.

If the attainment of virtue and Christian perfection requires *manly* courage and control and a rational soul that dominates irrational passions, in ascetic discourse the soul is also portrayed as a passive female receptacle or a structure vulnerable to both good and evil external forces. In Christian and pagan moral instruction directed to both male and female audiences the soul is often *effeminate* in relation to thoughts, passions and sensual stimulation. The soul is fertile ground awaiting good seed; it is subject to defilement or disease from bodily passions or wicked thoughts; it is the target of seductive intrusions by demon-inspired fantasies; it is stimulated by external sensations entering though the body's sense organs. Thus in relation to the external sights, sounds, tastes and sensations that can lead to sin, common metaphors for the soul or (depending on the text) for the ascetic body emphasize containment, intactness and protection. The soul or body is a house, a citadel, a city, or a temple. Passions are like invading soldiers, noxious smoke, or diseases against which the bodily senses are like windows that must be shut tight, walls that must be erected, doors that must be barred.[37] In her biography (probably written in the fifth century), the holy woman Syncletica, for example, teaches that the soul is like a house, and that the 'enemy' attacks the soul by whatever means necessary, undermining good works as if they were the house's foundation, challenging faith as if attacking the roof, or creeping in through the bodily senses like smoke through the windows.[38]

Moreover, passions can pollute the soul like male seed defiles a womb. The Neoplatonic philosopher Porphyry (ca. 232–305) argues that the soul is defiled both by mixing with body, through eating meat or through the emission of seed during sexual activity, as well as by passions such as anger and desire. To illustrate, he describes the female whose womb either receives the male seed – which pollutes whether or not conception takes place – or remains uncorrupted if it receives no seed. As mixing of soul and body is defiling, in the same way passions defile the soul by mixing the irrational with the rational part. For Porphyry the ideal soul is like the undefiled womb or the pure, clean stream running free of muck and mud.[39] Plutarch uses similar language of containment, vulnerability and pollution in his advice to

36 Clement of Alexandria, *Paedagogos* 1.4.10.1–11.2 (Henri-Irénée Marrou and Marguerite Harl, [eds], *Clément d'Alexandrie: Le Pédagogue* [SC 70; Paris: Éditions du Cerf, 1960], pp. 128–30).

37 For examples of these images see Basil of Ancyra, *De virg.* 15; 41 (PG 30.700C–704A; 749C–752B); John Chrysostom, *De inani gloria* 23–63 (Anne-Marie Malingrey [ed.], *Jean Chrysostome: Sur la vaine glorie et l'éducation des enfants* [SC 188; Paris: Éditions du Cerf, 1972], pp. 108–62); Pseudo.-Athanasius, *Vita et gesta Sanctae beataeque magistrae Syncleticae* 25; 46 (PG 28.1501B–C; 1513C–D); Jerome, *Adversus Jovinianum* 8 (PL 23.310B).

38 *Vita Syncleticae* 46 (PG 28.1513C–D).

39 Porphyry, *De abstinentia* IV.20 (August Nauck [ed.], *Porphyrii Philosophi Platonici opuscula selecta* [Bibliotheca Scriptorum Graecorum et Romanorum Teubneriana; Leipzig: Teubner, 1886; repr., Hildesheim: Georg Olms, 1963], pp. 262–64). Porphyry notes that the seed defiles if conception takes place, because of the association of soul and body, and if conception does not takes place, because the seed is left like a dead mass. In the same way male homosexual intercourse defiles because the seed is emitted into a dead receptacle.

a bride and groom, when he notes that a woman thinking without the guidance of her husband is like a womb without male seed. Just as the unfertilized womb might produce 'misshapen, flesh-like uterine growths originating in some infection', so also the woman's mind, left on its own, might 'conceive many untoward ideas and low designs and emotions'.[40] Here 'female interiority' provides the language for susceptibility in the mental process and emotional life, emphasizing not only entering and retention, but also the danger of both physically and mentally perverted 'conceptions'. Ruth Padel's description of what she calls the 'female model of mind' in fifth-century BCE Greek tragedy is helpful here. Padel describes the common use in tragic literature of the female metaphors of house, womb and earth to describe the mind, and notes that these images also informed later European literature, in which female interiority is 'a structure good to think with about the inner equipment, the mental and emotional experience'.[41] As the previous discussion demonstrates, the 'female model of mind' continues in the metaphors and preoccupations of late ancient moral and ascetic guidance. These metaphors and the ascetic imagery that they support exist along with and are interwoven with more overtly masculine metaphors of control, endurance and victory in the discourse on ascetic formation.

Turning now to focus closely on texts representing the Christian discourse on female virginity, we see how all of these themes become incorporated and modified in the delineation of the model of the female life dedicated to God. While dozens of texts could provide rich material for close analysis, I concentrate on just three sources in order to balance the wide-ranging nature of the previous discussion and to show how this discussion may be applied to closer textual readings. Gendered imagery for the threat of passions and the ascetic resistance to them characterizes the three Greek texts that are therefore the subjects of the remainder of this paper: Evagrius of Pontus's *Sententiae ad virginem*,[42] the anonymous *Life of Syncletica*[43] and the anonymous *Discourse on Salvation to a Virgin*.[44] These three texts probably date from the late fourth and fifth centuries CE, and they represent in their different genres – a set of short instructions, a hagiography and an extended discourse on the virginal life – the substantial body of literature from this period that focuses on female asceticism and the ideology and description of the virginal life. Ascetic works, they share a focus on the cure of souls through intentional bodily training (ἄσκησις) as well as prayer and careful attention to the influence of passions and passionate 'thoughts'.

40 Plutarch, *Coniugalia praecepta* 145d–f (trans. Babbitt, 2.339–341).

41 On female images for mind see Ruth Padel, *In and Out of the Mind: Greek Images of the Tragic Self* (Princeton, NJ: Princeton University Press, 1992), pp. 99–113.

42 Evagvius of Pontus, *Sententiae ad virginem* (Hugo Gressmann [ed.], *Nonnenspiegel und Mönchsspiegel des Euagrios Pontikos*, TU, 39, 4b [Leipzig: Hinrichs, 1913], pp. 146–51).

43 Pseudo-Athanasius, *Vita Sync.*, PG, 28.1488–1557. English translation: *The Life and Activity of the Holy and Blessed Teacher Syncletica*, in Vincent L. Wimbush (ed.), *Ascetic Behavior in Greco-Roman Antiquity* (trans. Elizabeth A. Castelli; Minneapolis, MN: Fortress Press, 1990), pp. 265–311.

44 Pseudo-Athanasius, *De virginitate* (Eduard F. von der Goltz [ed.], *Logos soterias pros ten parthenon (De virginitate): Eine echte Schrift des Athanasius*, TU, 29, 2a [Leipzig: Hinrichs, 1905]). English translation: *Discourse on Salvation to a Virgin*, in Richard Valantasis (ed.), *Religions of Antiquity in Practice* (trans. Teresa M. Shaw; Princeton Readings in Religions; Princeton, NJ: Princeton University Press, 2000), pp. 82–99.

Together, these features suggest another link among the three: the influence of the ascetic system associated with Evagrius of Pontus (ca. 345–399), who lived as a monk in Egypt and was distinguished by his highly developed, psychologically and cosmologically intricate ascetic theory. While Evagrius is known to be the author of the *Sententiae ad virginem*, the unknown authors of the other two texts show an interest in and familiarity with Evagrian ascetic theory and terminology.[45] Discussing the texts side by side therefore highlights both the tracings of Evagrian influence and the distinctive features of ascetic ethics promulgated for women. This female ascetic ethics mimics and builds on the Greco-Roman ideal of the virtuous woman possessing both σωφροσύνη and ἀνδρεία, while at the same time constructing a model of female virtue and achievement that rejects the social role of wife and mother and the social realm of the household, which previously defined the scope of the *virtus feminarum*. The features of the ascetic ethics include an emphasis not only on sexual chastity and the intactness of the body maintained by rigorous ascetic renunciations, but also the vulnerability of the senses and thoughts, the temptation wrought by the female form and female body itself, the danger of going out in public, speaking with men and raising one's eyes to a man, the importance of silence and holding the tongue as indicators of self-control, the concomitant ability of words to defile and corrupt, and the goal and reward of betrothal to Christ as the heavenly bridegroom.

One of the most distinctive aspects of Evagrius's ascetic vision is his highly developed and psychologically intricate understanding of the powerful effects of thoughts that take root and develop into passionate impulses, vice and moral enslavement to the worst human drives. In several of his key writings such as the *Praktikos*,[46] the *Antirrheticus*[47] and *On the Eight Spirits of Evil*[48] Evagrius articulates what becomes the organizing principle for his advice on the active ascetic life, that is, the eight passionate thoughts (which he also calls vices or evil spirits). The terms for passionate thoughts are λογισμοί or διαλογισμοί. Evagrius developed systematically the idea of a catalogue or list of vices, an idea – discussed above in relation to Stoic thought – which was widely present in earlier Hellenistic Jewish, Christian and pagan literature. He also built on the concept of ἀπάθεια or freedom

---

45 Scholars have previously recognized the Evagrian themes and terminology in both of the pseudo-Athanasius works. See for example Odile Benedicte Bernard (trans.), *Vie de Sainte Synclétique* (Spiritualité orientale, 9; Abbaye Notre Dame de Bellefontaine, 1972), pp. x–xiii; Ernesto Buonaiuti, 'Evagrio Pontico e il De Virginitate pseudo-Atanasiano', in *Saggi sul Cristianesimo Primitivo* (Castello: Il Solco, 1923), pp. 247–49. Buonaiuti outlines textual parallels between the *Discourse on Salvation* and Evagrius's *Sententiae ad virginem*, as does von der Goltz in his analysis of the *Discourse* (*Logos soterias pros ten parthenon*, pp. 73–74).

46 Evagrius of Pontus, *Praktikos* (Antoine Guillaumont and Claire Guillaumont [eds], *Évagre le Pontique: Traité pratique ou le moine*, [SC, 170–71; Paris: Éditions du Cerf, 1971]). English translation: John Eudes Bamberger (ed. and trans.), *Evagrius Ponticus: The Praktikos and Chapters on Prayer* (Cistercian Studies Series 4; Kalamazoo, MI: Cistercian Publications, 1981).

47 Evagrius of Pontus, *Antirrheticus*, in W. Frankenberg (ed.), *Evagrius Ponticus: Syrischer Text, griechische Retroversion* (Abhandlungen der königlichen Gesellschaft der Wissenschaften zu Göttingen, Philologisch-historische Klasse, Neue Folge, 13,2; Berlin: Weidmann, 1912), pp. 472–545.

48 Evagrius of Pontus, *De octo spiritibus malitiae* (PG 79.1145–1164).

from passions, especially as he found it in Clement of Alexandria.[49] Evagrius named the eight evil thoughts as gluttony, lust, love of money or greed, sadness, anger, listlessness, vainglory and pride. The passions affect both body and soul and are joined together like links in a chain, leading from one to the other by a progression of wicked thoughts brought on by demons inciting emotions and actions. Resistance to passionate thoughts and their consequences takes place by cultivating and applying opposing virtues in medical fashion, as Galen, Plutarch and others earlier advocated. For example, ἐγκράτεια (abstinence) is useful against gluttony, σωφροσύνη reduces the sting of πορνεία (lust), patience aids in the control of anger and humility thwarts the power of pride.[50] Fasting, vigils, prayer and constant effort are also essential physical and practical methods in the daily battle against the chain of vices. The goal of this daily practical effort is, therefore, by means of both physical ascetic exercise as well as careful observation of and resistance to tempting thoughts, to control and then eliminate passion. This ἀπάθεια (passionlessness) is only a preliminary step, however, to higher goals of ἀγάπη, pure prayer and contemplation.[51]

The three sources dealing with female ἄσκησις all give prominent attention to the danger of wicked thoughts (λογισμοί or διαλογισμοί), the cultivation of virtue, the particular danger of vainglory, the continual linking of prayer with physical asceticism and the active life, and the threat of defiling the mind, soul, or pure prayer by thoughts, words, or discussion. There are variations in these themes and the terminology among the three texts, and none – not even the *Sententiae ad virginem* written by Evagrius himself – is a blueprint for the entire Evagrian system. Moreover, the different genres and audiences influence the tone, emphases, level of detail and elaboration, and general content of the texts. For example, the *Sententiae ad virginem* consist of fifty-six short, memorizable and concise instructions ('Hunger and thirst quench evil desires, and a good vigil purifies understanding'),[52] while the *Discourse on Salvation* is an extended treatise and argument on the ideal of virginity and ascetic renunciation in general as well as the lifestyle and activities proper for a community of virgins, and the *Life of Syncletica* is in the genre of holy biography or hagiography and focuses on the life and teachings of one woman. Yet despite their different genres and modes of argumentation, they manifest a common understanding of the female ascetic project.

The *Sentences* and the *Discourse* focus primarily on the communal life of virgins, but Syncletica's teachings also deal in large part with interpersonal relations. The passionate thoughts that dominate in the three sources (greed, anger, sadness, vainglory and pride[53]) reflect the tensions inherent in a communal setting. These are the kinds of wicked temptations that the virgin living in community with other sisters may experience if the others achieve more than her, insult her, or ruin her with idle talk or

---

49 Guillaumont and Guillaumont, *Évagre le Pontique*, SC, 170. 63–112; Irénée Hausherr, 'L'origene de la théorie orientale des huit péchés capitaux', *Orientalia Christiana* 30 (1933), pp. 164–75.

50 The technique of applying virtues against vices is most explicitly discussed in *De octo spiritibus malitiae* and *De vitiis quae oppositia sunt virtutibus* (PG 79.1140–1144).

51 For a fuller discussion see Shaw, *Burden of the Flesh*, pp. 144–58.

52 Evagrius, *Sententiae ad virginem,* 40 (Gressmann, p. 149).

53 As noted above, none of these sources presents a systematic discourse on the eight passions (for example, the *Sentences* mention the vice of vainglory but not pride). Still the Evagrian concept of the passions and their connection to thought is clear.

seductive praise. The place of anger and its related emotions, sadness and resentment, also reflects community life. Syncletica states that the remembering of past insults and injuries is much more of a problem than anger. This is so because while anger dissipates like smoke, the memory of past injuries fixes itself in the soul. The *Discourse on Salvation* asserts that if one stores a past wrongdoing in one's heart rather than forgiving and enduring, one's prayers 'do not ascend pure'. Other sources in the Evagrian sphere, including those addressed to male monastics, likewise emphasize, using language of interiority and containment, the grave danger of holding a grudge in one's thoughts. Thus anger and resentment corrupt prayer by rooting in, being retained in, and defiling the interior spaces of heart and soul.[54] Here anger is not so much the displays of rage that threaten others with violence or abuse but rather the nagging resentments that eat away over time. But other instructions warn virgins against more explosive eruptions of anger that can spew out in words. The *Discourse on Salvation* reads, 'Do not raise your voice when you are angry at someone, for the servant of the Lord has no need to quarrel. Cursing shall not escape your mouth, nor insolence, nor abuse. For your mouth is sanctified by hymns and praises to God.'[55]

The idea of the sanctified mouth and instructions for the virgin to be silent or to keep her mouth closed and hold her tongue likewise characterize our three texts. Evagrius tells the virgin, 'Open your mouth with the word of God and prevent your tongue from too much talk'.[56] Here we find the powerful metaphor of the ascetic body as closed and intact, with orifices constrained by virginity. The symbolic connection between silence and virginity as the closing of mouths is found broadly in ancient literature and ethics.[57] And although the exhortation to guard the tongue is certainly found in instructions to male monastics,[58] both Christian and non-Christian moralists express the notion that silence is a virtue particularly appropriate to women and particularly linked with σωφροσύνη. Plutarch, for example, warns the new bride that the self-controlled (σώφρονος) woman's speech, like her body, 'ought not to be for the public, and she ought to be modest and guarded about saying anything in the hearing of outsiders, since it is an exposure of herself; for in her talk can be seen her feelings, character, and disposition'.[59] In the context of female asceticism, likewise, Basil of Caesarea observes that silence is one of the virtues that should be more studiously cultivated by women: 'The life among women demands greater and more extraordinary decorum in the virtues of poverty, silence, obedience, and sisterly love, and strictness in regard to going out in public, caution in associations,

---

54 Pseudo-Athanasins *Vita Sync.*, 63–65 (PG 28.1524C–1525C). See also Evagrius, *Sententiae ad virginem*, 8; 41 (Gressmann, pp. 146, 149); *De octo spiritibus malitiae* 9 (PG 79.1153C–D); *Sententiae ad monachos* 10; 13; 14 (Gressmann, p. 154); *Antirrheticus* 5.49 (Frankenberg, 519); Pseudo-Athanasius, *De virg.* 21; 22 (von der Goltz, pp. 56–58).

55 Pseudo-Athanasius, *De virg.*, 22 (von der Goltz, pp. 57–58).

56 Evagrius, *Sententiae ad virginem*, 15 (Gressmann, p. 147). See also *Sententiae ad virginem*, 33 (Gressmann, p. 148); Pseudo-Athanasius, *Vita Sync.*, 67 (PG 28. 1525D).

57 On the metaphorical associations of the female mouth with the other openings of her body and the symbolic linking of loose talk and loose sexual behaviour see Giulia Sissa, *Greek Virginity* (trans. Arthur Goldhammer; Revealing Antiquity, 3; Cambridge, MA: Harvard University Press, 1990); and Shaw, *Burden of the Flesh*, pp. 74–78.

58 See for example Evagrius's *Sententiae ad monachos,* 90; 91; 94 (Gressmann, p. 161).

59 Plutarch, *Coniugalia praecepta*, 142d (trans. Babbitt, 2. 321–23).

disposition towards others and not having split groups. In all these things the life of virgins should achieve a greater zeal.'[60]

If the proper virgin is silent, humble, modest and self-controlled, the public spaces are certainly no place for her. Advice not to go out of the home or community and the dangers awaiting the unwary woman who ventures out are fairly standard *topoi* in Christian sources on virginity. This is certainly the case with our three texts. The outside is the place of licentious sights and sounds, encounters with married women and worldly men, unguarded conversations and other sensory stimulations that creep through the senses into the soul like smoke through the windows.[61] The virgin is especially vulnerable to passion through her eyes and her ears, and she is herself responsible for tempting others with her eyes and her glances. This is why the virgin keeps her face and eyes down or focused only directly in front of her, whether on a street or in church. Evagrius tells the virgin not to speak a word in church or to lift up her eyes, and reminds her that the Lord knows her heart and all her thoughts.[62] And the author of the *Discourse on Salvation* instructs her to keep her face down if she should happen to encounter another person, and to listen with piety to the words of a visiting saint, while protecting her own σωφροσύνη.[63]

Comparing these warnings to women about encounters with men to parallel advice to men about encounters with women, we see that the responsibility for sexual temptation usually rests with the female. In his *Sentences to a Monk*, Evagrius tells a monk who goes into the village not to approach a woman or linger in words with her, warning that this encounter functions like a hook dragging down the soul.[64] In his treatise *On the Eight Spirits of Evil*, Evagrius warns monks who want to be self-controlled (σωφρονεῖν) against associations with women. In the beginning even ascetic women may seem pious or may in fact be pious, but later they are daring and shameless: 'At the first encounter they keep their eyes down, speak gently, and cry sympathetically; they assume a respectful manner, sigh, ask about purity and listen earnestly.' But on the next visit they lift their faces up a little, and on subsequent meetings they behave more shamelessly, laughing, fluttering their eyelids, displaying their bare necks and flaunting their whole bodies, and so on until the poor man's soul is 'in a state of siege'.[65] Indeed, the sight of a woman is like a 'poisoned arrow' wounding the soul. These passages illustrate the overlapping language and images related to σωφροσύνη as both 'self-control' in the broader, active sense, and the more narrow connotation of 'chastity' as intactness or sexual refusal. The self-control or self-mastery of the virtuous soul depends on the guarded purity of the physical senses.

But if physical sensations threaten the 'chastity' of the body and soul, each of our sources exhibits the distinctively Evagrian concentration on assaults of the more subtle variety. The virgin's soul is the interior space vulnerable to pollution and defilement by wicked λογισμοί. Evagrius notes that evil thoughts both stain

60 Basil of Caesarea, *Sermones ascetici*, 2.2 (PG 31.888A–B).

61 Pseudo-Athanasius, *Vita Sync.*, 24–25 (PG 28.1501B–C); Pseudo-Athanasius, *De virg.*, 22 (von der Goltz, pp. 57–58); Evagrius, *Sententiae ad virginem*, 26 (Gressmann, p. 148).

62 Evagrius, *Sententiae ad virginem*, 33 (Gressmann, p. 148).

63 Pseudo-Athanasius, *De virg.*, 11; 22 (von der Goltz, pp. 45, 57–58).

64 Evagrius, *Sententiae ad monachos*, 83 (Gressmann, p. 160).

65 Evagrius, *De octo spiritibus malitiae*, 4 (PG 79.1149A–B).

the soul and remove the virgin's pure prayer,[66] and Syncletica warns that thoughts 'lurk' or 'conceal' themselves in the 'enclosed areas' of intellect, waiting to do battle by means of visions and memories.[67] What is more, the seemingly pious activities of conversations and discussions, indeed words themselves, deceive and defile. Disguising the ravenous wolf beneath the soft sheep's clothing, the devil may lure the one pursuing abstinence by means of something that seems innocent and even virtuous, such as discussions of religious topics.[68] Evagrius claims that he personally has seen men 'corrupt' virgins with their 'dogmas' or opinions, so that the women's efforts to preserve virginity were rendered in vain.[69] Syncletica vividly describes the power of words to bring defilement in her warning that to listen to slanderous comments is to allow the 'foul-smelling impurity of words' to stain one's prayer through the workings of the λογισμοί.[70]

These graphic images of words, conversations, teachings and thoughts as deceptive sources of pollution suggest several points worth emphasizing. First, words – like thoughts – are alive, active forces. This point seems fundamental for our appreciation not only of the power of persuasive speech in late antiquity, but also of the warnings against heretical speech in so many Christian texts of the period. It also illuminates the fretting over women's speech and silence as well as the fear that some impious word or idea might take root in the fertile ground of her soul and produce, to borrow Plutarch's image, some perverted conception. Moreover, these images presuppose an interdependence of body and soul that reaches more deeply than the level of analogy or metaphor.[71] While the rhetorical association of bodily virginity and spiritual purity is common, there is something more profound at stake when we read, for example, 'Just as the body is defiled by a man, so also worldly habits defile the soul and body of the one who keeps abstinence',[72] or 'the desire to walk around ... upsets the condition of the soul'.[73] Indeed, this language reveals the common medical and philosophical understandings of the inter-dependence of bodily behaviour and psychological health.

Finally, what are the goals or rewards of the virginal life? Some have already been mentioned, and these again often reflect the influence of Evagrius. Freedom from passions (ἀπάθεια) and purity of prayer are interrelated goals, the former being necessary to protect the latter. Further, the pseudo-Athanasian sources and Evagrius's *Sentences* highlight purity or illumination of the mind or intelligence. In the *Discourse on Salvation*, for example, we read in the final exhortation, 'You, most precious sister who possesses this book, may God grant that you keep these words, that you live by them, that you abide in them, with an enlightened intelligence, a pure mind, and with the eyes of your understanding illuminated, so that you may receive the imperishable crown which God has prepared for those who love him.'[74]

---

66 Evagrius, *Sententiae ad Virginem*, 38 (Gressmann, p. 149).

67 Pseudo-Athanasius, *Vita Sync.*, 26 (PG 28.1501D–1504A).

68 Pseudo-Athanasius, *Vita Sync.*, 27 (PG 28.1504A–B).

69 Evagrius, *Sententiae ad Virginem*, 54 (Gressmann, pp. 150–51).

70 Pseudo-Athanasius, *Vita Sync.*, 66 (PG 28. 1525C–D).

71 See Padel, *In and Out of the Mind*, pp. 39–40.

72 Pseudo-Athanasius, *De virg.*, 2 (von der Goltz, p. 37).

73 Evagrius, *Sententiae ad Virginem*, 26 (Gressmann, p. 148).

74 Pseudo-Athanasius, *De virg.*, 25 (von der Goltz, pp. 59–60); Evagrius, *Sententiae ad Virginem*, 1; 40; 53 (Gressmann, pp. 146, 149, 150).

The *Discourse* further assures the virgin that the pure mind can discern 'even God himself with the interior eyes'.[75] And Syncletica offers instructions concerning the attainment of contemplation (θεορία) and knowledge (γνῶσις), arguing that the individual intent on contemplation must first take control of the reigns of the πρακτικὸς βίος, a term which is Evagrius's designation for the 'practical life' or 'active life' of ascetic disciplines directed toward the control of passions.[76]

While neither of these texts gives any particularly *lengthy* treatment to contemplation or knowledge, Evagrius's *Sententiae ad virginem* makes no specific mention of either, as Susanna Elm has demonstrated. This omission might be explained by the text's genre and its general focus on daily life, but it is especially curious and provocative if we compare the text to its parallel and companion piece, the *Sentences to a Monk*. In the *Sentences to a Monk*, practical details and advice relate systematically to a full emphasis on knowledge of God (γνῶσις τοῦ θεοῦ) as the goal of the ascetic life. Elm points that while both texts hold out union with God as the ultimate reward and end for both virgin and monk, nevertheless the text addressed to monks represents this union as γνῶσις τοῦ θεοῦ while the text addressed to virgins represents this union as marriage to Christ.[77] Marital union with the heavenly bridegroom is one of the consistent and dominant themes of early Christian discourse on virginity, and the three texts examined here are no exception.[78] In the *Sententiae ad virginem*, Evagrius's final exhortations set before the virgin the goals of an illuminated soul[79] and pleasurable union with Christ:

> Virginal eyes will see the Lord. The virgin's ears will listen to his words. The virgin's mouth will kiss the bridegroom, and the virgin's nose will rush toward the scent of his perfume. Virginal hands will stroke the Lord, and the purity of her flesh will be pleasing to him. The virginal soul will be crowned, and she will live forever with her bridegroom. A spiritual garment will be given to her, and she will celebrate a feast with the angels in heaven. She will light an inextinguishable lamp, and she will not lack oil in her vessels. She will receive everlasting wealth, and inherit the kingdom of God.[80]

Thus if Evagrius in his ascetic vision encouraged both male and female to a life of virtue, ἀπάθεια, purity of mind and prayer, and union with the divine, the textual

---

75 Pseudo-Athanasius, *De virg.*, 17 (von der Goltz, p. 52).

76 Pseudo-Athanasius, *Vita Sync.*, 43; 86 (PG 28.1512D–1513B; 1540B–C).

77 Susanna Elm, 'Evagrius Ponticus' *Sententiae ad Virginem*', *Dumbarton Oaks Papers* 45 (1991), pp. 97–120 (111–13).

78 On the goal of the bridal chamber and scriptural image of the wise virgins with oil in their lamps and foolish virgins lacking oil see Evagrius, *Sententiae ad virginem,* 17; 42; 43 (Gressmann, pp. 147, 149); Pseudo-Athanasius, *Vita Sync.*, 8 (PG 28.1489C–1492A); Pseudo-Athanasius, *De virg.* 23 (von der Goltz, pp. 58–59). See also the interesting parallel between *Sententiae ad virginem*, 52 (Gressmann, p. 150): 'Ἐγκράτεια is burdensome and chastity (ἁγνεία) is difficult to accomplish, but nothing is sweeter than the heavenly bridegroom' and Pseudo-Athanasius, *De virg.* 24 (von der Goltz, p. 59): 'Ἄσκησις is burdensome and ἐγκράτεια is difficult to bear, but nothing is sweeter than the heavenly bridegroom'. Two texts encourage the virgin to adorn herself for Christ with virtue and bodily mortification as a 'worldly woman' would adorn herself for her husband with jewellery, cosmetics and perfume (Pseudo-Athanasius, *Vita Sync.*, 92 [PG 28.1544C–1545A]; Pseudo-Athanasius *De virg.*, 6 [von der Goltz, p. 40]).

79 Evagrius, *Sententiae ad virginem*, 53 (Gressmann, p. 150).

80 Evagrius, *Sententiae ad virginem*, 55 (Gressmann, p. 151); Elm, 'Evagrius Prutious', p. 112.

metaphors and the vision of union with the divine are constrained, in this instance it seems, by more mundane social and cultural understandings. That is, as Elm has argued, the *Sententiae ad virginem* provide a remarkable instance of the power of gender to shape even the most radical ascetic eschatology. Even if Evagrius made no hierarchical distinction between male and female in terms of the ultimate goal of unity with the godhead, nevertheless for female ascetics that unity takes the familiar form of marriage. In this manner Evagrius's writings demonstrate both the ways in which Christian ascetic discourse could subvert late ancient social expectations by delineating a new model for the female ethical subject – a model that was not based on traditional roles of wife, mother and daughter – a well as the ways in which those social expectations with their supporting notions of male and female 'nature' can continue to determine the limits of the ethical and theological imagination.

In their description of the goals and methods of ascetic formation, the authors of the texts examined in this essay use gendered imagery for the soul, the body, the pursuit of virtue and the battle against vice. The Christian virgin as represented and idealized in ascetic literature is thus both the active, masculine charioteer who is in control of the passions and powers associated with embodiment, and she is also the bride of Christ who honours her spouse with her chastity, obedience, purity and reserved bodily decorum. In this way, while her rejection of the claims of human marriage and procreation represents a subversion of 'the moral language of σωφροσύνη',[81] she embodies the ideals of both ἀνδρεία and σωφροσύνη, achieving a harmony and balance in the tension between these virtues that would be the envy of any late ancient moral theorist or passion therapist.

---

81 Cooper, *Virgin and the Bride*, p. 15.

BIBLIOGRAPHY

Achelis, H., *Virgines Subintroductae: Ein Beitrag zum VII. Kapitel des I. Korintherbriefs* (Leipzig: Hinrichs, 1902).

Albrecht, R., *Das Leben der heiligen Makrina auf dem Hintergrund der Thekla-Traditionen* (Göttingen: Vandenhoeck & Ruprecht, 1986).

Althusser, L., 'Contradiction and Overdetermination: Notes for an Investigation', in *For Marx* (trans. Ben Brewster; London and New York: Verso, 1990).

— 'Est-il simple d'être Marxiste en philosophie?', *La Pensée*, 183 (1975), pp. 3–31.

— 'From Capital to Marx's Philosophy', in *idem* and E. Balibar, *Reading 'Capital'* (London and New York: Verso, 1979), pp. 11–70.

— 'Ideology and Ideological State Apparatuses (Notes Towards an Investigation)', in *idem Lenin and Philosophy and Other Essays* (trans. Ben Brewster; New York: Monthly Review Press, 1971), pp. 127–86.

Amand, D. and Matthew-Charles Moons, 'Une curieuse homilie grecque inédite sur la virginité adressé aux pères de famille', *Revue Bénédictine*, 63 (1953).

Amat, J. (ed.), *Passion de Perpétue et de Félicite suivi des Acts: Introduction, Texte Critique, Traduction, Commentaire et Index* (*SC*, 417; Paris: Les Éditions du Cerf, 1996).

Anson, J., 'The Female Transvestite in Early Monasticism: Origin and Development of a Motif', *Viator: Medieval and Renaissance Studies*, 5 (1974), pp. 1–32.

Arjava, A., 'Divorce in Later Roman Law', *Arctos: Acta Philologica Fennica*, 22 (1988), pp. 5–21.

— 'Jerome and Women', *Arctos: Acta Philologica Fennica*, 23 (1989), pp. 5–18.

— *Women and Law in Late Antiquity* (New York: Oxford University Press, 1996).

Atkinson, P.C., 'The Montanist Interpretation of Joel 2:28, 29 (LXX 3:1,2)', *SE*, Bd. 126.7 (1982), pp. 11–15.

Aubineau, M., 'Les écrits de Saint Athanase sur le virginité', *Revue d'ascétique et de mystique*, 31 (1955) pp. 140–73.

Babbitt, F.C. (ed. and trans.), *Plutarch's Moralia* (LCL; Cambridge, MA: Harvard University Press, 1927; repr., 2000).

Baer, R.A., 'Philo's Use of the Categories Male and Female' (*Arbeit zur Literatur und Geschichte des hellenistischen Judentums*, 3; Leiden: Brill, 1970).

Bagnall, R.S., 'Church, State and Divorce in Late Roman Egypt', in K.-L. Selig and R. Somerville (eds), *Florilegium Columbianum: Essays in Honor of P.O. Kristeller* (New York: Columbia University Press, 1987), pp. 41–61.

— 'Currency and Inflation in Fourth Century Egypt' (*Bulletin of the American Society of Papyrologists*, Supplement 5; Chico, CA: Scholars Press, 1985).

Bakhtin, M.M., *The Dialogic Imagination: Four Essays* (ed. M. Holquist; trans. C. Emerson and M. Holquist; Austin: University of Texas Press, 1981).

Bal, M., 'Metaphors He Lives By', *Semeia*, 61 (1993), pp. 185–207.

Balch, D.L., 'Household Codes', *ABD* vol. III, pp. 318–20.

— 'Let Wives Be Submissive'. *The Domestic Code in 1 Peter* (*SBLMS*, 26; Chico, CA: Scholars Press, 1981).

— 'Neopythagorean Moralists and the New Testament Household Codes', *ANRW* II.26.1 (1992), pp. 380–411.

— 'Zeus, Vengeful Protector of the Political and Domestic Order. Frescoes in Dining Rooms N and P of the House of the Vettii in Pompeii, Mark 13.12–13, and I Clement 6:2', in Annette Weissenrieder, Friederike Wendt and Petra von Gemünden (eds), *Picturing the New Testament. Studies in Ancient Visual Images* (Tübingen: Mohr-Siebeck, 2005), pp. 67–95.

Bamberger, J. E., (ed. and trans.), *Evagrius Ponticus: The Praktikos and Chapters on Prayer*, (Cistercian Studies *Series* 4; Kalamazoo, MI: Cistercian Publications, 1981).

Bardy, G., 'Aux origines de l'école d'Alexandrie', *RSR*, 27 (1937), pp. 65–90.

Barnes, T.D., 'Eusebius and the date of Martyrdoms', in *Les martyrs de Lyons* (177) (Colloque à Lyon 20–23 Septembre 1977; Paris: Centre National de la Recherche Scientifique, 1978), pp. 137–41.

Barrett, M., *The Politics of Truth: From Marx to Foucault* (Stanford, CA: Stanford University Press, 1991).

Barthes, R., 'The Discourse of History', trans. Stephen Bann, in E.S. Shaffer (ed.), *Comparative Criticism: A Yearbook* (25 vols.; Cambridge, UK: Cambridge University Press, 1981), 3, pp. 3–20 .

— *Mythologies* (trans. Annette Lavers; New York: Noonday Press/Farrar, Straus and Giroux, 1972).

— *The Pleasure of the Text* (trans. R. Miller; New York: Hill and Wang/Farrar, Straus and Giroux, 1975).

Barton, C., 'All Things Beseem the Victor: Paradoxes of Masculinity in Early Imperial Rome', in Richard C. Trexler (ed.), *Gender Rhetorics: Postures of Dominance and Submission in History* (Binghamton, NY: Center for Medieval and Early Renaissance Studies, 1994), pp. 83–92.

— 'Savage Miracles: The Redemption of Lost Honor in Roman Society and the Sacrament of the Gladiator and the Martyr', *Representations*, 45 (1994), pp. 41–71.

— *The Sorrows of the Ancient Romans: The Gladiator and the Monster* (Princeton, NJ: Princeton University Press, 1993).

Bartsch, S., *Actors in the Audience: Theatricality and Doublespeak from Nero to Hadrian* (Cambridge, MA: Harvard University Press, 1994).

Basil of Caesarea, *Epistolae/Lettres* (3 vols.; text established and French trans. Yves Courtonne; Paris: Societé d'édition 'Belles Lettres', 1957–1966).

Bassler, J., 'The Widows' Tale: A Fresh Look at 1 Tim. 5.2–16', *JBL*, 103 (1984), pp. 23–41.

Bateson, M., 'Origin and Early History of Double Monasteries', *Transactions of the Royal Historical Society*, n.s. 13 (London: Longmans and Green, 1899).

Batiffol, P., 'Le Livre de la Prière d'Aseneth', in *idem* (ed.), *Studia patristica: Ètudes d'ancienne littèrature chrétienne* 1–2 (Paris: Leroux, 1889–90), pp. 1–115.

Bauman, R.A., *Women and Politics in Ancient Rome* (London: Routledge, 1992).

Beaucamp, J., 'Le Vocabulaire de la faiblesse feminine dans les texts juridiques romains du IIIe au IVe siècle', *Revue historique du droit français et étranger*, 54 (1976), pp. 485–508.

Bedard, W., *The Symbolism of the Baptismal Font in Early Christian Thought* (Washington, DC: Catholic University Press, 1951).

Berchman, R.M., *From Philo to Origen: Middle Platonism in Transition* (BJS, 69; Chico, CA: Scholars Press, 1984).

Bernard, O.B. (trans.), *Vie de Sainte Sync.* (Spiritualité orientale 9; Abbaye Notre Dame de Bellefontaine, 1972).

Bernstein, M.J., 'Pseudepigraphy in the Qumran Scrolls: Categories and Functions', in Esther Glickler Chazon, Michael E. Stone, and Avital Pinnick (eds), *Pseudepigraphic Perspectives: The Apocrypha and Pseudepigrapha in Light of the Dead Sea Scrolls: Proceedings of the International Symposium of the Orion Center for the Study of the Dead Sea Scrolls and Associated Literature*, 12–14 January, 1997 (Leiden: E.J. Brill, 1999), pp. 1–26.

Best, S. and Douglas Kellner, *Postmodern Theory: Critical Investigations* (New York: Guilford Press, 1991).

Boatwright, M.T., 'Plancia Magna of Perge: Women's Roles and Status in Roman Asia Minor', in Sarah B. Pomeroy (ed.), *Women's History and Ancient History* (Chapel Hill: University of North Carolina Press, 1991), pp. 249–72.

Bobertz, C.A., 'The Role of Patron in the Cena Dominica of Hippolytus' Apostolic Tradition', *JTS*, 44 (1993), pp. 170–84.

Bohak, G., *Joseph and Aseneth and the Temple of Leontopolis* (EJL, 10; Atlanta: Scholars Press, 1996).

Bolgiani, F., 'La polemica di Clemente Alessandrino contro gli gnostici libertine nel III libro degli Stromati', *SMSR* 38 (1967), pp. 94–99.

Borgen, P., 'Philo and the Jews in Alexandria', in Bilde et al. (eds), *Ethnicity in Hellenistic Egypt* (Aarhus: Aarhus University Press, 1992), pp. 122–38.

Børresen, K.E., 'God's Image, Man's Image? Female Metaphors Describing God in the Christian Tradition', *Temenos*, 19 (1983), pp. 17–32.

— 'Recent and Current Research on Women in the Christian Tradition', in Elizabeth A. Livingstone (ed.), *Studia Patristica XXIX: Papers presented at the Twelfth International Conference on Patristic Studies held in Oxford 1995: Historica, Theologica et Philosophica, Critica et Philologica* (Leuven: Peeters, 1997), pp. 224–31.

Bourassa, F., 'Excellence de la virginité: Arguments patristiques', *Sciences ecclésiastiques*, 5 (1953), pp. 29–41.

Bowe, B.E., *A Church in Crisis. Ecclesiology and Paraenesis in Clement of Rome* (HDR, 23; Minneapolis, MN: Fortress Press, 1988).

Bowersock, G.W, 'Les églises de Lyon et de Vienne: relations avec l'Asie', in *Les martyrs de Lyons* (177) (Colloque à Lyon 20–23 Septembre 1977; Paris: Centre National de la Recherche Scientifique, 1978), pp. 249–55.

— *Fiction as History: Nero to Julian* (Berkeley: University of California Press, 1994).

— *Martyrdom and Rome* (Cambridge, UK: Cambridge University Press, 1995).

Bowman, A.K. and J. David Thomas (eds), 'Per Lepidinam': The Vindolanda Writing-Tablets (*Tabulae Vindolandenses*, II) (London: British Museum Press, 1994), no. 257 (inv. 85.117), pp. 230–31.

Bowman, A.K., *Egypt After the Pharaohs: 332 BC–AD 642* (Berkeley: University of California Press, 1986).

Boyarin, D., 'Gender', in Mark C. Taylor (ed.), *Critical Terms for Religious Studies* (Chicago: University of Chicago Press, 1998), pp. 117–35.

— *Carnal Israel: Reading Sex in Talmudic Culture* (Berkeley: University of California Press, 1993).

—*Dying for God: Martyrdom and the Making of Christianity and Judaism* (Stanford, CA: Stanford University Press, 1999).

— *Intertextuality and the Reading of Midrash* (Bloomington and Indianapolis: Indiana University Press, 1990).

— *Unheroic Conduct: The Rise of Heterosexuality and the Invention of the Jewish Man* (Berkeley: University of California Press, 1997).

Bradley, K.R., *Slaves and Masters in the Roman Empire* (New York: Oxford University Press, 1987).

Brakke, D., 'Canon Formation and Social Conflict in Fourth-Century Egypt: Athanasius of Alexandria's Thirty-Ninth *Festal Letter'*, *HTR*, 87 (1994), pp. 398–410.

— 'The Passions and the Social Construction of Masculinity', paper delivered at the American Academy of Religion Annual Meeting (Orlando, Florida, 1998).

— *Demons and the Making of the Monk: Spiritual Combat in Early Christianity* (Cambridge, MA: Harvard University Press, 2006).

Bregman, M., 'Pseudepigraphy in Rabbinic Literature', in E. Chazon et al. (eds), *Pseudepigraphic Perspectives: The Apocrypha and Pseudepigrapha in Light of the Dead Sea Scrolls: Proceedings of the International Symposium of the Orion Center for the Study of the Dead Sea Scrolls and Associated Literature*, 12–14 January, 1997 (Leiden: Brill, 1997), pp. 27–41.

Bremmer, J.N., 'Perpetua and Her Diary: Authenticity, Family and Visions', in Walter Ameling (ed.), *Märtyrer und Märtyrerakten* (Stuttgart: Franz Steiner Verlag, 2002), pp. 77–120.

Brennecke, H.C., 'Danaiden und Dirken. Zu 1 Clem 6.2', *ZKG*, 88 (1977), pp. 302–8.

Brock, S. and Susan Ashbrook Harvey (eds), *Holy Women of the Syrian Orient* (Berkeley: University of California Press, 1987).

Brock, S.P., 'Early Syrian Asceticism', *Numen*, 20 (1973), pp. 1–19.

Brooten, B., '"Junia ... Outstanding among the Apostles" (Rom 16.7)', in L. and A. Swidler (eds), *Women Priests: A Catholic Commentary on the Vatican Declaration* (New York: Paulist Press, 1977), pp. 141–44.

— 'Women Leaders in the Ancient Synagogue. Inscriptional Evidence and Background Issues' (*BJS*, 36; Chico, CA: Scholars Press, 1982).

— *Love Between Women: Early Christian Responses to Female Homoeroticism* (Chicago: University of Chicago Press, 1996).

— 'Mariage et famille chez Clément d'Alexandrie' (*Théologie Historique*, 11; Paris: Beauchesne et Ses Fils, 1972).

Brown, P., *Augustine of Hippo: A Biography* (Berkeley and Los Angeles: University of California Press, 1969).

— 'The Body and Society: Men, Women and Sexual Renunciation in Early Christianity' (*Lectures on the History of Religions*, 13; New York: Columbia University Press, 1988).

Brunt, P.A., '"Amicitia" in the Late Roman Republic', in Robin Seager (ed.), *The Crisis of the Roman Republic: Studies in Political and Social History* (Cambridge, UK: Heffer, 1969), pp. 199–218.

— '"Amicitia" in the Late Roman Republic', *Proceedings of the Cambridge Philological Society*, n.s. 11 (1965), pp. 1–20.

Buell, D.K., '"Sell What You Have and Give to the Poor": A Feminist Interpretation of Clement of Alexandria's Who is the Rich Person Who is Saved?', in Shelly Matthews, Cynthia Briggs Kittredge and Melanie Johnson-DeBaufre (eds), *Walk in the Ways of Wisdom: Essays in Honor of Elisabeth Schüssler Fiorenza* (Harrisburg, PA: Trinity Press International, 2003), pp. 194–213.

— *Making Christians: Clement of Alexandria and the Rhetoric of Legitimacy* (Princeton, NJ: Princeton University Press, 1999).

— *Why This New Race: Ethnic Reasoning in Early Christianity* (New York: Columbia University Press, 2005).

Buonaiuti, E., 'Evagrio Pontico e il De Virginitate pseudo-Atanasiano', in *Saggi sul Cristianesimo Primitivo* (Castello: Il Solco, 1923), pp. 247–49.

Burchard, C. (ed.), 'Joseph und Aseneth' (*Pseudepigrapha Veteris Testamenti Graece*, 5; Leiden and Boston, E. J. Brill, 2003).

Burrus, V., *'Begotten, Not Made': Conceiving Manhood in Late Antiquity* (Stanford, CA: Stanford University Press, 2000).

— 'Macrina's Tattoo', *JMEMS*, 33 (2003), pp. 403–17.

— 'Mimicking Virgins: Colonial Ambivalence and the Ancient Romance', *Arethusa* 38 (2005), pp. 49–88.

— 'Reading Agnes: The Rhetoric of Gender in Ambrose and Prudentius', *JECS*, 3 (1995), pp. 25–46.

— 'The Heretical Woman as Symbol in Alexander, Athanasius, Epiphanius, and Jerome', *HTR*, 84 (1991), pp. 229–48.

— 'Word and Flesh: The Bodies and Sexuality of Ascetic Women in Christian Antiquity', *JFSR*, 10.1 (1994), pp. 27–51.

— *The Making of a Heretic: Gender, Authority, and the Priscillianist Controversy* (The Transformation of the Classical Heritage; Berkeley: University of California Press, 1995).

— *The Sex Lives of Saints: An Erotics of Ancient Hagiography* (Philadelphia: University of Pennsylvania Press, 2004).

Burton-Christie, D., *The Word in the Desert: Scripture and the Quest for Holiness in Early Christian Monasticism* (New York: Oxford University Press, 1993).

Butler, C. (ed.), *The Lausiac History of Palladius* (2 vols.; Texts and Studies: Contributions to Biblical and Patristic Literature 6.1–2; Cambridge, UK: Cambridge University Press, 1898 and 1904).

— 'Chronicle', *JTS*, 7 (1906), Vita Olympiadis 6; Jerome, Epp. 66, 108; Vita Melaniae 41.

Butler, J., *Bodies That Matter: The Discursive Limits of 'Sex'* (New York: Routledge, 1993).

Camelot, T., 'Les traités De Virginitate au IVe siècle', *Etudes Carmelitaines*, 13 (1952), pp. 273–92.

Cameron, A., 'Desert Mothers: Women Ascetics in Early Christian Egypt', in E. Puttick et al. (eds), *Women as Teachers and Disciples in Traditional and New Religions* (Lewiston, NY: Edwin Mellen Press, 1993), pp. 11–24.

— 'Early Christianity and the Discourse of Desire', in Léonie J. Archer, Susan Fischler and Maria Wyke (eds), *Women in Ancient Societies: An Illusion of the Night* (New York: Routledge, 1994), pp. 152–68.

— 'Redrawing the Map: Early Christian Territory after Foucault', *JRS*, 76 (1986), pp. 266–71.

— 'Virginity as Metaphor: Women and the Rhetoric of Early Christianity', *eadem* (ed.), *History as Text: The Writing of Ancient History* (London: Duckworth, 1989), pp. 171–205.

Capper, B.J., 'Community of Goods in the Early Jerusalem Church', *ANRW*, 26.2 (1995), pp. 1731–74.

Cardman, F., 'Acts of the Women Martyrs', *ATR*, 70.2 (1988), pp. 144–50.

— 'Women , Ministry and Church Order in Early Christianity', in Ross Shepard Kraemer and Mary Rose D'Angelo (eds), *Women and Christian Origins* (New York and Oxford: Oxford University Press, 1999), pp. 300–29.

Casarico, L., 'Donne ginnasiarco', *ZPE*, 48 (1982), pp. 118–22.

Casey, R.P. (ed. and trans.), *The Excerpta ex Theodoto* (London: Christophers, 1934).

Castelli, E. and Hal Taussig, 'Drawing Large and Startling Figures: Reimagining Christian Origins by Painting Like Picasso', in *idem* (eds), *Reimagining Christian Origins: A Colloquium Honoring Burton L. Mack* (Valley Forge, PA: Trinity Press International, 1996), pp. 3–20.

Castelli, E., '"I Will Make Mary Male": Pieties of the Body and Gender Transformation of Christian Women in Late Antiquity', in J. Epstein and K. Straub (eds), *Body Guards: The Cultural Politics of Gender Ambiguity* (New York: Routledge, 1991), pp. 29–49.

— 'Visions and Voyeurism: Holy Women and the Politics of Sight in Early Christianity', *Protocol of the Colloquy of the Center for Hermeneutical Studies* n.s. 2 (Berkeley, CA: Center for Hermeneutical Studies, 1995).

— (ed.), *Women, Gender, Religion: A Reader* (New York: Palgrave, 2001).

— 'Mortifying the Body, Curing the Soul: Beyond Ascetic Dualisms in The Life of St. Syncletica', *differences: a Journal of Feminist Cultural Studies*, 4.2 (1992), pp. 134–53.

— *Imitating Paul: A Discourse of Power* (Louisville, KY: Westminster/John Knox, 1991).

— *Martyrdom and Memory: Early Christian Culture Making* (New York: Columbia University Press, 2004).

Castelli, E.A., and Daniel Boyarin (eds), *Sexuality in Late Antiquity*, Special issue of the *Journal of the History of Sexuality*, 10.3–4 (2001).

Chadwick, H., *Alexandrian Christianity* (London: SCM Press, 1954).

Chadwick, O. (ed.), *Western Asceticism* (Philadelphia, PA: Westminster, 1958), pp. 33–189.

Champlin, E., *Fronto and Antonine Rome* (Cambridge, MA: Harvard University Press, 1980).

Chesnutt, R.A., *From Death to Life: Conversion in Joseph and Aseneth* (*JSPSup*, 16; Sheffield, UK: Sheffield Academic Press, 1995).

Chitty, D.J., *The Desert as City: An Introduction to the Study of Egyptian and Palestinian Monasticism under the Christian Empire* (Oxford: Blackwell, 1966).

Chow, J.K., 'Patronage and Power: A Study of Social Networks in Corinth' (*JSNTSup* 75; Sheffield: Sheffield Academic Press, 1992).

Chrysostom, John, *Bapt Inst. 4.1*, in *St. John Chrysostom: Baptismal Instructions* (trans. P. Harkins; *ACW*, 31; New York: Newman Press, 1963).

— *De Virginitate/La Virginit* (text established by Herbert Musurillo; trans. Bernard Grillet; *SC*, no. 125; Paris: Cerf, 1966).

— educ. lib. 16 (B.K. Exarchos [ed.], *Johannes Chrysostomos, Uber Hoffart und Kindererziehung* [München: Max Hueber Verlag, 1955], pp. 42–43).

— *Epistolae ad Olympia/Lettres à Olympias*, 2nd edn., aug. with *Vita Olympiadis/ La Vie Ononyme d'Olympias* (text established and French trans. Anne-Marie Malingrey; SC, no. 13; Paris: Cerf, 1968).

Clark, C. and Margaret Haswell, *Economics and Subsistence Agriculture* (4th edn; London: Macmillan, 1970).

Clark, E.A., 'Theory and Practice in Late Ancient Asceticism: Jerome, Chrysostom, and Augustine', *JFSR*, 5.2 (1989), pp. 25–46.

— *Ascetic Piety and Women's Faith: Essays on Late Ancient Christianity* (Studies in Women and Religion, 20; New York: Edwin Mellen Press, 1986).

— '"Adam's Only Companion": Augustine and the Early Christian Debate on Marriage', *Rech. Aug.* 21 (1986), pp. 139–62.

— 'Ascetic Renunciation and Feminine Advancement: A Paradox of Late Ancient Christianity', *Anglican Theological Review*, 63 (1981), pp. 240–57.

— 'Devil's Gateway and Bride of Christ: Women in the Early Christian World', in *eadem, Ascetic Piety and Women's Faith: Essays on Late Ancient Christianity (Women and Religion*, 20; Lewiston, NY and Queenston, Ont.: Edwin Mellen Press, 1986), pp. 23–60.

— 'Foucault, the Fathers, and Sex', *JAAR*, 56 (1986), pp. 619–41.

— 'Friendship Between the Sexes: Classical Theory and Christian Practice', in *eadem, Jerome, Chrysostom, and Friends.*

— 'Holy Women, Holy Words: Early Christian Women, Social History, and the Linguistic Turn', *JECS*, 6.3 (1998), pp. 413–30.

— 'Ideology, History and the Construction of "Woman" in Late Ancient Christianity', *JECS*, 2.2 (1994), pp. 155–84.

— 'Patrons Not Priests; Gender and Power in Late Ancient Christianity', *Gender and History*, 2 (1990), pp. 253–73.

— 'Rewriting Early Christian History: Augustine's Representation of Monica', in J.W. Drijvers and J.W. Watt (eds), *Portraits of Spiritual Authority* (Leiden: E.J. Brill, 1999), pp. 3–23.

— 'Sex, Shame, and Rhetoric: En-gendering Early Christian Ethics', *JAAR*, 59 (1991), pp. 221–45.

— 'The Lady Vanishes: Dilemmas of a Feminist Historian after the Linguistic Turn', *CH*, 67.1 (1998), pp. 1–31.

— 'The Virginal Politeia and Plato's Republic: John Chrysostom on Women and the Sexual Relation', in *eadem, Jerome, Chrysostom, and Friends.*

— *History, Theory, Text: Historians and the Linguistic Turn* (Cambridge, MA: Harvard University Press, 2004).

— *Jerome, Chrysostom, and Friends: Essays and Translations* (New York: Mellen, 1979).

— *Reading Renunciation: Asceticism and Scripture in Early Christianity* (Princeton, NJ: Princeton University Press, 1999).

— *The Origenist Controversy: The Cultural Construction of an Early Christian Debate* (Princeton, NJ: Princeton University Press, 1992).

Clarke, J.R., *Art in the Lives of Ordinary Romans* (Berkeley: University of California Press, 2003).

Clarysse, W., 'Some Greeks in Egypt', in Janet H. Johnson (ed.), *Life in a Multi-Cultural Society: Egypt from Cambyses to Constantine and Beyond* (*SAOC*, 51; Chicago: Oriental Institute of the University of Chicago, 1992), pp. 51–56.

Clement of Alexandria, *An Exhortation to the Greeks, The Rich Man's Salvation, and the Fragment of An Address Entitled 'To the Newly Baptized'* (trans. G. W. Butterworth; LCL; London: Heinemann/New York: G.P. Putnam's Sons, 1919).

— *Stromateis: Books One to Three* (trans. John Ferguson; Fathers of the Church; Washington DC: The Catholic University of America Press, 1991).

Cohen, D., and Richard Saller, 'Foucault on Sexuality in Greco-Roman Antiquity', in Jan Goldstein (ed.), *Foucault and the Writing of History* (Oxford: Blackwell, 1994), pp. 35–59.

Constantinou, S., *Female Corporeal Performances: Reading the Body in Byzantine Passions and Lives of Holy Women*, (Acta Universitatis Upsaliensis Studie Byzantina Upsaliensia, 9; Uppsala: Uppsala University Press, 2005).

Cooper, K., *The Virgin and the Bride: Idealized Womanhood in Late Antiquity* (Cambridge, MA: Harvard University Press, 1996).

Corbett, P.E., *The Roman Law of Marriage* (Oxford: Clarendon Press, 1930).

Corrington, G.P., 'Anorexia, Asceticism, and Autonomy: Self-Control as Liberation and Transcendence', *JFSR*, 2.2 (1986), pp. 51–61.

Corrington, G.P., 'The "Divine Woman"? Propaganda and the Power of Celibacy in the New Testament Apocrypha: A Reconsideration', *ATR*, 70 (1988), pp. 207–20.

— 'The Milk of Salvation: Redemption by the Mother in Late Antiquity and Early Christianity', *HTR*, 82 (1989), pp. 412–13.

— *Her Image of Salvation: Female Saviors and Formative Christianity* (Louisville, KY: Westminster/John Knox, 1992).

Coward, R., and John Ellis, *Language and Materialism: Developments in Semiology and the Theory of the Subject* (London: Routledge & Kegan Paul, 1977).

Crook, J.A., 'Women in Roman Succession', in Beryl Rawson (ed.), *The Family in Ancient Rome: New Perspectives* (Ithaca, NY: Cornell University Press, 1986), pp. 58–82.

Crouch, J.E., *The Origin and Intention of the Colossian Haustafel* (FRLANT, 109; Göttingen: Vandenhoeck & Ruprecht, 1972).

Crouzel, H., *Virginité et mariage selon Origène* (Museum Lessianum section théologique, no. 58; Paris/Bruges: Desclée de Brouwer, 1963).

Daley, B., 'Position and Patronage in the Early Church: The Original Meaning of the "Primacy of Honour"', *JTS*, 44 (1993), pp. 529–53.

Danker, F.W., *Benefactor: Epigraphic Study of a Graeco-Roman and New Testament Semantic Field* (St. Louis, MO: Clayton, 1982).

Davies, J.G., *The Architectural Setting of Baptism* (London: Barrie and Rockliff, 1962).

Davies, S.L., *The Revolt of the Widows: The Social World of the Apocryphal Acts* (Carbondale, IL: Southern Illinois University Press, 1980).

Davis, S.J., *The Cult of Saint Thecla: A Tradition of Women's Piety in Late Antiquity* (New York: Oxford University Press, 2001).

Dawson, D., *Allegorical Readers and Cultural Revision in Ancient Alexandria* (Berkeley: University of California Press, 1992).

— *Cities of the Gods: Communist Utopias in Greek Thought* (New York: Oxford University Press, 1992).

de Beauvoir, S., *The Second Sex* (Le Deuxième Sexe, Paris: Gallimard, 1949).

de Certeau, M., 'History, Science and Fiction', *idem, Heterologies: Discourse on the Other* (trans. Brian Massumi; *Theory and History of Literature*, 17; Minneapolis: University of Minnesota Press, 1986), pp. 199–221.

de Faye, E., Clément d'Alexandrie. *Étude sur les rapports du christianisme et de la philosophie grecque au IIe siècle* (Paris: Ernest Leroux, 2nd edn, 1906).

de Jonge, M., *Pseudepigrapha of the Old Testament as Part of Christian Literature: The Case of the Testaments of the Twelve Patriarchs and the Greek Life of Adam and Eve* (Leiden and Boston: E. J. Brill, 2003).

de Mendieta, D.A., 'La virginité chez Eusèbe d'Emèse et l'ascétisme familial dans la première moitié du IVe siècle', *Revue d'histoire ecclésiastique*, 50 (1955), pp. 777–820.

Decarreaux, J., *Monks and Civilization: From the Barbarian Invasions to the Reign of Charlemagne* (trans. Charlotte Haldane; Garden City, NY: Doubleday, 1964).

del Tindaro Rampolla, M. (ed.), *Santa Melania Giuniore, senatrice romana: documenti contemporei e note* (Roma: Tipografia Vaticana, 1905).

deSilva, D.A., *Honor, Patronage, Kinship and Purity: Unlocking New Testament Culture* (Downers Grove, IL: InterVarsity Press, 2000).

Dexter, C., 'The Epigraphic Evidence of Pompeiian Women' (unpublished paper).

Dixon, S., 'A Family Business: Women's Role in Patronage and Politics at Rome 80–44 B.C.', *Classica et Mediaevalia* 34 (1983), pp. 91–112.

— 'Infirmitas sexus: Womanly Weakness in Roman Law', *Tijdschrift voor Rechtsgeschiedenis/Revue d'Histoire du Droit/The Legal History Review* 52 (1984), pp. 343–71.

— 'The Marriage Alliance in the Roman Elite', *Journal of Family History* 10 (1985), pp. 353–78.

— *Reading Roman Women: Sources, Genres, and Real Life* (London: Duckworth, 2001).

Dölger, F.J., 'Die Inschrift im Baptisterium S. Giovanni in Fonte an der Lateranensischen Basilika aus der Zeit Xystus III (432–440) und die Symbolik des Taufbrunnens bei Leo dem Grossen', *JAC*, 2 (1930), pp. 252–57.

Dronke, P., *Women Writers of the Middle Ages: A Critical Study of Texts from Perpetua († 203) to Marguerite Porete († 1310)* (Cambridge, UK: Cambridge University Press, 1984).

duBois, P., *Torture and Truth* (New York: Routledge, 1991).

Duncan-Jones, R., *The Economy of the Roman Empire, Quantitative Studies* (Cambridge, UK: Cambridge University Press, 1974).

— 'Costs, Outlays and Summae Honoriae from Roman Africa', *Papers of the British School at Rome* 30 (1962), pp. 47–115.

Durry, M., 'Le mariage des filles impubères dans la Rome antique', *Revue internationale des droites de l'antiquité*, 3d ser. 2 (1955), pp. 262–73.

Duval, N. and Françoise Baratte, *Les ruines de Sufetula, Sbeïtla* (Tunis: Société Tunisienne de Diffusion, 1973).

Eagleton, T., *Ideology: An Introduction* (London and New York: Verso, 1991).

Eckenstein, L., *Women Under Monasticism* (Cambridge, UK: Cambridge University Press, 1896).

Egger, B., 'Women and Marriage in the Greek Novels: The Boundaries of Romance', in James Tatum (ed.), *The Search for the Ancient Novel* (Baltimore, MD and London: Johns Hopkins University Press, 1994), pp. 260–80.

Eisen, U.E., *Women Officeholders in Early Christianity: Epigraphical and Literary Studies* (trans. Linda M. Maloney; Collegeville, MN: Liturgical Press, 2000).

Eisenbaum, P.M., *The Jewish Heroes of Christian History. Hebrews 11 in Literary Context* (SBLDS, 156; Atlanta, GA: Scholars Press, 1997).

Eisenstadt, S.N. and L. Roniger, *Patrons, Clients, and Friends: Interpersonal Relations and the Structure of Trust in Society* (Cambridge, UK: Cambridge University Press, 1984).

Elliott, J.H., 'Patronage and Clientage', in Richard Rohrbaugh (ed.), *The Social Sciences and New Testament Interpretation* (Peabody, MA: Hendrickson, 1996), pp. 144–56.

Elm, S., 'Evagrius Ponticus' Sententiae ad Virginem', *Dumbarton Oaks Papers*, 45 (1991), pp. 97–120.

— *'Virgins of God': The Making of Asceticism in Late Antiquity* (New York: Oxford University Press, 1994).

Elsom, H., 'Callirhoe: Displaying the Phallic Woman', in Amy Richlin (ed.), *Pornography and Representation in Greece and Rome* (New York: Oxford University Press, 1992), pp. 212–30.

Emmett, A.M., 'Female Ascetics in the Greek Papyri', *Jahrbuch der österreichischen Byzantinistik*, 32 (1982), pp. 507–15.

Engberg-Pedersen, T., 'Philo's De Vita Contemplativa as a Philosopher's Dream', *JSJ* 30 (1999), pp. 40–64.

Erskine, A., *The Hellenistic Stoa* (Ithaca, NY: Cornell University Press, 1990).

Eusebius of Emesa, 'Homiliae VI et VII', in E.M. Buytaert (ed.), *Eusèbe d'Emèse: Discours conservés en Latin* (*Spicilegium sacrum Lovaniense*, no. 26; Louvain: Université catholique et collèges théologiques O.P. et S.J. de Louvain, 1953).

Evans-Grubbs, J., 'Constantine and Imperial Legislation on the Family', in Jill Harries and Ian Wood (eds), *The Theodosian Code: Studies in the Imperial Law of Late Antiquity* (London: Duckworth, 1993), pp. 120–42.

— 'Review of Suzanne Dixon's The Roman Mother', in *Classical Philology*, 85 [1990], pp. 333–38.

— 'The Good, the Bad, and the Holy: Women in Late Roman Law', presented at the annual meeting of the American Philological Association, December 29, 1993.

— *Law and Family in Late Antiquity: The Emperor Constantine's Legislation on Marriage* (Oxford: Oxford University Press, 1995).

Fahey, M.A., 'Cyprian and the Bible: A Study in Third-Century Exegesis' (*Beiträge zur Geschichte der biblischen Hermeneutik*, 9; Tübingen: Mohr, 1971).

Fantham, E., Helene Peet Foley, Natalie Boymel Kampen, Sarah B. Pomeroy, and H. Alan Shapiro, *Women in the Classical World* (New York: Oxford University Press, 1994).

Farrer, J.A., *Literary Forgeries* (New York: Longmans, Green and Co., 1907).

Feichteinger, B., *Apostolae Apostolorum: Frauenaskese als Befreiung und Zwang bei Hieronymous* (Frankfurt am Main: Peter Lang, 1995).

Festugière, A.-J., *Antioche paienne et chrétienne* (Paris: de Boccard, 1959).

Fiedler, P., 'Haustafel', *RAC*, 13 (1986), pp. 1063–73.

Finn, T.M., *From Death to Rebirth: Ritual and Conversion in Antiquity* (Mahwah, NJ: Paulist Press, 1997).

Fitzgerald, J.T. (ed.), *Friendship, Flattery, and Frankness of Speech: Studies on Friendship in the New Testament* (Leiden: Brill, 1996).

— 'Haustafeln', *ABD*, vol. III, pp. 80–81.

Fontanille, M.-T., *Avortement et contraception dans la médecine gréco-romaine* (Paris: Searle Laboratories, 1977).

Foucault, M., *Power/Knowledge: Selected Interviews and Other Writings, 1972–1977* (ed. and trans. Colin Gordon; New York: Pantheon Books, 1980).

—*The Care of the Self. The History of Sexuality*, Vol. 3 (trans. Robert Hurley; New York: Pantheon, 1986).

—*The Use of Pleasure: The History of Sexuality* Vol. 2 (New York: Vintage Books, 1985).

Fowler, H.N. (ed.), *Plato: Euthyphro, Apology, Crito, Phaedo, Phaedrus* (LCL; Cambridge, MA: Harvard University Press, 1966).

Francis, J.A., *Subversive Virtue: Asceticism and Authority in the Second-Century Pagan World* (University Park: Pennsylvania State University Press, 1995).

Frank, G., *The Memory of the Eyes: Pilgrims to Living Saints in Christian Late Antiquity* (Berkeley: University of California Press, 2000).

Frank, K.S., *Grundzüge der Geschichte des christlichen Mönchtums* (Darmstadt: Wissenchaftliche Buchgesellschaft, 1975).

Frankenberg, W. (ed.), *Euagrius Ponticus: Syrischer Text, griechische Retroversion* (Abhandlungen der königlichen Gesellschaft der Wissenschaften zu Göttingen, Philologisch-historische Klasse, Neue Folge, 13, 2; Berlin: Weidmann, 1912).

Frankfurter, D., *Religion in Roman Egypt: Assimilation and Resistance* (Princeton, NJ: Princeton University Press, 1998).

Fraser, N. and Linda J. Nicholson, 'Social Criticism without Philosophy: An Encounter between Feminism and Postmodernism', in Linda J. Nicholson (ed.), *Feminism/Postmodernism* (New York and London: Routledge, 1990), pp. 19–38.

Frend, W.H.C., 'Blandina and Perpetua: Two Early Christian Heroines', *in Les martyrs de Lyon* (177) (Paris: Centre National de la Recherche Scientifique, 1978), pp. 167–75.

Friedan, B., *The Feminine Mystique* (New York: Norton, 1963).

Frilingos, C.A., *Spectacles of Empire: Monsters, Martyrs, and the Book of Revelation* (Philadelphia: University of Pennsylvania Press, 2004).

Fronto, M.C., *The Correspondence of Marcus Cornelius Fronto* (2 vols; trans. C. R. Haines; LCL; Cambridge, MA: Harvard University Press, 1962), 1, pp. 145–51.

Frow, J., *Marxism and Literary History* (Cambridge, MA: Harvard University Press, 1986).

Gaca, K.L., *The Making of Fornication: Eros, Ethics, and Political Reform in Greek Philosophy and Early Christianity* (Hellenistic Culture and Society, 40; Berkeley and Los Angeles: University of California Press, 2003).

Galen, *De Sententiis Politicae Platonicae, in De Placitis Hippocratis et Platonis* (ed. Iwanus Mueller; Leipzig: Teubner, 1874).

Gardner, J.F., *Women in Roman Law and Society* (Bloomington: Indiana University Press, 1986).

Garnsey, P., *Social Status and Legal Privilege in the Roman Empire* (Oxford: Oxford University Press, 1970).

Gaudemet, J., 'Tendances nouvelles de la legislation familiale au IVe siècle', in *Transformations et conflicts au IVe siècle ap. J.-C.* (Colloque organisé par la Fédération Internationale des Études Classiques, Bordeaux, 7. au 12. septembre 1970; Antiquitas 1, 29; Bonn: Rudolf Habelt Verlag, 1978), pp. 187–207.

— 'Sociétês et mariage' (*Recherches institutionnelles*, 5; Strasbourg: Cerdic-Publications, 1980).

Geffcken, J., *Die oracula sibyllina*, GCS, 8 (Leipzig: J.C. Hinrichs, 1902).

Gellner, E. and John Waterbury (eds), *Patrons and Clients in Mediterranean Societies* (London: Duckworth, 1977).

Giddens, A., 'Four Theses on Ideology', *Canadian Journal of Political and Social Theory/Revue canadienne de théorie politique et sociale*, 7 (1983), pp. 18–21.

Gill, C., 'The Emotions in Greco-Roman Philosophy', in Susanna Morton Braund and Christopher Gill (eds), *The Passions in Roman Thought and Literature* (Cambridge, UK: Cambridge University Press, 1997), pp. 5–12.

Glancy, J.A., *Slavery in Early Christianity* (Oxford: Oxford University Press, 2002).

Gleason, M., *Making Men: Sophists and Self-Presentation in Ancient Rome* (Princeton, NJ: Princeton University Press, 1995).

Goehring, J.E., *Ascetics, Society, and the Desert: Studies in Egyptian Monasticism* (Harrisburg, PA: Trinity Press International, 1999).

Gold, B.K. (ed.), *Literary and Artistic Patronage in Ancient Rome* (Austin: University of Texas Press, 1982).

Gorce, D. (ed.), *Vie de Sante Mélanie* (*SC* 90; Paris: Éditions du Cerf, 1962).

Gourevitch, D., *Le mal d'être femme: La femme et la médecine dans la Rome antique* (Paris: Société d'Edition 'Belles Lettres', 1984).

Grabar, A., *Le baptistère paléochrétien* (Mulhouse: Centre de culture Chretienne, 1980).

Gramsci, A., *Selections From the Prison Notebooks* (ed. and trans. Quintin Hoare and Geoffrey Nowell Smith; New York: International Publishers, 1971).

Grant, R.M. and Holt H. Graham, *The Apostolic Fathers. A New Translation and Commentary*. Volume 2: *First and Second Clement* (New York: Thomas Nelson & Sons, 1965).

Grant, R.M., 'Eusebius and the Martyrs of Gaul', in *Les martyrs de Lyons* (177) (Colloque à Lyon 20–23 Septembre 1977; Paris: Centre National de la Recherche Scientifique, 1978), pp. 129–35

Gregory of Nyssa, *De Virginitate/Traité de la Virginité* (text established and French trans. Michel Aubineau; *Sources Chrétiennes*, no. 119; Paris: Cerf, 1966).

— *Vita Macrinae/Vie de Sainte Macrine* (text established and French trans. Pierre Maraval; SC, no. 178; Paris: Cerf, 1971).

— *Vita Syncleticaea: Vita Olympiadis; Vita Melaniae/Vie de Sainte Melanie* (text established and French trans. Denys Gorce; Sources Chrétiennes, no. 90; Paris: Cerf, 1962).

Gressmann, H. (ed.), *Nonnenspiegel und Mönchspiegel des Euagrios Pontikos, TU* 39, 4b (Leipzig: Hinrichs, 1913).

Gruen, E.S., 'Heritage and Hellenism: The Reinvention of Jewish Tradition' (*Hellenistic Culture and Society*, 30; Berkeley: University of California Press, 1998).

Gryson, R., *The Ministry of Women in the Early Church* (trans. J. Laporte and M.L. Hall; Collegeville, MN: Liturgical Press, 1976).

Guillaumont, A. and Claire Guillaumont, *Évagre le Pontique: Traité pratique ou le moine*, (SC, 170–71, Paris: Éditions du Cerf, 1971).

Habermehl, P., *Perpetua und der Ägypter oder Bilder des Bösen im frühen afrikanischen Christentum. Ein Versuch zur Passio Sanctarum Perpetuae et Felicitatis* (Berlin: Akademie Verlag, 1992).

Halperin, D.A., 'Why Is Diotima a Woman?', in D. Halperin, J. Winkler and F. Zeitlin (eds), *Before Sexuality: The Construction of Erotic Experience in the Ancient Greek World* (Princeton, NJ: Princeton University Press, 1990), pp. 257–308.

Halperin, D.M., John J. Winkler and Froma I. Zeitlin (eds), *Before Sexuality: The Construction of Erotic Experience in the Ancient Greek World* (Princeton, NJ: Princeton University Press, 1990).

Halporn, J.W. 'Literary History and Generic Expectations in the Passio and Acta Perpetuae', *VC*, 45 (1991), pp. 223–41.

Hands, A.R., *Charities and Social Aid in Greece and Rome* (Ithaca, NY: Cornell University Press, 1968).

Hankinson, J., 'Actions and Passions: Affection, Emotion, and Moral Self-Management in Galen's Philosophical Psychology', in Jacques Brunschwig and Martha C. Nussbaum (eds), *Passions and Perceptions: Studies in Hellenistic Philosophy of Mind* (Cambridge, UK: Cambridge University Press, 1993), pp. 184–222.

Hanson, A.T., 'Rahab the Harlot in Early Christian Tradition', *JSNT*, 1 (1978), pp. 53–60.

Haraway, D., 'Cyborg Manifesto: Science, Technology, and Socialist-Feminism in the Late Twentieth Century', in *eadem, Simians, Cyborgs, and Women: The Reinvention of Nature* (New York: Routledge, 1990), pp. 149–82.

— 'Ecce Homo, Ain't (Arn't) I a Woman, and Inappropriate/d Others: The Human in a Post-Humanist Landscape', in Judith Butler and Joan W. Scott (eds), *Feminists Theorize the Political* (New York and London: Routledge, 1992), pp. 86–100.

Harkins, P.W., *Galen: On the Passions and Errors of the Soul* (Columbus: Ohio State University Press, 1963).

Harmand, L., *Le patronat sur les collectivités publiques, des origins au bas-Empire; un aspect social et politique du monde romain* (Paris: Presses Universitaires de France, 1957).

Harmless, W., *Desert Christians: An Introduction to the Literature of Early Monasticism* (New York: Oxford University Press, 2004).

Harpham, G.G., 'Ascetics, Aesthetics, and the Management of Desire', in Susan L. Mizruchi (ed.), *Religion and Cultural Studies* (Princeton, NJ: Princeton University Press, 2001), pp. 95–109.

— *The Ascetic Imperative in Culture and Criticism* (Chicago: University of Chicago Press, 1987).

Harries, J., '"Treasure in Heaven": Property and Influence Among Senators of Late Rome', in Elizabeth M. Craik (ed.), *Marriage and Property* (Aberdeen, UK: Aberdeen University Press, 1991), pp. 54–70.

Harrison, N.V., 'The Feminine Man in Late Antique Ascetic Piety', *Union Seminary Quarterly Review*, 48.3–4 (1994), pp. 49–71.

Hartsock, N.C.M., 'Louis Althusser's Structural Marxism: Political Clarity and Theoretical Distortions', *Rethinking Marxism* 4 (1991), pp. 10–40.

Hausherr, I., 'L'origene de la théorie orientale des huit péchés capitaux', *Orientalia Christiana*, 30 (1933), pp. 164–75.

Hawley, R., and Barbara Levick (eds), *Women in Antiquity: New Assessments* (New York: Routledge, 1995).

Hefele, K.J., *Histoire des conciles d'après les documents originaux* (trans. Henri Leclercq; Paris: Letouzey et Ane, 1907–1913), I: 1036–1039.

Heffernan, T.J., 'Philology and Authorship in the Passio Sanctarum Perpetuae et Felicitatis', *Traditio: Studies in Ancient and Medieval History, Thought, and Religion*, 50 (1995), pp. 315–25.

Heil, J.P., 'The Narrative Roles of the Women in Matthew's Genealogy', *Biblica* 72 (1991), pp. 538–45.

Hembold, W.C. (ed. and trans.), *Plutarch's Moralia* (LCL; Cambridge, MA: Harvard University Press, 1939; repr., 2000).

Hennessy, R., *Materialist Feminism and the Politics of Discourse* (New York and London: Routledge, 1993).

Heussi, K., *Der Ursprung des Mönchtums* (Tübingen: Mohr, 1936).

Hijmans, B.L., 'A!skhsiv: Notes on Epictetus' Educational System' (*Wijsgerige Teksten en Studies*, 2; Assen: Van Gorcum, 1959).

Hill, E. (ed. and trans.), *Sermons (51–94) on the Old Testament* (O.P. Series edited by John E. Rotelle; Brooklyn, New York: New City Press, 1991), III/3.

Himes, N., *A Medical History of Contraception* (2nd edn; New York: Schocken, 1970).

Honigman, S., 'The Birth of a Diaspora: The Emergence of a Jewish Self-Definition in Ptolemaic Egypt in the Light of Onomastics', in S.J.D. Cohen and E.S. Frerichs (eds), *Diasporas in Antiquity* (BJS, 288; Atlanta: Scholars Press, 1993), pp. 93–127.

Hopkins, M.K., 'Contraception in the Roman Empire', *Comparative Studies in Society and History*, 8 (1965/66), pp. 124–51.

— 'The Age of Roman Girls at Marriage', *Population Studies*, 18 (1965), pp. 309–27.

Horrell, D.G., *The Social Ethos of the Corinthian Correspondence. Interests and Ideology from 1 Corinthians to 1 Clement* (Edinburgh: T & T Clark, 1996).

Hultgren, A.J. and Steven A. Haggmark, *The Earliest Christian Heretics: Readings from Their Opponents* (Minneapolis, MN: Fortress Press, 1996).

Hunter, D.G., 'Resistance to the Virginal Ideal in Late-Fourth-Century Rome: The Case of Jovinian', *Theological Studies*, 48 (1987), pp. 45–64.

— 'The Language of Desire: Clement of Alexandria's Transformation of Ascetic Discourse', *Semeia*, 57 (1992), pp. 95–111.

Irelli, G.C., 'Archaeological Research in the Area of Vesuvius: Portraits from Herculaneum', in *Pompeii and the Vesuvian Landscape* (Washington, D.C.: Archaeological Institute of America and the Smithsonian Institution, 1979), pp. 16–24.

Irwin, M.E., 'Clement of Alexandria: Instructions on How Women Should Live', in Wendy E. Helleman (ed.), *Hellenization Revisited: Shaping a Christian Response within the Greco-Roman World* (Lanham, MD: University Press of America, 1994), pp. 395–407.

James, L. (ed.), *Women, Men and Eunuchs: Gender in Byzantium* (New York: Routledge, 1997).

Jameson, F., *The Political Unconscious: Narrative as a Socially Symbolic Act* (Ithaca, NY: Cornell University Press, 1981).

Jeffers, J.S., 'Jewish and Christian Families in First Century Rome', in Karl P. Donfried and Peter Richardson (eds), *Judaism and Christianity in First-Century Rome* (Grand Rapids, MI: Eerdmans, 1998), pp. 128–50.

— *Conflict at Rome. Social Order and Hierarchy in Early Christianity* (Minneapolis, MN: Fortress Press, 1991).

Jensen, R., *Living Water: Iconography and Architecture of Early Christian Baptism* (Leiden: Brill, forthcoming).

— *The Signs and Symbols of Baptism in the Early Church* (Peabody, MA: Hendrickson Press, forthcoming).

Jerome, *Epistolae/Lettres* (text established and French trans. Jerome Labourt; 8 vols.; Paris: Société d'Édition 'Belles Lettres', 1949–1963).

Jewett, R., 'Paul, Phoebe and the Spanish Mission', in Jacob Neusner, et al. (eds), *The Social World of Formative Christianity: Essays in Tribute of Howard Clark Kee* (Philadelphia, PA: Fortress Press, 1988), pp. 142–61.

Johnson, T. and Chris Dandeker, 'Patronage: Relation and System', in Wallace-Hadrill (ed.), *Patronage in Ancient Society*, pp. 219–42.

Jones, A.H.M., 'St John Chrysostom's Parentage and Education', *HTR*, 46 (1954), pp. 171–73.

— *The Later Roman Empire, 284–602: A Social, Economic and Administrative Survey* (Norman: University of Oklahoma Press, 1964).

Joubert, S.J., 'One Form of Social Exchange or Two? "Euergetism", Patronage, and Testament Studies', *BTB*, 31 (2001), pp. 17–25.

Judge, E.A., 'Cultural Conformity and Innovation in Paul: Some Clues from Contemporary Documents', *Tyndale Bulletin*, 35 (1984), pp. 3–24.

— 'Paul as a Radical Critic of Society', *Interchange* 16 (1974), pp. 191–203.

— 'The Early Christians as a Scholastic Community', *Journal of Religious History* (1960), pp. 4–15 and (1961), pp. 125–37.

— *The Social Pattern of Christian Groups in the First Century* (London: Tyndale Press, 1960).

Kasher, A., 'The Civic Status of the Jews in Ptolemaic Egypt', in Bilde et al. (eds), *Ethnicity in Hellenistic Egypt*, pp. 100–21.

Kearsley, R., 'Women in Public Life in the Roman East: Junia Theodora, Claudia Metrodora, and Phoibe, Benefactress of Paul', *Ancient Society: Resources for Teachers*, 15 (1985), pp. 124–37.

Kee, H.C., 'The Socio-Cultural Setting of Joseph and Aseneth', *NTS*, 29 (1983) pp. 394–413.

Khatchatrian, A., *Origine et typologie des baptistères paléochrétiens* (Mulhouse: Centre de Culture Chrétienne, 1982).

King, K.L., *'What is Gnosticism?'* (Cambridge, MA: Harvard University Press, 2003).

Klaw, S., *Without Sin: The Life and Death of the Oneida Community* (New York: Allen Lane, 1993).

Knowles, D., *Christian Monasticism* (New York: McGraw Hill, 1969).

Kraemer, R.S., 'A New Inscription from Malta and the Question of Women Elders in the Diaspora Jewish Communities', *HTR*, 78 (1985), pp. 431–38.

— 'Jewish Women in the Diaspora World of Late Antiquity', in Judith R. Baskin (ed.), *Jewish Women in Historical Perspective* (Detroit, MI: Wayne State University Press, 1998; 2nd edn), pp. 46–72.

— 'Monastic Jewish Women in Greco-Roman Egypt: Philo of Alexandria on the Therapeutae and Therapeutrides', *Signs*, 14 (1989), pp. 342–60.

— 'The Conversion of Women to Ascetic Forms of Christianity', *Signs*, 6 (1980/81), pp. 298–307.

— 'Women's Authorship of Jewish and Christian Literature in the Greco-Roman Period', in Amy-Jill Levine (ed.), 'Women Like This', pp. 221–42.

— *Her Share of the Blessings: Women's Religions Among Pagans, Jews, and Christians in the Greco-Roman World* (New York: Oxford University Press, 1992).

— *When Aseneth Met Joseph: A Late Antique Tale of the Biblical Patriarch and his Egyptian Wife, Revisited* (New York and Oxford: Oxford University Press, 1998).

— (ed.), *Maenads, Martyrs, Matrons, Monastics. A Sourcebook on Women's Religions in the Greco-Roman World* (Philadelphia, PA: Fortress Press, 1988).

— (ed.), *Women's Religions in the Greco-Roman World: A Sourcebook* (New York: Oxford University Press, 2004).

Kraemer, R.S. and Mary Rose D'Angelo (eds), *Women and Christian Origins* (Oxford: Oxford University Press, 1999).

Kraemer, R.S. and Shira L. Lander, 'Perpetua and Felicitas', in Philip Esler (ed.), *The Early Christian World* (London: Routledge, 2000), vol. 2, pp. 1048–68.

Krause, J.-U., *Spätantike Patronatsformen im Westen des Römischen Reiches* (Munich: C.H. Beck, 1987).

Krawiec, R., *Shenoute and the Women of the White Monastery: Egyptian Monasticism in Late Antiquity* (New York and Oxford: Oxford University Press, 2003).

Kristeva, J., 'Word, Dialogue and Novel', in Toril Moi (ed.), *The Kristeva Reader* (New York: Columbia University Press, 1986) pp. 36–41.

— *La Révolution du language poétique: L'Avant-Garde á la fin du XIXe siècle: Lautréamont et Mallarmé* (Paris: Editions du Seuil, 1974).

— 'Le Texte du roman: Approche sémiologique d'une structure discursive transformationnelle' (*Approaches to Semiotics*, 6; The Hague and Paris: Mouton, 1970).

Kuehn, R., *A Place for Baptism* (Chicago: Liturgical Training Publications, 1992).

Kugel, J., *In Potiphar's House: The Interpretive Life of Biblical Texts* (San Francisco, CA: Harper Collins, 1990).

Kugelman, R. and F. X. Murphy, 'Virgines Subintroductae', *New Catholic Encyclopedia* (New York: McGraw Hill, 1967).

Kühn, C.G. (ed.), *Galeni Opera Omnia* (Leipzig: K. Knobloch, 1823–1833; repr., Hildesheim: Georg Olms, 1965).

Laqueur, T., *Making Sex: Body and Gender from the Greeks to Freud* (Cambridge, MA: Harvard University Press, 1990).

Larmour, D.H.J., Paul Allen Miller, and Charles Platter (eds), *Rethinking Sexuality: Foucault and Classical Antiquity* (Princeton, NJ: Princeton University Press, 1997).

Larrain, J., *Marxism and Ideology* (Atlantic Highlands, NJ: Humanities Press, 1983).

Layton, B. (ed. and trans.), *Gnostic Scriptures* (Garden City, NY: Doubleday, 1987), pp. 314–15.

le Boulluec, A., 'L'École d'Alexandrie. De quelques aventures d'un concept historio-graphique', in *Alexandrina. Hellénisme, judaïsme et christianisme à Alexandrie: Mélanges offerts au P. Claude Mondésert* (Paris: Les Éditions du Cerf, 1987), pp. 403–17.

Leclercq, H., 'Cénobitisme', in Fernand Cabrol and Henri Leclercq (eds), *Dictionnaire d'archéologie chrétienne et de liturgie* (Paris: Letouzey et Ane, 1925).

— 'Vierge, Virginité', in Fernand Cabrol and Henri Leclercq (eds), *Dictionnaire d'archéologie chrétienne et de liturgie* (Paris: Letouzey et Ane, 1953).

Lefkowitz, M.R. and Maureen Fant (eds), *Women's Life in Greece and Rome* (1982; Baltimore: Johns Hopkins University Press, 1992; 2nd edn).

Lefkowitz, M.R., 'Did Ancient Women Write Novels?', in Amy-Jill Levine (ed.), *'Women Like This'*, pp. 199–219.

— 'The Motivations for St. Perpetua's Martyrdom', *JAAR*, 44 (1976), pp. 417–21.

Levine, A-J., 'Diaspora as Metaphor: Bodies and Boundaries in the Book of Tobit', in J. Andrew Overman and Robert S. MacLennan (eds), *Diaspora Jews and Judaism* (Atlanta: Scholars Press, 1992), pp. 105–17.

Levine, A-J., (ed.), *'Women Like This': New Perspectives on Jewish Women in the Greco-Roman World* (*Early Judaism and its Literature*, 1; Atlanta: Scholars Press, 1991).

— (ed.), *A Feminist Companion to the New Testament Apocrypha* (London: Continuum, 2006).

Levine, L.I., 'Women in the Synagogue', in *idem*, *The Ancient Synagogue: the First Thousand Years* (New Haven, CT: Yale University Press, 2000), pp. 471–90.

Levi-Strauss, C., *Elementary Structures of Kinship* (rev. ed.; trans. J.H. Bell; eds J.R. von Sturmer and R. Needham; Boston: Beacon, 1969).

Lewis, N., *Greeks in Ptolemaic Egypt* (Oxford: Clarendon Press, 1986).

— *Life in Egypt Under Roman Rule* (Oxford: Clarendon Press, 1983).

Leyerle, B., *Theatrical Shows and Ascetic Lives: John Chrysostom's Attack on Spiritual Marriage* (Berkeley: University of California Press, 2001).

Lightfoot, J.B., *Apostolic Fathers* (5 vols.; 2nd edn; London: Macmillan, 1889–1890).

Lindemann, A., *Die Clemensbriefe* (HNT, 17; *Die Apostolischen Väter*, 1; Tübingen: Mohr/Siebeck, 1992).

Long, A.A., 'Soul and Body in Stoicism', *in Colloquy 36 of The Center for Hermeneutical Studies* (Berkeley, CA: Center for Hermeneutical Studies, 1980).

— *Hellenistic Philosophy: Stoics, Epicureans, Sceptics* (New York: Charles Scribner's Sons, 1974).

Loraux, N., *Tragic Ways of Killing a Woman* (Cambridge, MA: Harvard University Press, 1987).

Lührmann, D., 'Wo man nicht mehr Sklave order Freier ist: Überlegungen zur Strucktur frühchristlicher Gemeinden', *Wort und Dienst*, 13 (1975), pp. 53–83.

Lutz, C., 'Musonius Rufus: The Roman Socrates', *Yale Classical Studies*, 10 (1947), pp. 3–142.

MacDonald, M. Y., 'Reading Real Women through the Undisputed Letters of Paul', in Ross Shephard Kraemer and Mary Rose D'Angelo (eds), *Women and Christian Origins*, pp. 199–220.

— *Early Christian Women and Pagan Opinion: The Power of the Hysterical Woman* (New York: Cambridge University Press, 1996).

Madigan, K. and Carolyn Osiek, *Ordained Women in the Early Church: A Documentary History* (Baltimore, MD: Johns Hopkins University Press, 2005).

Maier, H.O., 'Staging the Gaze: Early Christian Apocalypses and Narrative Self-Representation', *HTR*, 90 (1997), pp. 131–54.

— *Apocalypse Recalled: The Book of Revelation After Christendom* (Minneapolis, MN: Fortress Press, 2002).

Malingrey, A.-M. (ed.), *Jean Chrysostome: Sur la vaine glorie et l'éducation des enfants* (SC, 188; Paris: Éditions du Cerf, 1972).

Mannheim, K., *Ideology and Utopia: An Introduction to the Sociology of Knowledge* (trans. L. Wirth and E. Shils; New York: Harcourt, Brace & Co., 1946).

Marrou, H.-I., Marguerite Harl, Claude Mondésert (eds), *Clément d'Alexandrie: Le Pédagogue* (SC, 108; Paris: Éditions du Cerf, 1960).

Martin, D.B., *Slavery as Salvation* (New Haven, CT: Yale University Press, 1990).

Martin, D.B., and Patricia Cox Millers (eds), *The Cultural Turn in Late Ancient Studies: Gender, Asceticism, and Historiography* (Durham, NC: Duke University Press, 2005).

Martin, L.H., Huck Gutman, and Patrick H. Hutton (eds), *Technologies of the Self: A Seminar with Michel Foucault* (Amherst: University of Massachusetts Press, 1988).

Marx, K. and Frederick Engels, *Collected Works* (trans. Richard Dixon, et al.; 50 vols; New York: International Publishers, 1976).

Matthews, S., 'Thinking of Thecla: Issues in Feminist Historiography', *JFSR*, 17.2 (2001), pp. 39–55.

— *First Converts: Rich Pagan Women and the Rhetoric of Mission in Early Judaism and Christianity* (Stanford, CA: Stanford University Press, 2001).

McCutcheon, R.T., '"My Theory of the Brontosaurus...": Postmodernism and "Theory" of Religion', in *idem, Critics Not Caretakers: Redescribing the Public Study of Religion* (Albany: State University of New York Press, 2001).

McGinn, S., 'Perpetua', in Elizabeth Schüssler Fiorenza (ed.), *Searching the Scriptures: A Feminist Commentary*, vol. 2, pp. 800–28.

McVey, K., 'Christianity and Culture, Dead White European Males, and the Study of Patristics', *The Princeton Seminary Bulletin*, n.s. 15 (1994), pp. 103–30.

Meeks, W., 'The Image of the Androgyne: Some Uses of a Symbol in Earliest Christianity', *HR* 13.3 (1974), pp. 185–89.

— *The Moral World of the First Christians* (LEC; Philadelphia, PA: The Westminster Press, 1986).

Méhat, A., 'Études sur les 'Stromates' de Clément d'Alexandrie' (*Patristica Sorbonensia*, 7; Paris: Seuil, 1966).

Meier, H.O., 'Clement of Alexandria and the Care of the Self', JAAR 62 (1994), pp. 719–45.

Mélèze-Modrzejewski, J., 'How to Be a Greek and Yet a Jew in Hellenistic Alexandria', in Shaye J.D. Cohen and Ernest S. Frerichs (eds), *Diasporas in Antiquity* (*BJS*, 288; Atlanta: Scholars Press, 1993), pp. 65–92.

— *The Jews of Egypt: From Rameses II to Emperor Hadrian* (trans. Robert Cornman; French original 1992; Princeton, NJ: Princeton University Press, 1997).

Methodius, *Symposium Decem Virginem/Le Banquet* (text established and French trans. Victor-Henry Debidour; Sources Chrétiennes, no. 95; Paris: Cerf, 1963).

Metz, R., *La consécration des vierges dans l'Eglise romaine; Etudes d'histoire de la liturgie* (Paris: Presses Universitaires de France, 1954).

Metzger, B.M., 'Literary Forgeries and Canonical Pseudepigraphy', *JBL*, 91.1 (1972), pp. 3–24.

Miller, P.C., 'Desert Asceticism and "The Body from Nowhere"', *JECS*, 2 (1994), pp. 137–53.

— 'The Blazing Body: Ascetic Desire in Jerome's Letter to Eustochium', *JECS*, 1 (1993), pp. 21–45.

— *Dreams in Late Antiquity: Studies in the Imagination of a Culture* (Princeton, NJ: Princeton University Press, 1994).

Millett, P., 'Patronage and Its Avoidance in Classical Athens', in Wallace-Hadrill (ed.), *Patronage in Ancient Society*, pp. 15–47.

Mitchell, M.M., 'New Testament Envoys in the Context of Greco-Roman Diplomatic and Epistolary Conventions: The Example of Timothy and Titus', *JBL*, 111 (1992), pp. 641–62.

— *Paul and the Rhetoric of Reconciliation* (HUT, 28; Tübingen: Mohr/Siebeck, 1991).

Moine, N., 'Melaniana', *Rech. Aug.*, 15 (1980), pp. 3–79.

Moore, S.D. and Janice Capel Anderson, 'Taking it Like a Man: Masculinity in 4 Maccabees', *JBL*, 117 (1998), pp. 249–73.

Moulard, A., *Saint Jean Chrysostom: Le defenseur du mariage et l'apôtre de la virginité* (Paris: Lecoffre, 1923).

Murphy-O'Connor, J., *Paul: A Critical Life* (Oxford: Clarendon Press, 1996).

Musurillo, H. (ed.), *Acts of the Christian Martyrs* (Oxford: The Clarendon Press, 1972).

Nauck, A. (ed.), *Porphyrii Philosophi Platonici opuscula selecta* (Bibliotheca Scriptorum Graecorum et Romanorum Teubneriana; Leipzig: Teubner, 1886; repr., Hildesheim: Georg Olms, 1963).

Newsom, C.A. and Sharon H. Ringe (eds), *The Women's Bible Commentary* (Louisville, KY: Westminster/John Knox Press, 1992; rev. edn, 1998).

Norsa, M., 'Martirio Di Santa Christina', *Studi italiani di filologia classica*, 19 (1912), pp. 316–27.

North, H., 'Sophrosyne: Self-Knowledge and Self-Restraint in Greek Literature' (*Cornell Studies in Classical Philology*, 35; Ithaca, NY: Cornell University Press, 1966).

Nussbaum, M.C., *The Therapy of Desire: Theory and Practice in Hellenistic Ethics* (Martin Classical Lectures, n.s. 2; Princeton, NJ: Princeton University Press, 1994).

Okin, S.M., 'Philosopher Queens and Private Wives: Plato on Women and the Family', *Philosophy and Public Affairs*, 6 (1977), pp. 345–69.

Oldfather, W.A. (ed.), *Epictetus: The Discourses as Reported by Arrian, The Manual, and Fragments* (LCL; Cambridge, MA: Harvard University Press, 1966–1967).

Orfrasio, J.M., *The Baptismal Font: A Study of Patristic and Liturgical Texts* (Ph.D. diss.; Rome: Pontificio Instituto Liturgico, 1990).

Osiek, C., 'The Widow as Altar: The Rise and Fall of a Symbol', *Second Century* 3.3 (1983), pp. 159–69

— 'Women Patrons in the Life of House Churches', in *eadem*, Margaret Y. MacDonald, with Jane Tullock, *A Woman's Place: House Churches in Earliest Christianity* (Minneapolis, MN: Fortress Press, 2005), pp. 194–219.

Osiek, C. and David L. Balch, *Families in the New Testament World. Households and House Churches* (Louisville, KY: Westminster/John Knox, 1997).

Osiek, C., Margaret Y. MacDonald, with Janet Tullock, *A Woman's Place: House Churches in Earliest Christianity* (Minneapolis, MN: Fortress Press, 2005).

Padel, R., *In and Out of the Mind: Greek Images of the Tragic Self* (Princeton, NJ: Princeton University Press, 1992).

Palladius, v. Chrys. 61, in P.R. Coleman-Norton (ed.), *Palladii Dialogus de vita S. Joannis Chrysostomi* (Cambridge, UK: Cambridge University Press, 1928).

Parekh, B., *Marx's Theory of Ideology* (Baltimore, MD and London: Johns Hopkins University Press, 1982).

Patlagean, E., 'L'histoire de la femme deguisée en moine et l'évolution de la santéte féminine à Byzance', *Studi Medievali*, 3d. ser., 17 (1976), pp. 597–623.

— 'Researches sur les pauvres et al pauvreté dans l'empire roman d'orient' (IV–VIIe siècles) (*Civilisations et Sociétés*, 48; Mouton: Ecole des Hautes Etudes en Sciences Sociales, 1977).

Paulinus of Nola, *Epistolae/Lettres* (2 vols.; trans. P. G. Walsh; Ancient Christian Writers nos. 35, 36; Westminster, MD: Newman, 1967).

Pêcheux, M., *Language, Semantics and Ideology* (trans. Harbans Nagpal; New York: St. Martin's Press, 1982; French original, 1975).

Perkins, J., *The Suffering Self: Pain and Narrative Representation in the Early Christian Era* (New York: Routledge, 1995).

Peterson, J. M. (ed.), *Handmaids of the Lord: Contemporary Descriptions of Feminine Asceticism in the First Six Christian Centuries* (Kalamazoo, MI: Cistercian Publications, 1996).

Petroff, E.A., *Medieval Women's Visionary Literature* (New York: Oxford University Press, 1986).

Philonenko, M., *Joseph et Aseneth: Introduction, texte critique, traduction, et notes* (Studia Post Biblica; Leiden: E. J. Brill, 1968).

Pigeaud, J., *La maladie de l'ame: Étude sur la relation de l'ame et du corps dans la tradition medico-philosophique antique* (Paris: Les Belles Lettres, 1981).

Plaskow, J., 'What's Wrong with Hierarchy?' in *edem*, *The Coming of Lilith: Essays on Feminism, Judaism, and Sexual Ethics, 1972–2003* (Boston: Beacon, 2005), pp. 138–142.

Pleket, H.W., *Epigraphica II: Texts on the Social History of the Greek World* (Leiden: Brill, 1969).

Plumpe, J.C., *Mater Ecclesia: An Inquiry into the Concept of the Church as Mother in Early Christianity* (Washington, DC: Catholic University Press, 1943).

Poe, G.R., 'Spirituality of Fourth and Fifth Century Eastern Female Asceticism as Reflected in the Life of Saint Syncletica' (Ph.D. diss., Southern Baptist Theological Seminary, 1995).

Pohlenz, M., *Die Stoa: Geschichte einer geistigen Bewegung* (Göttingen: Vandenhoeck and Ruprecht, 1948–1949.

Poirier, M., 'Note sur la Passio Sanctarum Perpetuae et Felicitatis: Félicité était-elle vraiment l'esclave de Perpetué?', in Frank M. Cross (ed.), *Studia Patristica*, 10.1 (1970), pp. 306–9.

Pollard, E.A., 'Magic Accusations Against Women in the Greco-Roman World' (Ph.D. diss., University of Pennsylvania, 2001).

Pomeroy, S.B., *Women in Hellenistic Egypt: From Alexander to Cleopatra* (New York: Schocken Books, 1984).

Porphyry, *Ad Marcellam/Lettre à Marcella* (text established and French trans. Edouard des Places; Paris: Société d'Edition 'Belles Lettres', 1982).

Potter, D., 'Martyrdom as Spectacle', in Ruth Scodel (ed.), *Theater and Society in the Classical World* (Ann Arbor: University of Michigan Press, 1993), pp. 53–88.

Puech, A., *Histoire de la littérature grecque chrétienne depuis les origines jusqu'à la fin du IVe siècle* (3 vols.; Paris: Société d'Edition 'Belles Lettres', 1928–1930).

Quaegebeur, J., 'Greco-Egyptian Double Names as a Feature of a Bi-Cultural Society: The Case Ψοσνεύ ὁ καὶ Τριαδελφος', in J.H. Johnson (ed.), *Life in a Multi-Cultural Society: Egypt from Cambyses to Constantine (and Beyond), Proceedings of the Symposium held in Chicago, September, 1990 (Studies in Ancient Oriental Civilization*, Vol. 51; Chicago: The Oriental Institute of the University of Chicago, 1992), pp. 265–72.

Raitt, J., 'The Vagina Dentata and the Immaculatus Uterus Divini Fontis', *JAAR*, 48 (1980), pp. 415–31.

Rajak, T. and David Noy, 'Archisynagogoi: Office, Title and Social Status in the Greco-Jewish Synagogue', *JRS*, 83 (1993), pp. 75–93.

Rampolla, M. d. T. (ed.), *Santa Melania Giuniore, senatrice romana: documenti contemporei e nore* (Roma: Tipografia Vaticana, 1905).

Rawson, B., 'The Roman Family', in Beryl Rawson (ed.), *The Family in Ancient Rome: New Perspectives* (Ithaca, NY: Cornell University Press, 1986), pp. 1–57.

Reardon, B.P. (ed.), *Collected Ancient Greek Novels* (Berkeley and Los Angeles, CA and London: University of California Press, 1989).

Richlin, A., 'Approaches to the Sources on Adultery at Rome', in Helene P. Foley (ed.), *Reflections of Women in Antiquity* (New York, London and Paris: Gordon and Breach Science Publishers, 1981), pp. 379–404.

— 'The Ethnographer's Dilemma and the Dream of a Golden Age', in Nancy Sorkin Rabinowitz and Amy Richlin (eds), *Feminist Theory and the Classics* (New York: Routledge, 1993), pp. 272–303.

Rist, J.M., *Stoic Philosophy* (Cambridge, UK: Cambridge University Press, 1969).

Rist, M., 'Pseudepigaphy and the Early Christians', in David E. Aune (ed.), *Studies in New Testament and Early Christian Literature: Essays in Honor of Allen P. Wikgren* (Leiden: E.J. Brill, 1972), pp. 75–91.

Rives, J., 'Civic and Religious Life', in John Bodel (ed.), *Epigraphic Evidence: Ancient History from Inscriptions*, (London: Routledge, 2001), pp. 118–36.

Rizzerio, L., 'La notion de γνωστικὴ φυσιολογία chez Clément d'Alexandrie', in Elizabeth A. Livingstone (ed.), *Studia Patristica*, vol. XXVI: Papers presented at the Eleventh International Conference on Patristic Studies held in Oxford 1991. 'Liturgica, Second Century, Alexandria before Nicaea, Athanasius and the Arian Controversy', (Leuven: Peeters, 1993), pp. 318–23.

Robbins, B., 'The Politics of Theory', *Social Text*, 18 (1987/88), pp. 3–18.

Roberge, R.M., 'L'avortement dans le pensée chrétienne des premiers siècles', *Collection d'Etudes Anciennes*, 7 (1977), pp. 83–90.

Roberts, A. and James Donaldson (eds), *Fathers of the Second Century: Hermas, Tatian, Athenagoras, Theophilus, and Clement of Alexandria* (entire) (The Ante-Nicene Fathers; 1885; Peabody, MA: Hendrickson, 1995), vol. 2.

Rossi, M.A., 'The Passion of Perpetua, Everywoman of Late Antiquity', in R.C. Smith and J. Lounibos (eds), *Pagan and Christian Anxiety: A Response to E.R. Dodds* (Lanham, MD: University Press of America, 1984), pp. 53–86.

Rouselle, A., 'Observation féminine et idéologie masculine: le corps de la femme d'après les médicins grecs', *Annales* (Economies, Sociétés, Civilisations), 35 (1980), pp. 1089–1115.

— *Porneia: De la maîtrise du corps à la privation sensorielle IIe-IVe siècles de l'ère chrétienne* (Paris: PUF, 1983; English translation: *Porneia: On Desire and the Body in Antiquity*, trans. Felicia Pheasant; Oxford: Basil Blackwell, 1988).

Rousseau, P., *Ascetics, Authority and the Church in the Age of Jerome and Cassian* (Oxford: Oxford University Press, 1978).

Ruether, R., 'Mothers of the Church: Ascetic Women in the Late Patristic Age', in Rosemary Ruether and Eleanor McLaughlin (eds), *Women of Spirit: Female Leadership in the Jewish and Christian Traditions* (New York: Simon and Schuster, 1979), pp. 71–98.

Saller, R.P., 'Patronage and Friendship in Early Imperial Rome: Drawing the Distinction', in Wallace-Hardrill (ed.), *Patronage in Ancient Society*, pp. 49–62

— 'Familia, Domus, and the Roman Conception of the Family', *Phoenix*, 38 (1984), pp. 336–55.

— *Personal Patronage under the Early Empire* (Cambridge, UK: Cambridge University Press, 1982).

Salmon, G. 'Epiphases' in W. Smith and H. Wace (eds), *The Dictionary of Christian Biography* (London: J. Murray, 1880).

Schmitz, P., 'La première communautéde vierges à Rome', *Revue Benedictine*, 38 (1926).

Schneemelcher, W. and Edgar Hennecke (eds), *New Testament Apocrypha* (2 vols; trans. and ed. R. McL. Wilson; Philadelphia, PA: Westminster, 1966).

Schoedel, W.R., *Ignatius of Antioch: A Commentary on the Letters of Ignatius of Antioch* (Hermeneia; Philadelphia, PA: Fortress Press, 1985).

Schoellgen, G., *Ecclesia sordida? Zur Frage der sozialen Schichtung frühchristlicher Gemeinden am Beispiel Karthagos zur Zeit Tertullians* (Münster Westfalen: Aschendorffsche Verlagsbuchhandlung, 1984).

— *In Memory of Her: A Feminist Theological Reconstruction of Christian Origins* (New York: Crossroad, 1983).

Schüssler Fiorenza, E. (ed.), *Searching the Scriptures: A Feminist Introduction and Commentary* (2 vols.; New York: Crossroad, 1993, 1994).

Scott, J.W., 'Gender: A Useful Category of Historical Analysis', *American Historical Review*, 91 (1986), pp. 1053–75.

Shapiro, M.J., *The Politics of Representation: Writing Practices in Biography, Photography, and Political Analysis* (Madison: University of Wisconsin Press, 1988).

Shaw, B., 'Body/Power/Identity: Passions of the Martyrs', *JECS*, 4 (1996), pp. 269–312.

— 'The Passion of Perpetua', *Past and Present*, 139 (1993), pp. 30–33.

Shaw, T.M., *The Burden of the Flesh: Fasting and Sexuality in Early Christianity* (Minneapolis, MN: Fortress Press, 1998).

— 'Creation, Virginity, and Diet in Fourth-Century Christianity: Basil of Ancyra's On the True Purity of Virginity', in Maria Wyke (ed.), *Gender and the Body in the Ancient Mediterranean* (Malden, MA: Blackwell, 1998), pp. 155–72.

Singer, P.N. (trans.), 'The Affections and Errors of the Soul', in *Galen: Selected Works* (The World's Classics; Oxford: Oxford University Press, 1997), pp. 100–49.

Sissa, G., *Greek Virginity* (trans. Arthur Goldhammer; *Revealing Antiquity*, 3; Cambridge, MA: Harvard University Press, 1990).

Sivan, H., 'On Hymens and Holiness in Late Antiquity: Opposition to Aristocratic Female Asceticism at Rome', *JAC*, 36 (1993), pp. 81–93.

Smith, I.G., *Christian Monasticism from the Fourth to the Ninth Centuries of the Christian Era* (London: Innes, 1892).

Smith, M., *Clement of Alexandria and the Secret Gospel of Mark* (Cambridge, MA: Harvard University Press, 1973).

Soranus, *Gynaeciorum Libri IV*, ed. Ioannes Ilberg. *Corpus Medicorum Graecorum*, vol. 4 (Leipzig: Tuebner, 1927).

Spanneut, M., 'Le Stoïcisme des Pères de l'Église: De Clément de Rome à Clément d'Alexandrie' (*Patristica Sorbonensia*, 1; Paris: Seuil, 1957).

Speyer, W., *Die literarische Fälschung im heidnischen und christlichen Altertum: Ein Versuch ihrer Deutung* (Munich: C.H. Beck, 1971).

Spivak, G., 'The Politics of Interpretation', in W.J.T. Mitchell (ed.), *The Politics of Interpretation* (Chicago and London: University of Chicago Press, 1983), pp. 347–66

Stählin, O. (ed.), Clement of Alexandria, *Opera* (4 vols.; Die griechischen christlichen Schriftsteller der ersten drei Jahrhunderte, 12, 15, 17, 39; Leipzig: Hinrichs, 1905–1909).

Standhartinger, A., *Das Frauenbild im Judentum der hellenistischen Zeit. Ein Beitrag anhand von 'Joseph & Aseneth'* (Leiden: E.J. Brill, 1995).

Stanton, E.C., S.B. Anthony and M.J. Gage (eds), *The History of Woman Suffrage* (6 vols; Rochester, NY, 1881; repr., Salem, NH: Ayer Company, 1985).

Staples, A., *From Good Goddess to Vestal Virgins: Sex and Category in Roman Religion* (New York: Routledge, 1998).

Stauffer, S.A., *On Baptismal Fonts: Ancient and Modern* (Nottingham: Grove Books, 1994).

Stead, C., *Philosophy in Christian Antiquity* (New York: Cambridge University Press, 1994).

Stock, B., *Listening for the Text: On the Uses of the Past* (Baltimore, MD and London: Johns Hopkins University Press, 1990).

Talbot, A.-M. (ed.), *Holy Women of Byzantium: Ten Saints' Lives in English Translation* (Byzantine Saints' 'Lives in Translation', 1; Washington, DC: Dumbarton Oaks Library and Collection, 1996).

Taylor, G.H., 'Introduction,' in Paul Ricoeur, *Lectures on Ideology and Utopia* (New York: Columbia University Press, 1986), pp. ix–xxxvi.

Taylor, J.E., *Jewish Women Philosophers in First-Century Alexandria: Philo's 'Therapeutae' Reconsidered* (Oxford: Oxford University Press, 2003).

Thomas, G., 'La Condition social de l'êglise de Lyon en 177', in *Les martyrs de lyne (177)* p. 95 n. 5.

Thomas, Y., 'The Division of the Sexes in Roman Law', in P.S. Pantel (ed.), *A History of Women: From Ancient Goddesses to Christian Saints* (trans. A. Goldhammer; Cambridge, MA and London: Belknap Press of Harvard University Press, 1992), pp. 83–137.

Thompson, D.J., 'Language and Literacy in Early Hellenistic Egypt', in Per Bilde et al. (eds), *Ethnicity in Hellenistic Egypt* (*Studies in Hellenistic Civilization*, III; Aarhus: Aarhus University Press, 1992), pp. 39–52.

Thompson, J.B., *Ideology and Modern Culture: Critical Theory in the Era of Mass Communication* (Stanford, CA: Stanford University Press, 1990).

— *Studies in the Theory of Ideology* (Berkeley and Los Angeles: University of California Press, 1984).

Thurston, B.B., *The Widows: A Women's Ministry in the Early Church* (Minneapolis, MN: Fortress Press, 1989).

Tilley, M.A., 'The Ascetic Body and the (Un)making of the World of the Martyr', *JAAR*, 59 (1991), pp. 467–79.

Torjesen, K.J., 'Pedagogical Soteriology from Clement to Origen', in Lothar Lies (ed.), *Origeniana Quarta. Die Referate des 4. Internationalen Origeneskongresses* (Innsbruck, 2–6 September 1985), (Innsbruck: Tyrolia, 1987), pp. 370–73.

— *When Women Were Priests: Women's Leadership in the Early Church and the Scandal of Their Subordination in the Rise of Christianity* (San Francisco, CA: HarperSanFrancisco, 1993.

Treggiari, S.M., *Roman Marriage: Iusti Coniuges from the Time of Cicero to the Time of Ulpian* (Oxford and New York: Clarendon Press, 1991).

Tulloch, J., 'Women Leaders in Family Funerary Banquets', in Osiek, MacDonald and Tulloch, *A Woman's Place*, pp. 164–93.

Turner, C.H., 'The Lausiac History of Palladius', *JTS*, 6 (1905), pp. 352–54.

Ussher, R. G., *Aristophanes*, *Ecclesiazusae* (Oxford: Clarendon Press, 1973).

Vaage, L.E., and Vincent L. Wimbush (eds), *Asceticism and the New Testament* (New York: Routledge, 1999).

Valantasis, R. (ed.), *Religions of Late Antiquity in Practice*, (Princeton Readings in Religion; Princeton, NJ: Princeton University Press, 2000).

— 'Constructions of Power in Asceticism', *JAAR*, 63 (1995), pp. 775–821.

Van Bremen, Riet, 'Women and Wealth', in Averil Cameron and Amélie Kuhrt (eds), *Images of Women in Antiquity* (rev. ed.; Detroit, MI: Wayne State University Press, 1993), pp. 223–42.

van den Hoek, A., 'The "Catechetical" School of Early Christian Alexandria and Its Philonic Heritage', *HTR*, 90 (1997), pp. 59–87.

— 'Milk and Honey in the Theology of Clement of Alexandria', in Hans Jörg Auf der Maur et al. (eds), *Fides Sacramenti Sacramentum Fidei: Studies in honour of Pieter Smulders* (Assen: Van Gorcum, 1981), pp. 27–39.

— 'How Alexandrian Was Clement of Alexandria? Reflections on Clement and His Alexandrian Background', *Heythrop Journal*, 31 (1990), pp. 179–94.

— 'Techniques of Quotation in Clement of Alexandria: A View of Ancient Literary Working Methods', *VC*, 50 (1996), pp. 223–43.

Viller, M., 'Le Martyre et l'ascèse', *Revue d'ascétique et de mystique*, 6 (1925), pp. 105–42.

Vogel, C., 'Facere cum virginia (-o) sua(-o)annos … L'âge des époux chrétiens au moment de contracter mariage d'après les inscriptions paléochrétiennes', *Revue de driot canonique*, 16 (1966), pp. 355–66.

Vogt, K., '"Becoming Male": One Aspect of an Early Christian Anthropology', in Elisabeth Schüssler Fiorenza and Mary Collins (eds), *Women – Invisible in Theology and Church* (*Concilium*, 182; Edinburgh: T & T Clark, 1985), pp. 49–62.

von der Goltz, E.F. (ed.), *Logos soterias pros ten parthenon (De virginitate): Eine echte Schrift des Athanasius*, *TU* 29, 2a (Leipzig: J. C. Hinrichs, 1905). *Discourse on Salvation to a Virgin*, in Richard Valantasis (ed.), *Religions of Antiquity in Practice* (trans. Teresa M. Shaw; Princeton Readings in Religions; Princeton, NJ: Princeton University Press, 2000).

Wagner, W., 'Divine Femaleness: Two Second Century Contributions', *JRelS*, 17 (1991), pp. 19–43.

Wallace-Hadrill, A. 'Patronage in Roman Society: From Republic to Empire', in Wallace-Hadrill (ed.), *Patronage in Ancient Society*, pp. 63–87.

— (ed.), *Patronage in Ancient Society* (London: Routledge, 1989).

Ward, B., *The Harlots of the Desert: A Study of Repentance in Early Monastic Sources* (Kalamazoo, MI: Cistercian Publications, 1987).

Ward, R.B., 'The Public Priestesses of Pompeii', in Abraham J. Malherbe, Frederick W. Norris and James W. Thompson (eds), *The Early Church in Its Context: Essays in Honor of Everett Ferguson* (Leiden: Brill, 1998), pp. 323–27.

— 'Women in Pompeii: Work in Progress' (unpublished paper).

Weaver, P.R.C., *Familia Caesaris* (Cambridge, UK: Cambridge University Press, 1972).

Welborn, L.L., 'On the Date of First Clement', *BR*, 29 (1984), pp. 35–54.

Whelan, C.F., 'Amica Pauli: The Role of Phoebe in the Early Church', *JSNT*, 49 (1993), pp. 67–85.

White, H., 'The Historical Text as Literary Artifact', in R.H. Canary and H. Kozicki (eds), *The Writing of History: Literary Form and Historical Understanding* (Madison: University of Wisconsin Press, 1978), pp. 41–62.

— 'The Value of Narrativity in the Representation of Reality', *Critical Inquiry*, 7 (1980), pp. 5–27.

— *The Content of the Form: Narrative Discourse and Historical Representation* (Baltimore, MD and London: Johns Hopkins University Press, 1987).

White, L.M. (ed.), *Social Networks in the Early Christian Environment: Issues and Methods for Social History* (*Semeia*, 56; Atlanta: Scholars Press, 1992).

White, P., 'AMICITIA and the Profession of Poetry in Early Imperial Rome', *JRS*, 68 (1978), pp. 90–92.

Wicker, K.O., 'Mulierum Virtutes (Moralia 242E–263C)', in Hans Dieter Betz (ed.), *Plutarch's Ethical Writings and Early Christian Literature* (Leiden: Brill, 1978), pp. 106–34.

— 'Porphyry the Philosopher to Marcella, Text and Translation with Introduction and Notes' (*SBLTT*, 28; Atlanta: Scholars Press, 1987).

Wiedemann, T., *Emperors and Gladiators* (New York: Routledge, 1992).

Wilfong, T.G., 'Reading the Disjointed Body in Coptic: From Physical Modification to Textual Fragmentation', in Dominic Montserrat (ed.), *Changing Bodies, Changing Meanings: Studies on the Human Body in Antiquity* (New York: Routledge, 1997), pp. 116–36.

Wilkes, J.J., *Dalmatia* (Cambridge, MA: Harvard University Press, 1969).

Williams, M.A., *Rethinking 'Gnosticism': An Argument for Dismantling a Dubious Category* (Princeton, NJ: Princeton University Press, 1999).

Williams, R., *Marxism and Literature* (Oxford: Oxford University Press, 1971).

Wills, L.A., *The Jewish Novel in the Ancient World* (Ithaca, NY and London: Cornell University Press, 1995).

Wimbush, V.L. (ed.), *Ascetic Behavior in Greco-Roman Antiquity: A Sourcebook* (Minneapolis, MN: Fortress Press, 1990).

— (ed.), 'Discursive Formations, Ascetic Piety and the Interpretation of Early Christian Literature', *Semeia*, 57 & 58 (1992).

Wimbush, V.L., and Richard Valantasis (eds), *Asceticism* (New York: Oxford University Press, 1995).

Winkler, J.J., *Auctor and Actor: A Narratological Reading of Apuleius The Golden Ass* (Berkeley: University of California Press, 1985).

— *The Constraints of Desire: The Anthropology of Sex and Gender in Ancient Greece* (New York: Routledge, 1990).

Winter, B.W., *Roman Wives, Roman Widows: The Appearance of New Women and the Pauline Communities* (Grand Rapids, MI: Eerdmans, 2003).

Wire, A.C., *Corinthian Women Prophets. A Reconstruction through Paul's Rhetoric* (Minneapolis, MN: Fortress Press, 1990).

Wirth, A., *Danae in christlichen Legenden* (Prague: F. Tempsky, 1892).

Wolff, H.J., 'Doctrinal Trends in Post-classical Roman Marriage Law', *Zeitschrift der Savigny-Stiftung für Rechtsgeschichte, Romanistische Abteilung*, 67 (1950).

Wood, S.P. (trans.), *Christ the Educator* (Fathers of the Church Series: Clement of Alexandria; New York: Fathers of the Church, 1954).

Woodhouse, F.C., *Monasticism Ancient and Modern* (London: Gardner, Darton, 1896).

Yarbrough, A., 'Christianization in the Fourth Century: The Examples of Roman Women', *CH*, 45 (1976), pp. 149–65.

Yarnold, E. (trans.), *The Awe-Inspiring Rites of Initiation*, 2nd edn (Collegeville, MN: Liturgical Press, 1994).

Ysebaert, J., *Greek Baptismal Terminology* (Nijmegen: Dekker and Van de Vegt, 1962).

Zappella, M., 'A proposito di Febe PROSTATIS (Rm 16,2)', *RivB*, 37 (1989), pp. 167–71.

INDEX

1 Clement 5, 6, 7, 12, 15–25
  identity of author(s) 16

African theology *see under* baptism
ages of women devoting chastity to God
  89
Alexander 66, 71
Alexandria 44
Alexandria's relationship with Egypt 30
  influence on Clement's writings 30
allegory and interpreting the Old
  Testament 112, 113
analysis of Clement across the Corpus
  54–5
anger and grudges 206
asceticism 10, 72, 74, 81, 86, 87, 118, 120
  and liberation of women 92, 93
  attractiveness to women 93
  of women 10, 81, 86, 87
    and the rise of monasticism 87
  the roots of asceticism 76–86
Aseneth 1, 2, 158–66
  and ancient social reality 164–6
  and Joseph 158–62, 166
  her veil 163–4
  rejection of idolatory 1
Aseneth 1, 2, 7, 12, 158–66
  ancient social life 164–6
  readings by scholars 160–1
Attalus 65, 66

baptism 137–55
  African theology 145
  as generation from Mother Church
    139–40
  Jewish purificatory practices 137
  Mary and Eve 140
  Mother Church's children in North
    African polemic 140–4
  the Church as a *virgin* mother 140,
    145, 147, 152

  the Church's womb in Augustine's
    catechetical sermons 144–5
  the virginal Church's parturition
    in fourth-century catechetical
    discourse 145–8
baptismal fonts resembling wombs 3,
  138, 145, 146, 147, 152–5
  and poetry of the Latin West
    148–52
beasts, maulings by 65, 66
Biblis 56, 64
Blandina 65, 66, 67
bodily difference 49, 50
body, the 49, 50
breastfeeding 67

celibacy 10, 72
chastity 86, 87, 207
Christian sexual morality *see* sexual
  morality
Church Fathers, the, and womens'
  wealth 120–2
Clement 6, 12–14, 15, 16, 27–55, 82,
  127–8, 133–4
  as a Gnostic teacher 29
  disputation with Epiphanes 133–4
Clement of Alexandria 11, 26, 82,
  205
  and marriage 78
  and sexual morality *see under* sexual
    morality
Clement's context: late second-century
  Alexandria 28–32
Clement's works, commentaries 32
clothing 41, 42, 85
contraception 93, 93 n.107
convents, the first 87

Danaids and Dircae 19, 22
divine femaleness 54
double names 30

Ekklesia 3
erotic substitution 81
eroticism 81
Esther 21, 22
ethnic categories and social distinction
    30
ethnic markers 30
ethnicity, enslavement based on 31
Eve, identification of 'woman' with
    111–12; *see also under* baptism

familial imagery for the divine 39–41
family, leaving or hating 53
Favorinus 59
Felicitas 9, 68, 69, 169
Felicity 2, 9
female body, the 57
female martyrs 8, 19
'female model of mind' Padel's 203
female subjectivity 117
female virtue 193
feminine imagery for the divine 27
feminism, second wave 157, 157 n.6
font-womb *see under* baptism

gender 11, 12
gender and the passions in late ancient
    ethics 193–210
gender distinctions 70
gender norms and religious practices 33
gender roles and the household 22–5
Gnostic Christian
    process of becoming 51
    requirements for becoming a 48
    the ideal 13
    women's pursuit of the ideal 49
Gnostic/Gnostics 11, 27, 29, 45, 45
    n.50, 48, 119
    the Gnostic path 51
God, image becoming female 53
Golden Ass, Apuleius's 61

hair/coiffure 42, 84–5
    male hair removal 43
Haustafeln, the 22, 23
head covering 41–2, 163–4
Hellenism and social gradations 31

homoeroticism 42
household duties, codes of 22, 24, 25

ideology 102–24
    definition 102–4
    dominant ideology, a 123–4
    ideological literature and narrative
        106–8
    ideology of gender in the Church
        Fathers 109
    intertextual reading and writing 108,
        109
    intertextual writing and an ideology
        of gender 117–19
    of 'woman' 119
interiority, images of 57
intertextual exegesis 108
intertextual reading and writing *see
    under* ideology

jewellery 43, 44
Judith 21, 22

leadership by women 17, 27
*Letter of the Churches of Lyons and
    Vienne* 63–7, 68, 69, 70
Lot's wife 20, 22

Macrina 75, 81, 83, 84, 86, 89, 90, 91
magical arts, spells and rituals 171
manumission 58 n.10
markers
    ethnic 30
    racial 30
marriage 46, 47, 94, 116, 125, 165, 199
    and being continent 88
    at young age 90
    compared to virginity *see under*
        virginity
    patriarchal marriage and vices 133
    spiritual 82
    the pains of marriage 78–9
marriage with/brides of Christ 80, 81, 209
martyrdom 9, 50, 56–71
martyrs 50 *see also* female martyrs
    Christian martyrs 56–71
    gendering of 56

Mary and Eve *see under* baptism
maternal imagery for the divine 27, 54
maternal metaphors 40
Maturus 65
metaphors depicting educational
    process 51
Miriam 18–19, 22
monasticism
    practice of 'home monasticism' 88
    the rise of 87

narratives about women, in ancient
    literature 156–8
naturalizing of woman 109, 110, 112,
    123
'nature' in patristic literature 111

ownership of wives 132

Paidagogos 29, 38–45, 49, 51, 52, 54
papyrus documents 170
*Passio Sanctarum Perpetuae et
    Felicitatis* 2, 8
passion
    renunciation of 95
    restraint of 10
Passion of Perpetua and Felicitas 67–9,
    71, 166
passions
    of the soul 52
    the soul and the passions in ascetic
        literature 200–210
    yielding to 83
    see also gender and the passions
passions in late ancient ethics, the
    193–200
    lists of virtues and vices 197
    'passion' translated as 'emotion' or
        'disease' 194
patientia ('endurance') 60
patron saints 192
patronage by women 8, 120, 173–92
    alimentary programmes for poor
        children 181
    and martyrs 192
    and policies of church leadership
        186–7

and widows 190–1
    by Christian women 187–91
    Christians and the world of patronage
        184–91
    Latin patronage language 175
    non-elite women 179–80
    patron saints 192
    patron–client relations 173–5
    patronage in the early church 184–7
    patronage in the Early Roman
        Empire 173–7
    patronage of groups 180–4
    public patronage 176
    women's patronage in the Roman
        world 176–84
    patronage of individuals 177–80
perfection 48, 51, 52, 77
    attaining 50
    process of 48
Perpetua 2, 4, 7, 9, 67, 68, 69
    diary of 70, 71
    dreams of 67, 68
    the martyrdom of 166–71
philosophical schools 28
Pomponius 67, 69, 71
procreation 46, 47
Protreptikos 29, 32–8, 53, 54

race, enslavement based on 31
racial categories and social distinction 30
racial markers 30
Rahab 20, 21, 22
rich person being served, the 52–4

Sanctus 65, 66
sexual activity 47
sexual behaviour 42
sexual communalism 125, 127, 131
sexual desire 42, 46
sexual difference 13, 41, 55, 56, 83
sexual differentiation 42
sexual intercourse 3, 7, 47, 116
sexual morality, Christian 125–36
    and Clement of Alexandria 125,
        133–4
    and communal principles/social
        ideals 126

and Epiphanes 125–8, 132–3
  and augmentation of Christian
    communalism 132–3
  disputation with Clement; and
    valuable raising of ethical
    questions 133–4
  Epiphanes's sexual principles 126,
    128
and Plato 126
  appetitive desires 128–30
  communal reproduction 131–2
  communal sexual proposals 132
  Plato's communal social theory
    128–32
  communalising women 130–1, 132
  patriarchal marriage and vices 133
  points of agreement between
    Epiphanes and Clement 127–8
sexual mores/rules 125, 127
  and society and social justice 127
sexual norms and religious practices 33
sexual practices 46
sexual relations 122
sexual temptation 207
sexuality 122
slaves 43, 44
  ownership of 43, 44
social distinction
  by ethnic categories 30
  by racial categories 30
spiritual marriage 82, 83, 110
  with a female ascetic 110
spiritualized sexuality 81, 82, 86
status distinctions 31
stereotyping of female/woman
  characteristics 109, 110, 112, 123
Stromateis 29, 44, 45–52, 125
suffering body, texts on the 59–69
suspicion of the flesh and its passions
  82

texts on the suffering body *see* suffering
  body
torture 9, 56–71
  of Biblis 9
  of Blandina 9
  of Perpetua 9

of slaves, women, gladiators 56–63
public nature of 8
the free/slave boundary 58 n.11
typology and interpreting the Old
  Testament 112, 113

universalizing of woman 109, 110, 111,
  112, 123

veiling the face 41–2, 42 n.37
  Aseneth's veil 163–4
  by virgins 81
Vettius Epagathus 64, 66
virgins subintroductae, condemnation
  of 88–9
virginity 10, 11, 72–96
  and courage 85–6
  and liberation of women 92
  and mistrust of all flesh 80
  and rape and suicide 94–5
  and relationship with Jesus 94
  and spiritual fertility/fecundity 80, 82
  and suffering with joy for Christ 79
  and the celestial Bridegroom 94
  and transcending nature 84
  and transvestism 85
  and veiling 81
  and wealth 91–2
  and women's sexuality 72–96
  as liberation 80
  as marriage contract with Jesus 80
  Christian discourse on female
    virginity 203, 209
  intellectual and spiritual activities,
    pursuing 90–1
  lack of encouragement from parents
    and family 90
  marriage, compared to virginity 78,
    79
  of Christians 87
  rewards and golas 208
  the roots of the idea of virginity
    76–86
  women's experience of virginity
    86–92
virginity in early Christian writings
  193–210

virgins
  and continent men 88
  and public spaces 207
  and silence 206
  communities of 87–8
  encounters with men 207
  sexual temptation 207
  texts praising and regulating virgins 200
virtue
  cultivation and moral virtue and
    happiness 197
  equality in virtue 199
  training for virtue 198
virtues and vices, lists of 197

weakness of woman 6, 7
wealth 43, 52, 119–22, 184
  and the Church Fathers 120–2
  asceticism and virginity 91–2
  renouncing wealth 52, 53, 120
women
  and business dealings 91, 179
  and the development and spread of
    Christianity 92–3
  asceticism 10, 81
  celibacy 10

in *1 Clement* 18–22
in antiquity 1
in Jewish and Christian communities
    17–18
  leadership 17, 27
  martyrs *see* female martyrs
  of wealth 119–22, 184
    and the Church Fathers 120–2
  patronage 4, 8, 120; *see also*
    patronage by women
  politics/public appointments 177
  restraint of passions 10
  roles in first-century Diaspora
    Judaism 5
  weakness 6, 7, 109, 110
women's experience of virginity 86–92
women's historical experiences,
    understanding of 72–3
  the state of historical records 74
women's sexuality
  and the effects of virginity 92–6
  appropriated by men's power 94
  as token of exchange 94, 95
women's studies in antiquity 170
words, and the power to defile 208
writing using someone's name 167–9